THE POLITICS OF
THE SECOND ELECTORATE

THE POLITICS OF
THE SECOND ELECTORATE

Women and Public Participation

Britain, USA, Canada, Australia,
France, Spain, West Germany, Italy, Sweden,
Finland, Eastern Europe, USSR, Japan

Edited by

Joni Lovenduski
and
Jill Hills

Routledge & Kegan Paul
London, Boston and Henley

First published in 1981
by Routledge & Kegan Paul Ltd
39 Store Street,
London WC1E 7DD,
9 Park Street,
Boston, Mass. 02108, USA and
Broadway House,
Newtown Road,
Henley-on-Thames,
Oxon RG9 1EN
Printed in Great Britain by
St Edmundsbury Press,
Bury St Edmunds, Suffolk
Introduction, Conclusion and selection
© copyright Joni Lovenduski and
© Jill Hills 1981
Individual essays
© Routledge & Kegan Paul Ltd 1981

British Library Cataloguing in Publication Data

The Politics of the second electorate.
1. Women in politics
I. Lovenduski, Joni   II. Hills, Jill
324   HQ1236

ISBN 0-7100-0806-6

CONTENTS

HQ
1236
P64

FIGURES

TABLES

ACKNOWLEDGMENTS

A number of people gave valuable help in the preparation of this volume. We would particularly like to thank Professor Bo Särlvik, Bob McDermott, Judith Evans and Jill Crewe. Special thanks are due to Patricia Swift for her patience and cheerfulness when typing various drafts, and our editor at Routledge & Kegan Paul, Philippa Brewster, for her confidence in us and her reassurance when we most needed it. Mention should also be made of our long-suffering families who (fairly cheerfully) put up with a certain amount of neglect during the final stages of preparation.

NOTES ON CONTRIBUTORS

Anne M. Batiot (French) is a post-graduate student in the Department of Government at the University of Essex, Colchester.

M. Janine Brodie (Canadian) teaches in the Department of Political Studies at Queen's University, Kingston, Ontario. She is author of 'Crisis, Challenge and Change: Class and Party in Canada' and of several articles and conference papers on women in Canadian politics, recruitment and legislative behaviour and the Canadian party system.

Maud Eduards (Swedish) is a Research Assistant at the Department of Political Science, Stockholm University, where she has taught a course on women and politics since 1977. She is author of 'Petita-hur svenska myndigheter argumenter för högre anslag, Kvinnor och politikfakta och förlaringar', and 'Kvinnorepresentation och Kvinnomakt' and articles on women in politics and on the Arab world. She was treasurer and board member of the Swedish Political Science Association between 1978 and 1980 and is a member of the forum for female researchers at the University of Stockholm. Her current research is on Maghreb co-operation.

Judith Evans (British) is a lecturer in Political Science at Queen Mary College, London. She is author of articles on women and political science and a member of the Women's Group of the Political Studies Association of the United Kingdom (PSA).

Elina Haavio-Mannila (Finnish) is Associate Professor of Sociology at Helsinki University. She is currently president of the Finnish Sociological Association, was a board member of the Scandinavian Sociological Association between 1972 and 1976, and of the Finnish Political Science Association from 1977 to 1980. She was the Finnish Business and Professional Association Woman of the Year in 1969. She is author of 'Kylättappelut, Lääkarit tutkittavina', and numerous studies of women in Finnish and Scandinavian politics. Her current research is on family cycles in Europe and men and women MPs in Finland.

Jane Hall (British) is a lecturer in German Studies at Brighton Polytechnic. Her publications include articles on East and West German politics and she is currently working on a study of women in West German politics. She is a member of the Women's Group of the PSA.

Eileen Hargadine (American) is currently self-employed. She has published articles on Japanese women and is a member of the Association for Asian Studies and the American Political Science Association.

Jill Hills (British) was a Temporary Lecturer in the Department of

Government at the University of Essex. She is author of articles on government and industry in Britain and Japan and is currently preparing a book on women and British politics. She is convenor of the Women's Group of the PSA, and a member of the executive committee of the PSA. She is a member of the Labour Party, has been a borough councillor and stood as a parliamentary candidate in the 1979 General Election.

Joni Lovenduski (American) is a Lecturer in Politics in the Department of European Studies at Loughborough University (UK). She is co-author of articles on the Equal Opportunities Commission, on women and political science, and on the status of women in political science teaching in the UK. She has been a member of the executive committee of the PSA since 1978, is a member of the Women's Group of the PSA and on the editorial board of 'Woman's Studies International Quarterly'.

Catherine Matsell (British) is Head of Modern Languages at Burleigh Comprehensive School in Manchester. She has travelled extensively in Spain and lived in Madrid for several years in the early 1970's.

Janine Mossuz-Lavau (French) is a chargée de recherche at the Centre d'Etude de la view politique française in Paris. She is author of 'André Malraux et le gaullisme', 'Les Clubs et la politique en France', 'Les Jeunnes et la gauche', and joint author of 'Les Femmes françaises en 1978'. She is currently continuing her research on women in French politics (in collaboration with Mariette Sineau).

Marian Simms (Australian) is a lecturer in Politics at Canberra College of Advanced Education. She is author of 'A Liberal Nation', has written extensively on women in Australia and is currently undertaking research on the Australian Party System and working on a feminist analysis of women in Australian politics.

Mariette Sineau (French) is a chercheur at the Centre d'Etude de la vie politique française in Paris. She is joint-author of 'Techniques en uniforme', and 'Les Femmes françaises en 1978'. She is currently continuing her research on women in French politics (in collaboration with Janine Mossuz-Lavau).

Jill McCalla Vickers (Canadian) is Associate Professor of Political Science at Carleton University in Ottawa. She is joint-author of 'But Can You Type: Higher Education and the Status of Women in Canada' and has published articles on the control of election expenses, women in the Canadian universities, feminist theories of power and female participation in Canada. She was president of the Canadian Association of University Teachers in 1976–7, is a member of the National Policy Review Committee of the New Democratic Party and was a candidate for federal office in the 1979 General Election.

Maria Weber (Italian) is Assistant Professor of Comparative Politics at Bocconi University in Milan. She is author of 'It voto della donna' and other publications on women in Italian politics. Her current research is on women's voting behaviour in industrial societies and on party identification in Italy.

Sharon L. Wolchik (American) is Assistant Professor of International Affairs at the Institute for Sino-Soviet Studies at the George Washington University in Washington DC. She is a member of the Women's Caucus of the American Political Science Association and review editor of 'Women and Politics'. She is currently continuing her research on women and politics in socialist countries and on the role of professionals in policy formation in Eastern Europe.

ABBREVIATIONS

BRITAIN

AUEW	Amalgamated Union of Engineering Workers
COHSE	Confederation of Health Service Workers
GMC	General Management Committee
MP	Member of Parliament
NEC	National Executive Committee
NUT	National Union of Teachers
TGWU	Transport and General Workers' Union
TUC	Trades Union Congress
WSPU	Women's Social and Political Union

CANADA

CLC	Canadian Labour Congress
NAC	National Action Committee
NDP	New Democratic Party

AUSTRALIA

ACT	Australian Capital Territory
ALGWA	Australian Local Government Women's Association
ALP	Australian Labor Party
AWNL	Australian Women's National League
DLP	Democratic Labor Party
LWC	Labor Women's Committee
LWCOC	Labor Women's Central Organising Committee
MHR	Member of the Federal House of Representatives
NEAT	National Employment and Training Scheme
WEL	Women's Electoral Lobby

FRANCE

ENA	Ecole Nationale Administration
CDS	Centre des Démocrates Sociaux
CFTD	Confederation Française du Travail
CGT	Confederation Generale du Travail
FEN	Federation d'Education Nationale
FO	Force Ouvriér

HEC	Hautes Etudes Commerciales
MFPF	Mouvement Français pour le Planning Familiar
MLAC	Mouvement pour la Liberté de l'Avortement et pour la Contraception
MLF	Mouvement de Liberation des Femmes
MRG	Mouvement des Radicaux de Gauche
PCF	Parti Communiste Francais
PR	Parti Républican
PS	Parti Socialiste
PSU	Parti Socialiste Unifié
RPR	Rassemblement pour la République
UDF	Union pour la Democratie Française

SPAIN

CD	Colación Democratica
CiU	Convergencia i Unio (Cataluñnya)
CEDA	Autonomous Rightists
CNT	National Confederation of Labour
EE	Euskadico Esquerra
ERC	Esquerra Republicana
HB	Herri Batasuna
PAR	Partido Aragonés Reionalista
PCE	Partido Communisto de España
PNV	Partido Nacionalista Vasco
PSA	Partido Socialisto de Andalucía
PSOE	Partido Socialista Obrero Español
PSUC	Partido Socialista Unificat de Catalunya
UCD	Union de Centro Democratico
UGT	Unión General de Trabajadores
UN	Unión Nacional
UPC	Unión del Pueblo Canasio
UPN	Unión del Pueblo Navarro

WEST GERMANY

ASF	Arbeitsgemeinschaft Sozialdemokratischer Frauen
BDF	Bund Deutscher Frauenvereine
CDU	Christlich Demokratische Union Deutschlands
CSU	Christlich-Soziale Union in Bayern
DKP	Deutsche Kommunistische Partie
FDP	Frie Demokratische Partei
FV	Frauenvereinigung
KPD	Kommunistische Partei Deutschlands
NPD	Nationaldemokratische Partei Deutschlands
SPD	Sozialdemokratische Partei Deutschlands

ITALY

AC	Azione Cattolica
DC	Democrazia Cristiana
DN	Democrazia Nazionale
MSI	Movimento Sociale Italiano
PCI	Partito Communista Italiano
PDIUM	Partito di Unità Monarchica
PLI	Partito Liberale Italiano
PRI	Partito Republicano Italiano
PSDI	Partito Socialdemocratica Italiano
PSI	Partito Socialista Italiano
UDI	Unione Donne Italiane
WLD	Women's Liberation Movement

SWEDEN

LKPR	National Association for Women's Suffrage
SACO	Confederation of Professional Associations
SR	National Federation of Government Officers
TCO	Central Organisation of Salaried Employees
LO	Confederation of Trade Unions

EASTERN EUROPE

CSSR	Czechoslovakia
GDR	German Democratic Republic

USSR

CADETS	Constitutional Democrats
CPSU	Communist Party of the Soviet Union
NEP	New Economic Policy
PPO	Primary Party Organisation
RSFSR	Russian Soviet Federative Socialist Republic
VTsSPS	All-Union Central Council of Trade Unions

JAPAN

DSP	Democratic Socialist Party
JCP	Japanese Communist Party
JSP	Japanese Socialist Party
JWP	Japan Women's Party
LDP	Liberal Democratic Party
SOHYO	General Council of Trade Unions
WMB	Women's and Minors' Bureau

1 INTRODUCTION

Joni Lovenduski and
Jill Hills

Social science research and press commentary during the 1970s
generated a certain amount of contention over the nature and
extent of the direct contribution women in industrialised societies
have made to politics between the years when the suffrage was
first obtained and the 'second wave' feminism of the late 1960s
emerged. However there has been general agreement with the
results of the pioneering Duverger (1955) study that at the more
effective levels of activity women have participated less than men.
This discrepancy held across all types of societies and all types
of economic and political systems. To the extent that social scientists
in the 1950s and 1960s gave attention to the phenomenon of the
low levels of women's political activism, their explanations, such
as they were, tended to rest upon psychological assumptions.
Women were said to be more traditionalist and right-wing, to be
temperamentally unsuited to masculine styles of political activity,
to adopt unquestioningly their husbands' political allegiances, to
be more swayed by candidates than issues, to be more moralistic,
more emotional and less politically aware and interested than men
(see especially Goot and Reid, 1975).

The sources of these 'explanations' were to be found in the cultural environment of the social scientists themselves rather than
in the data under scrutiny. It is an important fact that until
recently few studies were primarily concerned with the political
behaviour of women. Apart from in Duverger's 'The Political Role
of Women' (1955), gender has been merely a 'background' variable
in most surveys of political behaviour, and women have rarely
been separately or extensively considered. Only in the 1970s,
when a growing interest in the relationship between sex roles
and politics emerged, was previously collected data systematically examined. Whilst early explanation had relied upon
psychological assumptions and further explanation was sought in
differential socialisation (see Welch, 1977), more recent work on
the aggregate level links such variables as electoral format, urban/
rural environment, and levels of public expenditure to such phenomena as women's formal representation in state legislatures (Rule,
1978). On the individual level, recent research has indicated the
importance of 'stake' in political outcomes and the consistent exclusion of issues of concern to women from the public sphere
(Jacquette, 1974). Lately, feminist movements have politicised
issues previously regarded as belonging to the private sphere,
and new research indicates that women are becoming increasingly
participant orientated. Anderson (1975) has noted that rises in

1

feminine participation rates are strongly associated with increasing women's activity in the labour market as well as with attitude
changes resulting from the impact of 'second wave' feminism.
Clearly aggregate analysis has complemented rather than challenged explanations on an individual level, enabling attention to
be given to individual resources of socio-economic status, education and income as primary determinants of recruitment to
political elites. Thus attempts to develop a feminist political
science have 'rescued' survey data on women's political roles, and
comparative studies have shown up both striking similarities and
striking differences in feminine political behaviour in different
political cultures (see particularly Rule, 1978; Welch, 1977, Hills,
1978).

The essays which follow were especially written for this volume
in an effort to map out the political behaviour patterns of women
in the twenty countries included. They represent an effort to
marry current research on women to traditional political science
preoccupations with the study of governments, legislatures, parties and electoral behaviour. Important background data are
included on national women's suffrage movements and on the contemporary economic and social position of women in each country.
These, in our view are essential to the understanding of women's
involvement in the political life of their countries.

Whilst considerable emphasis is placed on women's activity in
the formal political arena, attention is also given to their participation in the feminist campaigns of the 1970s. Where possible,
data on voting behaviour are included. We are aware that voting
behaviour studies often come under fire from feminist social
scientists on the grounds that such measurement of participation
is masculine biased in that traditional privatisation of women's
issues has resulted in a tendency for women to participate on less
formal levels. Certainly voting behaviour studies have produced
arguments by political scientists that at least in Western industrialised societies, women are more conservative in their belief
systems than men and that they uphold the very values and parties which make the reality of sex-equality unlikely (see Goot and
Reid, 1975). Whether such contentions are correct or incorrect -
and they may well be incorrect - it is our view that the recent
politicisation of issues in which women have a stake may change
traditional patterns of participation. There is also evidence that
instrumental considerations may make traditional political issues more
salient to women and voting behaviour studies are a good initial
indicator of such a change. We would contend that women's support for political parties and the legitimacy governments receive
from women's votes merit attention from both feminist and other
political scientists. It is no credit to our discipline that the political behaviour and preoccupations of over half the population
has been so inadequately documented.

This collection is more than simply a pursuit of the political
science of the measurable however, and there are a number of
more obvious reasons for investigating the pattern of women's

political activity across nations.

Political participation may be broadly defined as the 'activities by which members of a society share in the selection of rulers and, directly or indirectly, in the formation of public policy' (McCloskey, 1968, p. 252). Women's participation at the level of voting, standing for public office and entering the political elite are all sensitive indicators of their position and stake in a particular society. A person's willingness to engage in active politics is likely to be related to her economic, social and domestic status. Such growth in women's political activity rates as is discernible has taken place both in the formal political arena and in the less 'legitimate' areas of direct action. As the following chapters show, both areas of growth indicate a desire on the part of women to influence the public policy decisions which affect their lives. Matters which have previously been considered to be inappropriate targets of public policy are increasingly finding their way onto national policy agendas. Issues such as divorce, abortion, rape and the division of labour within the family are being aired in public debate while embarrassed (male) governments are being pressed to make decisions on issues previously relegated to the private sphere. Women's growing presence in the labour market, and greater access to education combine with modern methods of transport and communications to sharpen their appreciation of the importance of the traditional policy agenda with its emphasis upon the domestic economy and international relations. Hence a process of the de-privatisation of female roles coincides with a growing number of women perceiving themselves to have a greater stake in altering existing arrangements of public roles. At the same time male politicians (if only because of concern about such matters as falling birth rates) have been forced to give greater consideration to the needs and wishes of their women constituents.

Each contribution to this volume provides evidence of change in the pattern of women's participation in the nation(s) under consideration. Although it is a truism that the political activities of half of the population are a vital element in any national politics, it is far from easy to assess the implications of the changes which have taken place. Nor is it easy to forecast the pattern, direction or extent of future change. The results of research on women's political participation to date suggest that levels of political involvement are likely to vary directly by access to social and economic resources although this may not hold true in every political system. However, much of that research has compared women to men and not women to women, and there is evidence that even where women have similar resources to men they will participate less at the elite level (Rule, 1978, passim; Wolchik, 1979, passim). In concentrating on the lower visibility of women in politics, such research often minimises the fact that men and women normally have different life styles which may markedly affect the impact of a particular variable on political behaviour. Thus the complex of elements related to the understanding of political participation must be seen as requiring the addition of such considerations as

patterns of personal life, sex roles and the division of labour
within the family. Only when these and related factors are included will it be possible to produce a theory adequate to explain
why individuals or groups of individuals do or do not engage in
political participation.

To date attempts to produce such a theory have been either of
the psychologically based or economic variety. The psychologically
based theories such as those of McCloskey (1968), Milbrath (1965)
or Lane (1959, 1962) have provided only a partial explanation of
the phenomena toward which they are directed. They stress the
low incidence of individual need for political expression, often
concentrating on a 'political activist' personality type, but failing
to take sufficient account of the barriers to participation which
result from a lack of access to necessary resources or contextual
factors differing between societies.

Economic theories, such as that offered by Downs (1957) have
based explanations on the tenet that individuals will choose to
vote or to influence government policy in proportion to costs and
expected rewards. Clearly, political participation at any level
relies on an actor's motivation and perception of advantage. As
Salisbury (1975, p. 333) has written, implicit in the economic
theory of participation is the assumption that:

rationality entails voting in response to purposive or
instrumental motives or incentives which are related to the
interface between one's values and the available alternatives
of public policy.

But Downs found difficulty in accounting for any but minimal participation by the majority of a public, and specifically held that
the costs of more active participation would only be borne by
those standing to gain a direct economic benefit, that is, the pro-
ducers (Downs, 1957, pp. 251-9). It is, therefore, not surprising
that later advocates of Downsian rationality have tended to move
onto the explicitly psychological terrain to account for incidences
of participation beyond the formal voting or 'spectator' level (see
Dowse and Hughes, 1972, p. 218).

Besides the partial nature of the explanations produced, much
of the research on political participation has been static in time,
based on sample survey data, and we lack panel studies to determine how important 'time' is in individual choice. Not only may
some periods of a person's life demand greater presence at home
and increased time constraints, but political activity itself may
lead to commitments to other organisations which in turn provide
alternatives which may commensurately reduce the rewards to be
gained by formal political activity itself (see especially Salisbury,
1975).

A clear impediment to the understanding of women's political
role has therefore been the lack of dynamic theory of participation.
The inadequacy of existing theory is such that political science is
handicapped when attempting a systematic consideration of the
political participation of women. Additionally, the early data base
has been assembled in a way not conducive to the extrapolation of

sexually differentiated political behaviour, thereby making the determination of the evolution of the patterns of women's participation difficult.

Clearly the presentation of a fully fledged 'grand-theory-of-political-participation' is well beyond the scope of this volume. We would, however, argue that feminist political science has a contribution to make, and the essays which follow represent an effort in this direction. An outline of women's formal participation across several cultures should, at the very least, make a contribution to the comparative political study of those who are normally seriously politically under-represented. Furthermore, although the societies we have chosen for consideration exhibit a considerable variety of political and cultural arrangements, they all share characteristic features of developed states. Even the less developed countries considered such as Spain and some of the poorer East European nations may be seen to structure their political choices within a framework set by industrialism. All contain important core elements which imply key similarities and enable them to be classified as industrial or advanced industrial societies. These elements are, to borrow from Feldman and Moore (1962, p. 146), the dominance of

1 a factory system of production,
2 a stratification system based on the division of labour and a hierarchy of skills,
3 extensive commercialisation of goods and services and their transfer through the market,
4 educational systems capable of filling the various niches in the occupational and stratification systems; as well as
5 a social and domestic sector normally based on the nuclear family.

In other words, we are concerned with the study of a particular aspect of a particular syndrome in societies in which the social structure is rather atomised and in which the economic sphere has become paramount. These characteristics have emerged in each case because as Parsons (1960, p. 113) has written the state has 'at some time given special emphasis to the development of the economy and hence [has] accorded to the economy a special prominence in the structure of the society.'

Thus comparability is enhanced by the fact that our concern in each society is with a section of the population which is similarly, although not identically, located in socio-economic and political terms. To the best of our knowledge there is often no readily available comparative politics material on women's participation in the formal political arena which compares women with women. Hence students wishing to begin work on the topic have often been confined to the use of such raw data and official government statistics as are available on a state by state basis. Whilst such data may, for many countries, be quite extensive, it is often difficult and frustrating to use, even by those who possess the required linguistic and statistical skills. Specific and detailed direct

comparison of the economic, social and political statistics on the
women investigated in this volume is, of course, subject to caveats
concerning the different ways in which the individual nations,
institutions and social scientists collect and present statistics.
However the broader patterns suggested by these data are comparable. The similarities amongst women in the twenty nations
considered are striking. But situated within this similarity are a
number of substantial variations which may be directly linked to
particular domestic policies, traditions, cultures and political
arrangements. The presentation of both these similarities and
differences may throw some light on the key variables in the
determination of women's political behaviour. A comparative appreciation of the weights, directions, and interrelationships of these
variables may better place us to advance hypotheses which may be
used to begin constructing a systematic theory of political participation which has application for both sexes.

BIBLIOGRAPHY

Anderson, K. (1975), Working women and political participation
    1952-1972, 'American Journal of Political Science', XIX,
    pp. 439-54.
Downs, A. (1957), 'An Economic Theory of Democracy', Harper
    & Row, New York.
Dowse, R. E. and Hughes, J. A. (1972), 'Political Sociology',
    John Wiley, London.
Duverger, M. (1955), 'The Political Role of Women', UNESCO,
    Paris.
Feldman, A. S. and Moore, W. E. (1962), Industrialisation and
    industrialism, convergence and differentiation, 'Transactions
    of the Fifth World Congress of Sociology', Washington DC.
Goot, M. and Reid, E. (1975), 'Women and Voting Studies: Mind-
    less Matrons or Sexist Scientism', Sage Progessional Papers in
    Political Sociology, Sage, London.
Hills, J. (1978), Women in the British Labour and Conservative
    parties. Paper presented to the Annual Conference of the PSA.
Jacquette, J. (ed.) (1974), 'Women in Politics', John Wiley, New
    York.
Lane, R. E. (1959), 'Political Life', Free Press, Chicago.
Lane, R. E. (1962), 'Political Ideology', Free Press, Chicago.
McCloskey, H. (1968), Political participation in D. L. Sills (ed.),
    'International Encyclopaedia of the Social Sciences', Macmillan,
    New York.
Milbrath, L. (1965), 'Political Participation', Rand McNally,
    Chicago.
Parsons, T. (1960), Characteristics of industrial societies, in
    'Structure and Process in Modern Societies', Free Press,
    Chicago.
Rule, W. (1978), Socio-political environment and the eligibility
    and selection of women legislators. Paper presented at the 1978

Annual Meeting of the American Political Science Association.
Salisbury, R. H. (1975), Research on political participation,
   'American Journal of Political Science', XIX, May, pp. 323-41.
Welch, S. (1977), Women as political animals?, 'American Journal
   of Political Science', XXI, November, pp. 711-29.
Wolchik, S. (1979), Women and politics in Eastern Europe. Paper
   presented at the Joint Sessions of the European Consortium for
   Political Research, Brussels, 17-21 April.

2 BRITAIN
Jill Hills

BACKGROUND

Such emancipation as exists for British women has come through the economy's demands for labour, rather than through political pressure, alone. Legal emancipation has tended to follow rather than precede economic emancipation. As economic demands have fluctuated, and as wars or population trends have produced either a balanced population or 'surplus' women, so also has the progress of women towards equality with men fluctuated.

The period from the mid-nineteenth century to the outbreak of the First World War in 1914, was marked by the efforts of middle-class women reformers to change women's social and political status. The first petition for women's suffrage was presented to parliament in 1866, but progress came first at local government level. From 1869 unmarried women householders were allowed to vote in municipal elections. However, married women's property was still deemed to be represented by their husbands' votes (Morgan, 1975, pp. 10-13; Rover, 1970, p. 39).

Women's legal position as citizens, in Britain, has been intertwined with their legal status as wives. In the mid-nineteenth century property and marriage were indivisible. Any property, which a woman owned, became her husband's upon marriage, and a woman, herself, became her husband's property. But over the following twenty years, changes took place in the legal status of the married woman. In 1883 the Matrimonial Property Act allowed women to keep and control their own property after marriage. In 1891 Regina v. Jackson established the right of a woman to refuse to live with her husband. By the 1890s if her husband were convicted of assault on her, a woman could get a separation order, maintenance and custody of her children, and could claim maintenance, if he deserted her. But until the 1920s the laws on divorce operated a double standard, with husbands able to divorce wives for adultery, but wives needing grounds, such as assault, in addition to adultery, in order to obtain a divorce (Rover, 1970, pp. 25, 41-6).

The changes in married women's status were belatedly recognised in 1894, when wives holding property separate from their husbands were given the right to vote in municipal elections. Those who had no separate property continued to be represented by their husbands, by what was termed 'couverture'. The issue of 'couverture', bound up as it was, with all the traditional concepts of a woman's relationship of dependence on her husband, continued into the first decade of the twentieth century (Morgan, 1975, p. 20).

After forty years of struggle for the vote, the Women's Social and Political Union (WSPU) was formed, in Manchester in 1903, to campaign for women's parliamentary suffrage. Although Mrs Pankhurst and her two daughters, Christabel and Sylvia, are the most well known of the early suffragettes, the movement was also supported by working-class women in the North of England, and in the East End of London (Liddington and Norris, 1978, pp. 11-13). In 1906, having failed to achieve reform through established lobbying tactics, the WSPU began attacks on property. However, separate groups of 'constitutionalists', such as that led by Millicent Fawcett and that of the Women's Liberal Federation of the Liberal Party, also pressured peacefully for reform (Morgan, 1975, pp. 17-19). The women's suffrage movement drew support from some Liberal MPs and some of the new Labour Party, but was split, not only between the 'constitutionalists' and 'radicals', but also between those who wanted full adult suffrage, in which women should be included, and those content with some form of property qualification to enfranchisement.

Legend has it that Asquith, the Liberal Prime Minister, considered that the enfranchisement of women on the basis of a property qualification would have given the Conservatives an overwhelming majority in parliament, and opposed women's suffrage on those grounds. It is also true, however, that women's suffrage had to compete on the political agenda with problems such as that of Irish emancipation (Morgan, 1975, pp. 3, 155-7). The violence of the suffragettes had failed to break down the recalcitrance of the Liberal government by the outbreak of the First World War. In effect, war meant calling a halt to suffragist activities, and many of the leaders of the movement turned their attention to mobilising women for the war effort (Mitchell, 1966, pp. 301-46).

That war effort involved a demand for labour, which opened to women many of the jobs previously reserved for men. Before the war, the higher infant mortality rate for male children had produced a surplus of women, the majority of whom, either because of low pay or lack of available employment, were forced to rely upon a male relative to support them. For middle-class girls, paid employment was limited to teaching, clerical work and medicine (for a few) and for working-class girls, was restricted to factory work or household service. Because of economic necessity, the predominant concern for girls was to find a husband to support them (Adam, 1975, pp. 4-28).

Between 1914 and 1919 women's employment opportunities expanded into such areas as munitions, transport and agriculture (Adam, 1975, pp. 36-63). Thus, when women were given the right to vote in 1918, it was acknowledged that they had proved themselves equal to men and that their franchise had become inevitable (Harrison, 1978, p. 213). Hence, British women's enfranchisement came about less through the activities of the pre-war suffragette

movement than through the convergence of economic emancipation
of women with a change of political personnel (Morgan, 1975,
p. 161).
Originally the franchise extended only to those women who were
householders over 30 years old, or who were 35 and the wives of
householders. At the same time, it was extended to men over 21,
and to men over 19 who had served in the armed forces. At that
point, adult women outnumbered men by 2 million. Thus, had the
franchise been given to all adult women, the ensuing government
would have been elected mainly by women. The full franchise was
extended to women in 1924, when the composition of the electorate was more equal (Adam, 1975, p. 65).
With the demobilisation, returning soldiers claimed back their
jobs, and women returned to their homes. But, in the following
years, because of the lost generation of men, it became acceptable
for 'surplus' women to earn their own livelihood. Then the Great
Depression took men's jobs and women were deprived of employment in favour of men. Married women were forbidden to enter
such employment as teaching. In 1931 (on the assumption that
their husbands would support them) state unemployment benefit
was withdrawn from married women. In these inter-war years,
women became either wives or workers, but rarely both (Adam,
1975, pp. 121-5; Davies, 1975, pp. 81-90).
The Second World War again demanded the labour of women.
Women were conscripted and public facilities were set up to care
for children. But, once more, after the war, women were replaced
in their employment by men, and day nurseries closed down
(Davies, 1975, p. 97). By 1947 only 18 per cent of married women
were in paid employment (Adam, 1975, pp. 161-3). The welfare
state legislation of the 1940s was based on the presupposition that
'during marriage, most women would not be gainfully occupied'
and that paid employment undertaken by a married woman would
be intermittent (Beveridge, 1942, p. 50).
It was not until the late 1950s that it became respectable for a
middle-class woman to work in paid employment. Until that time,
to do so reflected her husband's incapacity to support her. A bi-
modal work profile, in which women work until the birth of the
first child and, then, subsequently, when children are at school
began to develop in Britain only in 1961, and was not firmly established until 1971 (Hakim, 1979, p. 12).

THE SOCIO-ECONOMIC ENVIRONMENT

The majority of women in paid employment still consider themselves
to be wives and mothers first and employed women second. Their
primary concern in employment is easy travelling distance from
home, rather than good wages or promotion prospects (NOP Bulletin 1971, pp. 1-31). The conception of woman as dependant and
husband as breadwinner is still embodied in much of the British
social security and tax legislation (Land, 1978, pp. 127-142;

O'Donovan, 1979, pp. 134-52). Two-thirds of British men recently
still preferred their wives not to work outside the home (EEC,
1975, p. 77). Should wives do so, although men may 'help' with
the household chores, women remain responsible for the running
of the household and care of children (EEC, 1979, p. 108).

Traditional attitudes reflect the opportunities for marriage available to British women. Since the Second World War a decrease in
male infant mortality has produced a population in which men and
women in the younger age groups have been more or less equally
balanced. Marriage rates have increased, so that, in 1971, 72 per
cent of women aged between 15 and 59 were married, and only 5
per cent were divorced or widowed. Following the easing of the
legal process for divorce, in the early 1970s divorce rates have
also increased, but, because over 50 per cent of divorced people
remarry within five years of their divorce, the proportion of
divorced people in the population is only 2½ per cent ('Population
Trends', Winter 1977, p. 18; Summer 1978, p. 8). In fact, marriage has never been so popular, nor, given the balance of the
genders, has it been so available for the majority of women.

Although the ideal size of family wanted by a British woman has
remained steady, for half a century, with a mean of two and a
half children, only 2 per cent of single women and 1 per cent of
married women want no children at all (Weightman, 1979, pp. 567-
8). Thus, the majority of women in Britain are likely, at some
time in their lives, to be married and to have children. In turn,
because neither men nor women consider it right for a man to
move house to facilitate his wife's employment, marriage cuts down
both the mobility and the career advancement of women (EEC,
1975, p. 57). The lack of adequate public day care facilities entails either a bi-modal career for a married woman or that she earn
enough money to pay for private child care. Hence, over the last
twenty years the major growth in women's employment in Britain
has taken place among the age group whose children are of school
age and above ('Labour Party Discussion Kit', 1975; Mackie and
Pattullo, 1977, p. 105).

In 1979 women employees formed 41 per cent of the total number
of employees and 36 per cent of the working population ('Employment Gazette', March 1980, p. 304). Despite the large numbers of
women in paid employment three-quarters were employed in a
narrow spectrum of jobs. Twenty-nine per cent were clerical
workers, 23 per cent were waitresses, cooks, canteen assistants,
maids, charwomen or hairdressers; 12 per cent were shop workers,
11 per cent were nurses, social workers, teachers and laboratory
technicians. And within that narrow spectrum of jobs, women competed mainly with women for employment. Ninety-nine per cent of
typists and secretaries, 97 per cent of canteen assistants, 92 per
cent of charwomen, 88 per cent of hairdressers, 82 per cent of
shop assistants, 92 per cent of nurses, 64 per cent of school
teachers and 62 per cent of social workers were women. But only
6 per cent of solicitors, 4 per cent of architects and 27 per cent
of doctors were women. A higher proportion of women work at the

bottom end of the occupational spectrum - as unskilled manual
workers - than do men (Hakim, 1979, p. 28). In 1971 84 per cent
of women in full-time paid employment worked in occupations
which were predominantly female, whereas only 16 per cent worked
in occupations which were predominantly male (Hakim, 1979, pp.
26-7).

The Equal Pay Act of 1970 gave employers five years in which to
ensure that equal pay was granted to women for the same work as
men. Following that legislation, non-manual women's salaries rose
faster than men's. Between 1970 and 1976, the index of male and
female non-manual workers' salaries showed an increase from 100
in 1970 to 132.6 for men and 176.6 for women. Similarly, in manufacturing industries, between 1970 and 1976 the average weekly
wage of women rose by 70 per cent as against a rise of 62 per cent
for men. But the average weekly earnings of women working full-
time in manufacturing industry in 1976 was still only 60 per cent
that of a man's and the average earnings of non-manually employed
women were 63 per cent of the earnings of similarly employed men.
If fringe benefits, such as membership of occupational pension
schemes, were taken into account, then the gap was wider still
('Annual Abstract of Statistics', 1978, pp. 177-9).

The Equal Pay Act and the Sex Discrimination Act of 1975 (which
outlawed discrimination in terms of entry, pay, conditions, or
promotion) have done little to restructure women's employment.
One estimate suggests that the Equal Pay Act applies to only one-
third of employed women (Mackie and Pattullo, 1977, p. 136). It
was officially admitted in 1980 that any further improvement in the
gap between men's and women's earnings must come from entry of
women into male-dominated employment ('Employment Gazette',
March 1980, p. 280).

The 1971 Census showed that 65 per cent of women who were
economically active in that year were married. Of that number 45
per cent worked part-time (under thirty hours per week). Part-
time work is normally undertaken because of family commitments
and, by 1978, 87 per cent of all part-timers were women. Part-
time employment limits both remuneration and promotion prospects
and precludes such benefits as membership of occupational pension
schemes (Mackie and Pattullo, 1977, p. 43). It also acts as a con-
straint upon the participation of women in trade unions, both
because part-timers lack status within their employment, and
because employers are less willing to give them the time off for
union activities (Fryer, Fairclough and Manson, 1978, pp. 101-74).
Thus the increasing trade unionisation of women in paid employment, from 22 per cent in 1969 to 44 per cent in 1979 (as against
a 56 per cent membership by men) has not led to the politicisation
of women which one might expect. Trade unions, with their predominantly working-class inegalitarian membership, have not
traditionally been the most sympathetic environments for women.
In 1979, despite the growth of white collar unionisation and despite the predominance in fifteen unions of women members, only
one in thirty-two trade union officials was a woman ('Labour Party

Discussion Kit', 1975; 'New Society', 6 September 1979, p. 510).
In terms of women's presence on the governing committees of
the trade unions the position is hardly better. In 1980 the National Union of Tailors and Garment Makers, with a 90 per cent
female membership, had 30 per cent of women on its executive
committee; the Confederation of Health Service Employees (COHSE)
with 75 per cent women members had 11 per cent on the executive;
the National Union of Teachers (NUT) with 70 per cent of women
members had 9 per cent on its executive, and the two largest
unions, the Transport and General Workers Union (TGWU) and
the Amalgamated Union of Engineering Workers (AUEW) had no
women on their executive, but 16 per cent of women members. In
the Trade Union Congress itself, two out of the forty-one places
on the General Council were reserved for women. In 1980, cap-
itulating to women's pressure, that number was raised to five
(Toynbee, 10 March 1980).
   Although the relationship between education and employment is
not as direct as it is for men, women's lower educational attainments help to structure their employment into lower status and
lower paid work. The proportion of women undergraduates has
risen by 11 per cent in the post-war years, but in 1976 only 36
per cent of undergraduate degrees awarded went to women. The
proportion of post-graduate degrees awarded to women was lower
still at 20 per cent ('Employment Gazette', March 1980, p. 269).
Men graduates were more likely to enter industry than women,
who tended to enter the public service - a trend which reflects
the Arts bias among women. At school leaving age, although over
a quarter of boys have specialised in maths and science, only 9
per cent of girls have done so (ibid.).
   Lower down the educational ladder, in 1971 40 per cent of boys
leaving school between the ages of 15 and 17 went into apprenticeships: only 8 per cent of girls did so. Of those girls, three-
quarters were apprenticed in one trade - hairdressing (Davies,
1975, p. 104). At school subjects may still be stereotyped 'girls'
and 'boys', and, particularly for working-class girls, the pressures to conform to a female role may induce under-achievement
and self selection out of the educational process (McRobbie, 1978,
pp. 96-108). Low educational attainment leads to low paid employment and to marriage at an early stage.
   A combination of gender stratification in schools, low educational
attainments, opportunities for marriage, the norms of 'good'
motherhood, lack of public child care facilities, low wages and a
stratified labour market combine to produce a host of intangible
barriers to women's political participation on equal terms with men.
Formal political participation is traditionally linked to high socio-
economic status and income, and the majority of women have
neither. In addition, differences in life style and attitudes separate working-class from middle-class women.
   Outside the formal political spectrum, the women's movement of
the 1970s was cut through by class cleavages, as well as ideological cleavages between Marxist and Radical feminists. A

decentralised organisational structure made it difficult to organise around anything but such specific issues as domestic violence and abortion (Rowbotham, 1972; 1979, pp. 21-156). Of the original four demands of the women's movement: for free contraception; for equal pay, equal education and job opportunity; for 24-hour day nurseries and for abortion on demand, only that of free contraception has been gained in substance. The Equal Pay and Sex Discrimination Acts, and the overseeing Equal Opportunities Commission, have proved ineffective in combatting both occupational segregation by sex and sex discrimination within schools. Future progress lies in individual action taken through the courts (Byrne and Lovenduski, 1978, pp. 163-5). The movement has also had to seek to convince the large majority of women, who do not enter into competition with men and, therefore, do not perceive themselves as unequal (EEC, 1975, p. 29).

Perhaps because most women in Britain are married, have been married, or expect to be married, the anti-male feminism of the early suffragettes and the anti-male image of the radical women's movement, appear to be inappropriate to many women (EEC, 1979, pp. 18-20). In a highly privatised society, the majority of women are too busy coping with the demands of home, family, husband and job to give the time necessary to regular political activity. Yet the abortion issue of the 1970s and 1980 polarised public opinion and brought many women into public demonstrations. For the first time, the women in the trade unions convinced their male colleagues both to adopt pro-abortion stances and to actively demonstrate on a non-economic and non-industrial relations issue (Toynbee, 10 March 1980). As in the USA, following a period of failed reformism, it may be that British women's political consciousness is awakening and a third wave of feminism was begun in 1980 (Bouchier, 1979, p. 399).

THE BRITISH PARTY SYSTEM

Since the early twentieth century, when the Liberal Party began to lose electoral support to the Labour Party, the predominant political cleavage in Britain has been along class lines. The British political system gradually evolved into one dominated by the two major parties - the Conservative Party, attracting the majority of middle-class support and the Labour Party, linked to the trade unions and seen as the party of the working class. The first past the post, simple majority, electoral system has operated to the disadvantage of third or minority parties, such as the Liberals, which are not geographically concentrated. For instance, although the Liberals gained almost 14 per cent of the total vote in the 1979 election, they gained only eleven of the 635 seats in parliament. On the other hand, the two nationalist parties, the Scottish Nationalist Party and the Welsh Nationalists, because of their geographic concentration, have taken approximately the same proportion of seats in parliament as their proportion of the total vote.

In the mid-1970s, it seemed that the two party system was dis-
integrating. The proportion of the total vote taken by the two
major parties had declined from 90 per cent in 1970 to 75 per cent
in October 1974. The Liberals and the two nationalist parties took
increased shares of the vote, and regional voting patterns became
increasingly apparent. This fragmentation culminated in the
election of a minority Labour government in October 1974 and its
maintenance in power through the medium of a pact with the Liberal Party in parliament. In 1979, the trend towards fragmentation
was somewhat reversed with a Conservative overall majority of 44
seats, and 81 per cent of the vote taken by the two major parties.
The nationalist parties lost ten of their fourteen seats and the
Liberals lost three of their fourteen. But regional variations in
voting behaviour had become even more pronounced. The Conservative Party became the party of the suburbs and rural areas,
strongest in the South of England, while the Labour party's
strongholds became confined to heavy industrial areas and urban
centres and geographically to the North of England and Scotland
(Crewe, 1979, p. 249).
    Explanations of the trend away from the two major parties bet-
ween 1970 and 1974, have centred upon the reduced saliency of
class-based politics, the weakening of voter identification with
either of the parties, and a general disillusionment with governments which have consistently failed to make the economy work
effectively (Crewe, Särlvik and Alt, 1974). Voter turnout at
general elections has more or less continuously declined from the
84 per cent of the period 1950 to 1964 to 73 per cent in 1979
(Crewe, 1979, p. 252). Women's contribution to this state of
affairs has been little studied by political scientists, who have
concentrated upon class, age, environment and political socialisation as the primary explanatory variables in British voting
behaviour. In general, however, women have been said to vote
less often than men, and, until 1979, were said to be more Conservative than men (King, 1972; Blondel, 1963, p. 60; McKie,
1978).

WOMEN AND VOTING

Because people do not admit to non-voting, a problem with data
collected from questionnaires after an election, is that it always
over-represents the turnout in that election. In a study which
attempted to outflank that problem, Crewe, Fox and Alt found
that in four elections between 1966 and 1974, non-voters were not
a discrete section of the electorate, and were likely to resume
regular voting in the future. Once those aged 75 and over were
excluded from the analysis, the three per cent superiority of men
in turnout narrowed to one per cent, reflecting the disproportionate number of women in the older age group. They concluded that
'the well known tendency for women to vote in Western Liberal
democracies in smaller proportions than men is not only statistically

insignificant in British elections, but attributable more to their greater longevity than to their sex, (Crewe, Fox and Alt, 1976, p. 59). Their conclusions are confirmed by those of Lansing (1977, pp. 6-12). At least since the 1960s British women have voted at the same rate as men.

Besides attributing women with failure to vote, political scientists and journalists have also attributed post-war Conservative victories to women's suffrage. Women have been presented as more Conservative than men and, in particular elections, such as that of 1970, have been considered directly responsible for a Conservative victory (King, 1972; McKie, 1978). Yet to talk of a 'women's vote' in contrast to a 'men's vote' is a nonsense, because women's voting pattern, in the mass, is affected by the disproportionate number of elderly women in the electorate (Rose, 1976, pp. 223-4).

Given the attributed importance of women to electoral outcomes it seems surprising that it was not until the late 1970s that the concept of 'Conservative woman' was specifically examined. Then, Lansing found that contrary to the myth, young women voted Labour in the 1964 election at a higher rate than young men. Although women seemed to become more Conservative in the older age groups, those over 60 years old were almost identical in their Conservatism to men in the same age group. She concluded that the apparent Conservative bias among women was no more than a generational artefact (Lansing, 1977, pp. 19-20).

There is evidence to show that, between 1970 and 1976, women's support of the Conservative Party declined (Durant, 1976). This decline might possibly have been related to the increased numbers of middle-class women in public sector employment - education, health and social work - to which the Conservative Party was less sympathetic than was the Labour Party. By 1979 even male political scientists could not ignore the evidence. Writing just after the election, with reference to the 'typical Conservative advantage among women' Crewe acknowledged that, in 1979, women in general were not more Conservative than men. He said of the election: 'the last minute surge of male chauvinism predicted by some never appeared, on the contrary, men swung much more strongly to the Conservatives (9.5%) than did women (3%)' (Crewe, 1979a, p. 26).

The 1979 election data in Table 2.1 shows that in the largest age group within the population, that between 30 and 59 years old, both men and women voted in similar proportions for the three major parties. In the youngest age group, from 20 to 29 years old, women supported both the Labour Party and the Conservative Party more than did young men, the difference being made up by less support of the Liberals by women. Only in the age groups over 60 years old was there, among women, both less support for the Labour Party and more support for the Conservative Party. Hence, once again, only in the elderly age group can women be said to be more Conservative than men. Even then, possibly attracting women to the Conservatives, a woman potential Prime Minister may have complicated this voting pattern. If British

women ever were more Conservative than men, they apparently
no longer are.

Table 2.1   Sex difference by age and party vote 1979 (% total sample)

Age	Sex	Conservative	Labour	Liberal
20-29	Men	25	27	21
	Women	30	30	13
30-59	Men	39	32	11
	Women	41	33	12
60-75	Men	40	36	8
	Women	46	32	10
75+	Men	40	26	12
	Women	52	18	3

Source: British Election Study Data, made available through the courtesy of Ivor Crewe,
Bo Särlvik and David Robertson, University of Essex.

WOMEN AND THE LABOUR AND CONSERVATIVE PARTIES

Part of the reason for the perpetuation of the 'Conservative
woman' myth may well have been the knowledge that, at local
level, women seem preponderant in the Conservative Party organisation. In total, probably less than 10 per cent of the population
belongs to a political party, of whom about 4 per cent are active
(Crewe, Fox and Alt, 1976, p. 59). But no firm figures are kept
of women's membership of the political parties, and even the numbers of total membership, publicised by the parties, have to be
treated with circumspection. The official figure for membership
of the Labour Party in 1978 was 676,000 individual members, but
this figure is based on a system whereby no local party may buy
less than 1000 individual membership cards from the Central Party
(Labour Party, 1980, p. 11). A more accurate figure is probably
that of 300,000 given by the Houghton Committee in 1977. A similar official figure for the Conservative Party is not available, but
the same committee suggested an average membership of a Constituency Association of 2,400 indicating a membership of 1.5 million
(Houghton, 1976, pp. 510-11; pp. 162-3).

Until 1970, Labour Party official figures suggested a woman's
membership running at 40 per cent of the total. Local studies of
Conservative Associations have reached the conclusion that women
slightly outnumber men, so it is probably accurate to suggest a
membership of 51 per cent of women in the Conservative Party
(Rush, 1969, p. 61). No figures are available for the Liberals and
minor parties.

An individual woman joining the Labour Party, may become a
member of her branch party and a member of a woman's section of

the party. The women's organisation of the Labour Party was
founded in 1906, as the Women's Labour League, and was formally
admitted to the party organisation in 1909 (Middleton, 1977, p. 28).
In recent years the numbers of women's sections in the Party has
been declining. In 1976, there was a total of 1,246 women's groups
of various types within the Party; by 1978, that number had declined to 1,165. The women's organisation is strongest in the rural
areas and the North of England, where traditional attitudes to
women's roles still tend to flourish. It sees its role as both a
training ground for women and as a pressure group for the presentation of problems, of special significance to women, to the
party policy-making machinery (McDonald, 1977, p. 153). But its
opponents see it as providing local groups with a social, rather
than a political purpose, and deride it for its positive discrimination in favour of women (Wulff, 1979, p. 16).

Each year the women's organisation holds its own national conference, to which all sections of the Party may send delegates.
But the resolutions passed at the conference have little political
force, they are treated with the same status as those passed by a
handful of party activists at a constituency party meeting. In the
late 1960s, and with renewed vigour after the passage of the Equal
Pay Act of 1970, a move began within the Party for the abolition
of the women's organisation (McDonald, 1977, pp. 152-3). The
abolition movement split women in the party, and feminists could
be found on both sides. The argument continues, paralleling a
similar debate on the women's organisation in the TUC, and has
crystallised around the numerical protection given to women in the
Party's policy making machinery (Hunter, 1980, p. 736: Toynbee,
1980).

At local level, the Labour Party is organised into branches which
correspond with a local government area. These branches, together with affiliated trade unions, women's sections and the youth
wing of the Party, send delegates to a constituency general management committee (GMC), whose area coincides with a parliamentary constituency. Recent evidence suggests that, even at this
local level, women form a smaller proportion on GMCs than they do
in membership. In a survey of eighteen constituencies, Denver
found 30 per cent of women on GMCs compared to a 40 per cent
membership of the Party (Denver, 1980).

From the GMCs one delegate is elected each year to the Party's
Annual Conference, which, formally, is the supreme policy making
organ of the Party. Resolutions passed by the Annual Conference
by more than a two-thirds majority become Party policy. Trade
unions, constituency parties and affiliated organisations send
delegates to Annual Conference, but trade unions dominate the
voting. In 1978 they held over six million votes compared to the
600,000 of the constituencies (Labour Party, 1980, p. 11). Women
are poorly represented at the Conference. In the 1970s only 5 per
cent of the delegates from the trade unions and 17 per cent of
those from the constituencies were women, so, in all, women represented about 11 per cent of delegates. Those who do manage to

become delegates are, however, more vociferous than men (Hills, 1978, p. 6).

The discrimination felt by women to exist at all levels of the Party, is combated at national level by the reservation on the highest elected committee of the Party, the National Executive Committee (NEC), of five seats for women. These five women members are elected by both the trade unions and the constit-uencies. Because the trade unions dominate the conference voting, the five women's seats allow control of the NEC by the trade unions. It has been around the abolition of these seats that de-bate has centred, but proposals for abolition have been defeated, and women have continued to have their own section on the NEC. Apart from these five seats, no woman has been elected to the NEC from the trade unions, and, since 1960, only two women have succeeded from the constituency section (Hills, 1978, p. 7).

Reflecting the fact that the mass membership of the Conservative Party arose after the Party was established in parliament, its organisation is split in two, with the Party headquarters, Central Office, under the control of the Party leader, and the mass mem-bership of the National Union of Conservative Associations under the control of an elected chairperson. The National Association and the Party organisation tend to have an almost military flavour of hierarchical progression within them, with higher committee membership dependent on achieved position at a lower level.

As in the Labour Party, at local level the Conservative Party is organised around parliamentary constituencies and the boundaries for local government elections. Such direct evidence as exists, suggests that, as in the Labour Party, a slightly smaller propor-tion of women are represented upon Conservative Constituency Association councils than are members of the Party (Rush, 1969, pp. 61-2). The women's organisation in the Conservative Party began in the late nineteenth century, when it became illegal for parties to pay for election canvassers and volunteers were there-fore needed. Each constituency association now has its women's constituency committee, and, since the mid-1970s the Party has set out to attract younger women by the establishment of informal social groups at local level. Unlike the Labour Party, the Conser-vatives believe that social activities are essential for the attraction of young people. Fund-raising is given considerable importance by the constituency associations, and the women's organisation plays an important part in both that activity and in conducting local surveys of 'women's problems' (Brown, 1980, pp. 19-20). In con-trast to the Labour Party, no internal debate on the role of the women's organisation seems to have taken place in the Conservative Party.

The Annual Conference of the Conservative Party does not have the policy making importance of that of the Labour Party. Although the conference provides a channel of communication between lead-ers and activists, increasingly its role has been to act as a public legitimation of the leadership (Wilson and Phillips, 1977). In order that women do not have to compete with men, specific places are reserved for them throughout the party hierarchy, including representation at the conference. In 1977 38 per cent of the representatives at the conference were women, a proportion higher than that at the Labour Party's conference. But, perhaps reflecting the lack of competition for places, the majority of Conservative women are silent, and organisers find it difficult to bring enough women to the rostrum (Hills, 1978, p. 6).

As in the Labour Party, the nearer to power the committee, the smaller the representation of women upon it. Thus the overall proportion of women on the Executive Committee of the Conservative National Union has remained at around 20 per cent since 1970. On the smaller and more powerful General Purposes Committee and on the even more powerful Advisory Committee on Policy of the Central Office, the proportion is smaller still at 18 per cent (Hills, 1978, p. 8). Therefore, in both major parties, the proportion of women in the top echelons of committees is about half that of the proportion of women in the constituency associations and parties. And even this small proportion is maintained in both parties by reservation of some seats to women.

That reservation has had the effect that some women have been able to achieve prominence in the parties. Eleven women have been chairperson of the Labour Party and seventeen women have occupied that position in the Conservative National Union (Labour Party, 1980, pp. 7-8; Brown, 1980, p. 28). In addition, a woman is always vice-chairperson of the Conservative National Union.

WOMEN CANDIDATES

At local level, the proportion of women contesting seats in local government elections is lower than women's proportion of party membership. The Labour Party fields between 12 and 15 per cent of women candidates in local elections, compared to the 20 to 25 per cent of the Conservatives. Greater London seems to have both the highest proportion of women candidates and the highest proportion elected, but, in general, women's success at local elections is slightly less than men's. In both the major parties, the proportion of women elected varies according to whether it is a favourable or unfavourable year for their party, suggesting that women are placed in marginal seats (Hills, 1978, pp. 10-18).

Between 1964 and 1976 the proportion of women councillors increased from 12 to 16 per cent. Data collected on local councillors suggests that both men and women councillors are older and more middle class than the population at large. Because of the rigid time constraints involved in this particular form of activity, where attendance at committee meetings, council meetings, caucus meetings and those of community organisations is obligatory, one might expec that the people of both sexes with the time available would be those past child-rearing age. Women councillors are appreciably older than women in the population as a whole, with a ratio of almost 2 to 1 in the 55-69-year age group, suggesting that for women, formal political activity may only be possible after children have grown up (Maud, 1967, pp. 15-16). More recent evidence, from a survey of women activists in the Labour Party, suggests that for some women, the time when children are small is when such women are most involved with the local community. They may then become local councillors during the years of childcare, despite the time constraints involved. It seems however that, possibly because of conflict with careers, few highly educated women become councillors (Hills, 1980, pp. 13-15). Of the women who become councillors few become chairpersons of local authority committees. In 1967, of 2,000 committees surveyed by the Labour Party, only 10 per cent overall (11 per cent in London) were headed by a woman (Labour Party, National Labour Women's Advisory Committee, 1968, pp. 18-19). In 1980, only 32 women Conservative councillors were chairpersons of committees (Brown, 1980, p. 31).

At parliamentary level, neither the two major parties, nor the Liberal Party have fielded more than a token number of women candidates. In absolute numbers for the first time in 1950, and then again in February 1974, the total number of women candidates rose beyond one hundred. Since then, the number has increased to 161 in October 1964 and to 210 in 1979.

It might appear that the influence of the women's movement in the early 1970s was the causal factor in the increase in the numbers of women candidates in February 1974. But, increased party competition favours women candidates. A major reason for the increase in their numbers in 1974 was the sudden growth in women standing for the Liberal Party. In that election, the number of women candidates fielded by the Liberals rose by 74 per cent to forty, whilst the number of seats fought by the Liberals increased by 56 per cent from 332 to 517. The numerical increase in women candidates, therefore, can be seen as a function of the relative hopelessness of the seats (none of the Liberal women were elected) and the larger number of seats fought. A similar feature is evident in the Scottish Nationalist Party's behaviour. In 1970, when the number of seats fought increased from 23 to 65, the number of women candidates increased from nought to ten. As chances of winning have increased, the number of SNP women candidates has since dropped.

Neither of the two major parties have made access to parliament easy for women, although, of the two, the Labour Party has been slightly more egalitarian in this respect. The number of women candidates for both Labour and Conservative varied little between 1945 and 1974. Following publicity within the Party on the need for more women candidates, the Labour Party fielded 50 per cent more in 1979 than in February 1974, but women made up only 9 per cent of the total number. The proportion of women candidates for the Conservatives at 5 per cent of the total, in 1979, was equal to the proportion of that party's candidates in 1950. Therefore, in sixty years, since women were given the right to vote their opportunity to enter the parliamentary elite hardly altered.

Looking at the success rate for women candidates in Table 2.2,

Table 2.2   Parliamentary elections 1945-74

| | CONSERVATIVE | | | |
	% men elected	No. of women candidates	No. of women elected	% women elected	Women's handicap ratio
1945	35	14	1	7	0.2
1950	54	29	6	21	0.4
1951	53	25	6	24	0.4
1955	58	33	10	30	0.5
1959	59	28	12	43	0.7
1964	48	24	11	46	1.0
1966	40	21	7	33	0.8
1970	52	26	15	58	1.1
1974(F)	49	33	9	27	0.6
1974(O)	46	30	7	23	0.4
1979	53	31	8	26	0.5

| | LABOUR | | | |
	% men elected	No. of women candidates	No. of women elected	% women elected	Women's handicap ratio
1945	66	41	21	51	0.8
1950	52	42	14	33	0.7
1951	49	41	11	27	0.5
1955	46	43	14	33	0.7
1959	42	36	13	36	0.9
1964	50	33	18	55	1.1
1966	59	30	19	63	1.1
1970	47	29	10	35	0.7
1974(F)	50	40	13	33	0.7
1974(O)	53	50	18	36	0.7
1979	45	52	11	21	0.5

Women's handcap ratio = $\frac{\% \text{ women elected}}{\% \text{ men elected}}$

Source: F.W.S. Craig (1976), 'British Electoral Facts' 1885-1975', London, Macmillan; 'The Times Guide to the House of Commons 1979', London, Times Books Ltd.

it seems as though women had an equal chance of election to men (with the exception of the Conservative women in 1964) when their party did well in the election. Thus women Labour candidates had a better chance of election than Labour men in 1964, when their party gained 56 seats, and in 1966, when it gained 48 seats. Similarly, in 1970, when 67 seats changed into Conservative hands, Conservative women had a better chance of election than Conservative men. But, in neither of the two 1974 elections, when the Labour Party formed the government, nor in 1979, when the Conservatives won the election, were women in those parties elected in the same proportion as their men colleagues.

The reason for this change of events revolves around 'marginal' and 'safe' constituencies. Between 1955 and 1970, out of the 635 seats in parliament, three-quarters never changed party allegiance, and a further 13 per cent were held by the same party in four elections out of five. In 1970 89 constituencies changed party control, but in the two 1974 elections only 30 seats moved from one party to another. The number changing allegiance in the 1979 election at 72 was higher than would have been expected from previous elections (Denver and Hands, 1977, p. 2; 'Times Guide to the House of Commons', 1979, p. 255). In the majority of seats, when the local ascendant party chooses its candidate, it also chooses its member of parliament (MP).

In order that some more women should have won seats in the 1979 election more would have had to be adopted in safe seats. Of the fifty-two Labour women candidates fifteen were incumbents seeking re-election. Of the thirty-seven non-incumbents, only one was adopted in a safe Labour seat, and only four women fought in marginal constituencies. In a year in which Labour lost the election, it could have hoped for a maximum of sixteen elected women. However, five of the incumbent women were in seats which Labour subsequently lost. It therefore ended the 1979 election with only eleven women MPs ('Times Guide to the House of Commons', 1979, passim).

In the case of the Conservatives, in 1979 7 of the 31 women candidates were incumbents. Of the rest, only 3 candidates were fighting in marginal constituencies. The Conservatives could have hoped for 10 women MPs. In fact, because of the regional variations in voting behaviour, only 1 of the non-incumbents won her seat, so, following the 1979 election the Conservatives had only 8 women MPs.

The lack of success of women in the 1979 election can be attributed to four factors. First, the party winning the election concentrated women candidates in unwinnable constituencies. Second, the losing party had some women in marginal constituencies, subsequently lost. Third, only one non-incumbent was adopted in a safe seat. And, fourth, the Scottish Nationalist Party lost several of its seats, including those of two of its women MPs.

Because the majority of British constituencies are safe seats, and, because unlike the primary system of the USA, the selection procedure of the British parties is private, that procedure is of considerable importance to women's access to parliament. Briefly, the selection process of the two parties is similar, in that constituency parties or associations choose their candidates with little interference from the central party organisation. Both central party organisations maintain lists of possible candidates. In the Labour Party the B list contains the names of those nominated by constituency parties, the A list contains the names of those nominated by trade unions. Trade union finance, to help local parties meet electoral expenses is available for A list candidates. In 1977, nine per cent of the 561 names on the B list, but only three out of 103 names on the A list were women. However, candidates who appear on neither list may be adopted by constituencies. The lists have only a consultative function. In the Conservative Party, with only minor exceptions, a candidate must have been interviewed by the central party and her name must appear on its list. The Conservative Central Office also intervenes to the extent that it expects constituencies to place the name of one woman on its short-list of candidates (Hills, 1978, p. 13). A similar proposal, made at the 1980 women's conference of the Labour Party, was rejected by the membership, as being an undue interference in local constituency affairs (Hunter, 1980, p. 736). No candidate for either party is required to live in the constituency for which he or she is selected, although a trend towards the adoption of such candidates may be emerging (Hills, 1978, pp. 13-14).

For a woman seeking to become a parliamentary candidate, there are four stages of the selection process. First, she must enter the pool of candidates; second, she must be nominated to a potential short-list; third, she must be selected for the short-list and fourth, she must achieve selection. For a woman in the Labour Party the process of entry is easy - she has only to write to the constituency concerned expressing her interest in becoming a candidate. In the Conservative Party, entering the pool of candidates may in the past have been more difficult than it is today (Stobaugh, 1978, p. 94). The proportion of women on the Party list, interviewed and passed as suitable for candidature by the Party organisation, increased from 10 per cent in 1965 to 15 per cent in 1977. In neither party are candidates expected to make heavy contributions to their own election expenses, although in the Labour Party trade union backing of electoral costs may help to win selection.

In both parties candidates are selected on the basis of a ten-minute speech and ten minutes of questions. Although candidates tend to stress their own opinions on political matters at these selection meetings, some evidence exists to suggest that conferences use wider criteria to select a candidate, and that a combination of attractiveness, status external to politics, personality and representation of opinions of activists may be used (Rush, 1969, pp. 61-75). Women in both parties have regularly claimed that they are discriminated against at selection conferences (Currell, 1978, pp. 3-4; Hunter, 1980, p. 736). In the Conservative Party, married men may be preferred, because they have a wife to look after the constituency in their absence (Rush, 1969, p. 66). Amongst Conservative selection committee members, many of them middle-class women, the perception of woman's role in the home and family makes it difficult for a woman to be seen as a legitimate candidate (Ranney, 1965, pp. 96-7). In particular, Conservative women candidates have alleged discrimination by women selectors against women candidates (Currell, 1978, p. 4). In the Labour Party a myth still lingers on, despite ambivalent evidence, that women are electoral risks and likely to lose votes (Masterman, 1978, p. 13).

Some indication of the problems which women have in establishing their legitimacy to fight in favourable seats is indicated in Stobaugh's analysis of the social backgrounds of women MPs in the 1970 parliament. Seventy-three per cent of women MPs had a university education; 66 per cent came from a professional background, and a further 15 per cent came from a political functionary position; 62 per cent had local government elective experience; 92 per cent had been party workers and only 31 per cent had been elected in their first parliamentary contest. In contrast, although 76 per cent of the men had had a university education, only 31 per cent had had local government experience, only 38 per cent had been party workers and 68 per cent were elected in their first electoral contest. The lower proportion of male MPs with professional background (59 per cent) can be attributed to the trade union sponsorship of over 100 Labour MPs who tend to come from working-class occupations (Stobaugh, 1978, pp. 108-9).

The analysis suggests that over and beyond higher education and professional status, in order to become an MP, a woman needs also to have had local government experience and to have fought a previous unsuccessful parliamentary contest.

Because non-incumbent candidates may be selected two or three years before an election takes place, the process of candidature is far from easy. The strain on the families of either sex may be heavy. In view of that strain and the prospect of repeating it, it is perhaps less than surprising that a large number of candidates of both sexes withdraw from the race after one attempt. But the wastage rate of women candidates is consistently higher than that for men. For instance, in 1974, when only a few months intervened between elections, 30 per cent of Conservative men and 21 per cent of Labour men withdrew from candidacy, but the proportions for women candidates' withdrawal were 43 per cent and 30 per cent respectively. A corollary of this high wastage rate of women candidates is that at each election a high percentage of the women candidates fielded by the two major parties are 'first-time' candidates. Thus, in 1979 70 per cent of the Labour and 89 per cent of the Conservative women non-incumbent candidates were fighting their first election. Only 20 per cent of the women candidates defeated in the 1974 elections were re-selected for 1979, and therefore had the qualifications demanded to fight more favourable constituencies.

Although no firm evidence exists which explains why women should drop out or be pushed out at such a rate, preliminary work by the author indicates that for both sexes, conflicts between home, family, and career are at the root of the problem. For women, the additional factor of perceived discrimination may also have an impact on career strategies (Hunter, 1980, p. 736). Because few women are adopted in safe seats, the most a woman can reasonably hope for is a marginal seat, from which she is likely to be swept at the next election. The risk is therefore high.

Concomitantly, the long-term prospect of reward of high office may be less, since it is unlikely that a woman will be in parliament long enough to attain a cabinet post.

WOMEN IN ELECTED OFFICE

Of the seventy Labour women MPs elected between 1919 and 1979, 7 per cent have become cabinet ministers. Of the forty Conservative women MPs, 5 per cent have entered the cabinet. The preponderance of women MPs representing marginal constituencies leads to a high turnover rate which precludes them from gaining the length of service necessary for a cabinet position. In 1979, at the same time as Margaret Thatcher became Prime Minister, the leading woman on the Labour front-bench, Shirley Williams, lost her seat.

Within the cabinet itself, women have tended to be placed in stereotyped positions, such as education, health and consumer affairs. But two Labour women, thirty years apart, Margaret Bondfield and Barbara Castle, became Ministers of Labour. Barbara Castle was also the first woman Minister of Transport.

It has been argued, from evidence of private members bills introduced by women MPs in the House of Commons, that they have also specialised in the stereotyped women's subjects (Vallance, 1979, p. 107). The argument does less than justice to women MPs of the 1970s. For instance, seven women served on the Select Committee on Violence in the Family, during the 1974 to 1979 parliament, and, in 1977, it was mainly women Labour members who spent all night sittings talking out, in standing committee, a bill which would have made abortion more difficult to obtain. Both marital violence and abortion, relating as they do to the private lives of women, are specifically feminist issues (HMSO, 1975, passim; 'Guardian', 23 June, 1977). In addition, in the same parliament a higher proportion of Labour women MPs were on the left-wing of their party. 12 per cent of women compared to 6 per cent of men were members of the Tribune ginger group, suggesting that for these women, areas of policy such as taxation, nationalisation and economic planning were of primary importance (Rendel, 1977, p. 7).

Just as women MPs are subject to the strains of a professionalisation which separates private from public lives, and makes them vulnerable to the charges of being bad mothers (Phillips, 1980, p. 8) so also are they subject to the strain of attempting to satisfy several different constituencies of interest, of which the feminist movement is only one (Vallance, 1979, p. 112). The data collected on public perceptions of women MPs suggests that whereas a large proportion of men expect a woman MP to be a steadying influence, and more consensus-oriented than a man, a similar proportion of women expect a woman to take up women's problems, thereby anticipating a less consensual approach (EEC, 1979, pp. 159, 161-3).

Nor is the general public confidence in women MPs high. In the egalitarian climate of the mid-1970s 53 per cent of men and 52 per cent of women spontaneously said that they had no more confidence in a man MP than a woman. By 1977 those proportions had decreased to 39 per cent and 37 per cent respectively; a reversion to patriarchal attitudes had taken place. The proportion of men with more confidence in a man had increased by 11 per cent to 48 per cent, and an increase of 4 per cent from 1975 showed 35 per cent of women favouring a male MP. Although women's preference for a woman MP had also increased by eight per cent to 20 per cent in the two years, the general flow of attitude can be said to have become much less egalitarian (ibid., p. 160). In view of the polarisation shown in these changing attitudes it is encouraging that women candidates are now emphasising in increased proportions, that they will fulfill the same role as a male MP, but also have additional value through their experience as women (Currell, 1978, p. 7).

WOMEN IN OTHER SECTORS OF POWER

Because the House of Commons is such a public forum, the access of women to it has particular importance. In the less public and less salient forum of the European parliament, women have done considerably better, with eleven seats out of eighty-one (14 per cent). But in other areas of power, women are tokens, at best.

In 1977, of 97 senior judges only two were women; out of 285 circuit judges seven were women. Even at the lay magistrate level of the law only just over 30 per cent were women ('Guardian', 13 March 1980). In the directorships of the top twenty companies in Britain, there are no women ('East Anglian Times', 11 September, 1978). In the lists of appointments to the boards of nationalised industries and quasi-government agencies, in 1977, 18 per cent were women, but one-third of their number of 3,000, were appointed by the Scottish Office (Equal Opportunities Commission, 1978, p. 76). In the civil service, in 1974, only 4 per cent of those in the senior administrative grades were women (Mackie and Pattullo, 1977, p. 87). In 1976, in local government, there were only two women chief officers out of over 500; two chief education officers out ot 116; 10 chief librarians out of 121; two chief planning officers out of 466, and 11 directors of social services out of 127 ('Guardian', 2 June, 1976). Yet education, libraries and social services are staffed mainly by women.

CONCLUSION

Laws in Britain are still predominantly made by men, interpreted by men, administered by men, and define women as dependants of men. That legal framework coupled with demographic balance in younger age groups, and cultural emphasis on the roles of wife

and mother, legitimates the structuring of women by men, and by
women themselves, into low grade or sex segregated employment,
thereby reinforcing their dependence. British women have become
increasingly important to a party's success or failure at elections.
Nevertheless, women in Britain continue to define themselves in
relation to their family rather than to their public, economic roles
(Fransella and Frost, 1977, pp. 116–17). Thus the legal gains
made in the period of the 1960s and 1970s, such as separate national insurance and better pensions for married women in paid
employment, under the 1975 Social Security Act, and protection
of a pregnant worker's job, under the 1975 Employment Protection
Act, may only have appealed to a minority of middle-class women.
Women's unemployment figures increased by 8 per cent between
January 1979 and January 1980, compared to a drop of 1.8 per
cent for men. (The women's figure takes no account of those
seeking paid employment who do not register for work.) But no
women's 'right to work' campaign has emerged to combat spokes-
men of both parties, who have presented the view, that, particularly in an economic recession, woman's place is in the kitchen
(Coote, 1980, p. 930). In the words of the Conservative Minister
for Social Services of 1980, quoted in an advertisement (NUPE,
'Spare Rib', June 1980, p. 16):
  I don't think mothers have the same rights as fathers. If
  the good lord had intended us to have equal rights to go
  out to work, he wouldn't have created man and woman.
In 1979, with a woman Prime Minister in office and sex equality
legislation on the statute books, British women appeared to have
all the legal and formal tools necessary to emancipation. Ironically
by mid-1980, immigration rules, admitted to be discriminatory to
women, had been introduced. Under a revision of the 1975 Employment Protection Act, protection for some pregnant workers had
been cut. Proposals had been made to cut the school day, for
women with small children to be unable to register for employment
and for school meals to be abolished in some areas ('Observer', 7
October 1979, p. 64; 'Daily Mirror', 12 July 1979, p. 15; 'Guardian', 15 July 1980, p. 1).
  In the same period, cuts in public expenditure reduced child
care facilities and provisions for the handicapped and elderly
affecting both the public employment of women and their private
lives. Because British women's public participation cannot be separated from the structure of their private lives, the prospects for
any increase in women's formal political participation are dim. As
money becomes tighter and family budgets stretched, so women
will feel less able to spend in order to undertake political activities.
As the public facilities for the care of the elderly, the sick and
children are reduced, so family commitments for all strata of women
will increase. The risk of a parliamentary career becomes greater
if the possibility of obtaining a job, after defeat, is reduced. The
more egalitarian party, the Labour Party, now has its safe seats
predominantly distributed in the North of England, where a less
egalitarian attitude to women exists. In addition, boundary changes

to parliamentary constituencies will relieve many incumbent male Labour MPs of their present inner-city seats, thereby increasing competition against women for the marginals.

Just as legal emancipation has followed economic emancipation for British women, so the economic recession of the 1980s has led to a reversal of trends in women's rights. On this basis, a down-turn in the rates of formal political activity and representation of British women could well be a feature of the next decade of Brit-ish politics. Paradoxically, women's success over the abortion issue of 1980 may lead to greater participation by women in direct action. Hence the ensuing decade may witness both an increased generalised response by women to issues which affect their private lives and a decrease in their formal representation in the political arena.

BIBLIOGRAPHY

Adam, Ruth (1975), 'A Woman's Place 1910-1975', Chatto & Windus, London.

'Annual Abstract of Statistics' (1978), HMSO, London.

Beveridge, Sir W. H. B. (1942), 'Social Insurance and Allied Services', HMSO, Cmnd 6404, London.

Blondel, Jean (1963), 'Voters, Parties and Leaders. The Social Fabric of British Politics', Penguin, Harmondsworth.

Bouchier, David (1979), The Deradicalisation of Feminism: Ideol-ogy and Utopia in action, 'Sociology', vol. 13, no. 3, pp. 387-402.

Brown, Rosemary (1980), 'Going Places. Women in the Conser-vative Party', Conservative Political Centre, London.

Byrne, Paul and Lovenduski, Joni (1978), Sex Equality and the Law in Britain, 'British Journal of Law and Society', vol. 5, no. 2, pp. 148-65.

Chambers, J. and Marsh, D. (1981), 'Abortion Politics', Junction Books, London.

Coote, Anna (1980), London Diary, 'New Statesman', vol. 99, 20 June, p. 930.

Crewe, Ivor (1979), The voting surveyed, 'The Times Guide to the House of Commons', May 1979, Times Books Ltd., London.

Crewe, Ivor (1979a), Who swung Tory?, 'The Economist', vol. 271, 12 May, pp. 25-7.

Crewe, Ivor, Särlvik Bo, and Alt, James (1974), The Why and How of the February Voting, 'New Society', vol. 29, 12 Sep-tember, pp. 669-72.

Crewe, Ivor, Fox, Tony and Alt, James (1976), Non-voting in British General Elections 1966-1974, 'British Political Sociology Yearbook', ed. Colin Crouch, vol. 3, pp. 39-109.

Currell, Melville (1974), 'Political Woman', Croom Helm, London.

Currell, Melville (1978), The Recruitment of Women to the House of Commons, Paper to the Political Studies Association Conference.

'Daily Mirror' (1979), 12 July.

Davies, Ross (1975), 'Women and Work', Hutchinson, London.
Denver, D. T. (1980), unpublished survey data.
Denver, D. T. and Hands, H. T. G. (1977), Recruitment to the
   Parliamentary Labour Party. Paper presented to the European
   Joint Sessions, Berlin, 1977.
Dunnell, Karen (1979), 'Family Formation 1976', HMSO, London.
Durant, H. (1976), Voting Behaviour in Britain 1945-1964,
   'Studies in British Politics', ed. Richard Rose, Macmillan,
   London, pp. 204-15.
'East Anglian Times', Ipswich, Suffolk.
EEC, (1975), 'European Men and Women', Commission of the Euro-
   pean Communities, Brussels.
EEC (1979), 'European Men and Women in 1978', Commission of
   the European Communities, Brussels.
'Employment Gazette', (1978, 1979 and 1980), HMSO, London.
Equal Opportunities Commission (1978), 'Third Annual Report',
   HMSO, London.
Fransella, Fay and Frost, Kay (1977), 'On Being a Woman. A
   Review of Research on How Women See Themselves', Tavistock,
   London.
Fryer, R. H., Fairclough, A. J. and Manson, T. B. (1978),
   Facilities for Female Shop Stewards, the Employment of Protection
   Act and Collective Agreements, 'British Journal of Industrial
   Relations', vol. 16, pp. 101-74.
Gibson, Colin (1974), The Association between Divorce and Social
   Class in England and Wales, 'British Journal of Sociology', vol.
   25, pp. 79-83.
Hakim, Catherine (1979), 'Occupational Segregation. A Compara-
   tive Study of the Degree and Pattern of the Differentiation
   between Men and Women's Work in Britain, the US and Other
   Countries', Department of Employment, Research Paper No. 9,
   London.
Harrison, Brian (1978), 'Separate Spheres. The Opposition to
   Women's Suffrage in Britain', Croom Helm, London.
Hills, Jill (1977), Women in the Labour Party. Paper presented to
   the European Joint Sessions, Berlin.
Hills, Jill (1978), Participation of Women in the Conservative and
   Labour Parties. Paper presented to Annual Conference of the
   Political Studies Association, Warwick.
Hills, Jill (1980), Life-style Constraints on Formal Political Par-
   ticipation. Why So Few Women Local Councillors in Britain?
   Paper presented to the Annual Meeting of the American Political
   Science Association 1980, Washington, DC.
HMSO (1975), 'Select Committees. Return for Session 1974-5',
   HMSO, London.
Houghton Committee (1976), 'Report of the Committee on Financial
   Aid to the Political Parties', HMSO, Cmnd 6601, London.
Hunter, Eveline (1980), Getting Out of the Back-Seat, 'New
   Statesman', vol. 99, 16 May.
King, Anthony (1972), A Sociological Portrait: Politics, 'New
   Society', vol. 19, pp. 57-60.

Labour Party, National Women's Advisory Committee (1968),
  'Discrimination Against Women', Labour Party, London.
Labour Party, National Women's Advisory Committee (1974),
  'Obstacles to Women in Politics and Public Life', Labour Party,
  London.
Labour Party (1975), 'Women in Society, Discussion Kit', Labour
  Party, London.
Labour Party (1980), 'Diary', Labour Party, London.
Land, Hilary (1978), Sex Role Stereotyping in the Social Security
  and Income Tax Systems, in J. Chetwynd and O. Harnett (eds)
  'The Sex Role System', Routledge & Kegan Paul, London, pp.
  127-42.
Lansing, Marjorie (1977), Comparison of the Voting Turnout and
  Party Choice of British and American Women. Paper presented
  to the European Joint Sessions, Berlin.
Liddington, J. and Norris, J. (1978), 'One Hand Tied Behind Us.
  The Rise of the Women's Suffrage Movement', Virago, London.
McKie, David (1978), The Hand that Rocks the Cradle, 'Guardian',
  5 May, p. 11.
Mackie, L. and Pattullo, P. (1977), 'Women at Work', Tavistock,
  London.
McDonald, Oonagh (1977), Women in the Labour Party, in Lucy
  Middleton (ed.), 'Women in the Labour Movement', Croom Helm,
  London, pp. 144-60.
McRobbie, Angela (1978), Working-class Girls and the Culture of
  Femininity, in 'Women Take Issue', Women's Studies Group,
  London, Hutchinson, pp. 96-108.
Masterman, Eileen (1978), Women in Elected Positions in Scotland.
  Paper presented to the European Joint Sessions, Grenoble.
Maud, John (1967), 'Committee on the Management of Local Gov-
  ernment', vol. 2, 'The Local Government Councillor', HMSO,
  London.
Middleton, Lucy (1977), Women in Labour Politics, in 'Women in
  the Labour Movement', Croom Helm, London, pp. 22-37.
Mitchell, David (1966), 'Women on the Warpath. The Story of the
  Women of the First World War', Jonathan Cape, London.
Morgan, David (1975), 'Suffragists and Liberals. The Politics of
  Woman Suffrage in England', Blackwell, Oxford.
'New Society' (1979), The Seventies Trade Union Boom, vol. 49,
  6 July, p. 510.
'NOP Bulletin' (1971), No. 102, Women and Employment, Oct./Nov.
  pp. 1-31.
NUPE (1980), Advertisement by National Union of Public Employees
  in 'Spare Rib', June, p. 16.
Oakley, Anne (1979), The Failure of the Movement for Women's
  Equality, 'New Society', vol. 49, 23 August, pp. 392-4.
'Observer', London.
O'Donovan, Katherine (1979), The Male Appendage - Legal Defin-
  itions of Women, in Sandra Burman (ed.), 'Fit Work for Women',
  Croom Helm, London, pp. 112-33.
Phillips, Melanie (1980), When a Woman's Place is in the Commons,
  'Guardian', 13 May, p. 8.

'Population Trends' (Winter 1977 – Spring 1980), HMSO, London.
Ranney, Austin (1965), 'Pathways to Parliament', Macmillan, London.
Rendel, Margherita (1977), Women and Feminist Issues in Parliament. Paper presented to the European Joint Sessions, Berlin.
Rose, Richard (1976), Social Structure and Party Differences, in 'Studies in British Politics', Macmillan, London, pp. 216–38.
Rover, Constance (1970), 'Love, Morals and the Feminist', Routledge & Kegan Paul, London.
Rowbotham, Sheila (1972), Women's Liberation and the New Politics, in 'Writings from the Women's Liberation Movement', compiled by M. Wandor, S. W. Litho Ltd, London, pp. 3–30.
Rowbotham, Sheila, Sega, Lynne and Wainwright, Hilary (1979), 'Beyond the Fragments: Feminism and the Making of Socialism', Merlin Press, London.
Rush, M. (1969), 'Selection of Parliamentary Candidates', Nelson, London.
Stobaugh, Beverly Parker (1978), 'Women and Parliament 1918–1970', Exposition Press, Hicksville, New York.
Toynbee, Polly (1980), Male Trade Unionists Weep Crocodile Tears, 'Guardian', 10 March, p. 8.
Vallance, Elizabeth (1979), 'Women in the House. A Study of Women Members of Parliament', Athlone Press, London.
Weightman, Gavin (1979), Women, Sex and the Family, 'New Society', vol. 49, 13 September, pp. 657–8.
Wilson, Elizabeth (1977), 'Women and the Welfare State', Tavistock, London.
Wilson, M. and Phillips, K. (1977), The Conservative Party: from Macmillan to Thatcher, in N. Nugent and R. King (eds), 'The British Right', Saxon House, London, pp. 29–63.
Wulff, Charlotte (1979), Women Activists in the Labour Party. Paper presented to the European Joint Sessions, Brussels.

3 USA

Judith Evans

Home of the contemporary feminist movement, the USA might be
thought to stand in the vanguard of female political emancipation;
and at the mass level, in many ways, it does. At the apex of
American politics, though, women are largely distinguished by
their absence; and it seems reasonable to assume that true political parity of the sexes will require further massive social change.
As I write, the chances of genuinely progressive female advance
do not seem good.

US POLITICS AND GOVERNMENT (1)

The American political system is vast and complex; its complexity
deriving partly from the fact that the USA is a federation of fifty
States, and that State and federal law and politics coincide, sometimes uneasily. It is highly democratic in form, from the extent to
which an enormous number of officers, including State judges, are
subject to election, to the way contenders for the presidency
must campaign for the popular vote in the smallest States before
they can even gain their party nomination. And yet so huge and
powerful is the country, so momentous the issues involved, that
despite remarkable strides towards open government the ordinary
citizen faces barriers to action and understanding capable of
negating democracy in practice.

Counties are the basic lowest unit of government in the USA;
they control local law enforcement, roads, education and welfare,
and are supervised by an elected board, and probably an elected
sheriff, and have a district or county attorney. Counties may have
only a few hundred inhabitants, or may comprise very large areas
including big cities. Next come the cities, again varying enor-
mously in size; most have an elected council, and a directly elected
mayor, the power of the latter differing greatly. The States have
elected governors whose power is growing, and elected legislatures
ranging from the properly salaried and professional to the 'citizen
legislatures' of, for example, New Hampshire; here there is a
general trend towards greater professionalisation (Epstein, 1978,
pp. 351-2). All but thirteen States choose their Supreme Court
judges by some manner of popular election; and all but seven
allow for popular election of judges in their lower courts (ibid.,
p. 349). Thirty-nine States provide for matters to be decided by
referendum, and in twenty-one there can be an initiative whereby
the people themselves put a proposal to the popular vote. The

States are governed by written constitutions; but State law is
subject to Federal law, and that is subject to its highest expression, the Constitution of the United States.

Integral to the framing of the American Constitution was the
avoidance both of too great a concentration of power in the hands
of a few, and of undue extension of power to the people; so that
the Federal Government consists of separate institutions designed
to act as checks upon each other. The President, elected quite
separately from the legislature, and in practice directly by the
people, is independent of the parties in Congress; and at the
same time, the latter can check his proposals; while the Supreme
Court rules on the conformity to the Constitution of the enact-
ments and actions of the other branches of government, as well
as being the court of ultimate appeal.

A nation of great cultural, ethnic and regional diversity, the
USA is nevertheless in practice a two-party system, with the
Democrats to the Left, standing for government action for welfare,
supported by the blacks and the urban working class whites; and
the Republicans to the Right, the party of big business and small
government, supported by the middle and upper class. However,
each party should be seen as a coalition – and in many ways an
ad hoc one, to elect candidates who will bring party stalwarts the
spoils of victory – of socially and ideologically disparate groups.

The President is elected every four years; all 435 Representatives and one-third of the hundred Senators, every two. Party
nomination is increasingly determined by primary elections where
all voters registered as supporters of the party concerned can
vote, rather than by the local party leaders. At the State level,
the primary can be the real arena of struggle, perhaps between
the party leaders' candidate, and a challenger; for it is common
for there to be a lack of genuine inter-party competition, one of
the two major parties effectively dominating the State (ibid., p.
355). Presidential candidates are nominated by enormous national
conventions; increasingly, State delegates will be bound by the
results of a primary. These tendencies weaken the parties – and
especially their local leaders – as power brokers and vote confer-
rers, while since 1971 limits on financial contributions and spending, and regulations making a large number of small contributions,
collected over a wide area, of vital importance in gaining State
funding, also lessen party control (ibid., pp. 241-2).

AMERICAN FEMINISM

As early as 1639 a woman demanded the right to vote in a State
Assembly; and women had the vote – though did not necessarily
use it – in many of the early colonies, e.g. in New Jersey, from
1776 to 1807 (Flexner, 1959, p. 164). By the early nineteenth
century, women and many free blacks had lost this right; the
campaign for female suffrage did not begin until the middle of the
century.

In July 1848, Elizabeth Cady Stanton and others organised the Seneca Falls Convention; and the American feminist movement began. Though the right to vote was only one of the resolutions passed - and indeed, by far the least supported - yet we can date the suffrage compaign from this time. This early movement was strongly associated with the cause of slavery, and its themes included a comparison, to which later feminists would return, of the position of women and blacks (Stanton, 1860, p. 119). As with later feminism, too, the actions of male liberators gave a crucial impetus to the movement. For in 1840 American women were denied participation in the World Anti-Slavery Convention in London; and at the end of the Civil War, the Fourteenth Amendment of 1868, enfranchising black Americans, for the first time put the word 'male' in the American Constitution. The Amendment brought controversy and a split between those women who thought its passing of paramount importance, and those who opposed it on feminist grounds. In 1869 Elizabeth Cady Stanton and Susan B. Anthony, leaders of the latter group, set up the National Woman Suffrage Association, confined to women, which was to press for the gaining of the vote by federal amendment, and to espouse a wide range of feminist issues; while later in the year emerged the more respectable American Woman Suffrage Association, concerned narrowly with the vote, and believing it best gained by changes State by State (Flexner, 1959, pp. 152-3; Sinclair, 1966, pp. 188-92).

Aspects of the early movement, and more especially of its radical wing, brought controversy; for example, the association of Anthony and Stanton with the 'charismatic clairvoyant and stockbroker and courtesan', Victoria Woodhull (Sinclair, 1966, p. 191), who ran for President in 1872. But by the 1880s the cause of women's suffrage was growing increasingly respectable; and the two wings were able to unite in 1890 in the National American Woman Suffrage Association (NAWSA). During the 1910s, the cause even became a little fashionable and the Association gained vast numbers of middle-class members (ibid., p. 226). However, the movement split again when the Congressional Union, set up by Alice Paul and Lucy Burns to press solely for a federal amendment, campaigned against the Democrats, as being responsible, as the party in power, for the failure to give women the vote. A further split occurred when the Congressional Union's successor, the Woman's Party, began a militant campaign of picketing, leading to arrests and forced feeding, which was disowned by the National Association under its leader Carrie Chapman Catt (Flexner, 1959, Ch. XXI).

Women did gain the vote in individual States before a federal amendment was finally passed; and, of course, support was needed within States before such an amendment could be ratified; and so to an extent, the policy of local campaigning, dominant from 1886 to 1913 (ibid., p. 175) made sense. But progress was painfully slow. Wyoming had granted female suffrage in 1869, while a Territory, and refused in 1889 to join the Union as a State without

maintaining it (ibid., pp. 177-8). State referenda gained the vote
for women in Colorado in 1893 and Idaho in 1896; but these were
the only successful referenda campaigns prior to 1910. Seven
States, in all, gave female suffrage before 1917; in that year, six
more gave the Presidential vote by legislation. A Bill for federal
action was first introduced in 1868. In January 1918 the President
declared for the federal amendment the day before the vote in the
House of Representatives; and it was passed, against opposition
mainly from the South, with Republicans overwhelmingly for, and
Democrats evenly split (ibid., pp. 291-3). The Senate delayed
the Bill until 1919; when they passed it, there began a long campaign for ratification. On 26 August 1919 American women were
formally enfranchised by the adoption of the Nineteenth Amendment, ruling that the right of citizens to vote should not adversely
be affected by their sex. One battle was over.

What kind of grouping was the American Women's Suffrage Movement? What type of women thus challenged the orthodoxy of their
day? Broad characterisations inevitably distort; attribute to individuals too narrow a stance, and deny the essential heterogeneity
of a movement. Also, to be a militant early feminist was not necessarily to make common cause with the poor, with immigrants,
blacks after enfranchisement, or even the working woman. And
history is still in large part the story of the articulate, and of
leadership. This account of workers for female equality is further
confined to the suffragists: medical pioneers, for example, or
trade union organisers, find no place here.

What can be said is that early feminist leaders were radical in
their broad attack on the oppression of women, carrying their
analyses far beyond the vote alone, raising issues that resound
today. Thus Frances Wright preached free love in the 1820s and
Angelica Grimke fought in the 1830s and 1840s for full and genuine
equality within marriage (Sinclair, 1966, pp. 36, 47). Thus, too,
Stanton and Anthony crusaded against the church, and Stanton
for better marital law (ibid., p. 190). On the other hand, the
mainstream leader Carrie Chapman Catt opposed immigration, and
asked in 1894 that politicians 'cut off the vote of the slums and
give it to women' (Chafe, 1972, pp. 14-15); and in the early 1900s
suffragists were offering a certain support to eugenics, viewing
it and the vote as moral matters, and ways of bettering the conduct of life (Sinclair, 1966, pp. 237-8). Moralism - as distinct from
the issue of sexual political equality - had been present among
feminists from the beginning, finding the height of its expression
in resonant statements of female political superiority (Elshtain,
1974, passim).

While the coming of female suffrage ushered in an era of political
quiescence, still feminism did not vanish totally, to rise from nowhere in the 1960s. Indeed, the immediate post-suffrage campaign
posed questions still at issue today; and that campaign still runs,
beginning to be as long lived as the struggle for the vote. For in
1923 the National Women's Party - the militant suffragists -
proposed the Equal Rights Amendment (ERA) to the American

Constitution; and it has been introduced at every following session of Congress, reading since 1943: 'Equality of rights under
the law shall not be denied by the United States or by any State
on account of sex'. Initially ERA was opposed by the League of
Women Voters, NAWSA's successor, which believed in a more
gradual approach, and wanted to keep the laws that protected
women, for example, on working hours, and that the Amendment
would sweep away (Chafe, 1972, p. 117). Though included in
every Democratic and Republican platform since 1944, ERA was
largely unknown to the new feminist movement of the 1960s,
partly because of the National Women's Party's preference for
elite lobbying tactics rather than mass mobilisation (Freeman, 1975,
p. 64). By 1970 protective legislation was perceived as being used
against women, and this objection to ERA lost its force (ibid.,
p. 212). The Amendment was passed by the House in 1970 and the
Senate in 1972; twenty-eight States ratified it in that year, but
the next January it met a national campaign to block it (ibid.,
p. 220). As I write, the time available for ratification has been
extended; just three States more are needed, but it looks as if
ERA will not succeed in the immediate future.

The modern feminist movement, which was to rally around ERA
(ibid., p. 238), grew up around 1963. There were two separate
wings, with different stimuli, though both for a long while were
white, middle-class and mainly college educated. The older and
more conventional wing includes such groups as the National
Organisation for Women (NOW), founded in 1966, a major co-
ordinating grouping; the National Women's Political Caucus, set up
in 1971 to get more women into public office and to further women's
interests generally; and the Women's Equity Action League,
founded in 1968, concerned basically with professional equality
(ibid., pp. 152-3). These organisations are interested essentially
in legal and economic affairs and the mobilisation of employed
women; and they are formally structured. Immediate stimuli for
this part of the movement were the 1961 President's Commission on
the Status of Women, and its 1963 report; and the publication, also
in 1963, of Betty Friedan's 'The Feminine Mystique', decrying the
home-centred 1950s. Additional stimuli were the retreat, if anything, of women in the professions; and the possibly joking
addition of 'sex' to the 1964 Civil Rights Act's Title VII, dealing
with discrimination in employment (ibid., Ch. 2). Given the generation and socio-economic background of this wing, it is not
surprising that their main concerns have been the gaining of
professional and economic redress by legal means, the liberalisation
of traditional marriage, and an escape from the bonds of 1950s
suburbia.

The younger section of the feminist movement, at its inception,
was even more exclusively white, middle-class, and well educated
than the older. It was, and is, in general formal terms more radical; that is, more of its members would espouse various causes
on the Left (ibid., p. 50). It is perhaps in tone, and area of concentration, that the difference between the two wings has lain; and

the tone of the younger grouping was set in its beginnings, anyway, by its major stimulus. Like the suffragists, these women
came to understand their own oppression by working for the
emancipation of others, for they were the product of the black
civil rights campaign. Also, though, they came from the student
and peace movements. They expected the society they were in
protest against to discriminate against them as women; it was the
sexism of the New Left, so contrary to its rhetoric of liberation
and participation, that led them first to rebel within existing radical organisations, and then to work on their own (ibid., pp. 56-9).
The waning of New Left activity in the late 1960s led to the growth
of this highly informal and unstructured wing of the women's
movement, the concern of which was initially less with economic
equality than with the politics of personal relationships. Its style,
in early years anyway, was characterised by the 'rap group' or
consciousness-raising session which, by free-ranging discussion,
sought to make women perceive that what they had thought to be
individual and personal problems, were shared and were political.
Characteristic, too, has been the exclusion of men from many
meetings and activities, though only a small part of the movement
was ever totally separatist. The movement's lack of structure, that
is, its avoidance of normal forms of political leadership, and its
attempt to avoid hierarchy and leadership, have been seen as contributing to a certain inertia and to the emergence of an informal
'star' system, which is as elitist as conventional structures, if not
more so (ibid., pp. 119f and 145).

In recent years the two wings of the movement have grown together. NOW's National Women's Strike in 1970 brought in many
previously unorganised and non-employed women, and with them
a demand for consciousness-raising. In 1967 NOW had 1,000 members; in 1974, forty times this number (ibid., p. 87). It is currently the major grouping.

It is difficult, obviously, to assess the achievements of the
modern American feminist movement. The Equal Employment Opportunity Commission, which oversees minority employment
generally, has been strengthened; and works more actively for
women than it did at first. The 1972 Congress passed a number of
women's rights measures including non-discrimination in health
training, child care deductions for the lower paid, and ERA; and
women were highly active within Congress in their initiation and
passing. Women's rights have become a matter of legitimate public
concern, and activism on their behalf has become accepted (ibid.,
Chs. 6, 7); though it has been suggested that women are successful precisely to the extent that they focus on narrow, non-
controversial considerations of equity, rather than issues that
involve role change, or challenge basic values (Gelb, 1979, p. 387f)
Less tangibly, petty sexism has become less easy to sustain; and
there is even - though not everywhere, or always - something of
a feeling of genuine support for women's endeavours, and of an
avoiding of previous power-laden behaviour. Much has changed
since the 1950s; and not only for women. The movement must ask

itself, though, as must those in all industrial countries, whether its gains can be maintained at a time of recession and potential new conservatism; whether, for example, attacks on affirmative action (Freeman, 1975, pp. 200-3) are the beginning of a serious backlash; and whether underprivileged groups in general can avoid isolation and selective attack.

WOMEN'S SOCIAL POSITION

Between 1950 and 1972, while the proportion of single women (2) in paid employment remained more or less the same, the figure for married women nearly doubled, and for married women with children under six years of age, nearly tripled (Barrett, 1976, Table 1, p. 80). In 1976 47 per cent of American women over the age of 16, and 56 per cent of those aged between 20 and 64, were employed or looking for employment ('Congressional Quarterly', 1977, p. 23). Economic need is thought to have been a major factor in the rise in female employment; and most recently, the rate of increase has been greatest among young married women (ibid., p. 6). There has not been a parallel improvement in women's occupational status relative to men's; for example, the differential between male and female pay has actually widened over the last twenty years. Women earn a lot less than men with similar educational qualifications: the average woman with a college degree earning less than a man who dropped out of high school (ibid., p. 26).

There is a similar disparity at the higher levels of the education system, reflected in an under-representation of women in certain professions. In 1975 men gained 79 per cent of all doctorates awarded, but over 90 per cent in business studies, computing and information sciences, engineering, law, physical sciences and economics. Business, engineering and higher level law, especially, were male ghettoes (US Bureau of the Census, 1977, pp. 153, 161).

Nearly 40 per cent of American marriages end in divorce, the highest proportion in the world, and the rate has risen sharply in recent decades, doubling between 1963 and 1975 (ibid., 1977, p. 3). Fewer than half of all American families now take the traditional nuclear form of husband and wife living with their children. These changes do not necessarily imply a drop in the number of births; indeed, this may be rising. Rather, an increase in the number of children may take place without a return to the home-centred values of the 1950s (ibid., pp. 18-19).

VOTER TURNOUT

Both suffragists and some of their opponents had believed that giving women the vote would change the conduct of public life. But it soon became clear that women did not in fact form a distinct block of voters; just like men, they were divided, and they divided along the normal party lines. And initially, their turnout was low (Chafe, 1972, pp. 30-1).

In 1952 and 1956 10 per cent fewer women than men voted in the presidential elections. Older, less educated and Southern women, and mothers of young children, were least likely to vote; childless women with a college education actually voted more than their male counterparts (Campbell et al., 1960, pp. 485-8). In 1964, among women voters under the age of 45, only in the South was there a difference of more than 1 per cent; elsewhere, the sexes voted at virtually identical rates. In 1964 and 1968 black women were more likely to vote than black men of the same age. In 1972 women under the age of 45 voted at the same rate as men or slightly higher (Lansing, 1974, pp. 10-14). In 1976 more women voted than men (Mezey and Mezey, 1979, p. 3).

American women's voting behaviour differs a little from men's, though not, as has conventionally been assumed, by any means always in the direction of greater conservatism. Twenty or so years ago, women were found to be 3 to 5 per cent more likely than men to be Republican voters, but this was explained by the fact that the women who were most likely to vote belonged to groups favouring the Republican party (Campbell et al., 1960, p. 493). Given changes in turnout, this partisan preference would be expected to change too; and indeed from 1964 women have been more likely than men to support presidential candidates of the centre and left (Lansing, 1974, p. 15). The McGovern campaign seems to have mobilised employed women, one-third of whom were self-identified liberals, as against 22 per cent of men and 18 per cent of housewives (Andersen, 1975, pp. 450-1, 452). But in 1976 women were more likely than men to support Ford against Carter (Kirkpatrick, 1978, p. 264). No simple evaluation of the difference between male and female voting behaviour can as yet be made.

CITIZEN ACTIVISM

If activity is measured by the number of political acts a person undertakes, then differences between the sexes are small, and among certain groups virtually non-existent. Where participation in one or more activities is the test, then among those with higher education, women were 13 per cent less active in 1952 and 1956, 6 per cent more in 1960, and 2 per cent less in 1964. If four or more activities are considered, then only in 1956 were highly educated men more active, by 2.7 per cent; women 0.1 per cent more active in 1952, 2.8 per cent in 1960, and 2.4 per cent in 1964 (Lansing, 1974, pp. 17-18). From 1960 employed women have taken part in campaigning more or less to the same extent as men, and in 1972 had a higher average number of campaign acts. In 1952 the average number of acts for all men was 0.24 higher than that for all women, in 1972, 0.1; in an effective range of 0.47 to 0.9 (Andersen, 1975, pp. 442-3).

Of course while the number of acts, and number of types of act, undertaken is important, it is a rather crude indicator of actual political performance and potential; and the relevance of action both for the person concerned, and for the conduct of politics, requires further investigation. A study of state party members found that women were less electorally ambitious, and undertook more routine work like attending meetings and telephoning, though Democratic women were less so inclined than Republicans. Suggested reasons for the sex difference are early socialisation into essentially subordinate female behaviour, and an adherence to expected female patterns for fear of reprisal. As the authors say, these findings point to the need for more research on the way established political structures, and current political contexts affect the behaviour of women (Fowlkes et al., 1979, pp. 777-80).

Differences in potential, measured by expressed readiness to engage in given types of political action, are small in America, and do not necessarily follow expected patterns. There is basically no difference in the number of men and women who are complete 'non-actives', that is, ready to engage neither in conventional nor in protest action; nor among those essentially committed to the conventional road. More men are 'progressives': the classic liberal citizen concerned with regular participation, but prepared for unorthodox action where necessary. The categories in which women are better represented than men are, interestingly, 'dissenters' who are mainly available for protest, and 'super-actives' who are high in expressed readiness for both types of action (Jennings and Farah, 1980, pp. 235-9).

WOMEN IN PUBLIC OFFICE

I turn from a near equality of the sexes to a massive disparity, for the proportion of women in public office in America is pitifully low. Carter's administration, 14 per cent of which was female, was the first to include two women cabinet ministers: Juanita Krebs, Secretary of Commerce, and Patricia Roberts Harris, Secretary of Housing and Urban Development. Before 1977 only three women had ever held cabinet rank. In the ninety-fifth Congress, there were eighteen female members of the House of Representatives; and two women Senators, Muriel Humphrey and Maryon P. Allen, both of whom were appointed after their (Senator) husbands' deaths (Johnson, 1978, p. 4). By 1977 only ten women had ever sat in the Senate, and all were filling the unexpired term of another legislator, mainly that of their husband; and only three had remained Senators for a full six-year term (Diamond, 1977, p. 9). In the ninety-fourth Congress, nineteen women held seats in the House of Representatives, none in the Senate; women comprised just 4 per cent of the combined membership of both houses (Johnson, 1976, p. xx). There has not been a simple linear rise in the number of women in Congress; the current figure is an improvement on the ten to twelve female members of the 1960s; but in three

Congresses of the late 1950s, seventeen women sat (Gehlen, 1977, p. 306). Finally among the judiciary, no woman has ever been a member of the US Supreme Court. In 1977 one woman only served as judge in US courts of appeals, eight in US district courts (Cook, 1978, p. 102).

In 1978 two women were governors of American States: Ella Grasso in Connecticut, and Dixie Lee Ray in Washington; and there were three female lieutenant governors, a rise from the figure of one governor and one lieutenant governor in 1975. In 1975 there were eighty-four, in 1977 ninety-seven, female members of state cabinets; in the latter year nearly 11 per cent of the total of nine hundred and four were female.(3) In 1975 women comprised 2 per cent of the membership of county governing bodies, in 1977 3 per cent; and female membership of school boards rose from 13 per cent in 1974 to 20 per cent in 1976, and 25 per cent in 1978 (Johnson, 1978, pp. 4-6). An especially large rise took place in mayoralties and municipal and township governing bodies, from 4 per cent in 1975 to 8 per cent in 1977; though part of the increase was due simply to more information being available, and thus a greater number being recorded (Johnson et al., 1978, pp. 6A, 7A). In 1977 2 per cent of judges in appeal courts and general trial courts were women (ibid., p. 4A), and nearly 6 per cent of all judges (Cook, 1978, p. 88). Four per cent of State legislators were female in 1969, 8 per cent in 1975, and 9 per cent in 1978; just over 5 per cent of senators, and nearly 11 per cent of Representatives (Johnson et al., 1978, p. 4A).

In political parties, formally, women are better represented; for most States have some form of rule providing for parity of male and female representation. In 1924 both major parties decided that the sexes should be represented equally on their national committees, and this principle has been extended either by State Law, or by the parties themselves, to the lower levels of party structure. Women comprise 34 per cent of the membership of American city parties (Clarke and Kornberg, 1979, p. 447). Since 1972 the Democrats have required their State parties to encourage the participation of women, the young, and minority groups in their delegations to the party convention; the Republicans have a similar though less formal principle of greater equality of participation (Ranney, 1978, pp. 213-4, 216-7).

What are the characteristics of female office-holders? How do political women differ from political men? What do male and female politicians think about women in office? What factors appear to favour the accession of American women to political office?(4) While data on these questions are far from comprehensive, a fair number of studies have now been carried out, and we begin to have something approaching a cumulative body of knowledge.(5)

I begin with social factors; and first, age. The finding for public office generally, for State legislators, for the US House of Representatives and for Congress as a whole is that women are first elected at an older age than men (Stoper, 1977, p. 324), though one study finds only a marginal difference (Johnson et al.,

1978, p. 16A). (Obviously a substantial age gap would give men a decided advantage in the race to establish themselves as legislators, for important committee posts, and for higher office.) Women tend to enter Congress in their early fifties, after the age of child-bearing and rearing (Werner, 1966, pp. 20-1). There is no firm evidence as to why women should enter politics at a later age than men. It could be that they have to spend their political youth caring for home and family; alternatively, it might take a woman longer than a man to become politically qualified, or be thought of as such (Johnson and Stanwick, 1976, xxvi). What is clear is that as long as a significant age gap exists and importance continues to be placed on political experience and seniority, women will be at something of a disadvantage.

My remarks assume that most female politicians are married; and indeed, this is the case. The proportion is much the same as that of the general population, except for women in Congress and in State executives; the difference between the latter two groups and others may not in fact be one of substance. It has been suggested that a high proportion of married women is what we should expect, given the importance for male politicians of a conventional family life (ibid., p. xxx).(6) Indeed, male legislators are even more likely than their female colleagues to be married. They are also more likely to have young children; perhaps because men marry women younger than themselves (Johnson, 1978, p. 9). It is not that a far greater proportion of political women remain unmarried; rather, at the Congressional level, anyway, we encounter the interesting and disputed phenomenon of the political widow (Gehlen, 1977, p. 307).

Seventy-three per cent of all female Senators, 50 per cent of all Congresswomen have been widows at the time they took office: 50 women in all, of whom 39 took the place of an incumbent Congressman on his death. Thirty-five of these replaced their own husbands (Kincaid, 1978, p. 96). There has been a tendency to regard these women as political ciphers; thus it has been noted that they have been less well educated than other Congresswomen, have had far less occupational experience, and have been much less likely to have a history of previous political work or public office. While 97 per cent of other Congresswomen wanted to serve another term, 55 per cent of widows retired at the end of their husband's term and had sometimes announced this intention even before they took up office (Bullock and Heys, 1972, pp. 417-20). This picture of the less qualified and relatively apolitical puppet has been challenged. It has been pointed out that of the four Senators who succeeded their husbands, Hattie Caraway, appointed in 1931, fought vigorously to retain her seat, and served two full terms. Margaret Chase Smith, one of America's most famous political women in her own right, was elected against opposition after her husband's death, and faced and defeated strong opposition from within her own party at a later election. Only five of the thirty-one political widows in the House of Representatives did not have to fight a contested election; and four of these served for a very

short time indeed. There were Congressional widows who tried
unsuccessfully to gain their husbands' seats; and one who refused
to stand down for her husband on his release from gaol. Further
a comparison of the activity rates and legislative behaviour of
widows and others shows no clear superiority of the latter (Kincaid,
1978, pp. 98-102).

The conventional view of political widows is seen as a product of
the general stereotyping of women as dependent, submissive, etc.
(Kincaid, 1978, p. 104); and whether this is so, or whether
there was a specific stereotype of these widows created from the
attributes of a few, Kincaid's correction is welcome. However, the
concern must be not only with the characteristics of women who
enter Congress by the various routes, but with what the routes
available tell us about the status of women in society, and its
relation to their political opportunities and role.(7) Viewed in this
light, the 'widow route' must be seen as an indicator that in the
past even more than now, women's standing has been a matter less
of their own accomplishment than of their association with the man
they married; that women have been seen as figureheads and political stop-gaps, as one-person front organisations for various
interests; and that in a not negligible number of cases, this view
has been correct. It is for this reason that we must welcome the
relative decline of this road to office. True, it has brought into
formal politics women lacking attributes - for example, a training
in law - whose status as qualifications for office we should perhaps reject; but it has done so in a way that has emphasised, if
not indeed reinforced, the subordinate place of women in American society.

Female legislators are well educated relative to the general population, but not compared with their male colleagues (Johnson,
1978, p. 9); the level of education rises with office (Johnson et
al. 1978, p. 9A). Congresswomen have been highly educated, more
than half having been college graduates, and two-fifths of these
having undertaken graduate work. As students they have specialised mainly in education and law, then in fine arts and business,
then in a range of social science disciplines. This is an unusual
profile for women, but it also differs from that of Congressmen,
who have been far more narrowly concentrated in business and law
(Werner, 1966, pp. 21-2).

As would be expected from their educational level, female office-
holders are relatively high in socio-economic status.(8) Their
husbands are highly educated and have occupations that are high
in prestige (Johnson, 1976, p. xxxi). Taken as a whole, they are
worse off financially than male politicians; among State legislators
50 per cent of women, as against 13 per cent of men, have an
individual yearly income of less than $5,000; 13 per cent of men,
and no women, of more than $25,000 (Diamond, 1977, pp. 38-9).
It is unmarried women who have less money than men; married
women, when family income is measured, have more. This could be
because they are at an age when family income tends to be at its
height; or because some, anyway, of male legislators' wives are

not employed; or it could reflect the tendency of women to marry
men of higher occupational status than themselves, whilst men
marry women of lower (Johnson et al., 1978, p. 18A).

By their own estimate, female office-holders have decidedly
helpful families. Most regard their husbands as supportive; a
greater proportion than that of men who so regard their wives
(Johnson, 1978, p. 9). Wives appear to give more actual help,
though the difference is not large; help is given along conventional sex lines, for example, men contribute money. More than
one-quarter of women do their own housework, and more than
one-third do some; only 16 per cent of men do any (Stoper, 1977,
pp. 326-9). It has been suggested that when evaluating their
wives' work, men do not take household matters sufficiently into
account (ibid., p. 331); and in this connection it is interesting
that another study, where again husbands are rated more highly,
finds that 42 per cent of female legislators, but only 29 per cent
of male, saw their spouse as taking on extra household work
(Johnson et al., 1978, p. 18A). It is a relevant question exactly
where the extra housework for these wives came from, given that
women do virtually all of it already.

Male legislators' wives view their husbands' political service
less favourably than female politicians' husbands (Stoper, 1977,
p. 330); and husbands were more supportive of absence from home
on political duties. Is this because only those women with helpful
husbands enter politics (Mezey, 1978b, pp. 494-5)? Certainly, in
most offices, three-quarters or more women report their husbands'
approval and interest; and the proportion rises with the status of
the post. Male legislators are more likely than female to see political life as harming the family; and this, whether the question
concerns the career of a woman, or a man (Johnson et al., 1978,
pp. 13A, 14A, 18-19A).

As I have said, female politicians have the relatively high social
and economic status associated with entry to political office; but
they have not, on the whole, engaged in the professions, of which
law is a prime example, that are conducive to success in politics.
Most have been teachers, nurses, secretaries, social workers;
occupations few male legislators have followed (Johnson, 1978, p.
9). With higher office, the picture changes a little. Most State
legislators have worked in business, public relations or teaching;
relatively few as lawyers or in the mass media (Werner, 1968, p.
46). In Congress, about one-third have worked in the field of
education, 20 per cent in communications; around 23 per cent have
been lawyers or public servants, and 8 per cent have worked in
business (Werner, 1966, p. 23). It is not that the occupational
difference between the sexes has been one of formal status; here
men and women have been roughly equal. So it is proposed that
female-dominated occupations are seen as lacking a preparation for
political life precisely because it is women who hold them; and also,
that they may not give access to the kind of contacts, or contact
networks, that further a political career (Johnson et al., 1978,
p. 17A).

Just as the proportion of female incumbents declines as the importance of the office rises, so within each type of office women's status is relatively low; and this is not accounted for by differences in men's and women's length of service (Diamond, 1977, p. 46). Are women less ambitious than men? Do they fail to gain higher office because they fail to seek it, or do not press for it strongly enough? It seems that women are as self-confident as men except with regard to their training and experience (Johnson, 1978, p. 10); and that they are at least as likely as men to want another term in their present post, and more likely to want to reach a higher office (Johnson et al., 1978, p. 52A). So even for those women who have gained public office, something intervenes between aim and attainment.

There are other attitudes, and sets of attitudes, on which male and female politicians differ; and among them are perceptions of women's assets and liabilities, as politicians, and of the existence and location of sex discrimination in politics. A very large number of female office-holders at State and local level believe that male party leaders discriminate against political women. A rather smaller number believe in voter prejudice; though the lower the office, the more likely this is to be perceived. At least half the women at every level - and as high as 78 per cent - report sex-related personal difficulties; and these are overwhelmingly concerned with their male colleagues', or other male politicians', discriminatory words and behaviour. Women, they feel, are treated frivolously, given menial work, and not given the office they deserve (Johnson et al., 1978, p. 39A). Even women who do not in any way emphasise the prevalence of discrimination, report various kinds of verbal harassment (Kirkpatrick, 1974, pp. 109-10). Male legislators are less likely to perceive discrimination against women - though they are very nearly as likely to think that women lack equality of opportunity - and more likely to believe in voter prejudices (Johnson et al., 1978, p. 42A).

Women are thought to have both advantages and disadvantages as politicians; responses differ by sex, with women emphasising women's good personal qualities as an asset, and sexism as the main liability; while men see, for example, housewives' leisure time as advantageous, and female lack of stamina as causing problems (Mezey, 1978b, p. 498). Women see women as having a better relationship with their constituents, as being more committed, more patient, and better able to understand the problems of minority groups. Men tend to see certain of women's characteristics as assets, but more in terms of traditional female qualities such as conscientiousness, and skill in personal relations (Johnson et al., 1978, pp. 40-43A).

There appear to be sex differences among politicians on various political issues; though on the whole, the differences are not large. One study finds female State legislators more in favour of women playing a greater part in politics, but not of policies that benefit women (Mezey, 1978a, p. 380).(9) Women at the same level of office elsewhere have been found to be a little more liberal than

men on a range of policies – for example, more likely to believe
that riots are better dealt with by removing their causes than by
the use of force, and more in favour of the provision of child day
care. Considerably more women think that abortion should not be
restricted by law; but equal proportions of men and women oppose
abortion completely, owing to a strong Catholic influence among
women (Diamond, 1977, pp. 49-50). Congresswomen are more liberal than their parties, and female State legislators, whatever
their party, have been more likely than men to vote for ERA.
Women office-holders are more likely than their male counterparts
to describe themselves as liberals, and less as conservatives.
Women are a lot more likely to support action by government and
industry for women's rights; and are more liberal on a number of
women's issues. They rather than men oppose harsher punishment
for crime, and an enforced retirement age; and support bussing
for racial integration. The sex difference holds within the self-
rated ideological categories; that is, conservative women are more
liberal than conservative men except on bussing and defence; and
liberal women than liberal men on all issues. Republican women
are as liberal as, or more liberal than, Democratic men on all
women's issues but government provision of child care (Johnson
et al., 1978, pp. 32-6A).

Do women behave differently from men as legislators? Do they
for example, concentrate on fields, like education and health,
which some have assumed to be the special province of women?
The answer is that there is something of a concentration, but its
direction is not intuitively obvious. Women in public office in general are indeed grouped in health, education and welfare committees; but the next clustering comes in the areas of finance, and
law and law enforcement (Johnson, 1976, p. xliii). Education and
health and welfare are fields of concentration for female State legislators; men range much more widely over the various committees
(Diamond, 1977, p. 45).

Certain attitudes relevant to a politician's behaviour in office
differ by sex. Women in State legislatures view the process of
bargaining and lobbying with less favour than do men, and think
that legislators should be independent of outside pressure. They
avoid lobbyists, or report that they are not so approached; but is
this because their relative lack of power makes them uninteresting
to those who lobby (ibid., pp. 47, 106-7)? More women, also,
stress the importance of having a good relationship with, and
helping, constituents (Johnson et al., 1978, p. 29A).

Female members of the House of Representatives are no more
dutiful in their attendance than men. They are not more likely
than men to vote with their party, but neither are they more independent; indeed, they are less likely than men openly to oppose
(Gehlen, 1977, pp. 311-4). At the State level, only women who
have no other paid employment, give more time to their office than
men (Johnson et al., 1978, p. 29A). In Congress, anyway, it does
not seem that there is a distinctive female political style (Gehlen,
1977, p. 317).

I have discussed various attributes of female politicians - relatively advanced education, fairly high socio-economic status, a supportive home environment - which appear to facilitate the entry of women to public office. But are there political factors, too, relevant to women's representation; apart, that is - or apparently apart - from the widespread discrimination so many politicians believe exists?

Various factors have been found; they mainly confirm the subordinate status of women. The higher a mayor's salary, the less likely it is that the post will be held by a woman; though the relationship is not strong. Also, women have more chance of gaining a mayoralty that is appointive, than one decided by popular election. Evidence on the effect of multi- as opposed to single-member constituencies is equivocal; multi-member seats are associated both with greater female representation, and with none. The relationship is in any event very weak. The representation of women is associated negatively with the status and importance of office; though not with the amount of competition for it (Welch, 1979, pp. 484-9). For State legislatures, the size of the House in relation to the population is a major factor; there are more women, that is, where constituencies are small. As it happens, this also means that women are more likely to serve in small Houses (Diamond, 1977, pp. 11-13). So women are concentrated in the traditionalist States of New England, and largely absent from the legislatures of, for example, California and New York. It is suggested that this is related to the greater ease and cheapness of campaigning in the former (Werner, 1968, p. 43). The attitude of political parties to female candidates is also important; there is evidence that women are given either undesirable seats, or ones the party sees no hope of winning (Diamond, 1977, p. 78); but also, that party attitudes may be becoming more favourable (Johnson et al., 1978, 21A).

In America today, there is a striking discrepancy between an apparent equality of the sexes at the level of grassroots politics, and the various social, economic and educational gains made by women, and their virtual exclusion from the upper levels of politics, the inner counsels of power. It may be that this is simply a matter of a time lag; that there is a move towards full political parity of the sexes, but it will take a long time. However, the 1980s seem set for a recession in the industrialised world. This will clearly not favour progressive social reform and it is therefore likely that American feminist practice will of necessity concentrate on holding the line rather than advancement.

NOTES

1 This account is, of necessity, highly simplified. For a more comprehensive view see, inter alia, Vile (1978).
2 This category includes all women not currently married and living with their husbands.

3 For these figures and those given below, the total number of
offices is occasionally an estimate.
4 I discuss here only the characteristics of American office-
holders, and factors that appear relevant to the representation
of women in America. General theories of female subordination
are not considered.
5 For ease of presentation, I give only one source for each finding; it should be noted that most are well confirmed by other
studies.
6 Governor Jerry Brown of California and Mayor Ed Koch of New
York are notable exceptions to this requirement.
7 Gruberg (1968, p. 120) points out that three types of women
have succeeded in Congress: Congressional widows, the rich
and wives of men with flexible occupations.
8 Feminists are rightly irritated by the tendency of researchers
automatically to classify a woman according to her husband's
occupation. However women's social positions often are derived
from marriage; and so I report spouse's status here.
9 Mezey strongly believes that differences in political attitudes
between men and women are few in number, and small in size.

BIBLIOGRAPHY

Andersen, K. (1975), Working Women and Political Participation,
'American Journal of Political Science', vol. 19, pp. 439-54.
Barrett, N. (1976), Women in Industrial Society: an International
Perspective, in J. Chapman (ed.), 'Economic Independence for
Women', Sage, Beverly Hills and London.
Bullock, C. and Heys, P. (1972), Recruitment of Women for Con-
gress, 'Western Political Quarterly', vol. 23, pp. 416-23.
Campbell, A., Converse, P., Miller, W. and Stokes, D. (1960),
'The American Voter', Wiley, New York.
Chafe, W. (1972), 'The American Woman', Oxford University Press,
New York.
Clarke, H. and Kornberg, A. (1979), Moving Up the Political
Escalator: Women Party Officials in the United States and Can-
ada, 'Journal of Politics', vol. 41, pp. 442-77.
Congressional Quarterly, Inc. (1977), 'The Women's Movement',
Editorial Research Reports, Washington DC.
Cook, B., (1978), Women Judges: the End of Tokenism, in W.
Hepperle and Laura Crites (eds.), 'Women in the Courts', Nat-
ional Center for State Courts, Williamsburg, Virginia.
Diamond, I. (1977), 'Sex Roles in the State House', Yale Univer-
sity Press, New York.
Elshtain, J. (1974), Moral Woman and Immoral Man: a Consider-
ation of the Public-private Split and its Political Ramifications,
'Politics and Society', vol. 4, pp. 453-72.
Epstein, L. D. (1978), Old States in a New System, in A. King
(ed.), 'The New American Political System', American Enterprise
Institute for Public Policy Research, Washington DC.

Flexner, E. (1959), 'Century of Struggle', The Belknap Press of Harvard University Press, Cambridge, Massachusetts.

Fowlkes, D., Perkins, J. and Rinehart, S. (1979), Gender Roles and Party Roles, 'American Political Science Review', vol. 73, pp. 772–81.

Freeman, J. (1975), 'The Politics of Women's Liberation', Longman, New York and London.

Gehlen, F. (1977), Women Members of Congress, in M. Githens and J. Prestage (eds.), 'A Portrait of Marginality', David Mc Kay, New York.

Gelb, J. and Palley, M. (1979), Women and Interest Group Politics, 'Journal of Politics', vol. 41, pp. 362–92.

Gruberg, M. (1968), 'Women in American Politics', Academia Press, Oshkosh, Wisconsin.

Jennings, M. and Farah, B. (1980), Ideology, Gender and Political Action, 'British Journal of Political Science', vol. 10, pp. 219–40.

Johnson, M. (1978), Elective and Appointive Office (mimeo), Center for American Woman and Politics, Eagleton Institute, New Brunswick, New Jersey.

Johnson, M. and Stanwick, K. (1976), 'Profile of Women Holding Office', repr. Center for American Woman and Politics, Eagleton Institute, New Brunswick, New Jersey.

Johnson M., Carroll, S., Stanwick, K. and Korenblit, L. (1978), 'Profile of Women Holding Office II', repr. Center for American Woman and Politics, Eagleton Institute, New Brunswick, New Jersey.

Kincaid, D. (1978), Over His Dead Body: a Positive Perspective on Widows in the US Congress, 'Western Political Quarterly', vol. 31, pp. 96–104.

Kirkpatrick, J. (1974), 'Political Woman', Basic Books, New York.

Kirkpatrick, J. (1978), Electoral Competition, in A. King (ed.), 'The New American Political System', American Enterprise Institute for Public Policy Research, Washington DC.

Lansing, M. (1974), The American Woman: Voter and Activist, in J. Jacquette (ed.), 'Women in Politics', New York, Wiley.

Mezey, S. (1978a), Women and Representation: the Case of Hawaii, 'Journal of Politics', vol. 40, pp. 369–85.

Mezey, S. (1978b), Does Sex Make a Difference?, 'Western Political Quarterly', vol. 31, pp. 492–501.

Mezey, S. and Mezey, M. (1979), The Effects of Government Policy on Feminist Attitudes and Voter Participation, 'International Political Science Association' Roundtable paper.

Ranney, A. (1978), The Political Parties, in A. King (ed.), 'The New American Political System', American Enterprise Institute for Public Policy Research, Washington DC.

Sinclair, A. (1966), 'The Better Half', Jonathan Cape, London.

Stanton, E. (1860), Address to the New York State Legislature, in M. Schneir, 'Feminism: The Essential Historical Writings', Vintage Books, New York, 1972.

Stoper, E. (1977), Wife and Politician, in M. Githens and L. Pre-

tage, 'A Portrait of Marginality', David McKay, New York.
US Bureau of the Census (1977), 'Statistical Abstract of the United
   States 1977', Department of Commerce, Washington DC.
Welch, S. and Karnig, A. (1979), Correlates of Female Office-
   holding in City Politics, 'Journal of Politics', vol. 41, pp. 478-
   91.
Werner, E. (1966), Women in Congress, 1917-1964, 'Western Pol-
   itical Quarterly', vol. 19, pp. 16-30.
Werner, E. (1968), Women in the State Legislatures, 'Western
   Political Quarterly', vol. 21, pp. 40-9.
Vile, M. (1978), 'Politics in the USA', Hutchinson, London.

4 CANADA

Jill McCalla Vickers and
M. Janine Brodie

HISTORICAL BACKGROUND

The campaign for the political emancipation of Canadian women
took slightly more than half a century. Ironically, the women of
Quebec, who had exercised an ancient right to vote on numerous
observed occasions (1) between 1809 and 1834 alone (Cleverdon,
1974, p. 214) were forced to mount a campaign that amounted to a
fight to regain that right - a fight that was not successfully won
in the provincial jurisdiction until 1940. In the federal jurisdiction,
women with close relatives in the British and Canadian forces were
given the right to vote in 1917 by a pro-conscription government
gambling that the women so favoured would support both the
government and its pro-conscription stand (see Geller, 1976). In
general, the history of the political emancipation of Canadian
women defies coherent analysis except within a framework of a
region-by-region assessment.

The fact that no coherent, country-wide campaign of any size
for suffrage was mounted by Canadian women reflects certain
features of the country's social and political life. Canada's character as a new country of vast proportions (2) sparsely settled by
many different and largely unassimilated immigrant groups has
always made country-wide organization difficult and this was more
particularly the case before the development of air travel and mass
media networks. In addition, the fact that Canada is administered
politically under a decentralized federal system with a complex
division of powers makes it necessary for movements which aim at
broad societal change to construct organizations which can effectively address both levels of the Canadian state almost simultaneously. Given the additional strains of a major linguistic division
and intense regional loyalties, this is a task which has proven to
be all but impossible even for major politicial parties and all but
the most economically powerful pressure groups (see Pross, 1975).

Although the campaign to achieve the vote for women began in
Ontario - Canada's most urbanized and industrialized province -
in the 1870s,(3) it achieved its most coherent form and its initial
successes in the most recently settled, largely agrarian provinces
of the Western prairies. Ontario (4) rapidly followed the western
lead, however, despite a longer and more difficult campaign faced
with more resistance (Gorham, 1976, pp. 23-56). In the long-
settled and economically declining Maritime provinces, there was
little apparent opposition but 'a weight of indifference' to the issue
on the part of all but a very few women (Cleverdon, 1974, p. 156).

The lack of a fight for the vote, except much later in Quebec, and the dominance of 'maternal feminism' over the fragile strain of Equal Rights Feminism (5) meant that no lasting political allegiances or alliances were formed as a result of the first wave movement. Political parties quickly learned that women were unlikely either to reward them or to punish them for their policies or for their willingness or refusals to field women as candidates. Few organizations created during these early campaigns survived (Teather, 1976, pp. 308-13) and as a result so little impact was made on the history of Canadians that subsequent generations of Canadian women lived their lives without ever realizing that a first-wave movement had existed.

Quebec women proceeded on their own belated timetable to mount a campaign for the provincial franchise well after the first-wave movement had sunk from view in the rest of Canada. The Quebec campaign was a protracted struggle against the most intense opposition encountered in Canada. It was not successful until 1940. The alliance formed between movement women and the provincial Liberal party in the struggle for political emancipation was sustained during the 'Quiet Revolution' when major changes in the legal, economic and social status of Quebec women occurred (Cleverdon, 1974, Ch. 7).

In general, the political impact of the campaign for emancipation in the rest of Canada was slight in the short run. The 'Report of the Royal Commission on the Status of Women' showed that from 1919 to June 1970 there had been 134 federal and provincial elections and of the 6,845 legislators elected only 67 were women. Women's political clout was apparently so slight that 90,000 were removed from their jobs between the end of the war in 1945 and May 1946 with impunity (ibid., p. 279). Indeed, until the 1960s and early 1970s there was little sense among Canadian women that their potential political power as citizens and as prospective legislators could be employed to alter their own status and condition. Rather, it was the progress of urbanization, economic development and the establishment of the welfare state which achieved most of what little change occurred in the status and condition of the women's movement.

SOCIO-ECONOMIC ENVIRONMENT

Urbanization, immigration and industrialization are key features of Canada's recent socio-economic history but their timing, character and political impact as well as their extent varies significantly from region to region. These regional differences may, in some circumstances, be more important in our assessment of their impact on women's political participation than national trends.

Canada's political life is limited and shaped by certain key features of its existence. With a landmass greater than that of the United States,(6) its sparse population (7) is concentrated in a band of settlement along its border with the USA.(8) Although in

relative terms, Canadians continue to enjoy one of the highest
standards of living in the world,(9) this standard is artificial in
many senses. Although resource-rich, the country remains relatively undeveloped in terms of the secondary processing of
resources and has a fragile manufacturing sector. Its economy,
moreover, is highly open to world economic trends and is especially susceptible to trends in the American economy.

In the settlement and development of Canada women have always
worked, although the proportion in the paid labour force was relatively small until the 1960s.(10) The dramatic increase in the
1960s and the 1970s moreover was accounted for largely by the
influx of married women into the paid workforce on either a full-
time or a part-time basis (Gunderson, 1976, pp. 93–103). As the
National Council on Welfare noted in its Report, 'Women and Poverty' (1979), a full 51 per cent of Canada's families with two
spouses working would have fallen below the official poverty line
in 1975 without the wives' income, demonstrating that most married Canadian women work because they must.(11)

While only 19 per cent of wives in families with incomes above
$25,000 participate in the paid labour force on a full-time basis,
31 per cent in the under $5,000 category participate in a full-time
job. The increase in mother-led, single-parent families also
requires note. As of 1977 8.6 per cent (502,000) of all families
were single-parent families and, of these, 85 per cent (427,000)
were mother-led.(12) While the average income of all Canadian
families at this point was $20,101, the average income of mother-
led, single-parent families was little more than half that sum -
$10,961.

In fact, this pattern prevails throughout the paid workforce.
An official publication of the Women's Bureau of Labour Canada
('Labour Canada', December 1979), sums the situation up as
follows:

In 1977, the average earned income of women employees who
worked 50 to 52 weeks was $9,143, compared with $15,818
for men. Therefore, in 1977 a woman working 50 to 52 weeks
earned 57.8 per cent of a man's earnings compared with 54.6
per cent in 1972.... In all categories, except the 0-9 week
group, *the difference between* women's and men's earnings
increased from 1972 to 1977. (Author's emphasis)

Moreover, the pattern of female poverty is even more extreme in
old age. As the National Council on Welfare concludes: 'After
fifty years or so of unpaid, faithful service a woman's only reward is likely to be poverty' (National Council on Welfare, 1979,
p. 32).

Over the past few decades, the Canadian family has undergone
significant changes - changes largely related to the increased
number of wives participating in the paid labour force. While
there is little evidence that more women are rejecting marriage as
a basic life style (Boyd, Eichler and Hofley, 1976, pp. 16-45),
decreased fertility accompanies the movement to a two-spouse-
earning family. A summary of the life patterns of Canadian women

shows that, of 100 single girls, 94 will marry and 85 of those who marry will have children. Of the married group, 79 will stay married and 53 of them will outlive their husbands. Of the 15 who will separate or divorce, twelve will have children.(13) Although there was a decline in marriage rates in the 1960s, attributable almost entirely to changes in the age structure, the corrected rate shows that Canadian women 'do not tend to avoid marriage now to any greater or lesser degree than previously' (ibid., p. 17). Nor are Canadian women delaying marriage (ibid.). The illegitimacy rate, on the other hand, increased from 40 per thousand total births in 1941 to 96 per thousand in 1970 and 93 per thousand in 1973 (Cook, 1976, pp. 19-20). The divorce rate index, moreover, rose sharply following the passage of more liberal legislation in 1968 and has continued to rise since, suggesting that the sharp increase was not simply a reflection of a backlog of cases from the pre-1968 period (ibid., Table 2.3, p. 22).

The combination of a fairly stable marriage rate with increased workforce participation by married women (largely for economic reasons) is reflected in some curtailment of the performance of the housewife and mother roles. Trends such as reduced fertility and delayed first childbirth are noticeable features of the last two decades. Although there is little evidence of a breakdown of traditional sex roles within the Canadian family, Canadian women are clearly responding to the strain of family work and paid work by reducing the extent of their child-care responsibilities (ibid., pp. 27-44). Increasing education, urbanization and workforce participation are all correlated with declining fertility and it seems likely that these trends will continue despite the pro-natalist character of Canada's political tradition. A full assessment of fertility trends, however, is difficult to make in terms of understanding the intentions of Canadian women because of the difficulty in assessing the abortion rates. Given restrictive Canadian legislation which has a highly differential effect from region to region, we may presume that fertility rates would further decline if equal access to abortion prevailed under the current legislation or if more liberalized legislation were passed.

The gradual change in Canada, at least in the urban areas, to a typical family which contains two wage earners seems largely to reflect economic pressures rather than major changes in the ideology of sex roles. This assumption is borne out by the fact that child-care and housework are still predominantly performed by women, and by the extreme sexual segregation obvious in the Canadian workforce (Armstrong and Armstrong, 1978, p. 40). Women without a high school diploma will spend most of their lives in the service sector - waitressing, cleaning or checking out groceries. Little more than one in ten will work in factories, and then largely in un-skilled jobs in a few industries such as textiles. Even women with high school diplomas are generally concentrated in clerical jobs in offices, banks and telephone companies or in the 'quasi-professions' of nursing and teaching (primarily of younger children) ('Labour Canada', 1977, Table 10). Canadian women are sparsely represented in the higher professions and in business management (Armstrong and Armstrong, 1978, passim). And while women in the 'professions' almost equalled men in actual numbers (526,000 women/567,000 men), they were largely lower-paid teachers (181,000) and nurses (205,000) with men predominating in the higher-paid and higher status 'higher' professions of doctors, lawyers, engineers, dentists, architects and scientists (see Gunderson, 1976, p. 113; Armstrong and Armstrong, 1978, passim; Vickers and Adam, 1978, Ch. 1).

While this extreme work-force segregation alone does not explain the male/female earning differentials in Canada - the differentials prevail even within occupations and professions ('Labour Canada', 1977, Tables 8A, 8B) - it is an important contributing factor. As the National Council on Welfare notes 'The relationship between women's work inside and outside the home is a vicious circle' (National Council on Welfare, 1979, p. 24). Most of the work done by Canadian women in the paid work force is an extension of women's home and child-care work. Unpaid in the home, it is given low value in the work force. Although Federal Human Rights legislation does involve the provision for 'equal pay for work of equal value' (which was introduced purportedly to overcome the negative effects of workforce segregation in the short-run) little movement in this direction is evident even within the federal civil service. Since the bulk of Canada's workers are covered, in terms of Labour Law and Human Rights Legislation, by the ten provincial governments rather than by federal legislation, any kind of national campaign to breakdown workforce segregation and to achieve 'equal pay for work of equal value' pay protection has been difficult to mount.

Union agitations for such changes are hampered by the fact that a small fraction of women are unionized (27 per cent in 1977 vs. 42 per cent of men) (National Council on Welfare, 1979, p. 24), that the unemployment rate for women is consistently higher than for men (one-third higher in mid-1979) (ibid.) and that such a large proportion of women work part-time. Despite recent important efforts on the part of women workers and some parts of the Canadian labour movement,(14) progress is at best slow. The Canadian labour movement is sharply fragmented, with the Quebec wing operating more or less independently. Educational workers are not included in the Canadian Labour Congress (CLC); nor are major unions like the Teamsters. Finally the relationship of many unions with International (generally American) unions is often more significant than their relationships with the CLC. Further hampered by the general organizational problems of Canadian political life and by the complexities of eleven different labour codes, the labour movement is unlikely to undertake a more vigorous organization of women in the future, although the picture is more optimistic in some provinces (British Columbia, for example) than it is nationally.

In terms of education, the past few decades have seen an enormous expansion in enrolment, for both men and women, at all levels.

Despite considerable federal funding, education in Canada is an exclusively provincial responsibility which means that basic regulations, standards and facilities vary on a province-by-province basis making generalizations difficult. In general, education is compulsory for girls and boys until about the mid-teens. The 1971 census data showed no significant difference between the proportion of girls (94 per cent) and boys (94.7 per cent) attending school at age 15 (Robb and Spence, 1976, Table 3.1, p. 57); (see also Vickers and Adam, 1978). At age 17, however, and in subsequent age cohorts, female participation declines. In the university undergraduate programme (18-21 age group) 22.9 per cent of the boys are enrolled but only 14.0 per cent of the girls (Robb and Spence, 1976, Table 3.6, p. 65). Equally important is the streaming and/or self-direction of most of those women who do obtain advanced education or training into the traditional female fields such as nursing, primary school teaching and the arts disciplines. Although the numbers of women enrolled in traditionally male-dominated fields have increased the numbers remain very small relative to male practitioners (ibid., passim; see also Vickers and Adam, 1978).

In general the number of Canadian women able to achieve economic independence and avoid poverty outside marriage or to achieve economic equality within marriage is small. With little breakdown in sex role assumptions either within marriage or in the paid labour force, women continue to perform typically female work whether paid or unpaid and those women who enter the paid workforce to augment family incomes reflect the strain of multiple roles in various ways including a marked reduction in fertility. Finally, the number of women with the skills, status and resources to undertake major tasks of organization – whether in unions, within the women's movement or in mainstream politics – is small indeed.

THE POLITICAL ENVIRONMENT

Canada is administered by three distinct levels of government – federal, provincial and municipal. Constitutionally, the federal and provincial governments each enjoy superior power and responsibility in distinct areas of activity and powers of taxation. The municipal level, on the other hand, is clearly a creature of provincial governments. Municipal governments enjoy only whatever legislative and taxing powers are permitted them by their provincial government. What is more, the partisan organizations which organize the electoral and legislative systems at the federal and provincial levels are largely absent at the municipal level of government and politics.

This structural anomaly means that elected or appointed offices at the municipal level command significantly less power and status (and remuneration in most cases) than federal and provincial offices. The contrast between the municipal level on the one hand and the partisan provincial and federal levels on the other, there-

fore, requires a distinct analysis of two quite different political
environments when we wish to consider the participation of women
in Canada. Hence we will first examine the environment of women's
participation at the municipal level, and then move to an examination of the partisan environment which prevails at the provincial
and federal levels.

The non-partisan environment
In Canada, it was until fairly recently a commonplace of political
wisdom that the advice 'start at the bottom and work your way up'
applied. In fact, our mapping of women candidates in Canada (15)
indicates clearly what is also now likely that case for male candidates - that the partisan and non-partisan arenas of Canadian
politics are largely disconnected and represent two distinct streams
of political recruitment for most people rather than an integrated,
hierarchical recruitment system. What is striking is the fact that
of the 219 women whose first candidacies were successful in the
period studied, only 55 (or 25.1 per cent) were contestants for
partisan offices, whereas 159 (or approximately 73 per cent) were
contestants for municipal office.(16) The pattern continues, moreover, for repeatedly successful candidacies, indicating that the
bulk of female candidacies and the bulk of successful candidacies
occur in the non-partisan environment of urban politics.

There are a number of features of this environment which must
be noted to begin to account for this streaming of women eager
for political office into the municipal arena. First, it is the level
with the least power and with the least status. In addition, most
municipal offices (except in the largest cities at the mayoralty
level) are part-time and involve a low level of remuneration in
comparison to provincial and federal offices. In general, this
reduces competition for municipal office especially since it is less
likely to serve as the bottom rung in a political career culminating
in a partisan arena than it is elsewhere or as it, perhaps, was in
the past. Largely because of the low level of power involved, the
political parties active at the provincial and federal levels have
made little effort to organize politics at this level.

Despite informal organization, no gate-keepers exist at this
level to control the first stage in recruitment - the nomination
process. Nomination at this level generally means simply getting
the required number of signatures to meet formal requirements.
Also, the election process at this level is normally relatively simple
and inexpensive making it quite possible for individuals to win
election successfully without the resources (financial or human) of
partisan or voluntary groups. In fact, an examination of the
recruitment and socialization experiences of the municipal women in
our sample showed that most municipal candidates funded their
campaigns with their own funds or with the assistance of a circle of
friends, and received relatively little non-financial support from
voluntary groups (see Brodie, 1979, pp. 18-19).

Apart from the environmental factors which have created a
vacuum into which prospective women candidates can move with

relative ease, we must also note other aspects of the municipal
environment which make it attractive for women. First, the size
of Canada (and of many of the provinces) dictates family dislo-
cation or separation for many successful legislative candidates.
The geographical proximity of municipal governments removes
this problem for candidates in municipal arenas. Further, the
curiously apolitical character of municipal government in Canada
is more likely to make it seem convergent with the private life or
professional concerns of the majority of women and to make their
credentials as home-makers, nurses, teachers and community
activists seem more appropriate. In addition, the anti-partisan
bias of maternal femininism in Canada has not disappeared from
the current movement and, for some women, the apparently non-
partisan character of Canadian municipal politics is a positive
attraction, despite the fact that the power to achieve the changes
they wish is generally not located at city hall.

In general, then, the environment of municipal politics and its
structural context do not foster movement upwards to the partisan arenas in most cases. What is notable, however, is movement
downwards. Some women who have run federally or provincially –
especially those running in lost-cause ridings – have shifted their
ambitions to the municipal arena in which their party label matters
very little. It is a mark of the profound difference between the
two environments, however, that women whose partisan candidacy
was a lost-cause at the provincial or federal level have been
elected as alder(wo)men and mayors at the municipal level by much
the same electorate.

Important regional differences are evident, even in the municipal
environment. Despite the relatively large number of successful
women candidates municipally in Ontario and in some Western
cities, such as Vancouver, Quebec and Maritime, cities have been
little touched by women's participation. In general, those cities
which have seen the greatest influx of women candidates are also
those cities in which community groups, concerned with quality-
of-life issues, have been the most active. In such cities the older
pattern, in which municipal government was largely dominated by
the business community and the developers, has been modified
and something of a Left/Right spectrum has emerged on community
development issues. If anything, this has increased the discord-
ance between the non-partisan political environments where it has
occurred, since the major parties in the partisan arenas generally
do not differ ideologically.

The partisan environment
In many ways, Canada's federal party system is an anomaly among
western liberal democracies. Since its conception in 1867 Canada
has had a parliamentary system, based on the British model, and
a single member plurality, first-past-the-post, electoral system.
This type of electoral arrangement, at least according to some
political observers, should maintain a two-party system and encourage the election of majority governments. To some extent these

generalizations apply to the workings of the Canadian electoral system. One of the two major federal parties, the Liberal or the Progressive Conservative party has always held power at the federal level but not always with the majority in the House of Commons. Since 1921, however, the federal party system has also accommodated a series of third party alternatives. These 'third parties' collectively capture 15 to 30 per cent of the popular federal vote, but only once in Canada's history has a third party gained sufficient electoral support to challenge the Liberals or Conservatives for the status of official opposition in parliament.

Another factor differentiating Canada's federal party system from those of other western systems is the regional basis of electoral support for all parties. The usual government party, the Liberal party, has mounted one electoral victory after another with the aid of its bastion of support in French-speaking Quebec. Most recently it has only been able to elect a handful of members of parliament in the western provinces. The Progressive Conservative party has had dismal electoral fortunes in the province of Quebec since the turn of the century while now it enjoys a predominant position in the western provinces.

A final factor contributing to the uniqueness of Canada's federal party system is the apparent absence of a class cleavage within the Canadian electorate and the lack of ideological distinctiveness between the two major parties. Unlike most other western nations with similar levels of economic development whose party systems reflect a fundamental electoral division between parties of the Left and Right, the Canadian electorate continues to divide against itself according to ethnic, religious and regional criteria (Brodie and Jenson, 1980, Ch. 1). The majority of Canadian voters tend to choose between two parties which resemble one another. Studies of the programmes and policies of the Liberal and Conservative parties reveal few real or consistent differences, especially in the class interests they claim to represent. Moreover, the two major parties tend to recruit their leadership from the same privileged strata of Canadian society and both derive most of their campaign finances from the business community, especially the corporate sector (see, for example, Paltiel, 1970, passim). In view of their policies, personnel and sources of funding, both of the major parties can be termed 'bourgeois' parties.

Canada's third parties, the Social Credit party and the NDP, differ from the two major parties in terms of organization and sources of finance. The NDP, in particular, more closely resembles the European mass party rather than the cadre organization of the two major parties. A great deal of its money is obtained from mass membership dues, particularly from affiliated union locals (Morton, 1977, passim). The political arm of labour, however, enjoys nowhere near a majority of the support of its claimed constituency - the Canadian working class. Rather, study after study has shown the bourgeois parties, and particularly the Liberal party, gain more votes from blue collar workers and trade unionists than Canada's self-styled social-democratic option (see Clarke et. al., 1979, pp. 93-130).

Canada's party system differs in a number of ways from other liberal democracies but in at least one respect it is very similar. Canadian women are almost totally excluded from positions of authority within government or their parties, as the following sections show.

CANADIAN WOMEN AS VOTERS AND CITIZENS

Gender differences in rates of citizen participation have been reported since the first voting studies were conducted in Canada in the early 1960s. Nevertheless, most of these differences are minimal and many, in fact, have now disappeared. The earliest election studies reported that women were slightly less likely to vote than men but the male rate did not exceed that of females by more than 5 per cent (see Regenstreif, 1963; Laponce, 1969; and 'Report of the Royal Commission on the Status of Women', 1970, pp. 353-5). Most of the studies conducted in the early 1960s did not employ statistical controls to determine whether other factors such as religion, education or the constraints of motherhood were important factors underlying the reported turnout differentials. Studies which did search for additional explanatory factors reported significant variations in turnout patterns among Canadian women. While one study found no differences in the turnout rates of married and non-married women, women with lower levels of education and those residing in small towns or Quebec were identified as Canadians least likely to vote (Laponce, 1969, passim). Education has been consistently identified an important factor levelling turnout inequalities in Canada as no gender differences are found in the highest education category (Van Loon, 1968, passim).

Similar to the American experience, gender differences in turnout have now all but disappeared and by 1974 were no longer in evidence (Thomson, 1977, passim). Thus, at level of voting, women can now be considered as fully integrated into the Canadian political system. Women still slightly trail behind men in other forms of citizen involvement in Canadian politics. Since the early 1960s women have been found to have lower levels of political efficacy and political knowledge, and less frequently campaign, contact public officials or attempt to convince others how to vote. These gender differences have been especially apparent among women in rural areas and Quebec, although they have narrowed considerably in the last decade, especially among young Quebec women (Black and McGlen, 1977, p. 19). Thus, over the last two decades there has been considerable mobilization of women into mainstream Canadian politics at the citizen level. The higher participation rates among young women, in particular, would suggest that this trend will continue, if not intensify.

The integration of women into citizen politics has not been as rapid in all regions of the country or at all levels of government. A multi-variate analysis of a scale of participation constructed

from the 1974 national election study indicates that sex is not a
significant predictor of differences in federal election participation
in any of Canada's five major regions. In terms of participation in
provincial elections, however, the participation rates of women are
significantly lower than those of men in the Atlantic region and in
Quebec (Burke et. al., 1978, pp. 61-75). Both regions have
tended to remain rural and traditional but in Quebec, at least,
these differences appear to be eroding with time and across generations (Black and McGlen, 1977, p. 22).

Voting studies have also found that Canadian men and women
have consistently differed in terms of partisan choice. While men
and women are equally likely to vote for the major parties, men
more frequently vote NDP than women. This finding, however,
should not be taken to mean, as it sometimes has been, that women
are more politically conservative than men (see Terry and Schultz,
1973, pp. 248-84). A large proportion of NDP voters are union
members and since far fewer female than male workers are unionized in Canada fewer women fit into this category of NDP supporters. In addition, there is some evidence to suggest that the view
that the NDP is a 'man's party' may be time-bound as young women
have been found to be more likely to vote NDP than older women,
at least in the more populous province of Ontario (Bashevkin, 1979,
pp. 42-5).

For those viewing political participation as a progressive continuum from voting to office-holding, data about women's citizen
participation lend little explanation to why only a few women move
up the political hierarchy to public office. In fact, the question of
women's involvement in Canadian politics has been increasingly
paradoxical. Few gender differences characterize citizen participation but few women gain public office. Thus, the obvious
question is: why are women rarely selected for political office when
they regularly choose to participate at rates similar to those of men?

CANADIAN WOMEN AS PARTY ACTIVISTS

Even before their enfranchisement, women served as the personnel of Canadian partisan politics. Reliable statistics indicating the
actual members of female party activists are not available but selective surveys or party organizations suggest that women comprise
one-fifth to one-third of Canadian party activists (Mishler, 1979,
p. 103; Kornberg, et. al., 1976, pp. 186-216; Brodie, 1975, p.
30). Although a large component of the parties' memberships,
women have not been fully integrated into party organizations.
Nor have they been provided with opportunities to pursue a career
in electoral politics. Political tasks within the party organization
tend to be differentiated on a gender basis. Women party activists
have generally been assigned the housekeeping and menial tasks
within the party organization while men have assumed the strategic and leadership roles.

The segregation of women from leadership roles has been facili-

tated and encouraged by the structure of the major party organizations. Both the federal Liberal and Conservative parties maintain separate women's auxiliaries which, while part of the overall
structure of the party at both the constituency and federal levels,
remain separate entities (Cochrane, 1977, p. 60).

Women's auxiliaries were initially formed at the constituency,
provincial and federal levels of the two major parties to integrate
newly enfranchised women into the party structure and to serve
as vehicles for political education. The first women's auxiliary
was established as early as 1913, some years before women's suffrage, but the first national organization, the Federation of Liberal Women of Canada, was actually launched in 1928, seven years
after all women were granted a vote in federal elections (ibid.,
pp. 59-60). Shortly after, a similar body was formed as an appendage of the Conservative party.

Auxiliary members, like most women party activists, generally
serve as party staffers - stuffing envelopes, distributing literature, answering telephones and minding campaign offices. Women
auxiliaries and women party activists, thus, are often credited,
albeit in a paternalistic manner, with the maintenance of Canada's
major parties between elections as well as successful electoral
campaigns.

The sexual division of labour institutionalized within Canada's
major party organizations has excluded many women party activists from important political tasks which may provide the recognition, skills and contacts necessary for political candidacy. The
essential tasks of developing elections strategies, party policies
and advertising campaigns, as well as the collection and dispersal
of party funds, have remained outside the range of political activities of a great many women party activists. Moreover, local constituency organizations select party candidates and women's
auxiliaries rarely attempt to contradict their choice or present
their own candidate for the party's nomination. As a result,
women auxiliaries have not acted as springboards either to party
office or to political candidacy and public office.

It is precisely the tendency of women's auxiliaries to lock women
party activists into a subordinate position within the major party
organizations which prompted the Royal Commission on the Status
of Women in Canada to recommend their dissolution in 1970. Their
'Report' (p. 346) revealed that none of the women candidates or
elected officials interviewed by the Commission 'considered that
membership in a women's association had been a determining factor
in her decision to run for office'.

Further evidence of the broken link between active participation
in women's associations and political candidacy is provided by a
sample of women candidates contesting election in the 1950 to 1975
period.(17) Among women candidates whose party did have a
women's association only 10 per cent had ever held an executive
post within this type of organization prior to their candidacy.

Despite the Royal Commission's recommendation to disband
women's auxiliaries, a decade later these associations remain in

place in the federal Liberal and Progressive Conservative parties
as well as many of their provincial counterparts although they
have diminished somewhat in importance. A few provincial women's
associations have disappeared and fewer women are joining these
organizations, preferring membership in the party's constituency
associations. An increasingly visible trend has been the formation
of women's caucuses within the main body of the party organizations. These ad hoc groups have been active in promoting
women's issues and lobbying for the nomination of more women
candidates for party and public office. There is little research,
however, exploring the activities and experiences of women within Canada's party organizations.

The few studies of Canadian women party activists which do
exist have tended to compare men and women in selected party
organizations to discover factors which might explain why so few
women seek and achieve public office. Their findings tend to be
inconclusive. One such study of the Ontario Liberal and Progressive Conservative party organizations reports only minimal differences in the backgrounds, political socialization and attitudes
of men and women party activists. As in Canadian society as a
whole, women party militants were less likely to be actively employed outside the home and exhibited slightly lower levels of
income and education than their male counterparts. In comparison
with the general population, however, both male and female party
activists were also found to be slightly more likely to have been
exposed to politics at an early age by politically active parents
and to join the party for partisan-related reasons. Nonetheless,
most men and women had similar backgrounds, motivations and
attitudes (Brodie, 1975, pp. 164-8). The few gender differences
which were reported certainly could not account for the apparent
inability of most women party activists to move up through the
party ranks to public office.

Another study comparing men and women party activists focuses
on all party officials holding positions above the level of poll cap-
tain in the two western cities of Winnipeg and Vancouver. Women
comprised only 19 per cent of this select group of party leaders
but their characteristics are very similar to those of the Ontario
sample of party activists. The Winnipeg-Vancouver study found
female party activists to be less of an elite group than their male
colleagues, even though both gender groups clearly were part of
the middle class (Kornberg et. al., 1976, p. 191). These western
party women were more likely to be raised in politicized childhood
environments than male party activists or neighbours in their
communities who were not party members. Again women party
leaders more frequently joined the party for partisan-related
reasons while men more often cited political career-related motivations for becoming party activists.

While the Winnipeg-Vancouver study found numerous similarities
between men and women party activists, there were significant
gender differences in terms of their activities and influence within the party organization. Approximately the same proportion of

men and women had an uninterrupted career as party militants,
but women spent more time between elections on party work than
their male counterparts. Moreover, women performed different
and less prestigious tasks and were ascribed less influence in the
party organization than men by their co-partyists. Most of the
women were party stalwarts in the bottom and middle level ranks
of the party, while the elite, holding the highest level positions in
the party, were disproportionately male. In fact, the ratio of
stalwarts to elites among women was almost fourteen to one whereas among men, it was approximately three to one (ibid., p. 108).
In short, far fewer women than men examined in this study gained
the types of party positions considered to be crucial springboards
for legislative office.

There is considerable evidence to suggest that elite positions
within the political party provide a bridge to legislative office for
both men and women. A study of federal legislators, for example,
reports that 77 per cent of officials - all male - held party office
before their election to the House of Commons. In fact, among
NDP members of parliament, all had held party office prior to
their election (Kornberg, 1967, p. 54).

Similar patterns can be observed among women legislative candidates. Among the survey of 163 women who contested provincial
or federal legislative office in the 1950 to 1975 period conducted
by the authors, only 21 had not been party workers prior to their
first candidacy.(18) Moreover, most of these women were not
simply party stalwarts within their respective party organizations.
Fully 64 per cent held elite positions performing such crucial
functions as collecting funds, managing campaigns and acting as
a candidate's official agent during elections.

Performing strategic tasks within party organizations, then,
appears to be a crucial first step for both men and women seeking
public office. Women party activists, however, whether isolated in
women's auxiliaries or excluded from party office by a more per-
vasive sexual division of labour, less frequently achieve strategic
positions within the party. Some studies have attempted to explain
women's inability to move up the party ladder with the same fre-
quency as men in a general way, in terms of sexual discrimination,
the lower occupational and educational status of women as a social
group or simply in terms of their apparent lack of motivation to
seek party and/or public office. The Winnipeg-Vancouver study,
for example, reports data indicating that women party activists
are much less likely to aspire to party and, particularly, public
office than male party activists (Kornberg et. al., 1976, p. 209).
Nevertheless, an important question which remains unanswered is
whether responses obtained from survey questionnaires actually
reveal a lack of political ambition among women or simply their
assessments of the opportunities that they perceive are available
to them. It is equally possible that 'political motives and desires
are molded by the *availability* of political opportunities and that
such opportunities are structurally determined' (Black, 1972, p.
144). The following section provides evidence which strongly

suggests that women's political opportunities are severely restricted by Canadian political parties, even after they have moved through barriers within the party to achieve the party's nomination for legislative office.

CANADIAN WOMEN AS CANDIDATES FOR LEGISLATIVE OFFICE

In few countries is the observation more true that the potential candidate remains on the sidelines, until and unless, some practical opportunity presents itself, no matter how strong the candidate's motives or how ready he (or she) stands to serve (Barber, 1965, p. 237). For the majority of women candidates and public officials, this opportunity presents itself at the municipal level of Canadian government where parties generally do not participate. Legislative candidacies are mediated and structured by the political party, which can serve either as a bridge or a barrier for aspirants to elected office. Local party constituency associations have the exclusive right to select the party's candidate for provincial or federal elections. Thus political parties are certainly influential actors in the recruitment of Canadian legislators, whether male or female. The evidence which is available concerning women's recruitment suggests that women often do indeed have difficulties achieving the party's nomination and, if successful, are most frequently recruited in constituencies where they have little chance of winning. For example, after completing extensive interviews with elected women, the Royal Commission on the Status of Women in Canada concluded its 'Report' (1970, p. 349):

> The constituency association has autonomy in the selection of the candidates and jealously guards this right. It is at the constituency level, according to the women interviewed, that the disparagement of women candidates and the belief that a woman candidate will lose votes are usually encountered.
> Women who have been successful at the polls confirm that winning the nomination is a more formidable hurdle than winning the election.

The Royal Commission's observation that nominations are difficult to achieve for women is only partially supported among the author's sample of candidates contesting provincial or federal office in the 1950 to 1965 period. Among these women office-seekers, 37 per cent indicated that their political careers were delayed because it was impossible to get the party's nomination. Less than 5 per cent of the sample, however, noted that this was the most important factor delaying their candidacy. Among this group of Canadian women candidates, factors such as perceived lack of political experience, difficulty in obtaining funding and fears that the community was unreceptive to women politicians were ascribed a salience as factors delaying their candidacies.

That far fewer women candidates than elected women mention that they had difficulty achieving the party's nomination should

not be surprising. In Canada, parties vary radically in strength
from one constituency to another and especially, from one region
to another. Some nominations are more desirable than others
because they promise greater chances for electoral victory. Given
the regional basis for support of both major and minor parties in
Canada, gaining the federal Liberal party's nomination in the
province of Quebec, for example, or the Progressive Conservatives' nomination in Alberta, virtually ensures the candidate's
success even before election day. A great many party nominations,
then, are for lost-cause candidacies, where the candidate waves
the party banner during the campaign but has no hope of election.
It is frequently observed that the dearth of women in Canadian
public office is not so much due to a shortage of women candidates,
although clearly there are fewer female than male candidates.
Rather women are generally found contesting office in marginal
ridings.

The study of women candidates contesting election between 1950
and 1975 confirms the conventional wisdom that women candidates
are most frequently the sacrificial lambs of Canadian elections. Of
146 candidates whose electoral districts were not redrawn over
the course of five campaigns, only 18 were nominated to constituencies where their party had won at least 3 of the last 5 elections,
while 92 were candidates in constituencies where their party had
won none of the previous five elections. Obviously, many women
contest office in Canada without any realistic expectation that
they will be elected.

Our sample of women candidates provided a variety of explanations for why they entered election campaigns with the certainty
of defeat. Fringe party candidates such as standardbearers for
the Communist or Marxist-Leninist parties cited reasons relating
to the education of the electorate while others mentioned specific
issue orientations. Many simply saw their candidacy as a necessary
expression of partisan loyalty. Others cited reasons relating to
the excitement of electoral campaigns. Still others saw their candidacy as an apprenticeship for future campaigns.

A crucial factor underlying the almost complete exclusion of
women from legislative office in Canada, then, had been the party's
unwillingness to extend and/or the woman candidate's inability to
win nominations in constituencies where their party is competitive.
Throughout the 1970s this tendency has persisted. The proportion
of women candidates in federal elections, for example, has increased at a rapid rate from less than 4 per cent of all federal
candidates in 1968 to approximately 14 per cent in 1979. Nevertheless a close examination of the candidacy patterns of women who
contested election in the 1979 campaign reveals that the increased
number of women's candidacies actually reflect two trends neither
of which are conducive to the election of women. There was a
greater willingness on the part of the Liberal, Progressive Conservatives and New Democratic parties to nominate women but, as
we shall see, primarily in lost-cause ridings. The greatest increases in women's candidacies are among the ranks of Independents

or fringe party candidates. This trend of women running for parties outside the main orbit of the federal party system can be traced back to the 1974 general election when 73 of the 125 federal women candidates ran as Independents or as Marxist-Leninists, Libertarians, Communists and other fringe party candidates. In 1979 106 of the 195 women candidates were not mainstream candidates and, as such, played little more than a symbolic role in the federal campaign. In the 1980 federal campaign, which was called unexpectedly after the defeat of the minority Conservative government's budget, approximately two-thirds of the women candidates were Independents or fringe party candidates and as such had no hope of becoming members of parliament.

The major parties have shown a greater tendency to nominate women in the 1970s but this growth has not been as rapid as in Independent and fringe categories. Between 1974 and 1979 the number of NDP women candidates increased but their numbers dropped considerably in 1980. The number of women candidates for the Liberal and Conservative parties has remained stable across the three election years. As a result, in all three elections, the NDP has run almost twice as many women candidates as the Liberal and Conservative parties combined.

The results of the 1979 and 1980 elections showed no departure from previous trends. Although fewer women were nominated in 1980, in 1979 the NDP ran nineteen of their forty-seven candidates in Quebec where the party is little more than a paper organization. Similarly the Progressive Conservatives ran three of their fourteen women candidates in 1979 and five of their fourteen in 1980 in Quebec where the party's fortunes have been dismal since the turn of the century. In contrast, it did not nominate any women in its prairie bastion of support in 1980. Only the willingness of the Liberal Party to recruit a small number of women to run in safe seats in Quebec has guaranteed a small representation of women in the House of Commons. In both 1979 and 1980, six Liberal women were recruited in Quebec: four were elected in 1979 and all six in 1980.

During the 1970s, the success rates of men and women candidates have shown considerable stability in their inequality. In the federal elections from 1972 to 1979, approximately one of every five male candidates has been elected. In contrast, less than one in ten of their female counterparts was successful (Brodie and Vickers, 1979). These probabilities of success clearly demonstrate that the 'women are not elected because they don't contest elections' type of explanation for the dearth of women decision-makers is clearly inadequate in the Canadian case.

The majority of Canadian women candidates are deprived of the most important recruitment opportunity leading to election to public office - the opportunity of contesting election where their party has at least a chance of victory. While the type of constituency to which a woman is nominated is the most crucial recruitment opportunity parties can extend to their candidates there are a variety of others. Even if a candidate is successful in securing

a nomination in a competitive electoral district, parties can expand
or contract her political opportunities by withholding or providing
the candidate with party resources such as moral support, campaign workers and financing. In this case, we find that the
recruitment opportunities for women vary with the competitive
position of the party.

Among the sample of women candidates contesting election between 1970 to 1975, the majority did not perceive their party to be
resistant to them simply because they were women. Nevertheless,
almost one-third of the women noted that they had experienced at
least one 'dirty trick' during the campaign, especially at the nomination stage. While these women most frequently mentioned that
they had received less financial support from the party than
previous male candidates, an almost equal number noted that the
party had actively sought a male candidate to oppose them for the
party's nomination. Also frequently mentioned were organized
attempts to block their candidacies. Some were confronted with a
combination of dirty tricks.

Most political observers would argue that when the party's nomination is contested by two or more political aspirants dirty tricks
invariably occur, regardless of the gender of the aspirants. Evidence from our sample of women candidates would seem to contradict this conventional wisdom. Women who won their nomination by
acclamation – having no competitors – still experienced discrepancies in the nomination procedure, received less funding or had
campaign workers desert them. Although a larger percentage of
women who competed for their nomination experienced these types
of incidents of negative support, fully 42 per cent of those who
were not contested also experienced dirty tricks. Being acclaimed
in a hopeless riding, however, does appear to make a difference.
Only 13 per cent of the non-contested lost-cause candidates compared to 40 per cent of the contested lost-cause candidates experienced incidents of negative support. In other words, when a
woman is the only potential candidate for a lost-cause riding, they
confront few barriers within the party, but, when their nomination is contested or, when the riding is competitive, evidence of
negative support increases substantially (Brodie and Vickers,
1978, pp. 18-20).

Surveying the experiences of women candidates in federal and
provincial elections, then, it would appear that Canadian political
parties do not allocate recruitment resources to men and women in
equal measure. First, and of primary importance to electoral success, is a nomination to a competitive constituency and, as we
have seen, few women actually are granted this opportunity in
Canada. As a result, women's chances for election are much lower
than their male counterparts. Nevertheless, a few women do move
through the party ranks, gain nominations to competitive constituencies and win the election campaign, and we now turn to a discussion of their experiences and characteristics.

CANADIAN WOMEN AS LEGISLATORS

Similar to all western democracies, statistically speaking, women
remain the single most underrepresented group in Canadian
elected assemblies today (Putnam, 1976, p. 32). Since women's
emancipation their integration into Canadian legislative assemblies
has been slow and tenuous. Most Canadian women gained the formal right to hold federal legislative office in 1921, while the
extension of the same rights in all the provinces was achieved
some time later. In the western provinces, for example, full emancipation in provincial politics was granted before federal emancipation. In contrast, women's right to hold provincial office was
withheld in New Brunswick until 1934 and until 1940 in Quebec
(Brodie, 1977, pp. 6 - 8). Nevertheless, only a few have been
elected to Canadian legislatures, even though the formal opportunity to do so has existed for more than a half-century (see
Table 4.1).

Canadian women have had a better history of electoral victory
at the provincial than federal level of government. Between 1920
and 1975, sixty-seven women have become provincial legislators
but most of these women (forty-four) were elected between 1950
and 1975. In some provinces, the election of a woman has been a
fairly recent phenomenon. While all the western provinces had
elected at least one woman by 1920, a woman was not elected in
Ontario until 1943, Quebec until 1961 and as recently as 1970 in
Prince Edward Island. More women have also been elected in the
western than eastern provinces. For example, in the 1950-75
period, thirteen women were elected to the British Columbia legislature and nine in the neighbouring province of Alberta; only
five were elected in Ontario, three in Quebec and two in each of
the three Maritime provinces (ibid., p. 9).

Why the western provinces should elect more women legislators
is not immediately clear. These provinces entered Confederation
later and their legislatures have been less professionalized than
some of their eastern counterparts, especially Ontario and Quebec.
Thus one might speculate that the role of legislator in the western
provinces has, until very recently perhaps, conferred less status
than in the eastern provinces, thereby allowing easier access for
women. In contrast, women in the older provinces may experience
more difficulty penetrating entrenched party organizations and
the recruiters' expectations of male incumbency. In the Maritimes,
in particular, the parochial 'father to son' flavour of political recruitment undoubtedly has presented an obstacle for women
aspiring to provincial office.

Fewer women have been elected to the federal House of Commons
than to provincial legislatures. Between 1921 when the first woman
was elected to the House of Commons and 1980, only thirty-four
women have been federal legislators. This is obviously a very
small proportion of the total number of politicians elected since
women's enfranchisement. Indeed, in the 1917-70 period, less than
one per cent of all Canadian legislators have been women ('Report

Table 4.1 The achievement of political emancipation of Canadian women

Jurisdiction	Suffrage granted	Eligibility to hold office granted	First women elected
Manitoba	1916	1916	1920
Saskatchewan	1916	1916	1919
Alberta	1916	1916	1918
British Columbia	1917	1917	1918
Ontario	1917	1919	1943
Dominion (Federal Government)	1917 relatives of service-men 1918- all quali-fied by age and citizen-ship	1919 re-affirmed and made permanent by the Dominion Elections Act, 1920	1921
New Brunswick	1919	1934	1967
Prince Edward Island	1922	1922	1970
Newfoundland[1]	1925	1925	1930
Quebec	1940	1940	1961

1 This was prior to Newfoundland's entry into Confederation.
Sources: Catherine Cleverdon, 'The Woman Suffrage Movement in Canada', p. 2. Janine Brodie, The Recruitment of Canadian Woman Provincial Legislators, 'Atlantis', Spring, 1977, passim.

of the Royal Commission on the Status of Women', 1970, Table 1,
p. 340). Moreover, while this proportion has increased modestly
in the 1970s, Canada's record of electing women still remains lower
than most western democracies. Although more women were elected
to parliament than ever before in the 1980 general election, less
than 5 per cent of federal members of parliament are now women.
Thus Canadian women remain conspicuously absent in both the
House of Commons and the ten provincial legislative assemblies.

The election of women has generally not brought debates about
women's status to the House of Commons. Although following
women's enfranchisement, there was a rash of legislation protect-
ing the rights of mothers and children, these reforms appear to
have emerged from the same social climate which enabled women to
vote rather than from the women politicians themselves. Two factors, in particular, are relevant to the limited articulation of
women's issues in the Canadian legislatures, especially by women
politicians. First, as already discussed, first wave feminism was a
weak and disjointed movement in Canada. Canadian women were
not mobilized as women at the time of their suffrage. Thus,
women's status throughout Canadian history has largely been
deemed a private rather than a public concern. Second, and more
important, elected women, like their male counterparts, are bound
by party cohesion in the parliamentary legislatures which requires
that they support the party's policies whether they agree with
them or not. Legislators wishing to have their concerns included
in the party's platform must first convince their fellow party members of their necessity. Unfortunately, Canadian parties have
generally not placed much salience on the question of the status
of women.

The first women to become legislative candidates in Canada were
not elected because they were women or because of their position
on women's issues. While many of the early suffragettes entered
municipal politics, of the first two women elected to provincial
legislatures, one was an armed forces representative and the other
was a member of the Non-Partisan League, elected on a prohibition
ticket (Cochrane, 1977, pp. 37, 40). The first woman elected to
the federal parliament, Agnes Macphail, was never a women's
rights activist. She was elected in 1921 as a member of the Progressive party and as a representative of the United Farmers of
Ontario. She acted as a spokesperson for agrarian interests, but
Macphail was the only woman in the House of Commons, a fact
which shaped her participation in the decision-making process.
As she recalled (quoted in Cochrane, 1977, p. 42):

I found that I couldn't quietly do my job without being
ballyhooed like the bearded lady.... I couldn't open my
mouth to say the simplest thing without it appearing in the
papers. I was a curiosity, a freak. And you know the way
the world treats freaks.

Few women followed Macphail to the House of Commons until
recently. In fact, she remained the lone woman in the House of
Commons for fourteen years and only ten more women were elected

before 1960. These pioneer women politicians shared many common characteristics which are less frequently found among today's women members of parliament. Like Macphail, three of the women elected before 1960 were teachers while four were home-makers. Unlike Macphail, however, many were elected in by-elections, four in all, and three gained their seats as widows of previous Members of the House of Commons. Of the 34 women elected to the House of Commons, 8 replaced their deceased spouses but only 2 of these remained MPs for more than one term.(19) This phenomenon, which is termed widow's succession, however, no longer appears to be a ticket for entry into the federal legislature as only one such widow has been elected since 1964.

Today's elected women have different backgrounds than their predecessors. Women legislators elected in 1979 were older than those before them; far fewer were teachers or home-makers prior to their election; none were elected in by-elections; and a great percentage are married. Moreover, these women were predominantly elected in urban ridings whereas their predecessors, especially those elected before 1965, generally represented rural constituencies. Today's women federal legislators are increasingly well educated professionals with independent political careers. They are, however, different from their male counterparts. While there is a high proportion of graduate degrees among both female and male legislators, a substantially greater proportion of male legislators hold law degrees and were practising lawyers before their election. A study of legislators in the 1972 Parliament indicates that one-third of the federal legislators surveyed held law degrees (Kornberg and Mishler, 1976, p. 65). In contrast, only three of all the women elected to parliament since 1921 (none presently in parliament) have a legal background. Three of the women elected in 1979 were associated with higher education, another three had journalism or public relations backgrounds while two others were involved in social work. Thus, while professionals, women legislators, by and large, are drawn from the upper ranks of the typically feminine sectors of the labour force while men tend to enter the legislature through the traditional male preserves of law and business (Brodie and Vickers, 1979).

Once in parliament, one finds few similarities in women's apparent patterns of interest of legislative behaviour. Most women have actively participated in the legislative committee system but the issue areas are as diverse as agriculture, prison reform, transportation and human rights. While some have shown interest in women's issues and rights, most have pursued the interests of their electoral districts. In fact, some have vigorously rejected a specific women's orientation to legislative work.(20)

A sizeable proportion of women legislators have also served as cabinet ministers. Among the 15 women belonging to the government party during their term and thereby eligible for a cabinet position, 6 were appointed. Nevertheless, women's access to the centre of parliamentary decision-making has been relatively recent, as all but 2 of these women have been appointed to cabinet since

1972. Again, there is little similarity in the nature of these appointments. While 2 have been Ministers of Health and Welfare, the others were appointed to direct the Post Office, and the Departments of External Affairs, Science and Technology, Sport and Indian Affairs and Northern Development. Thus prestigious and powerful portfolios concerning finance, industry and trade, the treasury and justice have not yet been filled by women. In 1980, however, the first female was appointed as Speaker of the House of Commons; a position which carries considerable prestige and control over the inner workings of the House of Commons.

This tendency for women, once elected, to move rather rapidly through the ranks of the parliamentary party also applies to the provincial level where approximately one-quarter of all women legislators have been appointed to cabinet (Brodie, 1975, Table 4, p. 15). Most of these women were appointed in their first or second terms and similar to the federal level, most have been appointed in recent years. Nevertheless, there is a strong tendency to appoint women either to the stereotypically housekeeping portfolios such as social services, consumer affairs or housing or to admit them into cabinet without a specific departmental responsibility. In fact, at one time five of the ten provincial ministers of social services were women (Cochrane, 1977, p. 73). Thus, there is some evidence of 'tokenism' in the nature of these provincial appointments. Women are quickly advanced to the highly visible cabinet but few are granted influential portfolios.

CANADIAN WOMEN AS PARTY APPOINTEES

Party appointments will be our final consideration of women's relationship with Canadian political parties. Women can be recruited to positions of influence within Canadian government by the governing party either by appointment to the Senate or to senior positions within Crown corporations. In both cases, as we shall see, parties in power generally pass prominent women by when appointed positions open up within the inner circles of influence.

Canada has a bicameral legislature, in which the federal House of Commons is comprised of elected officials, and the Senate is filled according to fixed regional proportions at the discretion of the Prime Minister. Since women gained the right to enter the Senate, however, few women have been selected by Canada's first ministers. Canadian women did not gain the right to become a Senator with their enfranchisement and how they achieved this right, as already discussed, is a celebrated case in Canadian constitutional history. The first woman senator was appointed in 1930 ('Report of the Royal Commission on the Status of Women', 1970, p. 338). Between 1930 and 1975, however, only fourteen women have been appointed to the federal Senate. The biographies of these women reveal a certain similarity in the nature of their appointments. Twelve of the fourteen had histories of party activism, holding senior leadership positions within their parties. (21) Thus, while women's auxiliaries appear to inhibit women party activists from pursuing legislative careers, they appear to be a pathway to the Senate for women, albeit for a minuscule and select proportion of their membership.

The government's appointment of women to Crown or public corporations is both less obvious and more difficult to assess. There are several forms of Crown corporations in Canada. At one extreme there are the departmental corporations which, except for directorships, are filled through the process of bureaucratic meritocracy. In contrast, agency corporations have a greater number of senior positions open to partisan appointment while a great many other positions, by their very nature, require clerical or technical staff. As might be expected, the great majority of women employed in federal Crown corporations are engaged in supportive roles such as data processing, clerical, secretarial and stenographic tasks. In fact, a full 82 per cent of women employed in agency corporations perform these types of supportive roles. In contrast, 96 per cent of the senior management positions, those most likely to be partisan appointments, are occupied by men (Dulude, 1977, pp. 3-6; and Rioux and Pearson, 1975, p. 24). Obviously, the Liberal party which has had almost uninterrupted control over patronage appointments since the Second World War has rarely employed its power to appoint women to decision-making roles within the federal bureaucracy.

Finally, only one woman - Pauline McGibbon - has been appointed to fill the largely ceremonial vice-regal office of Lieutenant-Governor. Legally a monarchy, Canadian jurisdictions each have a monarchical surrogate - Governor-General federally, Lieutenant provincially. Appointments to these offices are within the gifts of the government of the day.

SUMMARY AND DISCUSSION

The foregoing demonstrates that women's relationship with Canadian political parties varies substantially from one sphere of political activity to another. Some sixty years after their enfranchisement, Canadian women now appear to be integrated into politics at the citizen level, but their inclusion into other modes of political participation has been only partial. Many women, for example, are political party activists and, generally, they tend to devote more effort and time to the party organization than their male counterparts. The political party organization, however, does not exist in a social vacuum. Canadian women, in the party and outside it, are most often delegated low-prestige, 'housekeeping' and support tasks. Partially as a result, few Canadian women contest election with even a hope of electoral victory and even fewer are elected to the provincial and federal legislatures. Even though the formal right to share in the country's decision-making was extended to Canadian women some time ago, by all indicators they remain perennial onlookers, excluded from the centres of political authority.

Nevertheless, events of the late 1970s may suggest that some change in women's political status is under way. During the 1979 federal election, for example, the major parties did attempt to address a few of the problems confronting Canadian women. As the National Action Committee (NAC) observed:(22)

This was the first federal election in Canada in which women's issues played any role. The National Action Committee on the Status of Women does not think that any of the parties gave the issues the kind of attention they deserve, but *all* gave them much more consideration than ever in the past.

In fact, the major parties' definitions of women's issues concentrated almost exclusively on women's status (or lack thereof) in the federal bureaucracy and the paid workforce. Even on this, the proposals of the federal parties were limited and ambiguous. The Liberal party, which, as we have indicated, has taken greater effort to ensure the representation of a small but significant contingent of women in the House of Commons and in cabinet, did not issue a policy statement concerning women during the course of the campaign. They did, however, promise to act on their long-standing commitment to allow home-makers to contribute to the Canada Pension Plan. The NDP, in contrast, with the then lowest number of women legislators in the House of Commons, unveiled a variety of proposals including affirmative action programmes. The Progressive Conservatives also echoed some of the NDP's campaign planks.

Surprisingly, however, few women's groups actively intervened in the debate. Some small groups endorsed the NDP, and others actively lobbied local candidates, regardless of their party affiliations. The NAC, however, despite heated debate, refused to endorse any one party. This reflects the long-standing strategy of women's rights groups in English Canada to play among the major parties at both the federal and provincial levels for recognition and funding, rather than to work within a party to structure a clear partisan alternative for voters concerned with the status of Canadian women. This position was clearly articulated by Lynne MacDonald, President of NAC, on the eve of the election: 'We have decided that at no time will we support one party... Our members come from all political parties and we have to work with whomever is in government' ('Ottawa Citizen', May 16, 1979, p. 60). This is in contrast with the labour movement which, having held a similar position in the past, attempted to mobilize its membership behind the NDP in 1979. In fact, the Canadian Labour Congress undertook more actions to mobilize women to vote for their interests in 1979 than did mainstream groups of the women's movement.

CONCLUSION

Although, for analytic purposes, we have treated candidacies and issues separately, any survey of the history of parties shows that the content of electoral discourse and the nature of political recruitment are intimately tied. For example, it was only after the early trade union movement impressed their concerns on the dominant electoral debate (either through existing parties or with the establishment of new parties) that workers' issues and worker candidates were integrated into electoral parties. Similarly, we can observe both increased recruitment of women and legislation dealing with women's conditions shortly after women's enfranchisement was part of the dominant political debate ('Report of the Royal Commission on the Status of Women', 1970, p. 338). The 1979 election demonstrates in many ways the failure or inability both of party officials and of women's groups to forge the links that would enhance both women's recruitment opportunities and the passage of positive legislation. In 1979 there were greater numbers of women candidates and the women's movement was increasingly vocal. These factors, alone, however, are unlikely to lead either to a significant increase in the number of women elected or to concentrated legislative initiatives to improve the status of Canadian women. Most women candidates in 1979 had little chance of being elected and the most visible and established elements of the women's movement did not attempt to politicize and mobilize their substantial membership to force the major political parties either to recruit women in winnable constituencies or make the status of women a central issue in the campaign. Thus, most Canadian women chose between the parties without reference to their status as women or a clear estimation of the partisan options available to them. Changes in the political arena are unlikely without the crucial links first being drawn among organization, issue and party.

NOTES

1 While women in Nova Scotia and New Brunswick also appear to have had the legal right to vote during this period, if otherwise qualified, there is no evidence that the right was exercised.
2 See notes 6 to 9 for basic statistics on landmass, population, etc.
3 Dr Emily Stowe founded the Toronto Women's Literary Club in 1876 which, despite its name, was interested in the franchise. In 1883 its name was changed to the Toronto Women's Suffrage Club. Along with other groups, it was included in the umbrella group - Dominion Women's Enfranchisement Club - formed in 1889. To further confuse the issue, the umbrella group's name was also later changed to the Canadian Suffrage Association. See Cleverdon, 1974, chapters 1 and 2 and Geller, 1976, for a full account.

4   Ontario women presented petitions for the provincial fran-
     chise through the 1880s and the 1890s. By Gorham's (1976)
     account the petition campaign was largely dominated by the
     temperance forces.
5   See Gorham, 1976. Many of the maternal feminists were con-
     cerned with broader economic and social issues such as child-
     labour and factory legislation. Most Canadian women, however,
     saw their participation as a duty and few saw the vote as a
     tool to improve their own status and condition.
6   Canada's landmass is the largest in the Western hemisphere
     and the second largest in the world at 9,922,330 square kilo-
     metres but there is no permanent settlement in 89 per cent of
     this area. (See 'The Canada Year Book 1978-79' (Ottawa:
     Minister of Supply and Services, Canada, 1978) p. 3.)
7   Canada's population now exceeds 23 million. The last 'mini-
     census' showed a population of 22,992,604 on 1 June 1976
     (ibid., p. 135).
8   Using Statistics Canada's definition of urbanization ('an area
     having a population concentration of 1,000 or more and a pop-
     ulation density of at least 386 a square kilometre'), slightly
     more than 75.5 per cent of Canadians lived in an urban en-
     vironment as of 1 July 1976. Over half (55.7 per cent) lived
     in 23 metropolitan areas. See 'Canada Year Book 1978-79', pp.
     136, 137. Finally, 58 per cent of the population lives in a
     narrow band along Canada's border with the USA (ibid., p. 3).
9   In 1975 Canada's average family income (in current dollars)
     was $16,613 with significant regional variations from a low of
     $13,474 in the Atlantic Provinces to a high of $18,047 in On-
     tario. In the same year, the average family income of male-led
     families was $17,293 or almost twice the average income of
     female-led families at $9,291 (ibid., pp. 246-7). Canada's
     welfare state sytem is fairly extensive, although under attack
     at the time of writing. Globally, Canada ranks in the top ten
     in terms of living standards, according to the OECD.
10   In 1976 45 per cent of the adult female population was reported
     as participating in the paid labour force, in contrast with 77.7
     per cent of the adult male population (ibid., Table 8.2, p. 361).
     This data, however, must be seen in historical perspective, as
     even this level of female participation is a very recent phen-
     omenon.

Work-force participation by sex, 1901-76

Year	1901	1911	1921	1931	1941	1951	1961	1971	1976
% females in paid workforce	16	19	20	22	23	24	29	40	45
% males in paid workforce	88	91	90	87	86	84	81	76	78

Source: Gail A. Cook (ed.), 'Opportunity for Choice: A Goal
for Women in Canada' (Ottawa: Statistics Canada in association
with the C. C. Howe Research Institute, 1976), Table 4.1, p.
97, except for 1976 above.

11 Statistics Canada, 'The Labour Force', Catalogue No. 71-001,
    Ottawa: June 1979, Table 4.
12 Statistics Canada, 'Income Distribution by Size in Canada,
    1972', Catalogue 13-207. (Ottawa: August 1979).
    Annual and
    Canadian Council on Social Development, 'Canadian Fact Book
    on Poverty', (Ottawa: May 1979).
13 See National Council on Welfare, 'Women and Poverty', Table
    5, p. 26. This summary of life patterns is based on data
    derived from several sources: Statistics Canada, 'Vital
    Statistics: Volume II: Marriages'.
14 A series of recent strikes led by women have begun to break
    the image of women as strike-breakers or as willing to work
    for wages lower than men's wages. While attitudes are
    changing slowly, the picture of organizational success in
    units primarily involving women is mixed.
15 See note 17 for a description of the study and our sample of
    women.
16 It is important to note that our mapping of municipal candi-
    dates included only 24 sample municipalities, whereas our
    mapping at the provincial and federal levels included all
    women candidates. Hence, our data involve an under-estim-
    ation of the number of women active as candidates in all
    municipalities.
17 This sample of Canadian women candidates is part of a long-
    term project being conducted by the authors. The sample was
    drawn from a mapping which included all women candidates
    who ran federally and provincially between 1945 and 1976 and
    all women who ran municipally in 24 sample municipalities
    drawn from all ten provinces. For further details on the
    mapping, see Jill McCalla Vickers, Where are the Women in
    Canadian Politics?, 'Atlantis' vol. 3, no. 2 (Spring 1978)
    pp. 40-51. The sample, at the time of writing (Spring 1980)
    includes municipal, provincial and federal candidates from all
    provinces except Quebec (N-314). The data were derived
    from a mail questionnaire probing the backgrounds, social-
    ization, party and voluntary group apprenticeship and
    recruitment experiences of these women candidates for public
    office.
18 See note 17.
19 Compiled from Marion C. Wilson (ed.), 'Women in Federal
    Politics: A Bibliography', National Library of Canada, Ottawa,
    1975.
20 Observations based on personal interviews with women mem-
    bers of parliament.
21 As note 19.
22 The NAC is an umbrella organization consisting of 170
    women's groups. Quote is from a Press Release, Ottawa, 16
    May 1979, p. 3.

BIBLIOGRAPHY

Armstrong, P. and Armstrong, H. (1978), 'The Double Ghetto: Canadian Women and their Segregated Work', McClelland & Stewart, Toronto.
Barber, J. D. (1965), 'The Lawmakers', Yale University Press, New Haven, Connecticut.
Bashevkin, A. (1979), Women and Politics: Perspectives on the Past, Present and Future. Paper presented to the Annual Meeting of the Canadian Political Science Association, Saskatoon.
Black, G. (1972), A Theory of Political Ambition: Career Choices and the Role of Structural Incentives, 'American Political Science Review', 66, March, pp. 59-74.
Black, J. H. and McGlen, N. E. (1977), Changing Patterns of Political Participation between Canadian Men and Women, 1965-1974. Paper presented to the Annual Meeting of the Canadian Political Science Association, Fredericton.
Boyd, Eichler and Hofley (1976), 'Family', in G. A. Cook (ed.) 'Opportunity for Choice: A Goal for Women in Canada', Statistics Canada in Association with the C. C. Howe Research Institute, Ottawa.
Brodie, M. J. (1975), 'The Recruitment of Men and Women Political Party Activists in Ontario: A Four Variable Model', unpublished MA thesis, University of Windsor.
Brodie, M. J. (1977), The Recruitment of Canadian Women Provincial Legislators, 1950-1975, 'Atlantis', 2:2, Spring, pp. 4-17.
Brodie, M. J. (1979), Voluntary Groups and the Recruitment of Women in Canada: Some Preliminary Survey Findings. Paper presented at the Annual Meeting of the Canadian Political Science Association, June, Saskatoon.
Brodie, M. J. and Jenson, J. (1980), 'Crisis, Challenge and Change: Class and Party in Canada', Methuen, Toronto.
Brodie, M. J. and Vickers, J. M. (1978), Gates and Gatekeepers and Women Legislative Candidates. Paper presented at the Annual Meeting of the Canadian Political Science Association, London, Ontario.
Brodie, M. J. and Vickers, J. M. (1979), The More Things Change ... Women in the 1979 Campaign, in H. R. Penniman (ed.), 'Canada at the Polls: The General Election of 1979', American Enterprise Institute, Washington DC.
Burke, M., Clarke, H. D., and Le Duc, L. (1978), Federal and Provincial Participation in Canada: Some Methodological and Substantive Considerations, 'Canadian Review of Sociology and Anthropology', 15, February, pp. 61-65.
'The Canadian Yearbook 1978-9' (1978), Minister of Supply and Services, Ottawa.
Clarke, H. D., Jenson, J., LeDuc, L. and Pammett, J. (1979), 'Political Choice in Canada', McGraw-Hill Ryerson, Toronto.
Cleverdon, C. L. (1974), 'The Woman Suffrage Movement in Canada', 2nd ed., University of Toronto Press.
Cochrane, J. (1977), 'Women in Canadian Politics', Fitzhenry & Whiteside, Toronto.

Cook, G. A. (ed.) (1976), 'Opportunity for Choice: A Goal for Women in Canada', Statistics Canada in association with the C. C. Howe Research Institute, Ottawa.

Dulude, L. (1977), 'The Status of Women in Federal Crown Corporations', Action Committee on the Status of Women, Ottawa.

Geller, G. (1976), The War-Times Election Act of 1917 and the Canadian Women's Movement, 'Atlantis: A Women's Studies Journal', vol. 2, no. 1, pp. 88-106.

Gorham, D. (1976), The Canadian Suffragists, in G. Matheson (ed.), 'Women in the Canadian Mosaic', Peter Martin Associates, Toronto.

Gunderson, M. (1976), Work Patterns, in G. A. Cook (ed.), 'Opportunity for Choice: A Goal for Women in Canada', Statistics Canada in association with C. C. Howe Research Institute.

Kornberg, A. (1967), 'Canadian Legislative Behaviour', Holt, Rinehart & Winston, Toronto.

Kornberg, A. and Mishler, W. (1976), 'Influence in Parliament: Canada', Duke University Press, Durham, North Carolina.

Kornberg, A., Smith J. and Clarke, D. (1976), 'Citizen Politicians: Canada', Duke University Press, Durham, North Carolina.

Labour Canada (1977), 'Women in the Labour Force: Facts and Figures', Part II, Ottawa.

Labour Canada (Women's Bureau) (December 1979), 'Facts and Figures', Ottawa.

Laponce, J. (1969), 'People vs. Politics', University of Toronto, Toronto.

Mishler, W. (1979), 'Political Participation in Canada', Macmillan, Toronto.

Morton, D. (1977), 'Social Democracy in Canada', Samuel Stevens & Hakkert, Toronto.

National Council on Welfare (1979), 'Women and Poverty', October, Ottawa.

Paltiel, K. Z. (1970), 'Political Party Financing in Canada', McGraw-Hill, Scarborough.

Pross, A. P. (ed.), (1975), 'Pressure Group Behaviour in Canadian Politics', McGraw-Hill Ryerson, Toronto.

Putnam, R. (1976), 'The Comparative Study of Political Elites', Prentice-Hall, Englewood Cliffs, New Jersey.

Regenstreif, P. (1963), Some Aspects of National Party Support in Canada, 'Canadian Journal of Economics and Political Science', 29, February, pp. 59-74.

'Report of the Royal Commission on the Status of Women' (1970), Information Canada: Ottawa.

Rioux, M. and Pearson, M. (1975), 'A Review of Appointments Within the Power of the Federal Government to Boards, Commissions, Councils and Corporations', Action Committee on the Status of Women, Ottawa.

Robb, A. L. and Spence, B. G. (1976), in G. A. Cook (ed.), 'Opportunity for Choice: A Goal for Women in Canada', Statistics Canada in association with the C. C. Howe Research Institute, Ottawa.

Teather, L. (1976), The Feminist Mosaic, in G. Matheson (ed.), 'Women in the Canadian Mosaic', Peter Martin Associates, Toronto.

Terry, J. and Schultz, R. (1973), Canadian Electoral Behaviour: A Propositional Inventory, in O. Kruhlak et al., 'The Canadian Political Process: A Reader', 2nd ed., Holt, Rinehart & Winston, Toronto.

Thomson, A. (1977), Women and Canadian Politics. A Critique of the Adam's Rib Approach, unpublished MA thesis, Queens University, Kingston.

Van Loon, R. (1968), Canadian Electoral Participation: The Canadian Public in the 1965 Federal Election, unpublished PhD thesis, Queens University, Kingston.

Vickers, J. and Adam, J. (1978), 'But Can You Type', Clark Irwin, Toronto.

5 AUSTRALIA

Marian Simms

THE HISTORICAL, SOCIAL AND ECONOMIC CONTEXTS

Australia has been seen as a 'pure' (Kemp, 1976, p. 124) case of
an advanced industrial society. It was 'born modern' without
feudal remnants and with a free capitalist economy. Economically,
particularly since the Second World War, the tertiary sector has
been growing in importance vis-à-vis the manufacturing and rural
sectors. Socially, Australia has been one of the most urbanised
and suburbanised industrial nations. In sum it may be characterised as a small (population 14,000,000), rich (in world terms)
capitalist country. Women constitute 49 per cent of the population
but the incidence of women in positions of economic, political and
social power is 'statistically insignificant' (see Women's Advisory
Body Working Party, 1977, p. 5).

Discussion about women's political involvement in Australia must
be set in the context of certain methodological and historical
debates. One prevailing view is that after a time of hectic activity
around the suffrage campaigns women retreated to their kitchens
and did not emerge until western countries were re-radicalised
from the mid-1960s. For the Australian case, researchers are now
beginning to suggest that women were in fact active politically in
the interregnum between the suffrage movement and the second
wave of feminism. It is simply that their involvement took different forms.

First, women's organisations continued to exist but lacked a
single common objective and a shared ideology. Second, their
involvement was limited to two main types of issues, specifically
legal matters and social welfare problems. However, those efforts
to agitate on issues directly relevant to women such as marriage
and custody laws, maternal and child health and conditions of
female employment have been designated as community or voluntary
involvement around welfare reform rather than as politics. Politics
has been seen as being about the clash of material interests (see
Kemp, 1977). Consequently, employers and unions clashing over
material rewards and translating this into lobbying in the public
forum via organised groups has been seen as the prototype of
political behaviour.

The discriminatory impact of definitions of politics is an instance
of the case made by those criticising the sexist nature of much
social science and historical research (see Bourque and Grossholtz,
1974; Markusen, 1977; Roberts, 1976). Canons of relevance have
been determined by male-dominated professions. Women's activities

have been marginalised and stereotyped. Consequently, one must at least pose the question whether women's absences from the public sphere have been exaggerated by the presence of the biases of historical and political researchers. Responses by Australian women academics have been twofold. It has been maintained that the bias has not been in scholarship as much as it has been in actual political practices. Australian women have been designated the doormats of the western world (see Dixson, 1975), confined and constrained by a male-dominated mateship ethos. In response to that perspective others have pointed to the extent of women's political activities which are only now being unearthed and investigated by feminist researchers (Grimshaw, 1979; Lake, 1976; Reed and Oakes, 1977).

Table 5.1   Women's political rights in Australia

Colony/State	Suffrage	Office
South Australia	1894	No specific legislation
Western Australia	1898	1920
New South Wales	1908	1918 (Lower House)
		1926 (Upper House)
Tasmania	1903	1921
Queensland	1905	1915
Victoria	1908	1923

In contrast to these debates over origins and explanations there can be and has been little debate over the fact of women's absence from publicly-elected offices in Australia this century. Although enfranchised federally at the beginning of the century (in 1901, when they also gained the right to be elected to both Houses of Federal Parliament) and earlier in several of the colonies (Table 5.1) it was not until 1921 that women had a representative in an Australian parliament. A woman of conservative party affiliation, Edith Cowan, was the person concerned, having been elected to one of the State houses, the Western Australian Legislative Assembly (see Cowan, 1978). The two features, comparatively early and easily-won suffrage on the one hand and delayed political maturity on the other have been linked in the minds of some commentators. Hence the argument runs that Australian women, unlike their sisters in the USA and Great Britain, did not have to fight for the vote, did not appreciate its value and furthermore lacked the political schooling such a struggle might have provided (see Encel et. al. 1974, Ch. 14). Now, while it can be readily conceded that Australian women's groups were less obstreperous than their more militant counterparts in the USA and Britain they were still committed to women's legal, political and economic rights, and lobbied strongly and persistently for the vote. Australia did share with a range of other western countries the late nineteenth-century reform blaze whereby middle-class women became active in the public world. Temperance bodies and women's clubs had become established and proceeded to flourish (Bacchi, 1978; Cowan, 1978).

The legacy from the suffrage struggle may not have been a feminist political tradition, but it did leave a multitude of women's organisations active around women's rights and related issues. Given the federal structure of Australia a deal of the involvement has been at state and local levels. Examples include the state branches of the National Council of Women, established within the first decade of the century, and the various service clubs and guilds (see Norris, 1979). Their members were mostly middle-class social reformers who found radical socialist views anathema.

As well as being active in public life Australian women have always worked - in the home and in factories, as pioneers and convicts, as servants and schoolteachers. In fact in 1977 43 per cent of adult women constituted 35 per cent of the civilian labour force. Two-thirds of these women were married. The Borrie Report (the First Report of the National Population Enquiry) noted that workforce participation rates for married women between the ages of 25 and 34 years (the childbearing years) increased from approximately 25 per cent in 1964 to 39 per cent in 1973, with about 25 per cent of the married women concerned as mothers. Projections indicate that the trends for greater workforce participation will continue. Impetus is given by the declining birth-rate, which dropped from 21.6 per thousand (1971) to 18.1 per thousand (1973). In 1977 it had declined to 16.6 per thousand. The marriage rate is still high (95 per cent of women in 1977 contrasted with 75 per cent in 1900). Women are also becoming better educated - in 1975, 42 per cent of students within the technical and further education sector were women. In 1976 women comprised 37 per cent of university students and 46 per cent of college enrolments. However, opportunities may be limited by the slowing down of economic growth since the mid-1970s.

Most of those women already in paid employment are concentrated in the pink collar ghetto, in low-skill, low-paid occupations with poor expectations about prospects and careers. In fact in 1980, eight years after the Arbitration Commission (a quasi-independent federal wage-setting body) pronounced the principle of 'equal pay for work of equal value' and five years after this was enacted as law, women workers still only earned 78 cents for every dollar earned by men (see Schultz, 1980, p. 27). In the highest paid category of administrative executive and managerial positions, there is only 1.7 per cent of the female work force compared with 8.1 per cent of the male (Australian Bureau of Statistics figures for 1980).

As well as the lower wage structure of the female workforce, part of the blame must lie with the trade union movement which since the passage of the Equal Pay Act in 1975 has adopted a range of tactics to maintain (male) relativities. These include the reclassification of positions in which similar work is done and the promotion of males into positions from which women are excluded because of protective requirements (such as heavy lifting restrictions). This is but one instance of the significance of the labour movement in general and for women's position in particular. On the former it has been widely seen as an 'unusually powerful' (Kemp, 1976, p. 125) working-class movement. At an industrial level its power is mirrored in relatively high levels of unionisation (59 per cent in 1968 and 57 per cent in 1978). Incidentally, although women in 1978 comprised more than one-third of the trade union movement representing 47 per cent of Australian female employees (see Falkinder, 1978), they held only 12 out of 489 official positions. In the political sphere, Australia shares with four other nations (Britain, New Zealand, Norway and Sweden) the existence of a Labour Party. That party, the Australian Labour Party (ALP) has been one of the two major political groupings which have dominated Australian politics this century, first forming a government in 1904 and more recently in office from 1972-5. Labour has been traditionally viewed as embodying the mateship ethos, the peculiarly Australian syndrome seen in recent years as a major source of the invisibility of women in public life. The ALP has itself admitted the problems posed to women by the union link and associated traditions, calling for the party to become 'less confrontationist in political style, less urban, less industrial and less male-dominated' (APSA, 1979, p. 38).

The ALP's main opponent is provided by an alliance of two conservative parties, the Liberal Party and the National Country Party. (The Liberals have travelled under a variety of noms de plume, the current one having been adopted in 1945.) A coalition of those parties has been in government for most of the post-war years (1949-72, 1975-). There are a number of smaller parties. The Democratic Labour Party (DLP) was formed in 1955, after splitting from the ALP. It has averaged 7.4 per cent of the vote for the House of Representatives and 8.9 per cent for the Senate, between 1955 and 1970. Mainly on account of the electoral system for the House of Representatives (single-member constituencies and preferential voting) it has failed to gain representation. However it has been more successful in its bids for Senate seats (holding five out of sixty, between 1970 and 1974, when it was at its peak). Here the electoral system has worked to its advantage, with multi-member State-wide constituencies and proportional representation. To the left there has been a Communist Party, which splintered in the early 1970s. It has averaged only 0.5 per cent of the vote. Of more electoral significance have been the two 'middle-class' parties of the late 1960s and 1970s. The Australia Party first contested an election in 1969 and by 1979 seemed a spent force. The Australian Democrats were formed in 1977, largely out of disaffected elements within the Liberal Party. Because of two Senators changing their affiliation, the Democrats for a time had two Senate seats.

WOMEN AND PARTIES

At the level of membership there is a clear contrast between the
ALP and the Liberal Party. Approximately half of the Liberal
Party's members (between 20,000 and 25,000 over the past twenty
years) are women, although, as shall be discussed below, equal
representation has not percolated through into executive committees. For its part the ALP's membership figures appear to
validate the common view that it is a man's party - only about
one-quarter of the members are women. As with the Liberals an
even smaller proportion of party functionaries and parliamentary
representatives are women. Of the 49 delegates to the ALP's supreme policy-making body, the National Conference, in 1979, two
were women.(1) Women fare only slightly better in the States,
where about 11 per cent of all State Conference delegates are
women. There is only one woman on the National Executive (which
is composed of two representatives from each State, one from each
Territory, the four federal parliamentary leaders, the national
president and the national secretary - a total of twenty members).
A 1977 study of one State's (New South Wales) Annual Conference
estimated that of the 825 delegates from branches and affiliated
unions about 10 to 15 per cent were women. The low figure was
blamed upon women's poor representation among the trade union
delegations which account for 60 per cent of the total numbers,
whereas, among the branch delegates approximately one-third
were women. Within the category of the branch delegates, eight
places are reserved for members elected by the New South Wales
Labour Women's Committee. Women's lack of prominence in the
union movement also explains their absence from the ranks of full-
time party officers. The Education and Research Officer of the New
South Wales Branch of the ALP (Wise, 1977, p. 35) presented the
problem in the following terms:

> I understand that there was a woman Vice-President of the
> NSW Branch long ago, but generally speaking the officers
> have consisted of the General Secretary and Assistant
> Secretaries who are full-time Party officials (usually
> requiring a union power base), together with the President
> and Vice-President who are inevitably important union
> officials.

This situation has led to debate around the question of the des-
irability of a women's vice-president, but no clear line has emerged
amongst women on the issue. It has been felt by many women that
particular women's positions or organisations within the party do
not necessarily advance women individually or as a whole. This
position has been shared both by feminists who are opposed to
what they see as 'tokenism' and others who, holding to a sex-blind
ideology, believe that each case should be treated on its merits.

For historical rather than ideological reasons the Liberal Party
does have party offices reserved for women. Due to the prior
existence of a flourishing Victorian-based women's group, the
Australian Women's National League (AWNL), when the Liberal

Party was formed, the Victorian State Division incorporated the organisational doctrine of equal representation of men and women on executive bodies (see Simms, 1979). The doctrine of equal representation has stopped at a vice-presidential level. (There are two female and two male vice-presidents, one of each a metropolitan representative and a rural representative). Women State presidents and treasurers have been rare, although since 1976 a woman has been State president. Also the proportion of women on the range of executive committees has been very small.

The AWNL's political presence and clout was also reflected in the establishment of Women's Sections. These are formed on a State electorate basis from amongst ordinary branch members. In Victoria the peak organisation is the Central Committee, which is composed of three delegates from each Section - and ex-officio the two women State vice-presidents of the party, the immediate past chair of the Section and any Victorian women parliamentarians. The committee has many and varied functions (which will be examined more fully below) including what Betty Friedan has termed 'political housework' (1976, p. 225) but extending beyond that. Most significantly its elected chairman is a member of the State Executive and a Victorian delegate to the Liberal Party's national governing body, the Federal Council (see Aimer, 1974, p. 88).

The situation is different in the other States, lacking as they do the guarantee of equal representation. One partial exception is the New South Wales Division where the Constitution requires a minimum representation of women on the main deliberative body, the State Council and the State Executive.(2) Partly as a result of this requirement as at 1973 one-third of State Councillors and one-fifth of State Executive members had been women (see Encel et. al., 1974, p. 255).

An analysis (see Carlton, 1977, p. 26) of the composition of the New South Wales State Council in 1976 showed that out of a total of 831 members, 162 or only 19 per cent were women (Table 5.2).

In general, in all the State Divisions women, although comprising at least half the branch members (and in one State, South Australia, a clear majority of members in the metropolitan areas) and a presence in the State Councils are almost non-existent in the higher ranks. One would expect trends and patterns in the States to emerge at the national level, particularly as the party's key organisational historian has noted that one cannot see it as a single national party - instead, the Liberal Party is six State Divisions with a federal apex. The Federal Council has sixty members (ten from each state). The Victorian delegation has equal numbers of men and women (including the chairman of the Central Committee of the Women's Section). Women's voice is also projected through the Federal Women's Committee which discusses resolutions from all States, which if passed are then considered by the Federal Council.

The Country National Party has recently reacted against criticisms to the effect that 'little needs to be said except that women are free to join it' (Encel et. al., 1974, p. 256). It has responded

in two ways: by attacking the harshness of the Encel judgment; and by taking action to correct the imbalance of the sexes. The party's main historian (Aitkin, 1972, p. 126) has explained the subordinate role of women in the following way:
> While this situation reflects the patriarchal society in which the Country Party operates, and applies to some extent to all Australian political parties, it is a source of weakness in the party's organisation.

Table 5.2   Composition of the New South Wales Liberal Party State Council

Category of delegates	Number of delegates in category	Number of women delegates in category	Percent women
General branches	373	45	12
Women's branches	20	20	100
Young Liberal branches	54	7	13
State Electorate Conferences	217	68*	31
Federal Electorate Conferences	30	3	10
Parliamentarians	74	4	5
Miscellaneous	63	15+	24
Total	831	162	19

* Constitution requires a minimum number of women in this category.
+ Includes 7 Women's Group delegates.

The party itself admitted that the work of feminist groups, especially The Women's Electoral Lobby (WEL), has forced it to examine the state of its own house. In particular, impetus had come from women at a grass roots level who called for the establishment of a 'Committee which includes women to formulate policy on current issues and issues that arise with reference to women and that this Committee have direct access to our Parliamentary Leaders' (quoted in Briggs, 1977, p. 37). That was the substance of a resolution moved by the party's 1973 Annual General Conference, which was then examined by its hierarchy. It was felt that rather than establish a permanent structure to represent women, measures should be taken to increase the numbers of women on party bodies. Given that in 1974 there were only two women on the main extra-parliamentary body, the Central Council, out of a total of over sixty members it seemed a prime candidate for reform. Consequently in 1976 the Annual General Conference carried the following resolution (quoted in Briggs, 1977, p. 38):
> That for a trial period of three years:

(a) that there be from Federal Electorate Councils two
members of the Central Council, the Chairman and one
other who shall be elected by the Electorate Council;
(b) that the Electorate Councils be encouraged to elect
a woman to either one of the two positions carrying
representation on the Central Council.

By the device of increasing the total numbers the proportion of
women has increased significantly (in March 1980, 18 out of 43).
The spirit of equal opportunity trickled down to the party in general. For example, at the 1977 Annual General Conference 40 per
cent of the members were women (124 out of 314). In 1978 of 314
branches 13 had women chairs and 88 were women secretaries.

Given the Country Party's rural nature a male dominance is not
surprising. One would also expect the essentially Catholic origin
and nature of the DLP to have a similar effect. However, as Encel
et al. (1974, p. 256) have noted, circumstances have perhaps
ironically pushed women to the fore. In 1962 a woman was elected
as State president in Victoria (the party's heartland). Women have
also figured prominently on the Executive in Victoria and Tasmania
and have had a separate women's organisation. The newer parties
have eschewed sexual apartheid and women have also been a force
at all levels. In fact it would not be an exaggeration to say that
the Australian Democrats are seen as an avenue for women frustrated with the traditional parties.

At this juncture it is timely to ask whether women have had
cause to be dissatisfied with the mainstream parties? It can be
argued (see Summers, 1979) that when in power both major political groupings have subordinated women's concerns and interests
to economic considerations. For example, the McMahon government
enacted child-care legislation in 1972 and presented this in its
campaign of that year as a pro-woman initiative. Instead it was
seen as being linked to demands by manufacturers for more women
workers to cope with the shortage of labour. The election of 1972
marked the first intervention by WEL in the political process.
Having polled all candidates, the non-Labour parties fared badly
while the (then) Opposition Labour leader, Gough Whitlam, scored
the possible. After becoming Prime Minister he acted quickly to
translate theory into practice. Initiatives included applying to the
Arbitration Commission to reopen the National Wage (equal pay) case.
In its submission the government called for equal pay (in contrast
to its predecessors). (Here it is interesting to note that since the
late 1940s the platforms of the non-Labour parties had actually
committed them to equal pay.) Whitlam also early in 1973 abolished
a luxury tax on oral contraceptives and pledged the introduction
of paid maternity leave for employees of the Commonwealth Public
Service. Later that year he established the position of Adviser to
the Prime Minister on Women's Affairs.

The Labour government began to lose support from within the
women's movement over its handling of abortion law reform. In
1973 a private members' bill was introduced by two Labour back-
benchers, specifically to clarify the legal situation in the Australian

Capital Territory (ACT). (The Federal government lacking the
necessary constitutional powers to legislate nationally on the
question.) The bill was defeated on a 'conscience' vote. Anti-
abortion groups, particularly The Right to Life Association, had
lobbied strongly against it. Although the Prime Minister voted for
it, the majority of Labour members (including several front-
benchers) had opposed it. Parliament, instead of giving Australian women (at least those in the ACT) the right to control their
own bodies, presented them with a Royal Commission into Human
Relationships.

Criticism of the government mounted during 1974 with the onset
of the recession which hit in the second half of the year. Social
welfare programmes were pruned in an attempt to trim the deficit.
Amongst those affected were some specifically established to promote equal opportunity for women. In particular the National
Employment and Training Scheme (NEAT) which had been created
to 'aid the removal of past inequalities in employment opportunities' (quoted in Summers, 1979, p. 142) was fastened upon as a
device to alleviate male unemployment. The child-care programme
(administered via the Children's Commission) was reduced.

As well as being angered by cuts caused by the economic crisis,
women's groups had also been earlier critical of the implementation
of particular programmes. They had been grateful for the funding
of a range of undertakings, such as health centres, rape crisis
centres and women's refuges. But they viewed with some dismay
attempts by the government to claim credit for those initiatives.
Difficulties were compounded by the fact that feminists and government officials had different, and indeed competing notions, of
accountability and control.

Leaving aside the complex question of the fate of reform proposals, I will focus on the origins of those endeavours. This is
one way into discussing the role and impact of women's groups in
the ALP. To put it another way - why were the Whitlam (ALP)
government's policies on women different from those of their Liberal and National Country Party predecessors? Not all ALP state
branches had separate women's organisations. The New South
Wales one, the Labour Women's Central Organising Committee
(LWCOC) stands out with its record of continuous activity since
its formation in 1904. Although there were a handful of women who
rose to positions of power and influence within the ALP via the
LWCOC, in general, it had auxiliary functions (see Allen, 1977).
These included day-time campaigning, charity work, welfare
activities and strike relief. By the 1970s its character had begun
to change - reflected, in part, in the renaming of the group, now
known as the Labour Women's Committee (LWC). In the words of
one of its members (Allen, 1977, p. 14): 'it was evident by 1970
that an influx of younger women into the Labour women's organisation... was coinciding with an increase of criticism of women's
role in the Party generally, and with the activity of the LWC
specifically.' The new direction of the group and its growing political clout was reflected in the adoption by the 1973 Federal ALP

Conference of a child-care scheme initially drafted by the LWC.
The non-Labour parties have lacked, as one might expect of
conservative parties, radical feminist-inspired ginger groups.
This is not to deny that second-wave feminism has made its mark
upon the Liberal and National Country parties. Calls for internal
party reform have already been noted, as has the emergence of
several 'women's rights' type of feminists in the parties' front
ranks. The concerns of one of these, Beryl Beaurepaire (former
'chairman' of the Liberal Party's Federal Women's Committee), ex-
emplifies the strengths and limitations of the conservative feminist
perspective. She chairs a body, the National Women's Advisory
Council, which was established in 1977 by the Fraser (Liberal-
National Country Party) government in the wake of Whitlam's more
radical and spectacular initiatives. One suspects that the Council
was conceived of in largely symbolic terms and perhaps even as a
cipher for government policy, which given the persistence of
economic crisis, was largely about cutting costs. However, Beaurepaire has consistently publicly defended women's rights for
equal opportunity - legally, economically and educationally. Her
Council (see National Women's Advisory Council, 1979) has also
been concerned with improving the position of minority and disadvantaged women, particularly Aboriginal and migrant women as
well as country women facing problems of isolation.

WOMEN IN ELECTORAL OFFICE

At the federal level, 1943 saw the first woman member of the
House of Representatives (Dame Enid Lyons) and of the Senate
(Dorothy Tangney). As at the eve of the last federal election
(December 1977) there had been a grand total of twelve women
ever elected to the Senate and four women who had been successful in their bids for the Lower House. Then in 1980 in the thirty-
first parliament there were six women senators (there are 64
senators) and no women members of the House of Representatives
(which has 127 sitting members).
In all seven parliaments (State and federal) there has been a
total of only 57 women members. In 1977 there were 21 female
State parliamentarians, with a state by state breakdown as follows:

New South Wales	8
Victoria	1
Tasmania	2
South Australia	3
Queensland	2
Western Australia	5

Women have fared slightly better in the Territories where two
women were on the House of Assembly of the Australian Capital
Territory and two on the Northern Territory Legislative Assembly.
It might be expected that women would have a greater role to
play in local government. However available figures do not bear
this out. In December 1975 there were 5,811 members on local

government councils in New South Wales, Victoria, South Australia and the Australian Capital Territory. Less than 6 per cent,
only 330, were women (see Women's Advisory Body Working Party,
1977, p. 5). This seems to have been a fairly constant percentage.
For example, in 1960 of approximately 7,000 positions on local
authorities throughout the nation, women held 100. Then in 1968
it had increased to 178 and 315 in 1972 (see Encel et al., 1974,
p. 260).

Before returning to what are generally regarded as the more
significant State and federal arenas I want to make some more
comments about participation at the local level precisely because
women have been more visible there in an absolute even if not in
a relative sense. Furthermore, women's organisations of a type
mentioned in the first section of the chapter have focused upon
the local level. The National Council of Women and the Country
Women's Association have been particularly active - the former
also becoming involved in cases when it appeared that women
councillors were being denied their rights to rotating mayorships.
In this vein, the Australian Local Government Women's Association
(ALGWA) was established in 1951 in Canberra with state branches
being established soon afterwards. The most active of these was
the New South Wales one. It, in turn, established the Local Government Promotion Committee in 1958 to increase the numbers of
women. Not only did it meet with a measure of success (the numbers rose from 28 to 49), but it held a meeting to review the
campaign providing us with detailed information about 23 of the
52 candidates. Overall the numbers were small making general-
isation difficult. However, all of the group of 23 had been married -
two were divorced and three were widows. Sixteen had children,
suggesting heavy domestic commitments at the time of candidature.
To counterbalance this the majority had the active support of their
husbands. This was related to another significant shared characteristic, namely, a family political tradition. Fifteen of the women
had relatives who were involved politically - as civic officers,
party branch officers or party candidates.

Most of the women were also reasonably well educated. Of the
total group of 52, 2 had only primary school education but 15 had
completed secondary school, and 6 were university graduates.
They also tended to be employed in the paid workforce. Only 11
were engaged in home duties and the rest had a range of occupations (including grazier, hotel manager, nurse, teacher, sten-
ographer and librarian).

All were active members of public organisations (the 23 concerned between them belonged to 110 bodies). Most of these
organisations were what are commonly seen as community and
cultural bodies. This fits with a more recent study of women in
local government, although this time in Victoria (Bowman, 1972,
p. 10):

> Men councillors have probably been drawn into municipal
> circles through activity in locally-based organisations like
> APEX, Chamber of Commerce and Lions, where their potential

is not only displayed but noticed by those likely to give
them electoral support. Women, on the other hand, tend
to belong predominantly to charity and cultural groups often
consisting of women only. These are bad public showcases
for talent. The men accept, sometimes even gratefully
acknowledge, the funds raised, the help given, the job done,
but they aren't given the chance of seeing a potential colleague in action as an equal in a joint enterprise.

However, both the focus of local government and the thrust of
participation by women may be changing. The ALGWA has been
joined by consciously feminist groups such as 'Councillors for
Equal Opportunity' which was formed in Victoria in 1979 (see
Councillors for Equal Opportunity, 1979). The group, including
two women mayors, has direct links with WEL. As part of the same
process of change since the early 1970s local government is concerning itself with quality of life issues, including action around
the question of development in general and freeway construction
in particular. Residents' 'action groups' in Sydney, New South
Wales, have provided a base for women to become elected - after
one such struggle over development in the North Sydney municipality four women became elected to the Council of fifteen.

Moving to the federal level, where we have a grand total of sixteen women, one finds a blurring between the category of all
women federal MPs and particularly successful women. Even at a
State level there are still pathbreakers. For example, when Mrs
Mary Meillon (Liberal Party) was elected to the New South Wales
Legislative Assembly in October 1973, she became the first woman
to represent a country constituency in that legislature (see Meillon,
1977), its fourth female member and the first elected for the previous twenty-three years.

The first of the four women members of the federal House of
Representatives (MHRs) had special characteristics.(3) Enid
Lyons (MHR for Darwin, 1943-51) was the widow of a former Prime
Minister from the non-Labour side of politics (J. A. Lyons, Prime
Minister 1932-39, MHR for Wilmot 1909-39, who died in office).
She was the first woman to become a member of the federal cabinet, albeit of junior status as the vice-president of the Executive
Council, 1949-51 (minister without portfolio). In 1946 Enid Lyons
was joined by Doris Blackburn, who had inherited her husband's
seat - another instance of the widow factor. Both Blackburns had
been members of the ALP but they then became involved in the
breakaway group, the Independent Labour Party. Doris Blackburn
won and then lost (in 1946) her seat (a safe ALP one) as an Independent Labour representative. The third woman MHR, Kay
Brownbill (Liberal Party) was unmarried and a journalist. She did
not have family political connections. Her stay in parliament was
brief, 1966-69, as hers was usually an ALP seat, which she had
won as part of a swing to the Liberals in metropolitan Adelaide
(South Australia). A landslide back to Labour in 1969 saw her as
a casualty. Joan Child (married) who won Henty (Victoria) for the
ALP in 1972 suffered a similar fate. Henty was generally regarded

as a Liberal seat, having been held by the sitting member, M. E.
Fox, since 1955. There was a general swing to the ALP in 1972
which resulted in the first federal Labour government for twenty-
three years. However the swing in Child's seat was above the
Melbourne average (see Mackerras, 1977) and this was again the
case in the 1974 election. She lost in 1975 in a landslide against
Labour which caused the Whitlam government to lose office. Her
case has been cited (see Mackerras, 1977) to instance the fact
that women candidates do not lose votes. The pro-Labour swings
in her seat were above the metropolitan average, and when she
lost in 1975 her share of the vote was higher than the previous
Labour (male) candidate's had been in 1969.

The extraordinary fact is that three of the four women concerned only had one term in parliament. One was an unusual case,
related to problems of internal party conflict and factions. The
others are directly linked to the difficulties at the pre-selection
level, women have simply not been selected for safe seats.(4)

Women have been relatively more successful in the Upper House,
the Senate. (This has also been the case in the States.) 1943 saw
the first woman senator, there was also something of a minor influx after 1972 (since then six of the twelve have been elected).
Those two dates are important, both marking times of politicisation.
In 1943 more women contested the election than previously (see
Encel et. al., 1974, p. 250). There was a 'Women for Canberra'
movement (based on the English one). Its appearance was a high
point of women's broadly feminist activity, cutting across party
lines. The movement shared the rapid demise of one earlier similar organisation, the Women's Federal Political Association, which
had sponsored one of Australia's first women Senate candidates
(Vida Goldstein) in 1903. A third such group, the Women's Party,
was formed in time for the 1977 federal election. In common with
the Goldstein group it was grounded in the feminist movement, ran
candidates for the Senate and met with little success.

1943 also saw a shift in the direction of women's pursuit of
electoral office. Before then the majority of women candidates
sought office under 'non-party' labels. Since then there has been
a movement towards the party umbrella. This is an aspect of a
broader trend of the decline of the independent, partly given the
expense of running for office, but also due to the hegemony of
the main party.

The other key election, held in 1972, was the first 'post-second
wave feminist' election. Women's issues such as equal pay, contraception, child-care and abortion law reform were given prominence.
The parties were forced to examine their platforms and practices
in the light of those issues - we have already noted efforts by the
parties to increase female participation. There was a record number of candidates, 535 of which 38 were women. There were 14 out
of 60 candidates for the new party, The Australia Party, 7 out of
120 for the Democratic Labour Party, 4 out of 125 for the ALO, 3
out of 107 for the Liberals, and 10 others. The Country Party did
not nominate any.

This was not out of character for the Country Party - its anti-woman bias has already been hinted at. It has only mustered three woman MPs: Senator Agnes Robertson (Western Australia, 1955-62), Elizabeth Andrew (Northern Territory, currently a member of the Legislative Assembly) and Vicki Kippin (Queensland, currently a member of that State's Lower House). The ALP and the Liberal Party have fared equally well or badly depending on one's perspective. Of the pre-1972 Senators, four were Liberals, one was Labour and the sixth was the Country Party's Senator Robertson. Of those elected since 1972, three have been Labour, two Liberal and the final one, represented a minority party, The Australian Democrats. Of the post-1972 generation two (one Liberal and one Labour) are self-proclaimed feminists - who on account of this have become prominent even if not successful. One or two State women are in a similar position. For example, Rosemary Kyburz, Liberal Member for Salisbury in the Queensland House of Assembly (see Kennedy, 1979), has attempted to establish an Australia-wide association of women MPs. She has been able to raise little interest. In New South Wales, several members of the Legislative Council have been strong proponents of women's rights feminism, opposing discrimination and supporting maternity leave. In contrast others have cheerfully accepted the role of 'womanly woman - a sound home-loving woman' (Meillon, 1977, p. 23) or become conservative anti-feminists, like Western Australia's Winifred Piesse (see Bennett, 1979).

If we define successful as the achievement of ministerial office then there are few contenders for the title. Enid Lyons has had few successors. More recently, in 1975 Margaret Guilfoyle became a minister in the Fraser (Liberal-National Country Party) government. Her organisational stepping ladder was the Women's Section of the Victorian Division of the Liberal Party, where after serving on several sub-committees she was chairman from 1969-70 (and hence a member of the Federal Council). She also worked on the Federal Women's Committee from 1969-70 before becoming a Victorian Senator in 1970. As Minister for Social Security she is administering an area which can at least partly be seen as a woman's 'home and hearth' type of field. However Guilfoyle (see 1977) has been anxious to avoid that kind of characterisation for either her or her ministry, preferring to emphasise the economic policy-making aspects. (She is an accountant by profession.)

WOMEN AND VOTING

The existence of compulsory voting at the federal level since 1924 has resulted in comparatively high turnouts of over 90 per cent. One major study of political participation (Aitkin, 1977, p. 303) has suggested that 30 per cent of the electorate is 'politically active and aware', 37 per cent can be seen as a 'passive audience' and 33 per cent as 'quite indifferent and uninterested'. Almost 4 per cent of the electorate (over 250,000) belong to political parties.

Traditionally there has been seen to be a fit between on the one hand, the working class (or blue-collar voter) and the ALP, and on the other hand, the 'middle class' and the Liberal Party. The other smaller parties have represented residual sectional, sectarian and ideological interests. However, it is not (see Kemp. 1976) suggested that there has been a significant weakening in the class bases of support of the major parties in Australia from 1946 to 1972. This decline is believed to have two immediate causes. The steady movement of blue-collar voters away from the ALP, and the drift by upper white-collar voters away from the non-Labour parties.

Class and voting, and to a lesser extent religion and voting, have occupied the attention of Australian psephologists. The question of gender and voting has largely escaped their attention. For example, in one of the most recent and most significant voting studies (Aitkin, 1977) there is no entry for women in the index. In another (Kemp, 1978), generally deemed to be of similar significance, women rate two mentions but both concern their distaff functions (viz. the impact of women's incomes upon the affluence of the family unit and hence its embourgeoisement).

Consequently it would not be an understatement to say that the literature on women's voting is in an infant stage. On the one hand there is a number of small and scattered surveys, usually on an electorate basis (see Encel et al., 1974, pp. 257-9). On the other hand there are the beginnings of a critical practice through attempts to uncover sexist assumptions and neglect.

Such writers (see Goot and Reid, 1975; Gorring, 1977), largely inspired by the 'second wave' of feminism, have collected the stereotypes about women's political behaviour found in the literature of political science. Given the small size of the local literature compounded by its often derivative nature, they have focused on overseas (mainly American and British) works as well as available Australian material. There is broad agreement that the key clichés are the following: that children follow their fathers' voting habits; that wives imitate their husbands' political tendencies; that women are more conservative than men; and that women tend to personalise politics. The tendency of such critics is to reject those views and replace them with interpretations allowing women more independent, active and indeed critical stances. One obvious task is to ask whether this too does not involve mythologising about women?

Current survey analysis carried out at the Political Science Department, University of Melbourne, indicates that certain of these stereotypes no longer apply. Using this material, I have focused upon two firmly held views: one relating to voting behaviour - that women are more conservative than men; and the other dealing with political orientation in general - that women are less interested in politics. As well as presenting and analysing the available data it is also necessary to intervene in the more murky debates over interpretation. Here we find, in the existing literature, different views of preferred political norms for women.

These tend to mirror a great divide within the contemporary women's movement, namely, whether women are fundamentally like men (a sex-blind ideology) (see Francis and Peele, 1978) or that women are different (i.e. better) and should continue to construct their own alternatives (see Barnard, 1979).

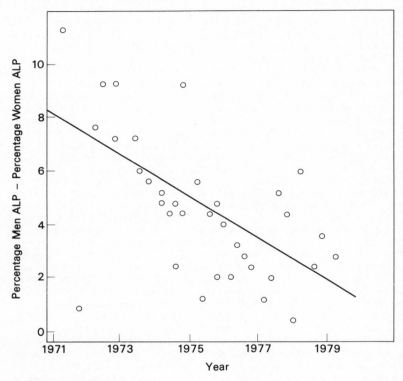

Figure 5.1:
Difference between percentage intended vote for ALP among men and percentage intended vote for ALP among women. Trend in the 'Age' polls, March 1971 to April 1979 (r = -0.61. Equation: Y = 61.02-0.7449X).

1 Are women more conservative than men?
Senator Susan Ryan (1979, p. 3) while calling for the ALP to take positive steps to appeal to the women voters decried the fact that their support for Labour had 'lagged several percent behind' that of men.

In order to examine her statement and ascertain recent tendencies I looked at 36 'Age' Polls (5) from March 1971 to April 1979, to try to map this difference between the sexes in their support

for the ALP. I wanted to see whether we could detect any pattern:
were the differences increasing or decreasing? Did it matter what
party was in government? Did the formation of the Australian
Democrats make an impact? I looked at the voting intention of the
respondents. The question used in each of the surveys: 'If a
federal election for the House of Representatives was held tomor-
row, for which political party would you probably vote?', and the
respondent was handed a card with the names of the parties. In
each survey I subtracted the percentage of women who intended
to vote for the ALP from the percentage of men who intended to
vote for the ALP (excluding 'Don't Know'). This measurement was
the only one that controlled for fluctuations in support on the
whole and was readily available at the same time. In Figure 5.1 we
can see that the difference is decreasing and, predicting the
future from the regression line fitted to the plotted values, that
it should disappear by late 1981. (It seems to make no difference
at all which party is in power.) The trend in Figure 5.1 raises
several questions: Why this is happening? Will the trend even out
around a couple of percent? Around zero? Increase again? Or will
women in the future support the ALP to a higher degree than men?
We will come back to some of these questions later.

When we look closely at the plotted values we find that in 1977
the differences suddenly increased only to start to decrease again
and had at the end of the whole period reached about the same
level as before the increase. In the June 1977 'Age' Poll a putative
'Centre Party' was mentioned for the first time and at the time of
the September 1977 poll the Australian Democrats had been formed.
In Table 5.3 we compare the two polls, before and after the Australian Democrats emerged. The Australian Democrats seem to have

Table 5.3   *Voting intention by sex, March 1977, September 1977*

	VOTING INTENTION			
	Men − Liberal %	Women − Liberal %	Men − ALP %	Women − ALP %
March 1977	40.0	42.0	46.4	45.1
September 1977	32.5	40.9	46.4	41.0
LOSS	7.5	1.1	0.0	4.1

Source: 'Age' Polls

attracted more male than female Liberal voters and more female
than male ALP voters, and as a consequence the differences with
the parties (ALP and Liberal) between men and women increased.
In Figure 5.2 there are two trend lines, before and after the
emergence of the Australian Democrats. It seems the Australian
Democrats put the trend back a couple of years but did not put a
stop to it or alter it.

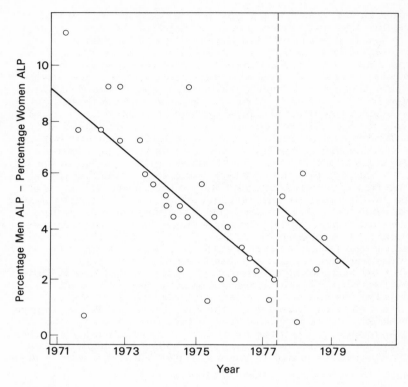

Figure 5.2:

   Difference between percentage intended vote for ALP among
   men and percentage intended vote for ALP among women. Trends
   in the 'Age' polls (March 1971 to April 1979), before and after
   the Australian Democrats were formed.
   (1971-7: $r = -.70$ Equation: $Y = 87.56-1.1047X$
    1977-9: $r = -.21$ Equation: $Y = 56.92-0.6778X$)
   Note: The second part of this scattergram has fewer observations than the first part and the trend line is therefore not as
   reliable. The latest 'Age' poll (late 1979) confirms the trend,
   however; the difference being zero.

   Why are the differences decreasing and is it a temporary phenomenon? The solution to the second part of the question probably
depends on the answer to the first part. For women to vote differently from men to a significant degree may be related to a
difference in 'life experience'. If men's and women's 'life experience' becomes less different, their voting differences ought to
diminish as well. Some of the aspects of 'life experience' can be
measured, others cannot, and of those we can measure the ones

Table 5.4   Attitudes towards sex role stereotypes in the family by sex, age, education and occupation

| | Men % | Women % | WOMEN ONLY | | | | | | | |
			Under 40 with tertiary education %	Under 40 with other education %	40 and over with tertiary education %	40 and over with other education %	Under 40 not home-maker %	Under 40 home-maker %	40 and over not home-maker %	40 and over home-maker %
False	48	62	83	67	74	43	76	64	64	43
True	52	38	14	33	26	57	24	36	46	57
N=	(246)	(244)	(46)	(95)	(19)	(84)	(97)	(44)	(52)	(51)

Statements: 'would you say whether each of the following statements about family life is true, or not true, as far as you are concerned?

   'The best arrangement for families is for the wife to run the home and the husband to earn the money.'

Source: Authority Survey (1974)

Table 5.5   *Attitude towards authority structures in the family by sex, age, education and occupation*

| | Men % | Women % | WOMEN ONLY | | | | | | | |
			Under 40 with tertiary education %	Under 40 with other education %	40 and over with tertiary education %	40 and over with other education %	Under 40 not home-maker %	Under 40 home-maker %	40 and over not home-maker %	40 and over home-maker %
False	74	82	94	88	90	66	92	86	74	67
True	26	18	6	12	10	34	8	14	26	33
N=	(247)	(243)	(46)	(93)	(19)	(85)	(96)	(43)	(53)	(51)

Statement: 'The father should be master of the house . . . the wife should be the helper.'

Source: Authority Survey (1974)

which have changed over the period (1971-9) are of most interest to us.

Belief in sex   _____   Identification
role stereotypes   with conservative parties

If the above hypothesis is true for women, then a rejection of traditional sex roles developed over time would lead to a radicalisation of women voters.(6) Here radical is used to denote a tendency to support the ALP and men's vote is taken as a reference point. It is also assumed that the parties will stay basically the same. Two questions in the Authority Survey dealt with sex role stereotypes in the family and traditional family authority.(7) Table 5.4 shows that men accept sex role stereotypes in family life to a higher degree than women, that younger women, women with tertiary education and women who are not full-time home-makers reject sex role stereotyping more than older women, women with lower education and women who are full-time home-makers (see Table 5.4).

The second statement about authority structure in the family, is regarded as false by a higher percentage of the respondents than the first one (Table 5.5). The pattern is otherwise the same: women reject it to a higher degree than men and young women, women with tertiary education, and women who are not full-time home-makers more so than others (see Table 5.5).

A third variable, combining the answers to the two statements, was computed and cross-tabulated with party identification.(8) The parties were divided into two blocks: the conservative block – Liberal (92), National Country Party (1); DLP (6); and the non-conservative block – ALP (113), Australia Party (7). (Figures in brackets refer to the number of female respondents in the survey.) There is a strong positive relationship between degree of acceptance of the two statements and identification with conservative parties (Table 5.6).

Table 5.6 *Party identification by attitudes towards the traditional family (women only)*

	Both statements FALSE %	One statement TRUE %	Both statements TRUE %
Conservative parties	38	50	60
Non-conservative parties	62	50	40
N=	(117)	(72)	(30)

Statements:
1. 'The best arrangement for families is for the wife to run the home and the husband to earn the money.'
2. 'The father should be master of the home . . . the wife should be the helper.'

Source: Authority Survey (1974)

Statements on the family have been used to measure traditional-
ism amongst women. Many other measures could have been used
but the one chosen is particularly apt given the current discussion about women's role in society (see Dworkin, 1979) with very
vocal anti-feminist groups (like Women who Want to be Women)
arguing for a return to the traditional family.

Age, education, and occupation appear to be important factors
in the formation of attitudes towards family structure. The correlation matrix (Table 5.7) shows the strength of the associations.
Party identification has been dichotomised as in Table 5.6 and
occupation is also a two value variable - full-time home-maker,
not full-time home-maker.

Table 5.7   Correlation matrix of party identification*

	A *Conservative parties not conservative*	B *Home-maker not home-maker*	C *Education (low/high)*	D *Age (young/old)*	E *Accept traditional sex roles in the family*	F *Accept traditional authority structure in the family*
A	1.00					
B.	.02	1.00				
C	.08	.29	1.00			
D	−.16	−.25	−.23	1.00		
E	−.13	1.16	−.22	.26	1.00	
F	−.13	−.12	−.15	.24	.29	1.0

*   not significant on .05 level
Source: Authority Survey (1974)

Only 'age' of our background variables has a significant correlation with party identification. Whether young women of today
will grow more conservative with age is impossible to answer at
this stage. Younger women are better educated than older women
and are more likely not to be full-time home-makers. Well educated
women are less likely to be full-time home-makers than women with
lower education.

2 Are women less interested in politics than men?

One implication behind the assumption that women derive their
voting preference from others (i.e. follow their husbands and
fathers) is that as well as being easily led they are apathetic.
Likewise, that they have been said to personalise politics also
implies a lack of political sophistication. Women's lack of interest
has also been suggested to explain their under-representation
within the political parties (and associated organisations) as well
as within elective institutions.

I decided to focus upon expressed interest in politics and to

examine the impact of age, education and occupation as well as
the salience of sex, using 'Age' Polls taken before the 1972, 1975
and 1977 elections and the Authority Survey. The respondents in
the 'Age' Polls were asked: 'How much interest have you taken in
the election campaign so far? Would you say you have taken: A
good deal; some; not much; or no interest at all?'

Table 5.8 shows that there is a slight difference between men
and women in their interest in the election campaigns. It is mainly
a question of differences at the 'interested' end of the scale, with
more men than women having 'a good deal of interest' and more
women than men having 'some interest'. At the 'uninterested' end,
'not much interest' and 'no interest at all', the differences between
the sexes are very small (Table 5.8).

Table 5.8   Interest in the election campaigns 1972, 1975, and 1977 by sex

	Nov. 1972		Dec. 1975		Dec. 1977	
	Male %	Female %	Male %	Female %	Male %	Female %
A good deal of interest	41	33	60	53	40	35
Some interest	35	39	26	31	33	36
Not much interest	19	22	11	13	21	22
No interest at all	5	6	3	3	6	7
N =	(1,249)	(1,251)	(999)	(1,001)	(1,003)	(997)

Source: 'Age' Polls (Irving Saulwick and Associates) Nov. 1972, Dec. 1975, Dec. 1977.

In the Authority Survey of 1974 the respondents were asked the
following question: 'How much interest do you generally have in
what's going on in politics – a good deal; some; not much; or no
interest in politics?' (Table 5.9).

Table 5.9   Interest in politics by sex

	Male %	Female %
A good deal of interest	53	32
Some interest	33	49
Not much interest	12	16
No interest at all	2	3
N =	(251)	(248)

Source: Authority Survey, (1974)

The differences between men and women are greater here than on 'interest in election campaigns', but the pattern is the same. More men than women say that they had 'a good deal of interest' and more women than men that they have 'some interest'. When we look more closely at the women in our sample we find no differences between younger and older women or between homemakers and those not full-time home-makers. Table 5.10 shows that education does make a difference to how interested women are in politics.

Table 5.10   Women's interest in politics by level of education

	Women with tertiary education %	Women with other education %
A good deal of interest	44	27
Some interest	48	49
Not much interest	8	14
No interest at all	0	10
N =	(66)	(177)

In the Authority Survey (see Table 5.11) the respondents were also asked: 'Would you like to have more influence in community affairs than you now have, or are you satisfied with what influence you have now?' There are no differences between men and women on this question nor any differences between educational groups or whether home-makers or not among women only. Age makes a difference, though, with younger women less satisfied than older.

Table 5.11   Satisfaction with influence in community affairs by age (women only)

	Women under 40 years old %	Women 40 and over %
Would like more	54	17
Satisfied now	46	83
N =	(140)	(103)

CONCLUSIONS

The portrait emerging is that women share many characteristics (such as increased participation in the workforce) but also exhibit tremendous diversity (of socio-economic status for example).

With the exception of a tiny handful of 'special' women they are uniformly absent from the corridors of political power and the organisational hierarchies of the political parties. For a time in the mid-1970s it appeared that women's issues had finally reached the political agenda. 'Second-wave feminist' groups (such as WEL) as well as ginger groups within the ALP must take some of the credit for this. Although some residual impact remains (women have become relatively more visible since that time) the onset of economic recession has signified a slowdown in the search for equality of opportunity.

The claim that Australian women are more conservative than men was, as far as voting is concerned, true for the first part of the 1970s. During the last decade this difference has been eroded. The implication of this malleability of women's vote is that women are neither naturally conservative in the sense of possessing an innate tendency to vote for the non-Labour parties, nor are they conservative in the sense of being afraid of change.

APPENDIX TO CHAPTER 5

Table 5.12   Women and the ALP (1979). Numbers of key party positions with figures for women in brackets

State	House of Reps	Senate	State Parliament	National Conference	National Executive	State Executive
NSW	17 (0)	4 (0)	73 (4)	7 (0)	2(0)	25 (2)
Vic	10 (0)	4 (1)	30 (1)	7 (0)	2 (0)	33 (2)
Qls	3 (0)	4 (0)	23 (0)	7 (1)	2 (0)	7 (0)
SA	6 (0)	4 (0)	37 (2)	7 (0)	2 (0)	24 (1)
WA	1 (0)	4 (1)	31 (2)	7 (0)	2 (0)	14 (1)
Tas	0 (0)	4 (0)	20 (2)	7 (0)	2 (0)	12 (1)
ACT	1 (0)	1 (1)		1 (1)	1 (1)	
NT	0 (0)	1 (0)		1 (0)	1 (1)	
TOTAL	38 (0)	26 (3)	214 (11)	44 (2)	14 (2)	115 (7)

The ALP has been the only major Australian political party to investigate and report upon the implications of social and economic change for its structure and policy. The National Committee of Inquiry was established in January 1978 and women and political change was one of its focusses. Consequently its information on women's contribution is more up-to-date and systematic than the other major parties whose records are relatively chaotic and information fragmented.

NOTES

* I am indebted to Ms Elsie Holmstrom, Research Assistant, Political Science Department, University of Melbourne for collection of data and assistance with Section IV.

1 The existing National Conference (APSA, 1979, p. 7). The basic structure of the ALP National Conference was laid down in 1902

and was strictly federal in principle with six delegates from each State elected in whatever way each State party determined. The only major change to occur in the composition of the Conference since 1902 took place in 1967, and these reforms did little to alter the basic structure established in 1902. In 1967 State delegations were increased from six to seven to allow the presence of the parliamentary leaders from the States; the four federal parliamentary leaders were also included; and representatives from the ACT, the Northern Territory and Young Labour were admitted. But these changes did little to alter the basic structure of the National Conference.

2 Liberal Party of Australia, New South Wales Division, 'Constitution', August 1974. Part XI State Executive Clause (160). 'The State Executive shall consist of President, 4 Vice-Presidents (2 men, 2 women), Treasurer, 6 country delegates (at least 2 women), 6 Metropolitan delegates (at least 2 women), Vice President Finance Committee, Immediate Past President (for following 12 months only), Young Liberal Movement representative, President of Women's Group, Regional Presidents, 3 State, 3 Federal Members of Parliament, President of Federal Council.'

3 Information on women MPs is based upon Rydon (1975).

4 On this point MacKerras (1977, p. 8) noted that over the previous five House of Representatives' elections 1 male candidate in four was elected, only 1 female in twenty-five was elected. Others have also pointed out that women do not put themselves forward. For example, Carlton (1977, p. 25) states that only twenty-six women nominated for Liberal preselection for Federal and NSW State Elections from 1973 to 1976 out of a total of over 600 candidates.

5 The 'Age' Polls used here were conducted by the Australian Sales Research Bureau, March 1971 to November 1974, and by Irving Saulwick and Associates, April 1975 to April 1979, for the 'Age' newspaper.

6 Here we are talking about general tendencies; these do not preclude the existence of conservative feminists. For details see Simms (1979).

7 The survey into attitudes to authority and politics, 1974 (henceforth called the 'Authority Survey') was carried out on a random sample of 500 Melbournians, stratified by sex. The chief investigators were David Kemp, Monash University, and Graham Little, Melbourne University, whom I thank for allowing access to part of this data.

8 The question in the Authority Survey on party identification was: 'Generally speaking, do you usually think of yourself as Liberal; Labour; Country Party; DLP; Australia Party; or What?'

BIBLIOGRAPHY

Aimer, P. (1974), 'Politics, Power and Persuasion', Bennett, Melbourne.

Aitkin, D. (1972), 'The Country Party in New South Wales', Australian National University Press, Canberra.

Aitkin, D. (1977), 'Stability and Social Change', Australian National University Press, Canberra.

Allen, P. (1977), The Role of Women in the NSW Branch of the Australian Labor Party, in 'The Women and Politics Conference Papers, 1875', vol. 1, pp. 12-15, Australian Government Publishing Service, Canberra.

Australian Political Studies Association (1979), 'Australian Labor Party, National Committee of Inquiry - Discussion Papers', APSA, Adelaide.

Australian Bureau of Statistics (1980), 'The Labour Force', Australian Government Publishing Service, Canberra.

Bacchi, A. (1978), The Impact of Scientific Theories on Attitudes towards Women in the Anglo-Saxon Community with Particular Reference to Australia. Women and Labour Conference Papers, unpublished, Sydney.

Barnard, J. (1979), Women as Voters: From Redemptive to Futurist Roles, in Lipmen-Bluemen, Jean and Barnard, Jessie (eds), 'Sex Roles and Social Policy', pp. 279-86, Sage, Beverly Hills.

Bennett, R. (1979), Focus on the Nation, 'Australian', 24 November, p. 11.

Bourque, S. and Grossholtz, J. (1974), Politics an Unnatural Practice: Political Science Looks at Female Participation, 'Politics and Society', 4, pp. 225-66.

Bowman, M. (1972), Women and Local Government, unpublished.

Briggs, P. (1977), The Role of Women as Policy Makers and Candidates in the National Country Party of Australia, 'Australian Quarterly', 49, pp. 36-41.

Carlton, J. (1977), The Role of Women in Political Parties as Policy Makers and Candidates, 'Australian Quarterly', 49, pp. 23-8.

Councillors for Equal Opportunity (1979), 'Submission to the Victorian Government Inquiry into Local Government', unpublished, Melbourne.

Cowan, P. (1978), 'A Unique Position', University of Western Australia Press, Perth.

Dixson, M. (1975), 'The Real Matilda', Penguin, Ringwood.

Dworkin, A. (1979), Safety, Shelter, Rules, Form, Love - The Promise of the Ultra-Right, 'Ms', 7, pp. 91-4.

Encel, S. et al. (1974), 'Women and Society', Cheshire, Melbourne.

Falkinder, L. (1978), Women Join the Union Movement, 'Age', 30 June, p. 16.

Francis, J. G. and Peele, Gillian (1978), Reflections on Generation Analysis: Is there a Shared Political Perspective between Men and Women?, 'Political Studies', 27, pp. 375-94.

Friedan, B. (1976), 'It Changed My Life', Dell, New York.

Goot, M. and Reid, E. (1975), 'Women and Voting Studies: Mindless Matrons or Sexist Scientism?', Sage, London.

Gorring, P. (1977), What Motivates Women to Political Office?, 'Australian Quarterly', 49, pp. 41-66.

Grimshaw, P. (1979), Women and the Family in Australian History - A Reply to 'The Real Matilda', 'Historical Studies', 18, pp. 412-21.

Guilfoyle, M. (1977), Women in the Parties, in 'The Women and Politics Conference Papers, 1975', vol. 1, pp. 25-31, Australian Government Publishing Service, Canberra.

Kemp, D. (1976), Social Change and the Future of Political Parties: the Australian Case, in L. Maisel and P. Sacks (eds.), 'The Future of Political Parties', Sage, Beverly Hills, pp. 124-64.

Kemp, D. (1977), Political Parties and Australian Culture, 'Quadrant', 21, pp. 3-13.

Kemp, D. (1978), 'Society and Electoral Behaviour in Australia', University of Queensland Press, St Lucia.

Kennedy, B. (1979), Queensland's Iron Butterflies, 'Australian', 16-17 February, p. 22.

Lake, M. (1976), To be Denied a Sense of Past Generations: A Review of Miriam Dixson's, 'The Real Matilda', 'Hecate', 2, pp. 68-73.

Mackerras, M. (1977), Do Women Candidates Lose Votes?, 'Australian Quarterly', 49, pp. 6-10.

Markusen, A. (1977), Feminist Notes on Introductory Economics, 'Review of Radical Political Economics', 9, pp. 1-6.

Meillon, M. (1977), Women and Representation, 'Australian Quarterly', 49, pp. 19-23.

National Population Inquiry (1975), 'First Report', Australian Government Publishing Service, Canberra.

National Women's Advisory Council (1979), 'First Annual Report', Australian Government Publishing Service, Canberra.

Norris, A. (1979), 'Champions of the Impossible', Hawthorn Press, Melbourne.

Reed, J. and Oakes, K. (1977), 'Women in Australian Society, 1901-45', Australian Government Publishing Service, Canberra.

Roberts, J. (1976), The Ramifications of the Study of Women, in J. Roberts (ed.), 'Beyond Intellectual Sexism', McKay, New York, pp. 3-13.

Ryan, S. (1979), Will Women Swing Back to Labour?, 'Kooyong News', pp. 3-7.

Rydon, J., (1975), 'A Biographical Register of the Commonwealth Parliament, 1901-1972', Australian National University Press, Canberra.

Schultz, J. (1980), Workforce, 'Australian Financial Review', 29 February, p. 27.

Simms, M. (1979), Conservative Feminism in Australia: A Case Study of Feminist Ideology, 'Women's Studies International Quarterly', vol. 2, no. 3, pp. 305-18.

Summers, A. (1979), Women, in A. Patience and B. Head (eds.), 'From Whitlam to Fraser', Oxford University Press, Oxford, pp. 189-200.

Wise, R. (1977), The Role of Women in the ALP as Policy Makers and Candidates, 'Australian Quarterly', 49, pp. 28-36.
Women's Advisory Body Working Party (1977), 'Report', Australian Government Publishing Service, Canberra.

6 FRANCE

Janine Mossuz-Lavau and
Mariette Sineau

Translated by Anne M. Batiot

THE SOCIO-POLITICAL ENVIRONMENT: WOMEN'S SUFFRAGE IN FRANCE: A LATE RECOGNITION

It was only in 1944, twenty-six years later than in England, that French women obtained the right to vote. Yet, in 1936, Léon Blum nominated three women as state under-secretaries. The situation was paradoxical. Women gained access to ministerial responsibilities before having exercised their rights as electors. This delay on the part of France to completely recognise universal suffrage is explained as much by the inadequacies of the feminist movement as by the characteristics of French political life itself.

If one ignores the revolutionary periods, during which women actively engaged in politics, there was negligible political activity among French women until 1870. The first suffragist movement, inspired by the English example, dates from the advent of the Third Republic. At first isolated within the women's movement, the suffragettes gained a limited audience only towards the turn of the century and that audience was owed to the rather extremist action of Hubertine Auclert (1848-1914). Suffrage associations were formed only during the period following her activities. Notably, in 1901, the National Council of French Women came into being. The suffrage organisations were very moderate and refrained from any violent action.

In fact as Théodore Zeldin (1978, p. 405) writes: 'it was clearly a middle-class movement, emanating from high society, conducted by republican politicians' wives, who showed no wish to endanger a regime to which they were deeply committed.' These characteristics of the French suffrage movement ultimately explain its failure. In addition, the majority of French women had no interest in their political rights. The experience of feminist Louise Weiss (1949, p. 14) illustrates this point: 'Peasant women stood open-mouthed when I spoke to them about the vote. Working women laughed, shop-keepers shrugged their shoulders and middle-class women rebuffed me, horrified.'

In the absence of mass feminism, the Senate met little difficulty in reiterating its opposition to women's suffrage over the following twenty years.

Just before the First World War, feminists won over some of the Socialists, in particular Jaures. In 1912, Jaurès unsuccessfully called for a debate on the question of women's suffrage. In 1919, following a proposal by Briand and Viviani, the Chamber of Deputies granted French women the right to vote, but the Senate

voted against it. This scenario was repeated five times between
1919 and 1937. During this period, in parliamentary debates every
argument was put forward to justify women's political incapacity –
their natural ineptitude, the possible division of the family, the
blow to the husband's authority, and the danger to moral life
(prostitutes would vote). In fact, in a Catholic country where the
separation between Church and State (1905) was still open to
question it was the fear of the Church's influence over women,
which blocked their suffrage under the Radical-Socialist Republic.
Those in power feared that women, most of whom were assiduous
church-goers, would favour the clerical parties and thus endanger
the Republic. Attached as it was to a very traditional conception
of feminine roles, the Catholic hierarchy was not, itself, unanimously in favour of women's suffrage. Hence, it was the Second
World War and the disappearance of the Radical Party which facilitated the events that enabled de Gaulle to decree political
equality.

WOMEN AND FRENCH SOCIETY

French women's past and present political participation can only
be understood in terms of their position in society. It was only
during the second half of the nineteenth century that women
gained educational equality with men. In 1867 women gained access
to primary schooling. In 1880 they were allowed entry to secondary education, and, in 1884, to university education. Since the
turn of the century there has been a continuous increase in the
proportion of educated women. At university level the proportion
of women increased from 2.4 per cent in 1900, through 25.7 per
cent in 1930 through 35 per cent in 1950, to 48.5 per cent in 1980.
Yet important forms of educational discrimination continue. In the
lycées, 75 per cent of girls opt for a philosophy specialisation at
the baccalauréat level and only 35 per cent specialise in science.
[The lycées are State-controlled secondary schools. Trans.] At
university level women represent two-thirds of humanities studies
but only 20 per cent of science and 14 per cent of economics and
law students. It is therefore understandable that so few women
attend the Grandes Ecoles (HEC, Polytechnique, ENA) from
which the country's economic and political elites are recruited
(Brimo, 1975, pp. 5-6; Sineau, 1974-5, pp. 63-110). [The
Grandes Ecoles are specialist higher education institutions. HEC
(Hautes Etudes Commerciales) is the School of Higher Commercial
Studies; the Polytechnic School is a very prestigious multi-
disciplinary school where many leading French political and economic figures have been educated; the ENA is the National Administration School.] Vocational training is equally segregated.
Fewer girls than boys sit the CAP (diploma for qualified workers/
artisans). When girls do hold the CAP it is usually in less marketable specialisations such as hairdressing, sales or pharmacist
assistantships. Only exceptionally do they hold it in an industrial

option. The results are distressing. Only 16 per cent of such
women exercise skills for which they have been trained (Le
Gendre, 1979, p. 45). In addition, parents still prefer to send
their daughters to Catholic schools. There they receive an education that often perpetuates a traditional view of women and of
their role in society (Mossuz-Lavau and Sineau, 1980, pp. 151-5).
This educational inequality is responsible for some of the most
serious discrimination in women's working lives.

In 1978, out of the 21 million French women (51.3 per cent of
the population) 8,261,799 were employed. Women comprised 39.4
per cent of the employed population. This percentage, although
hardly higher than that of 1900, has fluctuated a great deal since
then. Between 1946 and 1962 the rate of female economic activity
fell. Since 1962 it has continuously increased despite periods of
economic crisis. For young women the maximum rate of activity is
reached at the age of 23. In 1978 over 75 per cent of women aged
23 or over were in employment. In 1980 nearly half of mothers
with two children were also working. These two groups are responsible for the increase in employed women. Between the ages
of 20 and 54 years, there are fewer housewives than working
women; 77.6 per cent of women are waged rather than salaried
and more than a quarter of these (26.1 per cent as opposed to 19
per cent of men) are employed by the State ('Bulletin du Comité
du travail feminin', 1979, p. 3). In 1980 68.8 per cent of women
were employed in the tertiary sector, whereas in 1900 the majority
of the female employed population were in agriculture and industry (Table 6.1).

Table 6.1   Distribution by sectors of employment of the female population

Agriculture	8.40
Industry and Manufacturing	21.26
Construction, civil and agricultural engineering	1.56
Tertiary sector	68.80
	100.0

The discrimination that women suffer at work is well known. In
spite of the evolution noted since 1954, women still form a small
minority within the professions and higher management. Rather,
they are concentrated among shop assistants, office workers and
service personnel (Table 6.2). In industry and manufacturing
where occupations are categorised according to gender, women
hold the least qualified positions. They form 38 per cent of unskilled labour but only 5.9 per cent of forewomen. There are
fewer women than men in the professions: 67 per cent of the
women who teach are primary and apprentice teachers and only
35 per cent of teachers in higher education are women. Finally,
in the higher State bodies (State Council, Finance Inspection, the
Audit Office) women's presence is merely symbolic (Sineau, 1974-
5, pp. 75-7).

Table 6.2   Women's socio-economic position

	% women 1954-75	Rate of evolution 1954-75
Farmers	34.3	− 7.2
Agricultural salary-earners	11.6	− 3.4
Commercial and industrial employers	33.4	− 3.8
Professions and higher management	23.2	+ 9.4
Middle management	45.2	+ 8.5
Shop-assistants and office employees	63.9	+ 11.1
Industrial and manufacturing workers	22.4	− 0.3
Service personnel	77.9	− 7.0
Other categories (artists, clergy, army, police)	19.1	− 7.0
	37.3	+ 2.5

Source: Thevenot Laurent (1977), Les catégories sociales en 1975, 'Economie et Statistique', no. 91, July-August, p. 5.

The differences in men's and women's salaries although decreasing are still important in every occupation. This is especially true at the top of the hierarchy (Table 6.3).

Table 6.3   Salary differences* between men and women

	1951	1975
Higher management	58.6	36.0
Middle management	34.5	25.6
Shop-assistants and office employees	29.6	21.3
Industrial and manufacturing workers	31.5	29.5
All workers	35.1	31.6

* Salary differences = $\dfrac{\text{male monthly salary - female monthly salary} \times 100}{\text{male monthly salary}}$

Source: 'Economie et Statistique' (1979), no. 113, July-August, p.19.

At the beginning of 1980 the net average monthly salary in the commercial and industrial sectors was 4,420F for men and 3,335F [4,420F = approx. £480; 3,335F = approx. £329. Trans.] for women (including the thirteenth month). [An extra thirteenth month is now included in most salaries in France.] Of salary earners, 3 per cent are paid more than 10,000F [10,000F = approx. £1,086. Trans.] per month, of whom 4.2 per cent are men and 0.5 per cent are women. At the bottom end of the scale, 33 per cent earn only 2,680F [2,680F = approx. £291. Trans.]. One man out of four but one out of every two women were in this category, a situation which is explained mainly by women's lack of training (Mathieu, 1980, p. 23).

On 30 October 1979, 814,995 women were registered as seeking employment. They comprised nearly 55 per cent of the unemployed and 64 per cent of the 583,380 unemployed aged below 25 years were women. Moreover, the average duration of unemployment is longer for women. In March 1979, the proportion of women who had been unemployed for a year or more reached 32.8 per cent as opposed to 25.8 per cent for men ('Bulletin du Comité du travail feminin', 1979, p. 3).

WOMEN IN THE TRADE UNIONS

Exploitation, beyond a certain level, rarely favours consciousness raising and women's participation in the trade unions remains low. Yet the progress achieved since the turn of the century is considerable, according to Margaret Maruani (1979, p. 16):
    In 1900, women represented 6.3 per cent of the unionised
    work force and 34.5 per cent of the employed population;
    in 1975 these were respectively about 30 and 38 per cent.
    The disadjustment between the rate of women's unionisation,
    and their position within the employed population thus tends
    to disappear.
    Historically, women have had to fight against an anti-feminist tradition which, since Proudhon, has been firmly embedded in the unions. There are obvious reasons why women's rate of unionisation is low. Women are more likely to work in smaller firms or sectors, such as the textile industry, which are little unionised. The Confederation Générale du Travail (CGT) aligned with the Communist Party, estimates the proportion of women among its membership of 2,300,000 as 30 per cent. This estimate is similar to that of the Socialist, self-management oriented, Confédération Française Démocratique de Travail (CFDT). The more right-wing oriented Force Ouvriere (FO) claims to be well represented in sectors of high female employment, such as public offices and in the tertiary sector. Finally, there are a majority of women members in the Federation d'Education Nationale (FEN) (Guilbert, 1974, pp. 157 68). If the plurality of trade unions in France makes it difficult to give a precise account of the situation, it remains certain, that women's access to positions of responsibility is still difficult. As one looks from the bottom to the top of the hierarchy, women's representation decreases. Yet, since 1968, according to the thesis put forward by Maruani (1979, p. 116), 'Unionised women do not join in to merge quietly in a male union movement.... They ask *other* questions, propose other forms of militancy, formulate other struggle objectives.'

WOMEN IN POLITICAL PARTIES AND FEMINIST MOVEMENTS

Traditionally a multiparty electoral arena, France is characterised by a quadripolar partisan structure. The electoral system instituted by the Constitution of 1958 (a simple majority, uninominal system in two rounds) was strengthened by the reform of 1962 (election of the President of the Republic by universal suffrage) and has forced the parties to form alliances. So France has four large political groupings, which between them occupy almost the whole of the political spectrum. On the Left are the Communist Party (PCF) and the Socialist Party (PS) (which, at election time forms an alliance with the movement of Left Radicals (MRG)). In the Centre and on the Right are, on the one hand, the Union for French Democracy (UDF), and on the other hand the Rassemblement pour la République (RPR). The UDF includes the Republican Party of Valéry Giscard d'Estaing (PR), the Radical Party, and some centrists devolved from the Christian Democrats (CDS). The RPR is led by Jacques Chirac and claims affiliation with Gaullism. As Jean-Luc Parodi (1970, p. 107) comments:

This quadripartism is reduced in its turn to two large coalitions one of which unites all the left, and the other all the right, and which have confronted each other at every second round of electoral contests since 1965, with the exception of the presidential election of 1969.

Since France entered the post-Gaullist era, this confrontation has become increasingly sharp. The groups of the right and centre keep themselves in power with smaller and smaller majorities.(1) The left has gained just over 49 per cent of the total vote on several occasions. In addition, a very bitter struggle for the leadership sets the UDF against the RPR within the majority party, and the PS against the PCF within the opposition.

Consequently women, who form 53 per cent of the electorate, represent a very important prize for the parties, all the more so, because they are clearly less conservative than twenty years ago. In order to keep or to win their votes, most of the political groups therefore try to appear to support women's causes. However, none of the parties fully entrusts women with responsibility for themselves.

There are even fewer women in the higher echelons of the political parties than there are among activists and members (Table 6.4). The largest disparity between female membership and the number of women holding positions of responsibility is in the RPR. The RPR is the only party to refuse explicitly to take gender into consideration when assigning political responsibilities. The least disparity can be seen within the PS. The PS was the first party to establish a quota for women on its Executive and Legislative Committees, equal to the percentage of female membership. The quota was fixed at 10 per cent in 1974 and was increased to 20 per cent in 1979. Not a single major party has a woman as national leader. Only two extreme-left organisations, not represented in Parliament, were led by a woman in 1980. In 1974 Arlette Laguillier was the first woman to be a candidate for the presidential election for the Lutte Ouvrière (Trotskyist). And, since 1979, the Parti Socialiste Unifié (PSU) has been led by Huguette Bouchardeau.

This low representation of women cannot be explained solely by

Table 6.4   Percentage of women in the central councils and committees of four major French political parties

	Political parties	Female membership	'Legislative' councils	'Executive' committees
	Republican Party (PR)	37% (out of 170,000* members)	National Council 32%	Political Bureau 20%
Majority	Rallying For the Republic (RPR)	41% (out of 760,000* members)	Central Committee 8%	Political Council 14%
	Socialist Party (PS)	22% (out of 180,000* members)	Directing Committee 19%	Executive Bureau 19%
Opposition	Communist Party (PCF)	33% (out of 700,000* members)	Central Committee 21%	Political Bureau 19%

* Numbers are those given by the parties themselves and should therefore be treated with caution.

the misogyny of a nearly exclusively male political elite. This is also true of the non-Communist left; thus a genuine preponderance of the intelligentsia, always educational and often from management and technology can be observed within the leadership of the PS (Patrick Hardouin, April 1978, p. 252). The only exception is the PCF. It pays a full salary to most of its permanent staff and can, therefore, have a number of working-class militants among its cadres. However, because women are largely absent from the socio-economic elite, and more frequently tied to the home by their domestic and child-rearing responsibilities, they do not constitute the same pool of political personnel that men do. This inequality is aggravated by the specialisation of tasks among activists. Those rare women given party responsibilities are often in charge of such sectors as family, education and 'women's questions' (Mossuz-Lavau and Sineau, 1979). This situation does not always prepare them to defend the whole range of their party's policies and it publicly reinforces the traditional nurturing image of women.(2)

In every type of election there are few women candidates. Yet some progress has been made, in local as well as national elections. In the March 1979 District election, 9.6 per cent of women stood as candidates, an increase from the 5 per cent who stood in 1973. Similarly, in the 1978 legislative elections, 15.9 per cent of candidates were women as opposed to 3.3 per cent in 1968 and 6.7 per cent in 1973. But the 1978 figure is biased by the marginal parties

(Extreme Left, Ecologists, Feminists) who fielded 22 per cent
women candidates. The major parties showed little interest in
women. Five per cent of the candidates for the PR, 2.9 per cent
for the RPR, 5.9 per cent for the PS and 13.3 per cent for the
PCF were women (Fabre-Rosane and Guédé, 1978, p. 849). The
European elections of 1979 scored a spectacular advance, narrowly
linked, in the authors' opinion, to an initiative taken by the Ministry 'in charge of' Women's Condition. In the spring of 1979 the
Ministry tabled a motion which fixed at 'a minimum of 80 per cent
the number of persons of one sex on the candidate lists for
Council elections'. (3) This measure established a quota of 20 per
cent of women on candidate lists. In June 1979, especially since
the Giscardian list was conducted by a very popular woman,
Simone Veil, former Minister of Health, political parties anticipated
the application of this quota. The proportion of women candidates
rose to 27 per cent for the PCF, 25.9 per cent for the PS and
MRG, 25.9 per cent for the UDF and 16 per cent for the RPR.

Although the entry of women into politics has been gradual, it
has nevertheless been evident. Furthermore, the very active
campaigns conducted by feminists have progressively led both
those political parties in power and those in opposition to take
into account women's issues, which had previously been considered either as of minor importance, or as strictly private.

POLITICAL PARTIES AND THE WOMEN'S CAUSE

The first issue on which political leaders had to take a stance was
the repeal of the 1920 law forbidding abortion and contraceptive
information. This battle, spearheaded by Dr Andrée Weill Halle in
1955, was very unevenly supported by the political parties. The
non-Communist left showed immediate interest in legalising abortion and contraception and tabled several proposals to that end.
The Communist Party also demanded the liberalisation of abortion,
but, even in 1956, remained hostile to contraception (Mossuz, 1966).
The French Movement for Family Planning (MFPF) was created in
1958. Largely popularised in 1965, at the time of the campaign for
the first election of the Presidency by universal suffrage, the
efforts of the MFPF were supported by the Left in general, including the PCF. In 1967, under the Presidency of General de
Gaulle, these efforts led to the Neuwirth Law legislating contraception. From 1969 onwards (when Georges Pompidou became
President) the social equality of men and women acquired the
status of a political preoccupation. In December 1972 a statute
embodying the concept of equal pay for equal work was passed.

But it was only at the beginning of Valéry Giscard d'Estaing's
years of office that the political elites paid serious attention to
the position of women. As early as 1974 the new President created
a State Secretariat for Women's Condition (a position held by
Françoise Giroud, one of the personalities from the Radical Party.)
(4) In 1978 this State Secretariat became a delegate Ministry, 'in

charge of' Women's Condition. It was made the responsibility of Monique Pelletier, a member of the Republican Party's Political Bureau. In 1975 a series of laws were passed in an attempt to give equal rights to men and women. One forbade sex discrimination at work, a second gave mothers the equivalent rights to fathers in the running of everyday affairs; and a third law granted a wife the same rights as her husband in all decisions concerning the matrimonial home. Finally, divorce reform laws were passed which defined male and female adultery in the same manner. Previously female adultery had been subject to major sanctions, including imprisonment, whilst male adultery in practice benefited from penal immunity. But the most important law was that promulgated for a period of five years from 17 January 1975. From that date women were able to obtain abortions in either private or public health institutions up to the tenth week of pregnancy. This law was adopted in spite of very strong reservations expressed by deputies from the majority. Only 99 of 221 majority deputies voted for the measure, and its passage was secured by the support of the Left. Out of 180 Socialist, Communist and Left Radical deputies, 178 voted in favour of the law ('Le Monde', 5 October, 1977) which finally entered the statute books in the autumn of 1979.(5)

The juridicial resolution of the abortion problem cleared the political arena for other struggles. Hence issues of employment inequality (worsened by economic crisis) and bodily violence such as battering, rape etc. reached the agenda. A redefinition of rape and the sanctions to be incurred by it were voted into law on 11 April 1980.(6) As a general rule, the most marked split on women's questions occurred between the RPR and other political groups. The RPR, bastion of the most conservative Right, repeatedly questioned (7) the new law on divorce. On the Left, the PCF saw rape as resulting from a general climate of violence and pornography in capitalist society, while the PS placed emphasis on women's free sexuality.(8) The PCF was more suspicious of the feminist movement ('which diverts women from the class struggle') than the PS. Thus, whilst both parties denounced with equal vigour the non-application of the laws on equal pay and opportunity, they differed over enforcement strategy. The PCF wished to give the right to claim damages to the trade unions alone, while the PS demanded that this right be extended to other associations involved in the defence of the rights of women.(9) As it happened, these efforts were not sufficient to meet the demands of militant women.

Within the political Centre and Right, if one ignores complaints expressed by one or two personalities on particular occasions, women do not appear to be dissatisfied with their parties' policies. (10) On the Left, however, feminist agitation is more intense. In June 1977 the Socialist Party created a National Secretariat for Women's Actions. In January 1978 it organised a Women's National Convention. But, in the spring of 1978, believing themselves to be underrepresented and little heard within the higher echelons of the party, several militants created a 'women's current' to compete with other party 'currents' at the National Congress in Metz (1979). The militant women declared that 'it is as women that we wish to talk politics'. Their initiative lost some impact during preparation for the congress when the women responsible split over the motions to be presented. However the failure was not total, as resolutions voted on in Metz took up the demands put forward by the 'women's current'.

The Communist Party has been subject to a keen protest movement since its electoral defeat in 1978. The female 'rebellion' began with the publication of a text signed by five Communist women in 'Le Monde' (11-12 June, 1978). Lamenting their party's incompetence on women's problems, they claimed that the PCF's preoccupations were limited to women's working conditions. The party leadership severely condemned this initiative ostensibly because it was 'directed against men generally and not against those in power and the bosses' (Terrel, 1978, p. 992). The condemnation did not discourage the Communist women, who by the autumn of 1979 found themselves openly in conflict with the PCF leadership again. Thus women on the Left are questioning both the competence of their parties and of the feminist movement in defending the rights of women ('Le Monde', 13 November 1979; 19 March 1980; 'L'Humanité', 18 March 1980).

Until 1968 feminist campaigns were organised around single issues such as contraception and abortion, and one cannot speak of the existence of a feminist movement as such. The French women's movement only emerged in the wake of the events of May 1968 and first caught the public eye on 26 August 1970 when a few women laid a wreath to the wife of the Unknown Soldier (de Pisan and Tristan, 1977, p. 7). Named MLF (Movement de Libération des Femmes) by the media, but not in fact formally constituted as an association, the movement's first target was the legalisation of abortion. The struggle began in April 1971 with the publication of a manifesto signed by 343 women, who declared that they had all obtained abortions at some time in the past. Amongst them was Simone de Beauvoir, author of 'The Second Sex'. The 'movement' consisted of various small groups who were often in disagreement with each other. One of the better known of these groups was the 'Psychoanalysis and Politics' group which runs a women's publishing cooperative (les Editions des Femmes) and a bookshop in Paris. Groups branched out and new ones were set up throughout the early 1970s. For example, the MLAC (Mouvement pour la Liberté de l'Avortement et pour la Contraception) first appeared in 1973, and practised abortion by the Karman method in several cities. The Association 'Choisir', on the other hand, opted for a strategy of engaging in legal battles. Created by the lawyer Gisele Halimi to defend the women who signed the abortion manifesto, the group achieved notoriety through various important trials. Of these, perhaps the best known was the 1972 Bobigny trial in which Halimi defended women accused of having obtained abortions. 'Choisir' and the MLAC cooperated at first but soon split over the MLAC's illegal methods which, according to Halimi, could benefit only middle-class women.

For the movement as a whole, 1975 was a turning point. Feminists were divided into various factions and a break in the movement finally occurred in 1979. To the displeasure of other feminists the 'Psychoanalysis and Politics' group constituted the MLF as an association of the type regulated by a law of 1901, thereby appropriating to itself the title 'Women's Liberation Movement'. During this period 'Choisir' pursued its legal strategy and also publicised its position through elections and public discussion. First, it gave support in trials in which women were prosecuting men for rape. Second, it fielded 43 candidates in the 1978 elections. (None were elected and the 43 candidates attracted 1.5 per cent of the votes cast.) Finally 'Choisir' organised public meetings and conferences open to all political organisations.

The most recent co-operative effort of the French women's movement arose from the conjuncture of a crisis of left-wing militancy and the exhaustion of the feminist movement itself. In the autumn of 1979, in order to organise a march demanding definitive legalisation of abortion, a 'collective' gathered women from across the ideological spectrum for a mass protest demonstration. Included were women from the PCF (the protestors), from the PS (survivors of the 'women's current'), from the PSU, Family Planning, the MLAC, from Feminist journals and from the CGT and the CFTD. The demonstration took place in Paris on 6 October 1979 and brought 50,000 people together ('Le Monde', 9 October 1979). That demonstration may well have marked the beginning of a third phase of French feminism in which the division between feminists within the Left organisations and those from the women's groups will be overcome. A new cooperation might militate against at least two of the most flagrant deficiencies of contemporary feminism - its eschewal of traditional politics and its middle-class intellectual, Paris-centred character (Mossuz-Lavau and Sineau, 1980, p. 15).

WOMEN IN ELECTORAL OFFICE

There are few women in the political parties and even fewer in the elected assemblies in France. In 1980 twenty women (or 4 per cent) were members of the 491-member National Assembly, and seven (or 2.3 per cent) were members of the 295-member Senate. The 1979 elections returned only 120 women (or 2.3 per cent) to the General Councils (regional assemblies). The situation is only slightly more favourable at local level. In 1977 just over 8 per cent (8.4) of 460,000 town councillors were women. The percentage of women town councillors varies markedly by size of town. Although women's share of councillorships reaches 20 per cent in towns with more than 30,000 inhabitants and 17.4 per cent of those with populations of between 9,000 and 35.000 it is only 12.8 per cent in small towns with between 2,500 and 9,000 inhabitants.

In 1980 women were 2.9 per cent of 36,352 mayors and 6 per cent
of 8,430 assistants to the mayor, with the majority of women
mayors to be found in small rural parishes. In large urban centres
in which political problems take precedence over administrative
problems, women mayors are rare. In 1980 only twenty-three
women were mayors of towns with populations of over 30,000. The
election of 18 women out of 81 French representatives to the European Parliament thus seemed revolutionary. With women comprising
22 per cent of its elected European representatives (a proportion
reached in no other French Assembly) France was ahead of most
of her European neighbours.

French political personnel, at both local and national level, normally come from the more privileged social strata. The elitism in
the political class is clearly an obstacle to its feminisation. For
example, 62.5 per cent of deputies and 34 per cent of general
councillors come from the professions or from higher management.
Of the twenty women deputies in 1980, four had no stated occupations, eleven were from upper-middle-class occupations such as
the liberal professions and higher civil service, and only five (all
Communists) had more modest occupations such as dressmaking,
hairdressing and office work.

Elitism appears to be a less common feature of local assemblies.
According to the Ministry of the Interior, one-third of the 38,859
women town councillors in 1980 were not employed. Of the 25,949
in full-time employment, only 13.7 per cent were from higher
status occupations. Of the employed women, 7.7 per cent were
industrial and commercial employers, 6 per cent were from the
professions and higher management, 33.3 per cent were from
middle management, 21.6 per cent were shop assistants or office
employees and 3.7 per cent were industrial or manufacturing
workers, 15.9 per cent were rural workers, 7.7 per cent retired,
and 4 per cent had other occupations ('Bulletin d'Information du
Ministère de l'Intérieur', 1979, pp. 3-4). A great many women in
office, 5331 or 20.5 per cent of employed women councillors, are
teachers, and many of these are primary school teachers. That
profession offers low financial reward but ensures the free time
and economic security necessary for political involvement.

There are no systematic studies of the personal profiles of women
in elected office. It is known that most women deputies are married
and that they have an average age of 49. The same is true of
women members of the European Parliament. The average age of
women senators is 53 years. There have been more single women
in the Senate than in the National Assembly. Of the 32 women
senators between 1945 and 1974, 11 were married, 10 were single
(never married), 7 were widows and 4 were divorced (Geneviève
Bécane, 1974, passim.). An incomplete study of 353 men and
women mayors which was begun in 1975 revealed a profile of the
typical woman mayor. She administers a rural community of less
than one thousand inhabitants and like her male colleague is probably over 50 years old. She has a 40 per cent chance of being
either single or widowed compared with her male colleague's 90
per cent chance of being married (Cités Unies', 1975, pp. 6-9).

POLITICAL CAREERS

A parliamentary career in France is normally the outcome of a long cursus honorum: town councillor, mayor, general councillor etc. Having held at least one elected office is often necessary before becoming a deputy. Clearly this handicaps women candidates who lack the background and status necessary to compete with men at elections. Most of the women deputies in 1980 had held local electoral office (16) and some had held two (8). The office most often held was that of general councillor (9) followed by that of mayor (6). The political careers of the eighteen women deputies in the European Parliament had been more prestigious. Three were former ministers and six had held electoral office (two had been deputies). Moreover, practically all of them had held or continued to hold important positions within their own parties. Before entering office in 1971 only 30 per cent of women mayors, compared to 60 per cent of their male counterparts, had held either political, trade union or voluntary office. Only 5 per cent could be described as politically committed, and for 50 per cent of them it was their first electoral success (Cités Unies', 1975, p. 8; 'Vie Publique', 1980, pp. 19-28).

Since the Liberation the Communist Party has been the most feminist in terms of returning women deputies. Of the 20 women deputies and 7 women senators in 1980, 13 and 4 respectively were members of the PCF. Table 6.5 indicates that the PCF not only puts forward women candidates, it also places them in safe constituencies.

Table 6.5   The party affiliation of Parliamentary women in 1980

	National Assembly	Senate
Communists	13	4
Socialists	2	2
RPR	3	0
UDF	1	0
Independent	1	1
Total	20	7

Women town councillors are also mainly on the Left. In 1977 9.4 per cent were Communists, 9.9 per cent were Socialists and the 20.6 per cent of 'miscellaneous' affiliation were nearly all elected from the lists of the Union de la Gauche. [Union de la Gauche – Union of the Left – signed by the PCF, PS and Left Radicals (MRG) to stand at the 1978 elections. Trans.] Women fared considerably less well in the majority parties: 2.3 per cent of the RPR, 3 per cent of the PR and 2.7 per cent of the CDS

councillors were women. Although more than 44 per cent of all
women in office were of 'miscellaneous' party affiliation, this
nuance has no political significance. Women falling into this category were mainly in office in small parishes. Of the 22 women
mayors of towns with over 10,000 inhabitants, 16 were members
of the PCF (Ministère de l'Intérieur, 1977, p. 2).

Parliamentary women are no longer solely relegated, as they
were in the past, to 'social' commissions. They have begun to in-
filtrate the key areas of Foreign Affairs, Finance and Defence
(Table 6.6).

Table 6.6   Distribution of Parliamentary women among various commissions in 1980

	National Assembly	Senate
Cultural Affairs	6	4
Social Affairs	—	1
Foreign Affairs	3	1
Finance	1	—
Justice	2	1
Defence	2	—
Production	6	—

Source: Parliamentary documents.

However, sexual division in the distribution of tasks often seems
to be the case in local politics. A number of mayors assign elected
women to areas such as school meals and general social work problems, while men are given the more important (or at least more
prestigious) portfolios of security, economic and industrial development and transport ('Vie Publique', 1980, pp. 26-7).

In spite of considerable evolution, French public opinion remains
cautious about women assuming political responsibilities. Nevertheless a vast majority of French people now consider it appropriate for a woman to be elected mayor of a large city. A sample
survey carried out by 'Elle'/SOFRES in June 1976 found 80 per
cent of women and 88 per cent of men to be in favour of a woman
mayor. Such 'feminist' public consensus stops at that point, however. Similar agreement does not exist on a woman as President
of the Republic, for example. Only 42 per cent of women and 45
per cent of men would favour such an eventuality, suggesting
that in terms of attitudes toward women in public office, French
women are at least as sexist as French men (Mossuz-Lavau and
Sineau, 1980, pp. 6 and 299).

Yet the success of some of Valéry Giscard d'Estaing's women
ministers, and the particular popularity of Francoise Giroud and
Simone Veil have gone some way toward reducing these misgiv-
ings ('L'Aurore', 1975).(11) In January 1978 the Barre government counted 6 women in its total of 41 members. The 1980

government contained only three: Nicole Pasquier, State Secretary
to the Ministry of Employment and Participation; Alice Saunier-
Seité, Minister of Universities; and Monique Pelletier, Minister of
Women's Condition. It is to be hoped that the Ministry of Women's
Condition will be successful in accelerating women's political promotion. But the historical background is not encouraging. The
proportion of women in local assemblies has increased only slowly.
Women's participation in general councils rose from 0.8 per cent
in 1946 through 2.3 per cent in 1976 to 3.2 per cent in 1979. In
town councils the similar rise was from 3.1 per cent in 1947 through
4.4 per cent in 1971 to 8.4 per cent in 1977. Between 1946 and
1973 there was an almost continuous decrease in female representation in Parliament. In the National Assembly the number of
women declined from 40 in 1946 to 23 in 1951, to 19 in 1956 and to
6 in 1958. The crisis for women's political participation clearly
came with the advent of Gaullism and the adoption of a simple
majority electoral system. These led to a sharp fall in Communist
representation and consequently of women's representation. The
1980 figure of twenty women in the National Assembly, although
low in itself, represents a large increase and may indicate the
beginning of a return of the second sex to Parliament, (Brimo, 1975,
pp. 86-97).

POLITICAL BEHAVIOUR

Since first obtaining the vote women's political behaviour has been
said to be characterised by a low interest in politics, a tendency
to abstentionism and conservatism. Although that may have been
true of the 1950s, it no longer holds to the same extent. Women's
stated 'interest in politics', as expressed in public opinion polls,
gives us an indication of the changes which have occurred. In
1953 when 28 per cent of men declared themselves not to be interested in politics, 60 per cent of women did so. By 1969 34 per cent
of men and 47 per cent of women included in a sample survey said
they were uninterested in politics, indicating that the gap had
narrowed considerably ('Sondages', 1969, p. 13). Additional evidence of women's growing politicisation is also available. Far more
often than in the past women are prepared to answer political
questions asked in sample surveys, including complex questions
on issues such as nationalisation and tax on capital. Other evidence suggests that women now want to be better informed than
has been the case in the past. For example, the proportion of
women among the readership of the newspaper 'Le Monde' rose
from 32 per cent in 1974 to 43 per cent in 1972 (Brimo, 1975, p. 82).
    Change has been more rapid at the level of voting turnout.
Study of vote registers has regularly indicated that women abstain
from voting more often than men do. But the authors found that
women's turnout in Paris in the local elections of 1977 was, for the
first time, almost identical to that of men. Thirty-one per cent of
women and 30 per cent of men abstained in both the first and
second ballots (Mossuz-Lavau and Sineau, 1978, p. 87).

Recent enquiries also indicate the need to revise traditional views of women's conservatism. In 1956 47 per cent of men but only 34 per cent of women were in favour of the Left (Communist and Socialist) parties. By 1973, before the national elections, 51 per cent of men and 41 per cent of women intended to vote for the Left. By 1976 the gap was decisively reduced: 55 per cent of men and 50 per cent of women said they voted Left at the district elections. The same phenomenon was recorded a year later. Following local elections, 54 per cent of men and 50 per cent of women said they had chosen the lists of the Left. The gap slightly widened in the national elections of March 1978 (Table 6.7), when 52 per cent of men and 46 per cent of women voted for a Left

Table 6.7   Voting differences between genders at the first ballot of the legislative elections of 1978

Vote		Far Left	PCF	PS/Left Radicals	Misc.* Opposi-tion	UDF	RPR	Misc. Majority + Misc. Right
Men	(100%)	3	24	25	3	19	20	6
Women	(100%)	2	19	25	3	22	24	5

* Includes candidates from the Ecology Party, 'Choisir' and others.
Source: Post election survey by SOFRES in 'Le Nouvel Observateur', 24 April 1978, p. 59

candidate. The difference (6 percentage points) is to be found in the PCF vote. Traditionally that party has been less popular among women. Differences in the distribution of men's and women's votes are not large, however. Analysis of the composition of the electorates of the four major parties shows that the PCF is the most male favoured party whereas the UDF is the most female favoured (Table 6.8). There has been an evolution in the relative differences however. The traditional suspicion of the PCF expressed by French women voters is fading. Whereas over the previous twenty years the male/female ratio in hte PCF electorate was 60/40; in 1980 it was 54/46.

If women's relationship to politics has altered it is almost certainly due to changes in their socio-economic position. A sample survey of 2,200 persons (one-third men, one-third employed women and one-third housewives) carried out by the authors after the national elections of 1978 produced evidence on economic, cultural and social factors which structure women's exclusion from and integration into political life (Mossuz-Lavau and Sineau, 1980). To the extent that women in 1980 showed less interest in politics than men and tended to be more conservative, it was due to social and religious characteristics within the female population which strongly predisposed women toward such attitudes. The French population contains a disproportionate number of older people the

Table 6.8   Gender composition of the electorate of four major parties at the first ballot of the 1978 legislative elections

| | Parties | | | |
	PCF	PS	UDF	RPR
Men	54	48	43	44
Women	46	52	57	56
	100	100	100	100

Source: Post election survey by SOFRES in 'Le Nouvel Observateur', 24 April 1978, p. 59

women among whom are mainly housewives and, when employed, are confined to unskilled jobs. They also practise their Catholic faith more actively than men. Our research clearly showed that women who were or had been employed, even temporarily (the formerly employed), were often as politicised as employed men. By comparison to men these women were more in favour of women holding political office. Fifty-six per cent of employed women and 55 per cent of formerly employed women found it 'absolutely normal' that a woman should be elected Prime Minister. By contrast 42 per cent of employed men and only 37 per cent of full-time housewives found the notion agreeable. Full-time housewives were the group of women who were most traditional in their attitudes. Forty per cent of them, nearly twice as many as the 23 per cent of other women and the 22 per cent of men, considered that politics 'should be the business of men rather than women'. Furthermore it was from these women that the highest rate of 'no answer' responses to political questions in sample surveys came. Finally, the full-time housewives were less likely to express partisan positions. Twenty-three per cent said they did not support any party in comparison to 7 per cent of employed men, 9 per cent of employed women and 8 per cent of formerly employed women. These homemakers were also the most intransigent in matters of everyday morality and had particularly rigorous views on problems of sexuality. Thus there was a correlation between women's employment, their political concern and their refusal to remain confined to a child-rearing and domestic universe.

The effect of employment on women is not a unitary one. Only those women in the higher and middle level professions with a good education participate and commit themselves to the left to the same extent as men. For example, amongst higher managers and members of the professions, 32 per cent of men and 33 per cent of women often discussed political matters with the people around them. By contrast only 20 per cent of male and 14 per cent of female workers claimed to enter into such discussions. Twenty per cent of men and 18 per cent of women in higher management and the professions had taken part in demonstrations in

the two years preceding the survey. The comparable figures for
male and female workers were 29 per cent and 16 per cent. Finally,
at the first ballot of the 1978 national elections 47 per cent of men
and 56 per cent of women in higher management and the professions voted for a party of the Left, compared to the 62 per cent
of men and 45 per cent of women who were shop assistants or
office employees and the 72 per cent of male and 61 per cent of
female workers. This finding may be explained by the fact that
working-class women are cross-pressured. On the one hand their
class background predisposes them toward the Left, on the other,
a Catholic upbringing fosters traditional norms (ibid.)

Indeed the practice of Catholicism, which over the centuries has
inhibited the participation of women in public life, is an essential
element of the explanation of women's political behaviour. In France
it is known that women, including employed women, attend church
more frequently than do men. But it is important to note that
church attendance is still more frequent amongst women not employed outside the home. Thirteen per cent of employed men, 18
per cent of employed women, 17 per cent of formerly employed
women and 28 per cent of full-time housewives attend mass at least
once a month. Forty-three per cent of housewives also pray daily
or often in comparison to 26 per cent of employed women, 33 per
cent of formerly employed women and only 14 per cent of employed
men. Religious practice undoubtedly induces conservatism and
lack of political interest among women. When women are detached
from religion they are as much integrated into political life and as
committed to parties of the Left as men. Among people who do not
practise any religion 78 per cent of employed men and 76 per cent
of employed women stated that they had at least some interest in
politics. But among practising Catholics 67 per cent of employed
men, 56 per cent of employed women and 52 per cent of formerly
employed women expressed an interest in politics. Among those
who do not practise a religion 68 per cent of employed women and
74 per cent of formerly employed women voted for the Left in 1978.
Of practising Catholics the left gained 43 per cent of the votes of
the employed and formerly employed women, 40 per cent of the
votes of full-time housewives and 55 per cent of those of employed
men (ibid.). These figures suggest that the political integration
of French women (as well as their support for the Left) will come
with their professional integration, with their acquisition of higher
education and with their increased independence from the Catholic
Church.

CONCLUSIONS

In what manner will the political promotion of French women be
achieved? The evolution over the last decade appears to be linear.
Women are becoming increasingly politicised and opt more and
more for the Centre-Left. Will this tendency persist? Our enquiry
goes part way toward providing answers to these questions.

Political understanding goes hand in hand with exercising a public economic function. Employed women are the more radical, housewives the more conservative. If trends in women's employment persist the future will witness a decrease in the number of full-time housewives and married women will carry on in employment after the birth of their children. It is possible to predict that the most apolitical and conservative group of women will eventually almost disappear from the population. The entry of the majority of French women into active economic life will necessarily be accompanied by a deep transformation of attitudes and possibly by changes in the division of labour in the family. As women increasingly hold economic roles so they are likely to become more partisan. The evidence suggests that they are then likely to increase their rate of support for the Left. At that point women may contribute to a radical change in the political direction of France.

NOTES

1 The results of the first ballot of the 1978 legislative elections were: Communist Party - 20.6 per cent; Socialist Party and Movement of Left Radicals - 24.9 per cent; Far Left and Miscellaneous Left - 3.8 per cent; Ecologists - 2 per cent; Union for French Democracy - 21 per cent; Rallying for the Republic - 23 per cent; miscellaneous - 5.4 per cent.

2 For example, the highest committee in the Socialist Party, the Secretariat, at the beginning of 1980, comprised, apart from the First Secretary (François Mitterrand) and the Treasurer, 15 National Secretaries of whom two were women: a National Secretary for Women's Action and a National Secretary for the Quality of Life.

3 Draft bill modifying some clauses of the electoral law with the aim of encouraging the participation of women in municipal candidatures (Assemblée Nationale, number 1142, second ordinary session of 1978-9). The Bill was passed on 20 November 1980. It will concern localities having more than 2,500 inhabitants.

4 The President of the Republic has frequently stated his desire to help in the promotion of women. In particular, ('Le Monde', 3 October 1977): 'I wish my presidential mandate to be marked by the complete recognition of the rights and responsibilities of women in French society. I hope that of the dozen or so lines which future history books will devote to my presidential term in office, one or two will be reserved for my efforts to improve the condition of women.'

5 In spite of the opposition from one section of the Gaullists (in particular Jacques Chirac and Michel Debré) the definitive renewal of this law was voted on in November 1979. For a report on the Parliamentary proceedings see 'Le Monde' (1979), 30 November, 1-2 December.

6 The motion on the 'crime of rape' was unanimously adopted by

the deputies. A report of the proceedings and details of the vote appeared in 'Le Monde' (1960), 13-14 April.

7 The RPR tabled a motion (Assemblée Nationale no. 1161) on 8 June 1979, asking for the suppression of the clause which makes divorce automatic after a separation of at least six years. The RPR proposed that the only automatic grounds for divorce should be the insanity of a spouse.

8 This is shown by examination of the motions and official texts emanating from the two parties over the last five years.

9 In a motion (Assemblée Nationale, no. 1123) tabled 20 June 1979, the Socialist Party asked that it should be possible for the parity commission in charge of salary disputes to be referred to 'by any woman who feels herself unjustly treated in the establishment of her salary, by any trade union organisation representing workers, or any association of women which has been properly constituted for at least five years'.

10 For instance, Madame Alexandre-Debray (PR), went on hunger strike in protest against the absence of women candidates on the list presented for the Senate elections. In 1978, Florence d'Harcourt, President for five years of the Mouvement Femme Avenir (Future Women Movement), then General Co-Secretary of the UDF (now the RPR), maintained her candidacy against a media man presented against her by her own party.

11 Publimétrie survey of 3 and 4 February 1975. The French people interviewed were asked to answer the following question: 'What is your reaction toward each government minister: satisfaction, discontent, indifference?' They gave first place to Simone Veil and Françoise Giroud. See also SOFRES survey March 1979. In reply to the question 'For each of the following political personalities (13 names given), can you indicate if you wish to see him/her play an important part in the future?' Fifty-seven per cent of the answers given put Simone Veil ahead of all preferences, outdistancing Michel Rocard with 47 per cent, François Mitterrand with 40 per cent and Raymond Barre with 36 per cent.

BIBLIOGRAPHY

Association Choisir, (1973), 'Avortement: une loi en procès, l'affaire de Bobigny', preface by Simone de Beauvoir, Gallimard, Paris.

Bécane, Geneviève (1974), 'Les Femmes au Sénat', roneo, 18pp.

Blanquart, Lousette (1974), 'Femmes: l'âge politique', Editions Sociales, Paris.

Brimo, Albert (1975), 'Les Femmes françaises face au pouvoir politique', Editions Montchrétien, Paris.

'Bulletin d'information du Ministère de l'intérieur' (1979), no. 175 19 July.

'Bulletin du Comité du travail feminin' (1979), Actualités du travail des femmes, no. 23, December.

Charzat, Gisèle (1972), 'Les Françaises sont-elles des citoyennes?' Denöel-Gonthier, Paris.
'Cités Unies' (1975), Organe de la Fédération mondiale des villes jumelées, no. 84, April - July.
de Beauvoir, Simone (1949), 'Le Deuxième Sexe', Gallimard, Paris.
de Pisan, Annie and Tristan, Anne (1977), 'Histoires du MLF', preface by Simone de Beauvoir, Calmann-Lévy, Paris.
Dogan, Mattei and Narbonne, Jacques (1955), 'Les Françaises face à la politique. Comportement politique et condition sociale', Cahiers de la Fondation Nationale des Sciences Politiques, Armand Colin, Paris.
Duverger, Maurice (1955), 'La Participation des femmes à la vie politique', Unesco, Paris.
'F. Magazine' (1980), February.
Fabre-Rosane, Gilles and Guédé, Alain (1978), 'Revue française de Science Politique', October.
Guilbert, Madeleine (1974), Femmes et syndicats en France, 'Sociologie et Sociétés', vol. V, no. 1, May, pp. 157-68.
Hardouin, Patrick (1978), 'Revue française de science politique', April.
'L'Aurore' (1975), 5 February.
Le Gendre, Bertrand (1979), 'Le Monde', 8 May, p. 45.
'Les Cahiers du Grif' (1975), Les femmes et la politique, no. 6, March.
'Les Temps modernes' (1974), Les femmes s'entêtent, April - May.
Maruani, Margaret (1979), 'Les Syndicats à l'épreuve du féminisme', Syros, Paris.
Mathieu, Gilbert (1980), Combien gagnent les salariés français? 'Le Monde', 22 January, p. 23.
Ministère de l'intérieur (1977), Note relative aux femmes élues lors des élections municipales générales des 13 et 20 mars 1977, March, p. 2.
Mossuz, Janine (1966), La régulation des naissances. Les aspects politiques du débat, 'Revue française de science politique', October, pp. 913-39.
Mossuz-Lavau, Janine and Sineau, Mariette (1978), 'Revue française de science politique', February, pp. 73-102.
Mossuz-Lavau, Janine and Sineau, Mariette (1979), 'Le Monde', 7 April.
Mossuz-Lavau, Janine and Sineau, Mariette (1980), Les femmes françaises en 1978. Insertion sociale, insertion politique, CORDES, Paris, March.
Mossuz-Lavau, Janine and Sineau, Mariette (1980), A Proposal of the French Secretary of State for Women: the Quota of 20 per cent Opportunities, Content and Consequences. Paper presented to the ECPR Joint Sessions, Florence, 1980.
Mossuz-Lavau, Janine and Sineau, Mariette (1980), L'ouvrière française et la politique, 'Sociologie du travail', no. 2, pp. 213-31.
Parodi, Jean-Luc (1970), Le système des partis français à la veille des élections européennes, 'Les Partis politiques et les

élections européennes', Geneva, Dossiers de l'Institut univer-
sitaire d'études européennes, December.

Renard, Marie-Thérèse (1965), 'La Participation des femmes à
la vie civique', Editions Ouvrières, Paris.

Sineau, Mariette (1974-5), Les femmes et l'ENA, 'Annuaire International de la fonction publique', (4), Institut International
d'Administration Publique, Paris.

'Sondages', (1969), 1-2.

Sullerot, Evelyne (1973), 'Les Françaises au travail', Hachette,
Paris.

Sullerot, Evelyne (1978), 'Le Fait féminin. Qu'est-ce-qu'une
femme?' Fayard, Paris.

Terrel, Françoise (1978), Les femmes en politiques, l'autonomie
ou le ghetto?, 'Projet', September-October.

Weiss, Louise (1949), 'Ce que femme veut', Gallimard, Paris.

'Vie Publique' (1980), no. 90, March.

Zeldin, Théodore (1978), 'Histoire des passions françaises', vol.
1, Editions Recherches, Paris.

7 SPAIN

Catherine Matsell

'machismo igual a fascismo'

Partido Feminista, 31 May 1979

HISTORICAL BACKGROUND

The history of women's suffrage in Spain has been characterised
by frustration, manipulation and interruption. Spanish women
had their first opportunity to vote in the general elections of 1933.
The government which granted female suffrage was defeated, and
within six years universal suffrage was buried for almost forty
years under the dictatorship of General Franco. Such has been
the limited participation of women in the political process until
1977. In fact there has been little opportunity for political participation throughout the greater part of Spain's turbulent history,
the last 150 years being fraught with wars abroad, civil wars,
dictatorships, dethroned monarchs and two republics. From 1833
to 1919 Spain had 117 presidents, three of whom never actually
exercised the title, and the ministry of education, created in 1900,
had seen 41 office-holders by 1920.(1) The examples are numerous and point to the difficulties faced by successive Spanish
administrations in their attempts to devise lasting solutions to the
country's fundamental problems.
   Universal male suffrage was granted in the constitution of 1869.
That constitution contained no reference to women at all and was
only applied from 1889 until 1923 when the period of parliamentary
democracy came to an abrupt end with the dictatorship of General
Primo de Rivera. At the turn of the century two-thirds of the
adult population was illiterate (Payne, 1970, p. 22) and the
elections were rarely free from corruption.(2) Spanish men had
barely exercised their suffrage in general elections for thirty
years before the declaration of the Second Republic. Given that
Spain had little experience of parliamentary democracy, that universal male suffrage was not a reality until 1889, and bearing in
mind that less than 10 per cent of women could read in 1878
(Laffitte, 1964, p. 26), it is not surprising that no organised
feminist movement clamouring for suffrage ever emerged. There
were many famous and influential women (3) who campaigned for
many and varied issues, including suffrage, but such was the
political, economic and social climate that women's rights remained
firmly subordinate to those of men whose own rights were frequently denied.

Spain entered the twentieth century with a parliamentary democracy in its infancy and a population at an early stage of civic
development. Political stability, after the disastrous war with the
USA over Cuba, was the major preoccupation of the two main
ruling parties, the Liberals and the Conservatives, and the other
parties showed little interest in women's suffrage, with the notable
exception of the Socialists. On the formation of the Socialist Party
(PSOE) in 1879 universal suffrage was included as one of the
party's primary goals (Payne, 1970, p. 63-4). Shortly after its
foundation the PSOE set up their trade union, the Unión General
de Trabajadores (UGT), and membership of both the party and
the union was open to women but all posts within them were reserved for men. Of the other left-wing parties the Communist
Party of Spain (PCE) was not formed until 1921 when it immediately
set up a women's section. The anarchist National Confederation of
Labour (CNT), founded in 1911, had no political programme
(Kaplan, 1971, p. 103) and made no effort to organise the women
workers who at the time were employed in the textile, shoe and
tobacco industries. The Catholic church had a far more explicit
programme for women and organised women's sections of their
trade unions but, as with the parties of the Left, most of their
aims remained programmatic (Capel, 1975, p. 120-3). Nevertheless
the moderate interest shown by the various parties and unions is
important when one considers that these were not the result of
any sizeable campaign by women themselves for inclusion in
workers' organisations or for suffrage. Such few women's organisations as existed were formed by a tiny minority of liberal-
minded women mostly from the wealthier classes. The majority of
women were illiterate and familiar only with the teachings of the
church, and of those that worked only 13 per cent were employed
in industry in 1900 (Laffitte, 1964, p. 357). Most women were
homeworkers, the rest being employed in agriculture and domestic
service. There are numerous examples of women banding together
to seek improvements in their situation - particularly in campaigning for better working conditions and for equality of opportunity
in education (see Capel, 1975; Laffitte, 1964; Scanlon, 1976; and
Francos Rodriguez, 1920) but no large cohesive movement with
well-defined aims ever existed. The few organisations which did
form did not affect the vast majority of the population and it has
to be remembered that Spain was a long way behind the rest of
Europe in industrial development. In 1900 nearly 70 per cent of
the total population lived in rural areas (Sole-Tura, 1971, p. 102)
and of the total active population 63 per cent were engaged in
agriculture (Tamames, 1970, p. 26).

Despite the fact that there was no general demand for female
suffrage it was first debated in parliament as early as 1908 during
the discussion on the electoral reform of local government (Capel,
1975, pp. 155-7). A small group of liberal-minded politicians proposed the granting of an administrative vote to age-qualified
women heads of families. This did not, however, include the right
to be elected. In other words women would be able to vote in

municipal elections but could not be candidates. The proposal was
defeated because of the wider implications of opening the door to
the participation of women in national political life. The defeat is
not surprising for in many ways women's suffrage was in advance
of public opinion and was probably the result of the liberal ideals
of some politicians who were influenced by events in other
countries. In fact, the same could be said of most of the legislation
concerning women that was implemented in Spain. Liberal ideals
have often been far in advance of the general level of Spanish
women's consciousness and often far removed from reality in other
ways. The laws passed in the first twenty years of the century
improving the condition of women workers hardly touched women
at all as so few were employed in industry in the first place.

The first major 'gain' women experienced came from an entirely
unexpected quarter, from the dictator Primo de Rivera, who much
to everyone's surprise authorised by royal decree in 1924 the vote
for women over the age of 23 (ibid., p. 123). Primo de Rivera's
decree was, and still is, very difficult to understand; firstly,
because only the previous year he had closed the parliament indef-
initely, and secondly, because the suffrage decreed contained an
unusual exclusion, that of married women. His motivation was
obscure at the time, and, in any case, of restricted interest since
elections never took place. Instead a National Assembly was set up
in 1927 composed of non-elected representatives of various sectors
of society (Thomas, 1977, p. 28). The Assembly was purely consultative but it included eleven women representatives of women's
organisations and two ladies in waiting to the queen (Capel, 1975,
pp. 133-8). This was the first instance of women's participation
in the political arena, and together with the albeit strange decree
of 1924 may have influenced the thinking of some republican
parties in 1931.

With the departure of Primo de Rivera and the fall of the monarchy in 1931, the Second Republic was installed. General elections
were held in the same year. For these elections women could be
candidates but not electors (ibid., p. 155). The elections brought
victory to the republican parties of the Left, and for the first
time two women were elected to Parliament. Both Victoria Kent and
Clara Campoamor were from the left-wing coalition and were active
in drafting the new constitution. When the question of female suffrage came up only Clara Campoamor was totally in favour. Victoria Kent on the other hand expressed the fears felt by many on
the Republican Left that it was not safe for the Republic to admit
to the electorate a section of society so conservative that it might
cause Republican defeat (Scanlon, 1976, pp. 274-9; Capel, 1975,
pp. 167-82). In the event Article 36 of the Constitution was passed
giving universal suffrage to all citizens over the age of 23, but it
was only passed by a majority of forty and its support came mostly
from the Socialists and the right-wing parties (Capel, 1975, pp.
184-5).

Now that women had the vote the parties set about trying to
win their support. The parties of the Left needed women's votes

to stay in power and keep the Republic alive, whereas the right-wing wanted their vote for the opposite reasons. Of the left-wing parties it was the PSOE and the communists (PCE) who took the lead but the right-wing organisations were far better disciplined. Neither side seems to have been genuinely interested in feminine emancipation as both appealed essentially to traditional female roles: the right-wing stressing that in order to preserve their traditional values the left-wing had to be defeated, and the left-wing appealing to women to secure their families' future by voting for the Republican parties (ibid., pp. 230-3; Scanlon, 1976, pp. 283-90). The elections of 1933 were won by the right-wing. Of the six women returned to the Cortes (Parliament) three were socialists and three from parties of the Right (Capel, 1975, p. 242). The right-wing parties fought the elections as a united front led by the Spanish Confederation of Autonomous Rightists (CEDA) which probably attracted many women voters (Payne, 1970, p. 111). The Left was in complete disarray but in 1936 the tables were turned. As elections were again called the parties polarised into two broad fronts. This time the right-wing front collapsed and the Popular Front of the left-wing parties swept to power. All five women elected were from the Left including, for the first time, Dolores Ibarruri, 'la Pasionaria' of the PCE (Capel, 1975, p. 253). But the Republic's days were numbered and within six months the country was plunged into a civil war.(4)

During the civil war of 1936-9, the ideologies which separated the two sides, the Nationalists and the Popular Front, were clearly reflected in their attitude towards women. The Nationalists although composed of various sectional interests were united in their opinion that the traditional role of women, as mothers, companions of men and subordinates to men at all times should be upheld. The Falange, through its Feminine Section, organised support for the war on lines similar to the Nazi party in Germany. As the Nationalist women seemed to accept their subordination, their organisations were apparently acceptable to men (Scanlon, 1976, pp. 314-18). On the Republican side however the differences between the political parties which composed the Popular Front were reflected in numerous women's organisations, the diversity of which constituted a barrier to a single co-ordinated women's effort (ibid., pp. 291-5). The Anarchists in particular were suspicious of the Communists' efforts to enlist all women in their Mujeres Antifascistas organisation.(5) Federica Montseny, an Anarchist, became the first woman minister in Spain, in charge of Health and Social Service. Despite the war, the Anarchists were determined to keep up pressure for social change and so abortion was legalised in 1936, though this measure had little effect outside Barcelona (ibid., pp. 304-8). In summary it could be said that aspirations for sex equality became synonymous with the triumph of the Republic and that women were prepared to subordinate their demands to the more immediate task of winning the war. On the Nationalist side it was merely expected that women would support the war effort and sacrifice themselves for the sake of their children (Thomas, 1977, p. 763).

The Nationalist victory in 1939 did not prove in the long term to be all that the Nationalist side had bargained for. General Franco turned out to be far more durable than CEDA expected, and far less committed to the Falange than had been hoped. But if men were deprived of political and economic freedom women saw all the gains they had made in work, education and civil status swept away and all possibilities of a continued liberation movement destroyed. For women the situation was horribly familiar and their status reverted to that in force in the Civil Code of 1889 (Scanlon, 1976, p. 322). Divorce, abortion, co-education, the right to work and to strike, etc. were all rescinded in a series of laws promulgated by General Franco which establised the bases of his dictatorship.(6) Women were expected to stay at home and produce children, and up until recently prizes were awarded for the most 'numerous' families. Women could be dismissed from work on marrying until as late as 1961 (Bofill, 1968, p. 56). Spanish women were required to complete a form of compulsory social service, analogous to male military service. This social service programme was run under the auspices of the Feminine Section of the Falange, later to be incorporated into the 'Movimiento Nacional' of 1958 (Sole-Tura, 1971, p. 15) and consisted originally of three months of courses in the domestic arts (i.e. home management etc.) together with three months of practice, very often in a nursery or school. Only university students were exempted providing they had passed the domestic science course at secondary school level.(7) In this way the Franco regime hoped to preserve traditional Catholic feminine virtues and prepare women for their destiny as the future mothers of large families, and women themselves continued to accept this role because the majority had never really experienced anything different.

It was only during the 1960s that the situation for women was eased, reflecting the current needs of the Spanish economy. Economic development meant that women were needed to work and the laws of 1961-2 established women's rights to jobs and equal pay, but their civil status never changed. Hence women remained at a distinct disadvantage because of the persistence of other laws making them firmly subordinate to their husbands.(8) In the same period women were given some of the political rights enjoyed by men. In 1970 Spanish women obtained the right to vote for the 105 elected seats of the total 510 which comprised the Cortes in 1970 (ibid., p. 61). However only heads of families could vote and all political parties outside the official National Movement were banned, as were all trade unions except for the state-run syndicates. Despite the fact that strikes and demonstrations etc. were illegal, industrial unrest and political protest grew steadily throughout the 1960s and 1970s.(9) Spain could not remain isolated from the influence of other western countries nor could the institutions Franco created cope with the developments within the country, particularly the rapid industrialisation and urbanisation from the 1950s onwards. However no-one dared remove the General himself. He obliged all sides in November 1975.

SOCIO-ECONOMIC ENVIRONMENT

In 1960 women accounted for 18.2 per cent of the total workforce
in Spain, a mere 13.5 per cent of the total female population
(Maravall, 1970a, p. 105). By 1970 almost 18 per cent of all women
were in employment while over the same ten-year period they
accounted for over half of the total population of 34.75 million.(10)
This would seem to be a very small proportion compared to other
European countries (Maravall, 1970a, p. 105). The most striking
feature of the female workforce is its age. More women in the age
group 15-24 years work than in any other age group with 43 per
cent of women working between the ages of 20-24 years compared
with only 20 per cent between the ages of 25-34. This points to
the continuing practice of women giving up employment on marrying and is confirmed by the average age at which women marry.
In 1970 the average marriage age of women was 24. Other familiar
features of female employment in Spain are the higher proportions
of women working in urban areas, albeit with some notable exceptions, and their concentration in certain sectors of the economy.

During the last twenty-five years there has been a considerable exodus from rural areas resulting in the rapid growth of
urban areas. In 1970 over 44 per cent of the population was living
in towns with over 50,000 inhabitants compared with only 30 per
cent in 1950, and one of the consequences of this rapid rural de-
population is the increasing proportion of women employed in the
agricultural sector as compared to men. The overall proportion of
the active workforce in agriculture dropped from almost 50 per
cent in 1950 to 20 per cent in 1975. Over the same period the
proportion of women engaged in agriculture has risen from 7.9
per cent of the agricultural workforce to almost 30 per cent. As
the young, particularly young men of working age, leave to work
in the towns, the rural areas are left with only the old, the
women and children.

The process of urbanisation has led to an enormous imbalance
between those provinces essentially rural and those which are
becoming increasingly industrialised and urbanised. Only in 5 of
52 provinces, Madrid, Barcelona and 3 Basque Provinces is employment in agriculture insignificant. Twenty-one provinces
register over 40 per cent of their workforce engaged in the primary sector. If one looks at the employment of women in these
same provinces an interesting picture emerges. Though Barcelona
and Madrid employ more than the average proportion of their
female population, it is Lugo in the north-west which stands out
with a staggering 35 per cent. The north-west is a rural area but
so too is Jaen in the south which only employs a mere 6.53 per
cent of its female population. In summary the nine provinces
which employ the highest proportions of their female population,
i.e. over 15 per cent, are concentrated in the northern half of
Spain whilst the seven provinces which employ the lowest proportion i.e. around 6 per cent are in the south. The pattern of
female employment therefore reflects to a certain degree the

pattern of industrialisation and urbanisation in Spain. The southern half of the country is losing population and the fastest urban
growth is around Madrid, Barcelona and the Basque Provinces in
the north, with Bilbao having pushed Seville into fifth place. But
the pattern of female employment cannot be explained totally in
terms of economic development as shown by the differences between Jaen in the south and Lugo in the north-west, differences
which underline the social and cultural characteristics that so
separate the two halves of Spain.

Outside the agricultural sector, which is the single largest
employer of female labour, women are to be found mainly in commerce and personal services (including domestic service). These
three sectors accounted for over 60 per cent of all women workers
in 1970; and of the remainder, 18 per cent were in clothing, shoes,
textiles, tobacco and food industries with a mere 2 per cent employed in banking, insurance and public administration. Women
are therefore concentrated in the traditional 'women's' industries,
and in three constitute the majority of the workforce: personal
services, 63 per cent; leather, shoes and clothing, 66 per cent;
textiles, 53 per cent. A noticeable trend since 1960 has been the
considerable drop in the proportion of women employed in domestic
service, which in that year accounted for almost 34 per cent of all
women employed (Bofill, 1968, p. 44) as compared to 19 per cent
in 1970.

Throughout the decade under consideration the proportion of
women working has increased whilst that of men has decreased.
But women continue to be employed in those sectors of the economy which least require qualified personnel and which pay lower
wages. Wages in the agricultural sector are notoriously low and
those industries where women form the majority of the workforce
are poorly paid.(11) Between 1964-72 for example the shoe industry, already way behind most others in terms of pay, received
lower pay increases than most other sectors. Not only are women
in poorly paid employment they are not always paid an equal wage
for equal job though the principle was established in law in 1961.
During 1969 in the textile industry the wages received by a man
and a woman doing the same job could vary by up to 30 per cent
in the man's favour. In commerce, although pay was equal, in
two out of the four jobs compared in the lower and middle grades
the difference was 20 per cent (Maravall, 1970a, p. 117). In those
professions where one would expect a greater degree of equality
of pay and opportunity, e.g. amongst teachers, doctors etc.,
only 7 per cent of women workers were employed in 1960 (Bofill,
1968, p. 44).

The small proportion of women employed in the technical and
professional sector is largely explained by looking at the position
of women in the educational system. Lack of educational opportunity goes some way toward explaining women's firm entrench-
ment in the lowest paid jobs and in those where the fewest qualifications are required. In Spain education is compulsory between
the ages of six and fourteen but in 1970 there were still over half

a million children of school age with no schools to go to ('Cuadernos para el Dialogo', 1974, nos. 27-8, p. 14). Of those who had attended school almost 90 per cent did not go beyond primary (age fourteen since 1970, previously eleven) and almost 7 per cent of men and nearly 15 per cent of women had never been to school at all. Women outnumber men at the primary level and a higher proportion of women actually finish their basic schooling than men. However, of the 3 per cent in higher education in the course of 1971/2 only 28 per cent were women. Throughout the previous decade a higher proportion of women were passing through all stages of education but their numbers are still very low when compared with men's. In short not only is the population as a whole rather poorly qualified but women enjoy only extremely low average levels of education with almost 15 per cent totally illiterate.

For the minority of women who attend secondary schools (age 14-plus) the traditional subject division between the sexes is clearly reflected. Only 33 per cent of girls follow science courses. A similar pattern is apparent in higher education. Women account for 30 per cent of students enrolled in university science courses and only 15 per cent of those enrolled in Politics and Economics courses, but over 50 per cent of those enrolled in arts courses. In technical colleges women comprise only a very small proportion of the total number of students doing any course, the highest proportion being architecture with 9 per cent. As one would expect, in teacher training almost 60 per cent of all students are women. In the teaching profession itself women represent 64 per cent of all primary teachers, but only about 30 per cent of secondary teachers. Whilst the pattern of women's access to higher education in Spain is a typical one the very small proportion of women involved is remarkable.

The general level of education of the total population of Spain is slowly rising and with it that of women. Features particularly worthy of note are the high levels of illiteracy among women and the fact that of those who make it to university 12 per cent do not finish the courses and of those who do complete almost half never take paid employment (ibid., p. 26). The main reason for this would seem to be the propensity for women to give up work upon marriage. Although women degree-holders are substantially less likely to leave the labour market upon marriage, pressures on them to do so remain strong. The lower classes may have good reason to give up their education through economic necessity but higher education is still mainly the preserve of the upper and middle classes. University education is virtually free but maintenance grants are hard to come by and so unless there is a university within the province the expense is considerable. The fact that many women never use their higher qualifications has led some Spanish feminists to suspect the motives of those who bother to try. Is it, they ask, merely a pastime which has replaced the piano as the desired attribute of a marriageable young lady? (ibid., 1974, nos. 27-28, p. 26) Were those women who gave up their

university careers merely looking for a better class of husband?
(Bofill, 1968, p. 59).

It is obvious that Spain has a number of serious problems within the educational sector not least of which is the lack of schools
provision and the high rate of illiteracy. Both sexes need greater
encouragement to stay on at school to a later age but one of the
greatest inhibitors to the advance of women was the continued
emphasis by the Franco regime on their traditional role within the
home and it is this factor which is most reflected in the number of
women who seek education beyond the elementary stages and the
number of women who continue to work after marriage.

A further factor which affects the status of Spanish women and
which undoubtedly influences the political behaviour of Spaniards
is the role of the Catholic church. Data on the church's influence
on voting behaviour and party preference are not available but it
is a fact that the church in Spain has always exerted considerable
influence on Spanish society. Raised to supreme heights during
the Inquisition, the church was separated from the state briefly
during the Republic. The teachings of the Catholic church have
been preserved and enshrined in Spanish law. Under Franco, for
example, civil marriages were possible only for those who could
prove that they had not been baptised. According to official
statistics 95 per cent of the population was baptised in the Catholic faith. The church has provided much of the education available in Spain and though the state now provides 65 per cent of
all school places the religious instruction received by pupils has
always referrred exclusively to the Roman Catholic faith with its
emphasis on the sanctity of marriage, virginity, etc. Although
the influence of the church is reflected in social attitudes it has
never managed to control its flock completely. Religious beliefs
have remained on the personal level and a Spaniard may be nom-
inally Catholic while at the same time expressing antagonism towards the church and its clergy. Spain has been the home not
only of the Inquisition but also of numerous outbursts of violence
against the institutions of Catholicism.

The Catholic church is used for the formal expression of faith
(i.e. baptism, first communion, marriage, death) and for the
formal acquisition of Catholic principles and moral attitudes, but
Spain is not a nation of church-goers. A survey carried out in
1974 showed that 89 per cent declared themselves to be Catholics
but only 32 per cent of men had communion more than three times
a year. This figure is almost doubled for women, and the statistics show clearly that rural areas attend more than urban, and
the least educated more than the professional classes. Regional
differences are also apparent. Spanish women's relatively (to men)
stronger adherence to Catholicism suggests that the national religion is a more salient political variable for women than for men.
Thus, although we are short of the necessary information to
measure its precise influence, the probable importance of the role
of Catholicism should be borne in mind in any discussion of the
political behaviour of Spanish women.

PARTY SYSTEM AND ELECTIONS

Within two years of Franco's death Spain held its first democratic
elections for over forty years. From a dictatorship the country
passed relatively smoothly into a constitutional monarchy and by
the end of 1978 had a new constitution which separated church
from state, gave suffrage to all over the age of 18 and established
the equality of all Spaniards before the law ('Gaceta de Madrid',
1978). Despite the fact that all political parties except the official
National Movement had been outlawed since the civil war, a prolif-
eration of parties covering the complete political spectrum from
extreme Right to extreme Left were ready to contest the elections
in 1977. Some of the parties were new and others familiar, but
what is interesting is the emergence of two main parties in the
parliament out of a total of over sixty, many of which bear similar titles. What would have discouraged Franco most is the fact
that forty years of authoritarian central government has not
dampened the regionalist spirit at all; if anything it is more vigorous than ever.

Spain has adopted a two chamber parliament, Congress and
Senate, with Congress being the most important and taking precedence over the Senate. Congress has a total of 350 seats and
Senate 208. The electoral system for Congress is one of proportional representation and constituencies are whole provinces
which return a number of members which varies according to population. The Senate is made up of four Senators from each
province, regardless of population, and each elector has four
votes. Voters are obliged to choose a party list and thus independents are excluded unless they can form a list between them. This
was the system, complicated by a vast array of political parties,
which faced the Spanish electorate in 1977 and 1979. The only
difference between the two elections was the 1979 inclusion of the
eighteen-year-old voter. The results for the March 1979 Parliamentary elections for a term of four years are given in Table 7.1.

The victorious UCD party is a mixed coalition broadly covering
the spectrum of political opinion from Centre-Left to Centre-Right.
The PSOE, the second largest party is a traditional European
Socialist party. On the extreme Right are the CD and UN. On the
extreme Left are the PCE, PSA, UPC, and two Basque parties HE
and EE.(13) The remaining parties occupy various positions on
the Centre Left. Data on women's voting behaviour are not available, nor is systematic information on women candidates and office
holders at sub-national level. However, it is possible to outline
the position of women office-holders and candidates for office at
national level. Of the 350 congressmen elected in 1979 nineteen
were women (5 per cent of the total) and of the 208 senators six
were women.(14) Compared with 1977 women have lost two seats
in Congress but gained two in the Senate. These small numbers,
at three times the number ever returned during the Republic, are
actually a healthy showing for women in Spain. All the congresswomen are from the main parties and coalitions: UCD 10, PSOE 5,

Table 7.1   Main parties and coalitions 1979

	Seats in Congress 1979
Democratic Centre (UCD)	167
Socialists (PSOE)	121
Communists (PCE/PSUC)	23
Democratic Coalition (CD/UPN)	10
Basque Autonomists (PNV/HB/EE)	11
Catalan Autonomists (CIU/ERC)	10
Socialist Party of Andalucia (PSA)	5
Regionalist Party of Aragon (PAR)	1
Canary Autonomists (UPC)	1
National Union (UN)	1
Total	350

Source: Diplomatic Information Office, Spain 79, no. 69, April 1979; 'The Economist', November 1979, pp. 12-14, 'Cambio', 16, no. 380, 18 March 1979, pp. 26-9.[12]

PCE 2, CIU 1, CD 1, and the distribution of women members roughly reflects the party composition of parliament. In Congress women account for the following percentages of seats: UCD 6 per cent, PSOE 4 per cent, CIU 11 per cent, PCE 9 per cent and CD 11 per cent.

According to the weekly magazine 'Cambio', (no. 376, February 1979, pp. 14-18) a total of 1,290 women were candidates for the 1979 elections to Congress which represents 22 per cent of all the candidates as compared to 15 per cent in 1977. If this is the case then their success rate was rather poor obtaining, as they did, only 5 per cent of the seats. But far more important than the number of women fielded is their position on the party lists and it does not appear that they have been well placed. Whether women have been included to display the egalitarian qualities of the parties, to attract the female voter, or more cynically to fill the lists is difficult to say without seeing all the party lists which were presented in each province. Nevertheless it seems that at least two women were placed at the top of the list presented, CD in La Coruna and CIU in Lerida. The UCD would appear to have placed their female candidates better than the PSOE, but the parties may well be short of suitable and willing women candidates.

The regional distribution of seats shows that all but five elected women came from the northern half of Spain, possibly reflecting the more traditional attitude towards women so prevalent in the southern rural areas. That Barcelona and Madrid should each return three women is to be expected from the two largest cities which had a total of 65 seats available. More surprising are the four women returned from the region of Galicia with a total of 27

congressional seats between the provinces of La Coruna, Lugo,
Pontevedra and Oreñse. La Coruna with only nine seats returned
two women, one from the UCD and one from the CD. Lugo and
Pontevedra with five and eight seats respectively each returned
one UCD female candidate. These three small provinces in the
north-west of Spain demonstrate the influence of regional differences and characteristics. The three provinces, particularly Lugo,
employ a higher proportion of their female population than any
other province with the exception of Barcelona, but they are
essentially rural with most of the women employed in agriculture
and related industries. Also, of the 27 congressional seats allocated to Galicia, 21 went to the UCD and the right-wing CD
parties. The area presents an interesting contrast to Andalucia in
the south which only returned two women (PSOE and UCD) out of
a total of 56 seats. Both regions are experiencing rural depop-
ulation in their interiors though this is far more acute in Andalucia. Galicia employs a high proportion of its female population
whilst Andalucia employs one of the lowest proportions. Explanation for the differences between the two regions may well be
found in the different agricultural pattern which differentiates
the north from the south. In the north the land tenure is based
on small-holdings whilst in the south it is divided into enormous
estates. Thus the north-west is traditionally more conservative
than the south where during the early part of the century the
Anarchists had considerabie support. Galicia was also Franco's
birthplace and very much his territory. Galician women –
'gallegas' – are apparently known for their 'sweet but persistent'
natures. Therefore though both regions may be considered as
backward they are different in crucial ways. It may well be that
in the north-west the female peasant has not lost her original
status because she is still working on family land whereas the
position of the landless labourer and his family produces an
entirely different pattern in the south. It is not difficult to understand why Galicia would both appeal to, and also vote for the
right wing, and the CD were obviously behaving rationally in
placing a woman candidate at the top of the list in La Coruna.
This region may well have been one of the few where the women's
vote was actively and successfully fought for.
   The attitudes of the various parties towards women's issues
and hence their vote is perhaps best demonstrated by looking at
two issues which directly affect women, divorce and abortion.
Both these issues illustrate the persisting non-egalitarian nature
of Spanish society. As neither issue has yet been resolved both
also underline the difficulties faced by parties which adopt policies
which imply fundamental changes in attitude.

DIVORCE

During the Republic, Spain possessed a very advanced divorce
law which admitted divorce by mutual consent or on the petition of

either party, but since 1938 divorce has not been recognised, although legal separations and annulments are possible. Up to the present day both the civil and penal code have been heavily weighted against married women particularly as regards adultery which is an acceptable reason for legal separation and punishable in law by a prison sentence. The most significant distinction in legal terms has been that between adultery and concubinage (Bofill, 1968, pp. 152-4). Women could be punished for simple adultery but men only if notoriety or concubinage could be proved. In a society where sexual liberation for men has been encouraged and considered part of the natural 'macho' makeup notoriety was obviously difficult to prove. The sexual exploits of a married man outside the home have always been indulged rather than frowned upon and considered by many, including women, as the natural activity of a healthy male. By contrast the honour of the family has always resided firmly on the shoulders of women.(15) These two attitudes have been enshrined by the church and in the law itself though most women have probably not been aware of their appalling legal position.

The church itself, however, has recognised that not all marriages are made in heaven and annulments have been relatively easy to obtain for those who can afford them. The Association of Separated Women estimates that half a million marriages have been dissolved, are in legal separation or in dispute at the present time. The issue is, of course, as much of interest to men as women. All the major parties included divorce in their political programmes with only the CD declaring themselves to be the 'custodians of Christian morals' ('Cambio', 1979, 16, no. 408, p. 17). The main difference from the situation in the 1930s is that the parties now know they have public opinion on their side. Surveys carried out during the 1960s and 1970s show that a majority is in favour of divorce (ibid.). Both the PCE and PSOE have plans for a divorce law and they both coincide on the main and most controversial point, that of mutual consent which the UCD does not recognise. In the event it was the PSOE who made the first move in Congress. This was a response to UCD inactivity and also a device intended to force the UCD's hand in the knowledge that the UCD had problems with its own right wing (ibid., p. 18). The debate ended with Socialists defeated by a very narrow margin of eight votes. The UCD reacted by unveiling their own proposals which involved rather long waiting periods and fell rather short of PCE and PSOE demands. By May 1980 UCD proposals had not been placed before Parliament, possibly because of the fear of reaction from within the party and from the Catholic church. The bill could well be defeated and the party also faces problems over other issues such as regional autonomy for Andalucia, unemployment and the continuing terrorism in the Basque Provinces. Sooner or later the UCD will be forced into action by the other parties whose motives for pushing divorce are obviously not solely related to the issue itself. In the meantime a million Spaniards await the happy day with growing impatience and frustration ('The Economist', 3 November 1979, p. 11).

ABORTION

The question of abortion is, in a largely Catholic country, if anything more controversial than that of divorce and it was so even
during the Republic, when it was legalised by the anarchist
Federica Montseny, then Minister of Health and Social Services
(Scanlon, 1976, p. 308). That measure was superseded by the
law of 1941 which instituted far harsher penalties than any previous legislation, increasing prison sentences from six months to
six years (Bofill, 1968, p. 155). At the moment Spain is the European country which most protects the unborn foetus but yet some
300,000 Spanish women have abortions every year, most of them
within Spain but with an estimated 13,000 going to London in 1978
alone. In the same year 3,000 women died from illegal abortions
('Cambio', 1979, 16, no. 413, p. 17). Yet despite the necessity
for some action only the PCE included abortion reform in its programme. A motion for its inclusion in the PSOE electoral platform
was defeated at a delegates conference ('The Economist', 3 November, 1979, p. 11).
    Very much a taboo subject, it is only since Franco's death that
abortion has received any publicity. The mere mention of contraception in the media was grounds for immediate censorship, as
was experienced by the magazine 'Triunfo' in the early 1970s.
Attention has now been focussed on the issue by the trial of
eleven women from Basuri under the 1941 law. The nine women
who had abortions, plus the two abortionists, face a prison sentence of six years unless the law is altered quickly. Public opinion
however is not in their favour and in 1977 a survey showed that
60 per cent were against legalised abortion and that opinion
against it was strongest among women. On the question of whether
abortion should be available where the mother's or the child's life
is in danger almost 60 per cent of women answered affirmatively
('Cambio', 1979, 16, no. 413, pp. 16-23). It would seem therefore
that at least some reform would receive public support.
    An enormous amount of publicity has been given to the trial
which attracted a great deal of feminist protest, culminating in an
occupation of the Palace of Justice in Madrid. Equal publicity was
attracted by the violent dispersal of the female protesters by the
police amid a flurry of insults and beatings. Over 4,000 women
have signed a document stating that they too have had abortions
and among them are some well-known figures including two congresswomen, trade union officials, lawyers, etc. The aim of the
exercise is to challenge the authorities and to bring publicity to
the plight of the eleven women due to go on trial. The response
of the UCD has been to defend the trial and so it appears there
are no reforms in the pipeline. The communists have given notice
of their intention to seek the depenalisation of abortion under the
reform of the penal code when it comes to Congress and to seek
legislation to legalise abortion (ibid.). The most that can be expected in the short term would seem to be the removal of the
prison sentences or their reduction, as it seems doubtful whether

the PCE could rely on the PSOE for support for complete legalisation - at least not at present. The strength of opinion both in
and out of Congress against legalised abortion is very great.
Feminist groups face great difficulties in canvassing support,
though they may be able to sway some of the left-wing parties. A
return to the situation of 1936 is not imminent.

The reluctance of the major parties to give greater priority to
women's rights has not gone unnoticed by the feminists. In Cataluña the Feminist Party was formed in June 1979 by some well-
known activists, including Lidia Falcon, the lawyer. Disillusioned
by the attitude of the parties of the Left they have formed their
own party whose four main aims are the reform of the civil code,
divorce, legalisation of abortion and a campaign to establish family planning centres which at present are mostly run by volunteers and only exist in the major cities. The Partido Feminista
also intends to establish links with the left-wing parties in Congress ('Vanguardia', 1 June, 1979).

Response to the two issues of abortion and divorce suggests
that where a solution will directly benefit both sexes, as in the
case of divorce, it is more likely to be resolved in the immediate
future. Abortion however is always more problematical for it
involves wider issues which tend to divert attention away from,
for example, the problem of unwanted children. At present all the
ethical and moral questions which accompany any debate on abortion are diverting Spanish attention away from the fact that it is
only lower-class women who are affected by such a law and who
have recourse to the back-street abortionist in the first place.
The cost of an abortion in London is much cheaper than going
privately to those Spanish doctors willing to perform them ('Vanguardia', 1 June, 1979). Thus, it is only those of very slender
means who are forced to seek help outside the medical profession.
But Spain is a very Catholic country often considering itself as
'more papist than the Pope himself'. It would seem unlikely therefore that any mass support for abortion will be forthcoming even
from the left wing. That the ruling UCD would risk a stand on the
issue is even more unlikely.

CONCLUSIONS

Parliamentary democracy in Spain is still in its infancy and its
survival not altogether guaranteed. Issues dominating political
discussion at present are regionalism, with Cataluña and the
Vascongadas already having their own assemblies but the UCD
dragging its feet over Andalucia, terrorism, membership of the
Common Market, growing unemployment and inflation and falling
tourism etc. all of which have pushed women's issues into the
background. This is true for all parties, and with the occasional
exception, and it is true for women themselves be they in Congress or not. Once again, women have allowed other national
issues to take precedence over their own, presumably believing

as they did during the civil war that survival of the system itself comes first and their rights only later. Only a minority of women think the two go hand in hand and as yet there are no cross-party links between women politicians.

The UCD, which accounts for half of the congresswomen, is considered very much a 'macho' party having no feminine organisation within it. Only one woman is on the party executive ('Cambio', 1979, no. 314, p. 39) and the inclusion of any at all is seen as adornment. It would seem optimistic therefore to predict the promotion of any women politicians to ministerial status in the near future.

The very electoral system adopted by Sapin (The D'Hondt system) (16) with its emphasis on party rather than candidates makes it difficult to measure the extent to which a party may be trying and succeeding at attracting the female vote. It inevitably de-personalises the campaign in that the voter chooses a party and not a particular representative. This fact may be working in the favour of Spanish women at the moment, given the traditional male-oriented society in which they are trying to make their mark. Any electoral success by women in Spain is worthy of note and those few women who have achieved elected office represent an advance which should not be undervalued. But it remains to be seen whether feminine issues stay firmly in the background or come to the fore as they have in other European countries.

The serious nature of difficulties facing Spanish feminists must inform any analysis of their success. The word 'macho', now incorporated into English usage to symbolize the excesses of the male sex, is merely the Spanish word for male and as such still signifies the qualities that a true male possesses and of which he is proud, above all it expresses his ability to dominate women both sexually and intellectually. This view is still held by most Spaniards, both men and women. Without a major change in the attitudes of a large number of Spanish women, it is unlikely that 'macho' will be seriously challenged. Unlike in the Republican days, women are having to fight for their rights. The experience of having to mobilise and organise themselves and of being able to do so for the first time in many years without fear of censorship may mean that improvements, although harder-won, will be more permanent.

NOTES

1 See Chapter 2 ('Inconsistencia Politica') in Francos Rodriguez, 'La Mujer y la politica espanolas', Writing in 1920, the author answers critics of women's inferiority by citing the examples of male inconsistencies throughout Spanish history. He says that women could not have performed any worse.
2 See S. G. Payne, pp. 22ff in 'The Spanish Revolution', and G. Brenan in 'The Spanish Labyrinth', pp. 6ff for examples of election corruption.

3 See M. Laffitte, 'La Mujer en Espana: cien anos de su historia' and Rodriguez op. cit., for examples of famous women such as Emilia Pardo Bazan, Concepcion Arenal, et. al.
4 For an analysis of the social conflict and origins of the civil war see Brenan (1971) and Payne (1970).
5 See E. T. Kaplan, 'Spanish Anarchism and Women's Liberation' for differences between the Communists and Anarchists.
6 See Jorge Sole-Tura (1971) for legal bases of Franco regime.
7 For details of the courses see Scanlon in 'La Polemica feminista', pp. 326-35.
8 For details of civic status see Chapter 4 of Bofill (1968).
9 For industrial unrest in the 1960s see Maravall, 'El Desarollo econòmico y la clase obrera'. For political unrest see Maravall, 'Dictatorship and Political Dissent'.
10 Statistics employed throughout this chapter are from Fundacion FOESSA (1976) unless otherwise stated.
11 Maravall, pp. 112-14 in Aspectos del empleo feminino en Espana, lists areas where statistics are needed.
12 Full results of the Congressional elections 1977-9

Main parties and coalitions		Seats 1979	Seats 1977
UCD	Unión de Centro Democrático	167	166
PSOE	Partido Socialista Obrero Espanol	121	124
PCE	Partido Comunista de Espana	23	20
PSUC	Partido Socialista Unificat de Catalunya		
CD*	Coalición Democrática	10	16
UPN	Unión del Pueblo Navarro		
CiU	Convergenica i Unió (Catalunya)	9	–
ERC	Esquerra Republicana (Catalunya)	1	1
PNV	Partido Nacionalista Vasco	7	8
HB	Herri Batasuna (Pais Vasco)	3	–
EE	Euskadico Esquerra (Pais Vasco)	1	1
PSA	Partido Socialista de Andaluciá	5	–
PAR	Partido Aragonés Regionalista	1	1
UPC	Unión del Pueblo Canario	1	–
UN	Unión Nacional	1	8
	Others	–	5
	Total	350	350

* Alianza Popular in 1977

Senate results 1979 (Senate was reduced from 248 in 1977 to 208 in 1979.)

Main parties and coalitions	Seats
UCD	119
PSOE	68
PNV	8
CiU	1
HB	1
CD	2
Others	8
	207

13 See Chao (1976) for political parties formed in 1975-6.
14 Candidates taken from election lists supplied by Spanish Embassy, Eaton Square, London. Confirmed verbally by 'Cambio' 16, May 1980.
15 Honour is a recurrent theme throughout Spanish literature from the Golden Age onwards. See works by Lope de Vega, Lorca and Galdos as examples.
16 For a full explanation of the D'Hondt system see T. Burkett (1975), 'Parties and Elections in West Germany', C. Hurst & Company, London, Appendix A, pp. 131-5.

BIBLIOGRAPHY

Alba, V. (1978), 'Transition in Spain', Transaction, New Jersey.
Alvarez, L. (1970), Mujer y aceleractión histórica, 'Cuadernos para el dialogo', Colección los supplementos, nos. 27-28.
Bofill, (1968), 'La Mujer en España', Madrid.
Brenan, G. (1971), 'The Spanish Labyrinth', Cambridge University Press.
'Cambio', 16, no. 376, 18 Feb. 1979, pp. 14-18 'Dígaselo con votos'.
————— no. 38, 28 Mar. 1979, pp. 26-9, 'Atlas Electoral'.
————— no. 408, 20 Sept. 1979, pp. 16-25, 'El divorcio que viene'.
————— no. 413, 4 Nov. 1979, pp. 15-55, 'Porque abortamos'.
Capel, R. Ma. (1975), 'El Sufragio femenino en la segunda república espanola', University of Granada, Granada.
Chao, R. (1976), 'Después de Franco', Espana, Ediciones Felmar, Madrid.
Diaz del Moral, J. (1967), 'Historia de las agitaciones campesinas andaluzas', Edit. Alianza, Madrid.
Diplomatic Information Office, Spain 79, no. 69, Year VII, Madrid.
'The Economist' (3 November, 1979), All the Spains: A Survey.
Francos Rodriguez, J. (1920), 'La Mujer y la política espanolas', Editorial Pueyo, Madrid.
Fundacion FOESSA (1976), 'Estudios sociológicos sobre la situación social de Espana 1975', Euramerica, Madrid.

Gaceta de Madrid, Boletin Oficial del Estado (29 December 1978),
no. 311.1, 'Constitución Espanola'.
Juglar, A. (1971), Ideologías y clases en la España Contemporánea,
(1874-1931), 'Cuadernos para el dialogo', Madrid.
Kaplan, T. E. (1971), Spanish Anarchism and Women's Liberation,
'Journal of Contemporary History', 1, no. 2, pp. 101-10.
Laffitte, M. (1964), 'La Mujer ne España: cien años de su historia,
1860-1960', Aguilar, Madrid.
Maravall, J. M. (1968), 'Trabajo y Conlicto Social', Edicusa,
Madrid.
Maravall, J. M. (1970a), Aspectos del empleo femenino en Espana,
in 'Revista española de la opinión pública', vol. 19, pp. 105-23.
Maravall, J. M. (1970b), 'El Desarollo económico y la clase obrera',
Ariel, Madrid.
Maravall, J. M. (1978), 'Dictatorship and Political Dissent', Tav-
istock, London.
Martinez Cuadrado, M. (1969), 'Elecciones y partidos políticos de
Espana', Taurus, Madrid.
Migeul, Amando de (1975), 'El Miedo a la igualdad', Grijalbo,
Barcelona.
Nelken, M. (1975), 'La Condición social de la mujer en Espana',
Coleccion Ateneo, Madrid.
Payne, S. G. (1968), 'Franco's Spain', Routledge & Kegan Paul,
London.
Payne, S. G. (1970), 'The Spanish Revolution', Weidenfeld &
Nicolson, London.
Scanlon, G. (1976), 'La Polémica feminista en la España contem-
poránea, (1868-74)', Siglo XXI de España, Madrid.
Sole-Tura, J. (1971), 'Introducción al régimen político espanol',
Ariel, Barcelona.
Tamames, R. (1970), 'Introducción a la economiá española',
Alianza, Madrid.
Thomas, J. (1977), 'The Spanish Civil War', Penguin.
'La Vanguardia' (1 June, 1979), 'Constitución de Partido Fem-
inista', no. 35.135.

8 WEST GERMANY

Jane Hall

HISTORICAL BACKGROUND

Although a women's movement emerged in Germany in the latter half of the nineteenth century it was for the most part divided and ineffective, and the granting of the vote to women was not the result of efforts by the women themselves but of the particular circumstances prevailing in Germany after the First World War.

The failure of the 1848 liberal revolution in Germany to break the domination of the traditional ruling classes and elites of Prussia led to the domination of militarist and authoritarian values in the German Empire from its inception in 1871. The attitudes of the leadership of the Second Reich were hostile to women's emancipation and it was not until 1901 that the first federal state, or Land, Baden, allowed women to study at university (1908 in Prussia), while entry to most professions was restricted or forbidden for women. The Imperial Civil Code (Bürgerliches Gesetzbuch) of 1900 reflected the prevailing ideology: husbands had the right of decision in all matters affecting the marriage and children, and the wife could work only 'in so far as this is compatible with her duties in marriage and the family' (Paragraph 1356). These and similar provisions remained in force in West Germany at least until the 1950s.

The Prussian 1851 Law of Association forbade women, along with the mentally ill, schoolchildren and apprentices, to join political parties or attend meetings where political subjects were discussed. Other Länder had similar laws and only in Hamburg, Bremen, Baden and Württemberg could women participate in political activity and express political opinions publicly. It was not until 1908 that the Imperial Law Association lifted this ban.

The women's movement that emerged in Germany thus developed in a hostile atmosphere and the risk before 1908 of being banned for discussing political matters resulted in a timidity in proposing anything more than moderate demands.(1) The liberal middle-class women's movement was characterized by two approaches: those who saw women's suffrage as the first step towards a greater influence of women in public life and so demanded its immediate introduction, and those who felt that the time was not yet ripe for such an extreme demand and that women first had to gain recognition in society through achievements in the social welfare spheres.

The second approach was adopted by the Bund Deutscher

Frauenvereine (the Federation of German Women's Associations) or BDF, established in 1894. Although the BDF passed a resolution in 1902 demanding female suffrage, its leadership later passed to more moderate and conservative elements who were supported by the many member-associations opposed to female suffrage. The first approach was represented by the Deutscher Verband für Frauenstimmrecht (German Union for Women's Suffrage), founded by radical liberals in 1902. However, differences over whether to demand universal suffrage, which even men did not have, or merely the property suffrage (which was employed in many sub-national elections) on the same terms as men, led to a split and by 1914 there were three suffrage associations, more concerned with their mutual hostility than with obtaining female suffrage.

The Social Democratic Party of Germany (SPD) was the first, and for many years the only, German party to demand equal rights for women and universal suffrage for both sexes. However, the BDF decided to refuse membership to social democratic women's organizations and the SPD rejected co-operation with the bourgeois women's movement so that, apart from co-operation between individual SPD members and radical liberal feminists, the two did not come together.

Women's suffrage only came when a revolutionary situation in Germany after the First World War led to the establishment of the ill-fated Weimar Republic. The provisional government, the Council of Peoples' Delegates, announced in its programme of 12 November 1918 that all men and women over twenty would have the vote in all elections. This took effect for the elections to the National Assembly in January 1919 and was incorporated into the Weimar Constitution. That Constitution also contained provisions stating that men and women had 'fundamentally' the same rights and that marriage rested on the equality of the sexes. But without corresponding changes to the Civil Code such provisions were meaningless.

The idea that politics was a sphere for women did not take firm root before the Nazi Third Reich reversed much of what little had been achieved. Women did not lose their right to vote but could no longer stand for election, and although this restriction was of limited significance in a totalitarian one-party state it reinforced the still prevailing view that politics was not for women. The Weimar Republic years could, therefore, be regarded almost as a deviation from the 'norm' as far as women's political participation was concerned and although a new start could be made in 1945 by both men and women, women were starting with a far greater handicap.

SOCIO-ECONOMIC ENVIRONMENT

The Federal Republic of Germany today has an advanced industrial economy and is among the world's leading trading and manufacturing nations. With a population of 61.3 million (32.1 million women and 29.2 million men),(2) it is a densely populated and urbanized country, although many rural areas exist. The two main religions are more evenly balanced than in pre-1945 Germany, with 40 per cent of the population Protestant and 44.6 per cent Catholic (1970). These proportions are not, however, evenly distributed; the northern Länder are mainly Protestant, Bavaria and the Saarland are mainly Catholic, while the remaining four Länder have more evenly balanced proportions.

The proportion of women in the labour force, at 37.3 per cent in 1978, was only slightly above that at the turn of the century. Forty-nine per cent of all women between the ages of 15 and 65 work, about one-third in part-time employment. The increase in the proportion of married women at work has been considerable: in 1950 they constituted 34.6 per cent of all women working, and in 1978 61 per cent. About 3 million women at work in 1978 had children under 15, with just under a million having children less than 6 years old.

Women in the labour force are more likely to be affected by unemployment and although women account for just over a third of the labour force they constitute over a half of those registered as unemployed. Despite Article 3 of the West German constitution, the Basic Law, providing for equality between men and women, and interpreted by court decisions to include equal pay for equal work, women earn between a quarter and a third less than men, with the average pay for skilled women in industry below that of the average unskilled male industrial pay. Women are spread over a narrower range of sectors than men and tend to predominate in areas such as the textile and clothing industry, retail trade, hairdressing, administrative and clerical work, social and welfare work, and as medical assistants and nurses.

In the teaching profession women constitute 63.8 per cent of primary school teachers, 36 per cent of grammar school teachers (1977), about 10-20 per cent of university teachers (the higher proportion in the lower-scale positions) and about 2 per cent of university professors (Wisniewski, 1979, p. 7) Although the proportion of women in the professions is rising, they are still in a minority and in the lower-level positions, constituting 12.2 per cent of judges (1979), 17 per cent of tenured civil servants (1978), and 2.3 per cent of top managers (Näser, 1978).

Despite equal educational opportunities, the proportion of women being educated decreases the higher the level of education. Girls now constitute 48.9 per cent of all grammar school pupils (1977) and 42.5 per cent of those obtaining the Abitur, the certificate required for university and college entrance (1978). 35.3 per cent of students in higher education are women (1978) although they are concentrated in certain subjects, particularly the humanities (56 per cent), and in teacher training colleges (67 per cent). Proportionately fewer women than men complete their course, for women account for 22.5 per cent of those obtaining first degree, 15.8 per cent of those obtaining their doctorate

and 50.4 per cent of those obtaining teacher qualifications (1977).
Although women have been traditionally less willing to join trade
unions than men, increasing numbers of women have joined a
union during the 1970s. In 1978 women accounted for 19.1 per
cent of members of trade unions affiliated to the Federation of
German Trade Unions, the Deutscher Gewerkschaftsbund, and
55.7 per cent of the 1978 membership increase. In the Deutsche
Angestellten-Gewerkschaft, the white-collar union, women constituted 37.4 per cent of members in 1979, and 99.4 per cent of
the 1979 membership increase. Women are underrepresented within the trade union hierarchies and on works' councils but their
representation is increasing steadily.

The level of marriage in West Germany has dropped steadily
from 9.4 marriages per thousand inhabitants in 1960 to 5.4 in
1978, while the number of divorces has risen from 9.2 per hundred thousand marriages in 1966 to 17.5 in 1976. The birthrate has
declined from its postwar peak of 17.7 births per thousand inhabitants in 1965 to 9.4 in 1978, one of the lowest birth rates in the
world. The number of deaths has, since 1972, been exceeding
that of births, a fact causing consternation among some politicians
who are convinced that measures should be adopted to reverse the
trend. One consequence of the declining birth rate has been the
decrease in average family size: of the 8.5 million families with
children under eighteen in 1978 16.7 per cent had three or more
children, a third had two children and 47.9 per cent had one
child.

PARTY AND ELECTORAL SYSTEMS

The establishment of a parliamentary democracy under the aegis
of the Western allies has stood the test of time and can no longer
be regarded as a 'fine weather' democracy unable to withstand
any substantial crisis. The position of President is primarily symbolic and the centre of the political stage has moved to the Chan-
cellor, elected by the Lower House, the Bundestag. He is responsible for the general policy guidelines of the government and
appoints the ministers (at present fifteen). In the federal system
each Land has its own parliament and the Upper House, the
Bundesrat, is composed of forty-five members delegated by the
Land governments.

The postwar party system in West Germany has displayed fewer
of the divisions characterizing the Weimar Republic. The parties
licensed by the allies in their zones represented the four main
strands of European ideological development: Communism, Social
Democracy, Liberalism, and Christian Democracy.

The Christian Democratic Union, CDU, which was established
after 1945 was intended to appeal not only to all social groups but
to both Catholic and Protestants, and thus emerged as the first
'catch all' party in West Germany. The party was established with
a commitment to 'Christian values', it supported the free market

economy and alliance with the West, and as a basically conservative force has displayed considerable hostility to Communism.
The Christian Social Union, CSU, is confined to Bavaria, where
the CDU does not organize or campaign. The CSU has its origins
in the separatist tendencies of Bavarian politics and the strong
identification of Bavaria with its own traditions and history. It
represents the right wing of Christian Democracy in West Germany, with stronger nationalist, anti-Communist and more traditionally conservative views than the CDU. The CDU and CSU
form a joint parliamentary group in the Bundestag and as the
main parties in government from 1949 to 1969 played a significant
role in determining the course of the new West German state.

The Social Democratic Party, SPD, re-established itself after
its years of exile and developed a programme based on the planned
economy, support for the nationalization of production, and
opposition to the incorporation of West Germany into the Western
alliance. However, the CDU's success forced the SPD to widen
its basis of support with its 1959 Godesberg Programme, which
facilitated identification with the pluralist society of West Germany,
after which the SPD emerged as a moderate, reformist party.

The Liberal Party, FDP, was heir to both the right- and left-
wing Liberals of the Weimar Republic. In the early years the
national, more conservative wing dominated, supported particularly by Protestants among the old middle class. The FDP was
in several government coalitions with the CDU/CSU but during its
period of opposition at the time of the Grand Coalition CDU/CSU
and SPD government, 1966-69, its left Liberals came to predominance, enabling the FDP to enter into a coalition with the SPD
in 1969.

The Communist Party of Germany, KPD, was already a weak
force before the anti-Communism of the Adenauer era led it to be
banned in 1956. A new Communist party, the DKP, was established in the late 1960s, but it has been unable to obtain even 1
per cent of the votes at Bundestag elections.

After the decline of several smaller parties during the 1950s
the only significant movement in the party system of the 1960s
was the rise and fall of the right-wing NPD. In the late 1970s
some new parties emerged, notably the various environmental
groups which have formed into 'The Greens'. In October 1979 a
Women's Party, the Frauenpartei, was established. This party,
open to both men and women, is demanding the equality of women
in all areas of life, the end of role clichés for both men and
women, and the establishment of a more humane society for all
people, and intends in the long run to participate in Land and
Bundestag elections.

The electoral system used for Bundestag elections is that of
'personalized proportional representation'. Half of the 496 Bundestag seats (excluding the twenty-two Berlin MPs who are not
directly elected) represent constituencies and the other half is
filled from the party Land lists, so that the final number of seats
obtained by each party reflects its proportion of votes. Each

voter has two votes, one for the constituency, won by simple majority, and the second for the Land list, this second vote determining the proportional representation of each party in the Bundestag. There are no by-elections; a vacant seat is allocated to the next name on the relevant Land list of the party concerned. Parties obtain Bundestag representation only if they obtain 5 per cent of the total second vote or three constituency seats.

Constituency candidates are selected by the local party organizations. The vested interests of each local group play an important role in selection in addition to such criteria as previous parliamentary experience of the candidate (especially prestige gained as an existing Bundestag MP), party work and positions held, ability to attract as many voters as possible, contacts with local interest groups and with party groupings, qualifications and career. The party lists are composed at Land level and reflect the regional party organizations within the Land as well as interest groups both inside and outside the party. The Land lists allow the parties to include a particular expertise or interest group representation not included among the constituency candidates, and criteria such as age, sex, education, profession, region are also considered. However, there is an increasing tendency to secure the constituency candidates on the Land list first regardless of these criteria. Competition for selection has increased considerably in recent elections, in the constituencies incumbent candidates for re-election more frequently encounter competition rather than being re-selected unopposed, and more intense lobbying for the list positions takes place.

There is no financial restriction on election campaign expenses. Each party with at least 0.5 per cent of the second vote is entitled to 3.50 DM from the state for each vote received. In addition, the parties rely on their own funds and outside contributions. The election campaigns are professionally organized, with public relations and advertising firms being hired by the parties to run their campaigns.

OTHER RELEVANT FACTORS

Despite the modernization of West German structures since 1945 the historical background of conservatism and reaction continued to manifest itself in various ways. In the case of women, traditional views survived and official policy adopted the ideal of housewife at home with the three Ks of Kinder, Küche and Kirche. Although the West German Basic Law of 1949 contained the statement that men and women have equal rights and that no one may be prejudiced on the basis of sex (Article 3), included only after consistent lobbying on the part of women representatives (Vogelheim, pp. 446-67), little was achieved to realize this provision. In 1969 the comment could be made that 'so far as women's advancement is concerned, West Germany presents the picture....of a country stumbling backwards out of tradition into a pattern of

modernization of which it has no very clear conception and to
which it adapts only half-heartedly and under the pressure of
events' (Sommerkorn, et al., 1970, p. 2). The traditional socialization of women into a role of submissive and inferior housewife
and mother in the private sphere is still part of the dominant
culture in West Germany.

Attitudes are changing towards the role of women, but slowly,
and more slowly than in other countries. For example, in 1965
72 per cent of men and 68 per cent of women felt that it was 'not
normal' for married women to be employed, and in 1976 42 per
cent of men and 35 per cent of women expressed this view
(Claessens et al., 1979, pp. 409-10). A survey undertaken for
the Ministry of Youth, 'Family and Health' ascertained that the
majority of married couples adopted the traditional division of
labour, with the wife responsible for the home and family and the
husband for the public sphere, and that 88 per cent of women and
92 per cent of men were satisfied with this division of labour.
Seventy per cent of husbands and 69 per cent of wives felt that
one of the main tasks of the wife was to look after the family,
even where the wife had an outside job, with the result that 72
per cent of working wives and 16 per cent of husbands spent
their evenings doing housework, and only 5 per cent of working
wives, compared to 18 per cent of husbands, went out in the
evenings (see Burkhardt and Meulemann, 1976). West German men
are less likely to take over household jobs than their British
counterparts, and German women are less likely to expect this
than British women, as European Community Surveys have
shown.(3)

This 'double burden' for German married women who also have
a job is a barrier to their participation in public life, particularly
as the prevailing culture has not been conducive to women in
public life. Thirty-five per cent of married men would not agree
with their wives becoming politically active (von Meibom, 1980,
p. 7), and within the EEC West German men come after those only
of Ireland and Luxembourg in expressing more confidence in a
man MP - 56 per cent in 1977. West German men are second only
to Luxembourg men in agreeing that politics should be left to men
- 51 per cent in 1975, and West Germany and Luxembourg have
the lowest proportion of men who agreed that men and women
should play the same role in politics - 47 per cent in 1977.(4)

These attitudes are complemented by the relative lack of interest and activity of German women in politics. In 1952 11 per cent
of women and 46 per cent of men replied that they were interested
in politics, and in 1977 33 per cent of women and 66 per cent of
men replied thus.(5) Opinion polls show that women are less prepared to join a party than men, show less interest in election
campaigns than men and are less well informed than men. Although
the proportion of women showing an interest and becoming active

in politics is increasing and a greater acceptance of women in politics is evident, it cannot be denied that the prevailing climate of opinion was for many years opposed to this.

WOMEN AS PARTY PARTICIPANTS

After the war when political activity was re-established many Germans, and particularly women, turned away from all political activity after their experiences in the Third Reich. Information on the numbers of women party members in these early years is not always obtainable and not necessarily consistent. However, it appears that the proportion of women party members declined from the mid-1950s to the late 1960s, and increased steadily from the late 1960s onwards.

THE CHRISTIAN DEMOCRATIC UNION OF GERMANY (CDU)

The figures available for the early years show a decline in the proportion of women members in the 1950s and 1960s, followed by a steady increase not only in the proportion but also in the actual numbers of women members (Table 8.1). There are wide regional variations within the CDU, which has a higher proportion of women members in the industrial and urban areas than in the more agricultural and thinly populated regions.

Table 8.1   CDU members by sex and year

Year	Men	%	Women	%
1957				17
1962	212,453	85.5	36,031	14.5
1964	242,651	86.7	37,119	13.3
1966	242,865	86.5	37,916	13.5
1968	249,406	87.0	37,135	13.0
1970	284,425	86.4	44,816	13.6
1972	357,950	84.6	65,018	15.4
1974	437,355	82.4	93,145	17.6
1976	523,234	80.2	128,776	19.8
1978	536,381	79.4	138,905	20.6
1979	540,531	79.2	142,250	20.8

Source: Fülles (1969), p. 25; Philipp (1972), p. 21; and Frauenvereinigung der CDU

Women are under-represented in the CDU hierarchy in relation to their membership proportion. A provision that women should be 'adequately' represented on all party organs was removed from the CDU Statute at the 1967 Party Congress and since then women have had to be voted on to party organs in their own right.

Since 1967 a woman has always been elected as one of the (in 1980 seven) deputy chairpersons of the Federal party and in addition two women were elected as ordinary members on to the Federal Executive Committee in 1979, so that this committee has three women members representing 9.4 per cent of the total. The proportion of women on the executive committees of the regional associations (Landesverbände) ranged from 4.2 per cent to 16.7 per cent in 1979, with an average of 9.9 per cent. There were eight women deputy chairpersons at this level but no women chairpersons. At the next level down, the district (Kreisverband), the number of women chairpersons doubled from three in 1973 to six in 1977, or from 0.9 per cent to 2.3 per cent of the total. The proportion of women selected as delegates to the Federal Party Congresses rose slowly, from 8.1 per cent in 1971, to 9 per cent in 1978, but then increased to 12.0 per cent in 1979.

THE CHRISTIAN SOCIAL UNION IN BAVARIA (CSU)

The CSU is active only in Bavaria, much of which is predominantly Catholic, agricultural and rural. Information on women members is not available for the early years, but the number and proportion of women members have increased throughout the 1970s (Table 8.2).

Table 8.2   CSU members by sex and year

Year	Men	%	Women	%
1964	80,267	86.3	12,821	13.7
1974	109,992	89.5	12,880	10.5
1976	129,028	88.1	17,405	11.9
1978 (June)	142,648	87.4	20,592	12.6
1979	147,245	87.0	22,002	13.0

Source: A. Mintzel (1977), 'Geschichte der CSU. Ein Uberblick', Westdeutscher Verlag, Opladen, pp. 129 and 133; and CSU–Landesleitung

Although the proportion of women members is low compared with the other parties being examined, it corresponds to the proportions within the CDU in similar socio-economic regions. Also, unlike the CDU and SPD, the CSU women's organization accepts non-CSU members, so that additional women (8,786 in 1979) are closely associated with the CSU.

The CSU still has provisions in its Statute for the representation of women in the party hierarchy, namely one woman deputy Land chairperson and at least one woman on all executive committees. In addition, one woman must be included in every four persons elected as representatives and delegates to higher organs. Since 1974 three women have been represented on the Land Executive Committee, including a woman deputy chairperson, representing

7.0 per cent of the total. At the next two levels, the Bezirk and the Kreis, there are no women chairpersons although about one-third of the associations at these levels have women deputy chairpersons.

THE SOCIAL DEMOCRATIC PARTY OF GERMANY (SPD)

The number of women members in the SPD fell between 1947 and 1955, although as the number of men members fell more rapidly the proportion of women members was higher in 1955 than in any postwar year until 1974. During the 1970s, however, both the number and the proportion of women members rose steadily (Table 8.3). Variations in the proportions occur between the regions, with higher proportions in the urban areas.

Table 8.3   SPD members by sex and year

Year	Men	%	Women	%
1948			159,479	19.2
1951			121,986	18.7
1955			114,347	19.5
1958	503,708	80.7	120,108	19.3
1962	527,306	81.6	119,278	18.4
1966	602,308	82.7	125,582	17.3
1970	677,186	82.6	143,016	17.4
1972	775,882	81.3	178,512	18.7
1974	770,462	80.5	186,791	19.5
1976	772,472	79.0	205,465	21.0
1978 (July)	777,848	78.0	219,110	22.0
1979 (March)	771,664	77.6	222,171	22.4

Source: Fülles (1969), p. 25; Philipp (1972), p. 37; and Frauenreferat, SPD-Parteivorstand.

Until 1971 the SPD Statute included provisions for the representation of women in the party, including at least four women on the Federal Executive Committee. The effect of removing these provisions was seen immediately on the Federal Executive Committee, which from 1948 onwards had always had more than the minimum number of women, either five or six. In 1971 the number fell to two. It rose to three in 1975 and fell back to two in 1977. Concern within the party about the representation of women led to the decision to increase the number of seats by four and to vote an additional four women onto the Committee. A slate of 6 women was proposed at the 1979 Party Congress, 5 of whom obtained seats, and in addition another 2 women proposed by other groupings within the SPD were elected, thus bringing the total number of women to 7, or 17.5 per cent of the total, a considerable increase over the previous 5.6 per cent.

The proportion of women on the regional executive committees (Bezirke and Landesverbände) varies from 5.9 per cent to 21.6 per cent with an average of 12.9 per cent. Three women are deputy chairpersons but there are no women chairpersons at this level. Although the proportion of women chairpersons at the lower levels of the party (Unterbezirk, Kreis and Ort) is gradually increasing, it is still low, ranging from 2.5 per cent to just over 4 per cent, depending on the level. The proportion of women delegates to Federal Party Congresses was 5.3 per cent in 1971 and 8.5 per cent in 1977 but rose to 14.0 per cent in 1979.

This increase at the 1979 Party Congress was one of the results of the SPD's concern over the continuing under-representation of women within the party. After the 1977 SPD Congress a working group, 'Equality of Women', was set up to examine the position of women in the party and its report of October 1978 made suggestions for aiding women to become more active in the party and for increasing the representation of women in party offices and as candidates for parliamentary elections. At the 1979 SPD Congress a resolution incorporating many of these suggestions was passed, but the extent to which they can be effected remains to be seen.

THE FREE DEMOCRATIC PARTY (FDP)

The FDP does not distinguish between men and women party members in its own statistics, which are all estimates made by the party itself. During the 1950s the proportion of women members was lower than in the SPD and CDU but has risen since then to equal them (Table 8.4).

Table 8.4   FDP members by sex and year

Year	Total	Men	%	Women	%
1956					10-15
1965				6,500	7-8
1971	ca 60,000			ca 8,400	14.0
1974	68,000			12,220	18.0
1977	79,174	61,756	78.0	17,418	22.0
1979	ca 81,000				ca 23.0

Source: Bremme, 1956, p. 194; Fülles, 1969, p. 25; 'Frauen in der Bundesrepublik Deutschland', 1974, p. 21; 'Handbuch Frauen', 1978, p. 114; and FDP-Bundesgeschäftsstelle.

A protective statutory clause ensuring the representation of women on the Federal Executive Committee was removed as early as 1954. Since 1977 the FDP has had a woman as one of its deputy chairpersons and three women were elected as ordinary members

of the Federal Executive Committee in 1978, bringing the number
of women to four, or 10.8 per cent of the total.

At the Land level the proportion of women on the executive
committees ranged from 6.7 per cent to 35.7 per cent in 1978,
with an average of 12.1 per cent. The FDP had a woman chairperson at this level, Helga Schuchardt, from 1975 to 1980. At the
levels of Bezirk, Kreis and Ort the proportion of women chairpersons ranges from 2.5 per cent to nearly 8.0 per cent depending on the level. The proportion of women delegates to the 1979
Federal Party Congress was 9.75 per cent. Although women continue to be under-represented within the FDP hierarchy in relation
to their membership, they have made good progress particularly
at the lower levels in increasing their representation among office-
holders.

The FDP is the only party of the four being surveyed that does
not have a women's organization. It dissolved its women's organization during the 1950s and has integrated women within the
main party.

The CDU women's organization was founded in 1948 and since
1956 has been known as the Frauenvereinigung der CDU, or FV
(Women's Association of the CDU). All CDU women members are
also automatically members of the FV without paying an additional
subscription. This contrasts with other CDU associations which
have their own membership and a separate membership subscription. The aims of the FV are to represent the concerns of women
in the party, encourage the participation of women in party work
and support the representation of women on party organs and as
parliamentary representatives.

Since 1972 the FV has pursued a systematic policy of recom-
mending women as potential parliamentary candidates at the
relevant level of the party organization.

The CSU's women's organization was set up in 1947 and since
1968 has been known as the Frauen-Union der CSU. Both members and non-members of the CSU can join the Frauen-Union
although non-members can hold office only at the lower levels.
The aims of the Frauen-Union are to represent the women's point
of view within the CSU, and to encourage women to be active
within the CSU.

Although the SPD established women's committees at the various
levels of the party, these had little organizational independence
and were appointed by the executive committee at the relevant
level. The 1971 Party Congress decided to set up additional interest groups within the party, one of which was to represent women
SPD members - the Arbeitsgemeinschaft Sozialdemokratischer
Frauen or ASF (Working Group of Social Democratic Women). A
more democratic organization was thus set up, with women able to
vote for their own officials.

All women SPD members are automatically members of the ASF
and pay no additional subscription. The aims of the ASF are to
represent the views of women members to the main party, to develop policies and programmes on issues of especial concern to

women, to help engage women in political activity and political responsibility, and to encourage women to stand for election to party posts and parliamentary candidatures.

The ASF has been closely involved in the SPD's concern to open up greater opportunities for women and provided half the members of the working group 'Equality of Women'. Dissatisfaction had been increasingly expressed by SPD women members, and disappointment at the bad placings of women on electoral lists led to threats by women to split from the main party.(6) This implies that the ASF has not had the influence within the SPD expected by many SPD women, and although the ASF is no different here from the other women's organizations, SPD women have been more vocal in expressing their dissatisfaction.

Responses given in interviews and questionnaires of women party members (7) revealed that the attitude of many women towards the women's organizations is ambivalent; many feel that they are necessary to help involve women in party politics in a more helpful and sympathetic atmosphere, others feel that they hive women off into a ghetto away from the activities of the main party. On one hand, the women's organizations can provide support and solidarity for women seeking party office and parliamentary seats. On the other hand, women find it harder to obtain support as representatives of other party groupings because many men feel that as women represent the women's organization, men should represent other groups, such as the youth. The women's organizations have not been able to obtain much increase in the parliamentary representation of women and they do run the risk of becoming an end in themselves. However, while politics is still dominated by men it is difficult to see how the women's organizations could play a more satisfactory role.

One of the most frequent complaints heard in recent years from women party members is the failure of the parties to select as many women as candidates for parliamentary elections as wanted by the women. A second complaint is that even when women are selected they are placed more disadvantageously on party lists than men so that a lower proportion of women than men is successful in obtaining a parliamentary seat.

Table 8.5   Women constituency candidates and MPs in the 1976 Bundestag election

Party	Candidates			MPs		
	Total	Women	%	Total	Women	%
CDU	204	12	5.9	94	2	2.1
CSU	44	0	0.0	40	0	0.0
SPD	248	12	4.8	114	5	4.4
FDP	248	23	9.3	0	—	—

Source: 'Die Wahlebewerber für die Wahl zum 8. Deutschen Bundestag'; and Amtliches Handbuch des Deutschen Bundestages, 8. Wahlperiode.

Although an equal number of Bundestag MPs represent constituencies as enter via the Land lists the number of women MPs
winning a constituency seat is very low, dropping from twelve in
1949 (when 60 per cent of MPs represented constituencies, and
not 50 per cent as in later elections) to four (all SPD) in 1972,
compared with twenty-three women MPs who entered via the lists
in 1972. In 1976 the number of women constituency MPs rose to
seven (Table 8.5) compared to twenty-eight women list MPs (Table
8.6). One of the reasons for this low number of women constituency MPs is that few women obtain selection as a constituency
candidate, and the majority of those who do, do so in 'unwinnable'
constituencies.

Table 8.6   Women Land list candidates and MPs in the 1976 Bundestag elections

| Party | Candidates | | | MPs | | |
	Total	Women	%	Total	Women	%
CDU	545	76	13.9	96	13	13.5
CSU	73	7	9.6	13	2	15.4
SPD	629	64	10.2	100	9	9.0
FDP	333	34	10.2	39	4	10.3

Source: 'Die Wahlebewerber für die Wahl zum 8. Deutschen Bundestag'; and Amtliches
   Handbuch des Deutschen Bundestages, 8. Wahlperiode.

However, the fact that parties have increasingly favoured constituency candidates for good list positions means that selection
even for a hopeless constituency can be important for entering
the Bundestag as a list MP. Of the 35 non-Berlin women MPs
elected to the Bundestag in 1976 10 had a list position only,
whereas 18 of the 28 women list MPs had also been constituency
candidates.

The proportion of women obtaining selection as list candidates
is higher than for the constituencies and close to the proportion
of women list MPs but does not compensate for the very low number of women entering from the constituencies (Table 8.6). The
Land party organizations vary in regard to their attitude towards
women candidates and their positioning on the list. Four of the
nine women SPD list MPs in 1976, for example, came from Baden-
Württemberg, thus accounting for 44 per cent of all women SPD
list MPs, although Baden-Württemberg itself contributed only 22
per cent of all SPD list MPs. This high proportion of women MPs
was achieved not by a high number of women candidates, five out
of forty-nine, but by a more favourable distribution of the women
on the list itself.

In 1976 the average age of women candidates ranged from 40.0
years (CSU) to 44.6 years (SPD), compared with 46.0 years (SPD)
to 49.6 years (CDU) in 1969. It is not always possible to ascertain
from the professions given by candidates the exact nature of their

job or qualifications but from the information available the majority
would be classified as new middle class, with very few from the
working or old middle classes or independents (Table 8.7). The
majority have had either a post-school training or higher education and are in white collar jobs. They are likely to have held
party positions, more usually as an ordinary committee member
than as an office-holder, although positions in the women's organizations at higher levels than in the party will probably have been
held. Many candidates have also had some parliamentary experience, usually at local council level. The majority of women candidates stand just once for Bundestag elections and the turnover of
women candidates is fairly high.

Table 8.7   Professions given by women candidates at the 1976 Bundestag election

Profession	CDU	CSU	SPD	FDP	Total
Housewife	27	1	12	9	49
Teaching, research	13	3	15	10	41
White collar employee	8	1	13	2	24
Medical professions	5	0	2	2	9
Journalism, publishing	1	0	6	1	8
Welfare, social professions	4	0	2	0	6
Legal professions	2	0	1	3	6
Secretary	1	1	4	0	6
Tenured civil servant (Beamtin)	4	0	0	0	4
Independent	2	0	0	2	4
Political party/Interest group employee, politician	1	0	1	1	3
Student/trainee	2	0	0	0	2
Trade union employee	0	0	1	0	1
Diverse professions for which academic study is required	8	1	2	7	18
Other	0	0	5	0	5

Source: 'Die Wahlebewerber für die Wahl zum 8. Deutschen Bundestag'

PARTY ATTITUDES TO WOMEN'S ISSUES

Although no party in West Germany today would deny women the
vote or equal rights, differences of emphasis exist between the
parties as to the role of women in society. The CDU and CSU tend
to emphasize the role of women as housewife and mother who
should be given every chance to choose to stay at home, and
work only if she really wants to. The view that women cannot
find real fulfilment in a career, however successful, but only in
their 'natural abilities of creating life and looking after life', as
expressed by Bavarian CSU Minister for Labour and Social Affairs,
Fritz Pirkl ('Süddeutsche Zeitung', 5 November 1979) still prevails within the Union parties. The SPD tends towards the view
that women should be given all opportunities to work, and to stay

at home only if she really wants to. The FDP emphasizes the view that both partners should decide whether to work or stay at home and that this should be a personal decision, with no disadvantages ensuing for either sex whatever the decision taken. It is, however, worth noting that women from all parties tend to be more flexible on the role of women than party policies indicate and expressions of the view that either parent should be able to stay at home and look after children have been heard from the SPD and CDU as well as from the FDP.

The falling birthrate, coinciding with the period of SPD/FDP government, has led the CDU/CSU opposition to criticize the government for failing to remedy the decrease in births and even to have caused it by its emphasis on women at work. Whereas the SPD and the FDP want to ease the double burden of the working mother, the CDU and CSU regard any measure in this direction as discriminating against non-working mothers. A law of 1 July 1979 enabling women to take four months' leave with a payment of up to 750 DM per month and the right to their job back in addition to their fourteen weeks' maternity leave was criticized by the CDU and CSU for discriminating against housewives who could not receive such a payment. In response, one CDU-governed Land, Baden-Württemberg, introduced from 1 September 1979 a payment of 2,000 DM to all non-working mothers on the birth of a child.

Strong differences have existed between the parties over the abortion law reform which was passed in July 1974 by the SPD and FDP but which was prevented from coming into effect when CDU and CSU Land governments and the CDU/CSU Bundestag party group took the law to the Constitutional Court. The Court ruled, in February 1975, against abortion on demand in the first three months of pregnancy, and in February 1976 a law was passed under which women have to fulfil specific medical, genetic, criminal or social criteria before being allowed an abortion. The reform is still the subject of dispute and is opposed particularly by the Catholic Church. An attempt to bring the subject into the 1980 election campaign was made when the chairperson of the CSU health policy group, Hartwig Holzgartner, compared abortion to the Nazi killing of the Jews and when the chairperson of the German Bishops' Conference, Cardinal Höffner, also referred to abortion as murder. Such statements have been a matter of embarrassment for the Union parties and, indeed, the chairperson of the Frauen-Union, Ursula Krone-Appuhn, publicly criticized Höffner and stated that the law would be retained if a CDU/CSU government came to power in 1980 ('Süddeutsche Zeitung', 5 October 1979).

Theoretically, all parties support the concept of equal pay for equal work and oppose discrimination on the basis of sex even where this is not covered by the constitution, as in private contracts. The influence of employers has, however, led the CDU and CSU in the Bundesrat to attempt to weaken a government proposal to legislate on equal pay according to European Community guidelines ('Spiegel', 18 February 1980, p. 26). This influence has also resulted in an unsuccessful attempt by the FDP to weaken the same proposal so that the 'burden of proof' in equal pay cases would have lain with the women and not, as originally foreseen, with the employer ('Spiegel', 2 June 1980, p. 44). The SPD, under the initiative of Annemarie Renger set up a project 'Benachteiligung von Frauen im Erwerbsleben' ('Discrimination of women at work') which has supported women taking cases of unequal pay to court. The FDP has been the most forthright in demanding an anti-discrimination law to cover constitutional loopholes, and both FDP General Secretary, Günter Verheugen, and FDP Minister of the Interior, Gerhart Baum, have been among the few men who have publicly supported such a law.

WOMEN IN ELECTORAL OFFICE

Table 8.8   Percentage of women councillors in West German towns

Size of town	1 Jan. 1973	4 May 1975	1 Jan. 1977	1 Oct. 1979
1 million and over			11.8	14.0
500,000–1 million	12.3	13.2	13.8	14.7
200,000–500,000	11.6	12.2	12.7	14.7
100,000–200,000	10.7	12.1	12.4	14.5
50,000–100,000	9.1	10.1	11.0	12.0
30,000–50,000		8.3	9.3	
20,000–50,000	6.9	—	—	10.3
Total	8.3	10.0	10.8	11.4

Source: 1973 and 1975 — 'Parlamentarierinnen in deutschen Parlamenten 1919-1976', p. 75; 1977 and 1979 — 'Der Städtetag', NF 30(10), 1977, p. 67, and 33(1) 1980, p. 59.

The highest proportion of women in electoral office is at local council level where 11.4 per cent of all councillors in West German towns with at least 20,000 inhabitants in 1979 were women, with the highest proportions in towns of 100,000 to one million inhabitants (Table 8.8). The trend throughout the 1970s has been upwards and particularly in those Länder where the voter can vote for individual candidates on the list. The one council with over 30 per cent women (Heidelberg with 32.5 per cent) is in Baden-Württemberg and the seven councils with at least 25 per cent women are either in Baden-Württemberg or Bavaria ('Der Städtetag', 33 (1980), pp. 59ff).

At the Land level the proportion of women Landtag deputies is just over 8 per cent and has increased only slightly over past averages. The city states of Hamburg and Bremen are the only two Länder where the proportion of women deputies has been consistently at least 10 per cent since the early 1950s.

In the other Länder slight increases in the proportion of women deputies have occurred at the most recent elections but only Rhineland-Palatinate has achieved 10 per cent of women deputies. The proportion of women in the Bundestag increased throughout the first three legislative sessions, declined during the following four sessions and then rose again in the eighth session (Table 8.9). More women have been MPs at the end of most sessions than at the beginning because women have frequently been placed on the Land lists in positions where they just miss entering the Bundestag on election day but replace a serving MP in their party and Land who resigns or dies during a session. Nevertheless the proportion of women Bundestag MPs is below that at both Land and local level.

Table 8.9   Women MPs in the Bundestag

Year	Total	Women voted in on election day	%	Women at end of session	%
1949	410	28	6.8	38 (total = 421)	9.0
1953	509	45	8.8	52	10.7
1957	519	48	9.2	49	9.4
1961	521	43	8.3	49	9.2
1965	518	36	6.9	41	7.9
1969	518	34	6.6	32	6.2
1972	518	30	5.8	36	6.9
1976	518	38	7.3	41	7.9

Source: 'Parlamentarierinnen in deutschen Parlamenten 1919-1976', p. 5 and Bundestag handbooks.

Traditionally the SPD has had the highest proportion of women in electoral office although this is no longer true at national level. At local council level 12.8 per cent of SPD local councillors in 1979 were women, compared with 11.4 per cent of FDP councillors and 10.5 per cent of CDU/CSU councillors. The SPD had the highest proportion of Landtag deputies in the 1950s and 1960s but was overtaken by the FDP for much of the 1970s, while the CSU continues to have the lowest proportion (Table 8.10). In the first six sessions of the Bundestag the SPD had the highest proportion of women MPs but has since dropped to third place behind the FDP and the CDU, while the CSU is in fourth place (Table 8.11). The FDP has the highest proportion at national level, although the small numbers involved can create a distorted picture. The Union parties have tended to return lower proportions of women than the other parties although this is no longer true of the CDU at national level.

In the early Bundestag sessions a distinction could be noted between the backgrounds of women MPs according to a party, but this is no longer true. MPs, both men and women, come from various backgrounds, regardless of party, and they themselves are

Table 8.10   Percentage of women Landtag deputies according to party and legislative period

Year of election	CDU	CSU	SPD	FDP
1946-48	5.2	2.9	9.8	9.0
1949-52	6.2	1.6	9.3	8.3
1953-56	6.0	2.1	9.6	5.8
1957-60	6.8	3.0	9.2	9.1
1961-65	6.0	4.6	9.3	7.3
1966-69	6.7	2.7	7.9	7.6
1970-73	6.2	6.5	6.9	9.7
1974-77	6.3	6.1	7.4	12.0
1978-Mar. 1980	6.8	5.4	10.0	6.3

Source: 1946-65 — Fülles (1969), p. 85; 1966-80 — Landtag handbooks and Land statistical offices

Table 8.11   Percentage of women Bundestag MPs at the beginning of each legislative session according to party (including Berlin MPs)

Year	CDU	CSU	SPD	FDP
1949	8.5	4.2	9.6	0.0
1953	8.1	5.8	13.0	5.7
1957	8.6	5.5	12.2	7.0
1961	7.5	6.0	10.3	6.0
1965	5.9	6.1	8.8	4.0
1969	6.0	4.1	7.6	6.5
1972	7.5	2.1	5.4	4.8
1976	8.5	3.8	6.7	10.0

Source: Bundestag handbooks

increasingly members of the educated new middle class. Thirty-four of the forty-two women (8) MPs in the eighth Bundestag session had obtained the Abitur and undertaken further study and the remaining seven had all had access either to training or to apprenticeships.

Of the forty-two women MPs from the eighth Bundestag session eleven worked in the area of teaching, lecturing and research, eight were housewives, six worked for the public service, three came from party political work, three were engaged in welfare or social work, two had legal professions and two were independent. The remaining seven had diverse occupations, most of which had required an academic training. In contrast to men Bundestag MPs a lower proportion of the women have studied law and fewer are from the private sector of industry and its interest groups.

In earlier Bundestag sessions over half the women MPs were single, divorced or widowed but by the eighth session over half the women MPs were married - in contrast, however, with the men

MPs, of whom about 90 per cent are married. Of the thirty women MPs who were married, divorced or widowed, six had no children and the remaining twenty-four averaged 2.5 children, including two with six children each (one SPD and one CDU). Thus, the traditional view of women in politics as unmarried or childless is no longer true.

The Bundestag has a number of standing committees to deal with legislation on which all MPs, except important office-holders, serve. In the early Bundestag sessions women tended to be concentrated on a few committees, partly because of the previous experience of many women in the social, welfare and educational areas, but also because of the unwillingness of their male colleagues to make way for them on what were considered the more prestigious and influential committees. Women now not only have qualifications in other areas they are also not so willing to be pushed into these traditionally 'female' areas and, as a result, they are distributed over a far wider range of committees.

Women were also chairpersons and deputy chairpersons of committees most frequently in the social and welfare areas, with the petitions committee being the only one that has always had a woman chairperson. It was not until the seventh Bundestag session that a committee outside these areas was chaired by a woman, when Liselotte Funcke (FDP) became chairperson of the important finance committee, a post that she held until her resignation in November 1979, when she was replaced by another woman, Ingrid Matthäus (FDP). Women became deputy chairpersons of committees outside the welfare and social areas from 1961 onwards and in the eighth session women were deputy chairpersons of three out of nineteen committees, namely foreign affairs (SPD), legal matters (SPD), and youth, family affairs and public health (CDU/CSU).

The Bundestag elite includes the positions of Bundestag President and Deputy President, posts which were held exclusively by men in the early sessions. In the fifth session (1965) the CDU/CSU nominated Maria Probst as a Deputy President, and in the sixth session (1969) Liselotte Funcke (FDP) was nominated a Deputy President, a position she held until November 1979 when she was replaced by a man. After the 1972 election the SPD became the largest party group in the Bundestag for the first time, and by convention thus had the right to nominate the Bundestag President. As the proportion of women MPs in 1972 was lower than ever before it was decided to make a 'gesture' and nominate a woman. Annemarie Renger proved that she was more than a 'token' woman and as Bundestag President contributed much towards acceptance of the view that women can achieve high office and towards arousing in women an interest in politics. In the eighth session she became a Deputy President.

It was not until 1961 that a woman became a federal minister when consistent lobbying by CDU/CSU women MPs led Adenauer to create a new ministry and appoint Elisabeth Schwarzhaupt Minister for Health, a position she held until 1966. In the Grand Coalition government two women became ministers, one (CDU/CSU)

as Minister for Health and one (SPD) as Minister for Family and
Youth. In 1969 the two ministries were merged into the Ministry
of Youth, Family and Health and a woman has always been appointed as Minister. In 1976 Marie Schlei refused this 'token' women's
ministry, which was then given to Antje Huber, and Marie Schlei
became Minister for Economic Cooperation, the first time that a
woman obtained a federal ministry outside the traditional 'women's'
area. However, the appointment was premature in that wide areas
of society were unwilling to accept a woman in such a post, and
after a particularly hostile campaign from the media Marie Schlei
was forced to resign in February 1978.

There have been few women ministers in Land governments and
if at all, then in the family, health, education or social areas.
However, in 1975 the SPD/FDP government in North Rhine Westphalia included Inge Donepp (SPD) as Minister for Federal Affairs
and in 1978 she became Minister of Justice there. In 1978 the CDU
government in Lower Saxony included Birgit Breuel as Minister
for Economic Affairs and a few months later the SPD/FDP government in Hesse included Vera Rüdiger (SPD) as Minister for Federal Affairs. After government reshuffles in November 1979
Liselotte Funcke (FDP) became Economics Minister in North Rhine
Westphalia until May 1980, and Eva Leithäuser (SPD) became Senator for Justice in Hamburg. After the 1980 election in Baden-
Württemberg Annemarie Griesinger (CDU), previously Minister for
Social Affairs, became Minister for Federal Affairs. There are no
women ministers in Bavaria, Bremen and Schleswig-Holstein, and
in the remaining three Länder women ministers are responsible for
social, health or education areas.

Women MPs indicated during interviews that most feel that they
are treated as equal partners by their male colleagues, that the
prejudices against women are at the lower levels of political activity. Having finally passed all the hurdles on the way to the
Bundestag they find fewer disadvantages and even some advantages in being a woman MP. Because there are so few women MPs
they stand out, are remembered more easily and can occasionally
progress more quickly than men. On the other hand, women MPs
find it harder than men to be accepted as experts in their own
field and to gain support for an opinion and are often assumed
not to be striving for higher office. Also, they are often expected
by their male colleagues to be informed on issues concerning
women and the family in addition to their own specialist areas of
work.

WOMEN AND VOTING

Since the first elections in 1919 a lower proportion of women than
men have voted although the gap has narrowed with every election.
The greatest differences in the proportions of men and women
voting are to be found in the older age cohorts, for example, in
1924 the difference in the proportions of men and women over 70

voting was 20.6 per cent, in 1953 it was 14.6 per cent and in 1976 5.2 per cent. In certain of the younger age cohorts a higher proportion of women than men now vote, in 1972 this was so for women aged 21-35 and in 1976 for women aged 25-40. Taken overall, the difference between the proportions of men and women voting has narrowed from 6.5 per cent in 1953 to 0.8 per cent in 1976, when 90.8 per cent of men and 90.0 per cent of women voted.(9)

Voting participation figures in the Federal Republic of Germany are based on representative electoral statistics obtained by selecting specific voting areas for random samples. In these areas voting cards are coded for sex and age group and as 2.8 per cent of those voting are 'surveyed' a high degree of accuracy is achieved. Only sex and age group are included in order that the vote may be secret, other factors such as marital status, religion and educational level are excluded. Postal votes are also excluded.

Although a higher proportion of women than men vote for the CDU or CSU the gap has been closing, and the fact that many women switched from the CDU/CSU to SPD in 1972 was a major factor in the final election result. The proportion dropped in the 1976 election but did not fall back to the 1969 levels and the proportions of men and women voting for each party were close (see Table 8.12). Studies have shown that women and men of the same age groups and educational and social background are more likely to vote in the same way than members of the same sex from different age groups and educational and social backgrounds, and that although differences in voting behaviour still exist between the sexes these are of less significance than other factors.

Table 8.12   Voting behaviour of men and women at the 1953 and 1976 Bundestag elections

Party	1953 Men	1953 Women	% difference	1976 Men	1976 Women	% difference
SPD	32.5	27.6	−4.9	43.6	43.1	−0.5
FDP	11.7	10.4	−1.3	8.1	7.6	−0.5
CDU	38.9	47.2	+8.3	36.8	38.0	+1.2
CSU				10.4	10.8	+0.4
Other	16.9	14.8	−2.1	1.2	0.5	−0.7

Source: 'Wirtschaft und Statistik', 1977, no. 1, p. 17, Table 5

The evidence available shows that the sex of a candidate does not alter basic voting intentions. The view that women do not vote for women is disproved by Cologne constituency statistics where voting is monitored according to sex and where the SPD and the CDU usually have a woman candidate in one of the constituencies. Women constituency candidates at the 1976 election fared as well as their party overall throughout the Federal Republic.

Women show less interest in election campaigns and are less

prepared to become actively involved in them than men although
the numbers of women prepared to participate actively is increasing. Patterns of issue orientation are also different, and an
analysis of North Rhine Westphalia, whose population structure
closely parallels that of the Federal Republic, found that women
attach less importance than men to election campaign issues such
as foreign policy, economic policy, social policy, and intra-German
relations, and more importance than men to the following areas
only: measures against price increases, pollution, criminal activity,
and attainment of equal rights for women (Wilms, 1978, pp. 86-7).
This suggests that women are in general more concerned with
issues they see as closest to their everyday lives. However,
increasing numbers of women are recognizing that politics affects
them, that their environment and quality of life, their housing
and the education of their children are political issues and that
change can be effected only be engaging in party political activity.
The new women's movement has had an impact not only in the
party political area but also in women's attitudes to education,
career planning and trade unions. This has resulted in a turning-
away of some women from the established political parties, which
they see as part of the patriarchal structure, towards the protest
parties or 'apolitical' activity. This too has had an impact on the
established parties. Both the CDU and the SPD women's associations have arranged meetings with feminists in an attempt to find
common ground, and the fact that a survey has revealed that 38
per cent of women did not think that they and their concerns were
sufficiently represented by the Bundestag parties led D. Wilms, a
CDU MP, to urge her party to enter into a dialogue with the
younger women and to take their attitudes and views seriously
(Wilms, 1979, p. 11). Willy Brandt, too, warned the SPD that it
must not provide arguments for the Women's Party by nominating
only token women as candidates for the 1980 Bundestag election.
   Before the 1976 election a campaign 'Vote for Women' was
launched by the Deutscher Frauenrat (German Women's Council)
and the mass circulation young women's magazine 'Brigitte'. A
campaign for the 1980 election was launched in 1979 with the slogan
'More women in the parliaments'.
   Little of this would have happened without the increase in awareness and change in attitudes of the 1970s. The fact that there are
more women voters than men, that women can decide the election
result, and that women are increasingly aware of their influence
has caused the parties to ensure that they are at least seen to be
promoting women's interests, even if only by using women politicians 'as fig-leaves to cover up the patriarchal structure' of the
parties, as one woman CDU MP expressed it in an interview with
the author in 1978.

CONCLUSIONS

A survey of the West German political scene reveals that women play a very subordinate role in the decision-making organs of the political process. West German politics is populated by men; women appear as isolated individuals with little influence and, lacking the presence of other women, able to effect changes only with the support of their male colleagues.

The parties are democratic institutions in that the majority decision is adhered to, and so while the numerical inferiority of women in the parties exists no woman can be voted into office or selected as a candidate without the votes of men. This numerical inferiority thus has an effect through all levels of the parties up to the top where women do not have the support they need because of the minority position of women throughout the lower levels.

In all three major national parties, SPD, CDU and FDP, the proportion of women members is between 20 and 25 per cent and, thus, there is no significant difference in terms of women's membership.

The decrease in the significance of sex as a variable in voting participation and behaviour has led some observers to the conclusion that women no longer constitute a particular target group for the parties and that the idea of women as a target group is a relic from the days of discrimination against women (see, for example, Rühle and Garding, 1980). However, although sex may have lost its significance as a variable in voting, women are in general far less interested in politics than men, are less prepared to be politically active, and are far from achieving equality of opportunity in most areas of life. Many women are unlikely to be attracted by politics and political issues while this area is still regarded mainly as a matter for men and to suggest, as Rühle and Garding do, that specific institutions for women are no longer necessary in the age of equality is to ignore the difficulties still encountered by many women in participating in male-dominated structures and institutions.

Rising participation rate of women in the political parties will doubtlessly continue, for women form a higher proportion of new members joining the parties than their proportion of existing members. However, the problems facing women who wish to be politically active have not disappeared, particularly the double burden of women and the unwillingness of many men to share the running of the household, even when their wives are in paid employment outside the home.

Although the parties are male-oriented, run for and according to a masculine life-style and measuring the achievements of the individual according to male standards, the increase in the awareness of women during the 1970s has had some impact. This awareness, and the knowledge that women can decide the election result, has meant that the parties can no longer ignore the interests of women and their demand for greater political representation. The

strong criticism that the SPD faced in the late 1970s from its
women members and its attempt at remedial action is indicative of
the change that is underway.

However, an important point at issue is the extent to which men
are prepared to give up rights and privileges that they have until
now considered to be theirs. Although men pay 'lip-service' to
the idea of more women office-holders and candidates they do not
wish to be personally affected. A higher number of women as
constituency candidates, for example is supported by men MPs,
'but not in my constituency'. Also, the fact that the SPD decided
to create an additional four Federal Executive Committee members
in order to accommodate more women is indicative of this unwillingness, present not only in the SPD, to concede existing positions held by men to women.

Thus, despite the many fine words expressed by party leaders
supporting a higher number of women office-holders, candidates
and MPs, the proportion of women holding office will increase only
very slowly. Although it is unlikely that the proportion of women
Bundestag MPs will fall again to the 1972 level, the increased com-
petitiveness and aggressiveness of the candidate selection process
will probably ensure that the existing proportion will increase by
very little at each election.

Possible solutions to the problem of women's underrepresentation
could involve giving women candidates on the Land lists more
favourable positions, and a 'quota' of one woman for every five
positions instead of one for every ten positions, which is the unofficial 'quota' often used at present. Such a change would
require the constant lobbying and solidarity of existing women
members. But the long-term solution can only come from an increase in the proportion of women party members. While women
members are in a numerical inferiority they can effect only a little
change, and it is significant that the influx of women joining political parties during the 1970s has already begun to have an impact on the internal running of the parties and the atmosphere in
which party business is handled. Parties reflect society, but the
under-representation of women in the political parties has also
been a contributory factor in the slowness of West German society
to realize the constitutional provision for equality of the sexes.

NOTES

* I wish to express my gratitude to the German Academic Exchange
  Service (DAAD) for their grant enabling me to undertake research in Bonn, to all the women members of the Bundestag and
  political parties who gave so much of their time in answering my
  questions, and to the Bundestag library and the parties for
  responding to my numerous requests for information.
1 For fuller details on the bourgeois and socialist women's movements in Germany see: R. J. Evans (1976 and 1977); C. Koepcke
  (1979); S. Miller (1978a and 1978b); and W. Thönnessen (1973).

2 The statistics in this section are from the 'Statistisches Jahrbuch 1979 für die Bundesrepublik Deutschland', Kohlhammer,
Stuttgart, unless otnerwise stated.

3 E.g. 'European Men and Women in 1978. A Comparison of Their
Attitudes to Some of the Problems Facing Society', (1979),
Brussels, Commission of the European Communities, especially
p. 112.

4 Ibid., p. 160; and 'Men and Women of Europe: Comparative
Attitudes to a Number of Problems of Our Society' (1975), Commission of the European Communities, pp. 104 and 109.

5 'Information für die Frau' (1976), no. 1, p. 18; and 'Allens-
bacher Jahrbuch der Demoskopie 1976-1977', ed. E. Noelle-
Neumann (1977), Fritz Molden, Vienna, p. 63.

6 As happened after the disadvantageous positions obtained by
SPD women on the list for the Hesse Landtag election in 1978.
Reinhard Voss, SPD-Frauen küdigen Zerreissprobe an, 'Frank-
furter Rundschau', 10 March 1978.

7 Questions on general opinions about women in politics and the
political parties as well as on the personal political career of the
respondent were sent in 1978 to as many women candidates for
the CDU, CSU, FDP and SPD in the 1976 Bundestag election,
and former women MPs of these parties, as it was possible to
trace. Similar questions were asked during interviews with
many of the women who were Bundestag MPs in the summer of
1978 (14 CDU/CSU, 12 SPD and 4 FDP women MPs were interviewed). Responses given in the questionnaires and interviews
provide the source for the personal experiences and attitudes
and some of the personal data referred to in this chapter.

8 Forty-two women and not 41 as in Table 8.7 because after 1976,
when 38 women were elected, 4 women took up vacant seats and
1 woman resigned, so that a total of 42 women were MPs in the
eighth session.

9 Bremme (1976), p. 41; and Wilfried Linke (1977), Wählerver-
halten nach Geschlect und Alter bei der Bundestagswahl 1976,
'Wirtschaft und Statistik', no. 1, p. 16, Table 4.

BIBLIOGRAPHY

Berger, L., von Bothmer, L. and Schuchardt, H. (1976), 'Frauen
ins Parlament? Von den Schwierigkeiten, gleichberechtigt zu
sein', Rowohlt, Reinbek.
Brandt, W., ed. (1978), 'Frauen heute. Jahrhundertthema Gleich-
berechtigung', Europäische Verlagsanstalt, Cologne.
Bremme, G. (1976), 'Die politische Rolle der Frau in Deutschland.
Eine Untersuchung über den Einfluss der Frauen bei Wahlen
und ihre Teilnahme in Partei und Parlament', Vandenhoeck und
Ruprecht, Göttingen.
Bruer, L. (1975), 'Frauenhandbuch', Frauen-Verlag, Koblenz,
2nd ed.
Burkhardt, W. and Meulemann, H., (1976), 'Die "Rolle des Mannes"

und ihr Einfluss auf die Wahlmöglichkeiten der Frau', Kohl-
hammer, Stuttgart.
Claessens, D., Klönne, A. and Tschoepe, A. (1979), 'Sozialkunde
der Bundesrepublik Deutschland', Diederichs, Düsseldorf, 9th
ed.
Däubler-Gmelin, H. (1977), 'Frauenarbeitslosigkeit oder Reserve
zurück and den Herd!', Rowohlt, Reinbek.
Deutscher Bundestag, Pubd. (1953-76), 'Amtliches Handbuch des
Deutschen Bundestages. 2. (-8.) Wahlperiode', Neue Darm-
städter Verlagsanstalt, Darmstadt/Rheinbreitbach.
Erst gemeutert, dann gesiegt, 'Briggite', 3 May 1978, pp. 203-7.
Evans, R. J. (1976), 'The Feminist Movement in Germany 1894-
1933', Sage, London.
Evans, R. J. (1977), 'The Feminists. Women's Emancipation Move-
ments in Europe, America and Australasia 1894-1920', Croom
Helm, London.
'Frau und Gesellschaft. Zwischenbericht der Enquete-Kommission,
Deutscher Bundestag' (1977), Kohlhammer, Stuttgart.
'Frauen in der Bundesrepublik Deutschland. Ihre Situation. Ihre
Möglichkeiten. Ihre Rechte. Ihre Bemühungen' (1974), Bundes-
ministerium für Jugend, Familie und Gesundheit, Bonn.
Fülles, M. (1969), 'Frauen in Partei und Parlament', Wissenschaft
und Politik, Cologne.
'Handbuch Frauen' (1978), Presse- und Informationsamt der
Bundesregierung, Bonn.
Heinz, M. (1971), 'Politisches Bewusstsein der Frauen. Eine
Sekundäranalyse empirischer Materialien', Wilhelm Gilldmann,
Munich.
Hellwig, R. (1975), 'Frauen verändern die Politik. Eine gesell-
schafts-politische Streitschrift', Bonn Aktuell, Stuttgart.
Herve, F. (1976), Frauen und Bundestagswahlen, 'Marxistische
Blätter', 14, no. 4, 5-9.
Herve, F. (1978), Frauen und Politik, 'Blätter für deutsche und
internationale Politik', 23, 489-99.
Jochimsen, L. (1978), 'Sozialismus als Männersache oder Kennen
Sie "Bebel Frau"?' Rowohlt, Reinbek.
Koepcke, C. (1979), 'Frauenbewegung. Zwischen den Jahren
1800 und 2000', Glock und Lutz, Heroldsberg.
Kunkel, K. (1973), '"Politik ist Sache des Mannes."' Wie Arbeit-
erinnen über Ihre Arbeit, den Unternehmer und die Wirtschaft
denken. Darstellung und Interpretation einer psychologischen
Untersuchung', Informedia, Cologne.
Kutsch, M. (1979), 'Die Frau im Berufsleben. Der Weg der Chan-
cengleichheit am Arbeitsplatz', Herder, Freiburg im Breisgau.
Laurien, H-R. (1976), Die Union und die Frauen, in 'Union alter-
nativ', ed. G. Mayer-Vorfelder and H. Zuber, Seewald, Stuttgart, pp. 440-53.
Liepelt, K. and Riemenschnitter, H. (1973), Wider die These vom
besonderen Wahlverhalten der Frau, 'Politische Vierteljahres-
schrift', 14, 567-605.
Mabry, H. (1974), 'Unkraut ins Parlament. Die Bedeutung

weiblicher parlamentarischer Arbeit für die Emanzipation der
Frau', Ernst Vögel, Munich, 2nd ed.
Männle, U. (1976), Weibchen oder Feigenblatt - die Frau in der
Politik, in 'Für eine humane Gesellschaft', ed. M. Wissmann
and W. Schönbohm, Ullstein, Frankfurt am Main, pp. 94-100.
von Meibom, I. (1980), Mehr Frauen in die Parlamente, 'Inform-
mation für die Frau', 29, no. 1, 6-7.
Miller, S. (1978a), Frauenfrage und Sexismus in der deutschen
Sozialdemokratie, in 'Sozialismus in Theorie und Praxis. Fest-
schrift für Richard Löwenthal zum 70. Geburtstag am 15. April
1978', ed. H. Horn, A. Schwan and T. Weingartner, Walter de
Gryter, Berlin, pp. 542-71.
Miller, S. (1978b), Frauenrech is Menschenrecht. Zue Frauen-
programmatik der Sozialdemokratie von den Anfängen bis
Godesberg, in 'Frauen heute. Jahrhundertthema Gleichberech-
tigunt', ed. W. Brandt, Europäische Verlagsanstalt, Cologne,
pp. 52-72.
Näser, C. (1978), Selten, tüchtig, unterbezahlt. Frauen im Man-
agement, 'Die Zeit', 5 May.
'Parlamentarierinnen in deutschen Parlamenten 1919-1976', Wissen-
schaftliche Dienste, Deutscher Bundestag, Materialien No. 42,
1976.
Philipp, I. (1972), Frauen in den Parteien der BRD, unpublished
MA dissertation, University of Giessen.
Pross, H. (1973), Demokratie und Frauenemanzipation in der
Bundesrepublik, in H. Pross, 'Kapitalismus und Demokratie.
Studien über westdeutsche Sozialstrukturen', Athenäum, Frank-
furt am Main, pp. 68-81.
Riedel-Martiny, A. (1975), Genosse Hinderlich und die Frauen -
Die Situation Weiblicher Mitglieder in der SPD, 'Die Neue
Gesellschaft', 22, 731-4.
Rühle, H. and Garding, S. (1980), Wahlkämpfer müssen umdenken:
Es gibt keine 'Zielgruppe Frauen', 'Die Welt', 12 February.
Schlaeger, H. (1978), The West German Women's Movement, 'New
German Critique', no. 13, pp. 59-68.
Schlei, M. and Brück, D. (1976), 'Wege zur Selbstbestimmung.
Sozialpolitik als Mittel der Emanzipation', Europäische Verlag-
sanstalt, Cologne.
Schmid-Burgk, A., ed. (1978), 'Mut zur Offentlichkeit. Briefe
an junge Frauen', Herder, Freiburg im Breisgau.
Smith, G. (1979), 'Democracy in Western Germany. Parties and
Politics in the Federal Republic', Heinemann, London.
Sommerkorn, I., Nave-Herz, R. and Kulke, C. (1970), 'Women's
Careers: Experience from East and West Germany', PEP Broad-
sheet 521, London.
Stern, C., ed. (1976), 'Was haben die Partein für die Frauen
getan?', Rowohlt, Reinbek.
Strecker, G., revised by Lenz, M. (1975), 'Der Weg der Frau in
die Politik', Eichholz, Bonn, 3rd ed.
Thönnessen, W., trans. de Bres, J. (1973), 'The Emancipation
of Women. The Rise and Decline of the Women's Movement in

German Social Democracy 1863-1933', Pluto Press, London.
Vogelheim, E. (1979), Der Emanzipationsbefriff im Grundgesetz. Zur Entwicklung des Gleichberechtigungsgrundsatzes, 'Die Neue Gesellschaft', 26, 466-8.
Wilms, D. (1978), Die ältere Frau in der Politik, 'Zeitschrift für Gerontologie', 11, 80-9.
Wilms, D. (1979), Protest der jungen Frauen gegen politische Parteien?, 'Frau und Politik', 25, no. 4, 11.
Wisniewski, R. (1979), Frauen als Hochschullehrer, 'Frau und Politik', 25, no. 7, 7.
Witting, G. (1969), 'Rolle und Einfluss der Frauen in der Politik der Bundesrepublik', Gewerkschaft öffentliche Dienste, Transport und Verkehr, n.p.

9 ITALY

Maria Weber

HISTORICAL BACKGROUND

In Italy the women's struggle for the right to vote began later
than in other European countries. This was largely due to the
fact that the Italian national unification process left few openings
for movements other than the Risorgimento. 1848, a milestone year
in international feminism, was in Italy the year of the First War
of Independence. Only after unity was achieved did Italians begin
to speak of feminine suffrage, and then only in a negative way.
An 1861 bill specified that 'neither women nor people affected by
mental illness can have the right to vote'. A noblewoman, the
Countess of Belgioioso (quoted in Parca, 1976, pp. 50-1), who
had become prominent during the Risorgimento, wrote in 1866
that

> the woman, who remained for centuries without culture,
> responsibility in public and family affairs has not aimed
> at equality of rights . . . (if she now wants a new way)
> . . . she must have patience and abnegation and she has
> to be content to prepare the ground for it.

To Belgioioso's suggestion of patience, the middle-class Anna Maria
Mozzoni sharply replied, 'women will not have other rights than
those they will conquer' (Mozzoni, 1892, p.15). Mozzoni stood
alone in the struggle for women's emancipation. In 1870 she translated John Stuart Mill's work on the subject of women, adding a
passionate preface in which she invited politicians, priests, jurists
and free thinkers to meditate on the subject. The translation
caused heated debate amongst Italian intellectuals and even those
who appeared enlightened rebelled against the ideas it contained.
Gioberti, for example, believed female weakness to be such that
'the woman is in relation to the man what the vegetable is in
relation to the plant, she relies on and hangs from him'. (Quoted
in Parca, 1976, p.52.)

Meanwhile, the industrialisation process based on a large use of
female labour, particularly in the textile sector, was modifying the
traditional structure of the working class and bringing many women
into social and trade union struggles. Anna Kuliscioff acted as a
spokesperson and interpreter for those struggles. In 1897 she
made an impassioned appeal for votes for women, believing that
it was possible to use the ballot box, previously a means of oppression, as a means of emancipation. The socialist Anna Kuliscioff
and the illuminist Anna Maria Mozzoni were precursors of the two
main tendencies of the future women's movement: that which saw

work as a means to emancipation and the vote as a device for the
defence of working class rights; and that which considered the
vote as part of the struggle against society and the family. The
latter view held that the employed woman is doubly oppressed, by
the husband in the family and by the employer at work. The
dilemma posed by the juxtaposition of sex and class was resolved
by Kuliscioff in the classic style of European socialism, that is
that the needs of the revolution should take priority over the need
for women's emancipation. Mozzoni, on the other hand, was a more
articulate precursor of later feminist radicalism.

The ideas expounded by Mozzoni and Kuliscioff set off debate
amongst intellectuals at the end of the nineteenth century; but it
was only at the beginning of the twentieth century that newspapers
started to give space to the 'woman question'. It was at this time
that the first women's associations were born. The National Association for Woman was founded in Rome in 1897, the Feminine
National Union in Milan in 1899, and the National Council of Italian
Women in 1903. February 1906 saw the appearance of an article by
Maria Montessori in the 'Vita' (Life) review which invited women to
enter their names as candidates for the coming general elections
(as no bill prohibited it). A group of women students replied to
this appeal and produced a poster to which hundreds of women
responded. From this emerged the Committee for Feminine Suffrage.
Although the authorities did not accept women's inscription on
electoral lists, the ball had been set rolling at last and the women's
suffrage movement finally took off in Italy. Conferences and public
debates were organised by suffragists all over the country and
these obliged parliament and the parties to generate discussion on
the rights of women. In 1908, the National Council of Italian Women
met in Rome in the presence of Queen Helen. Aiming for compromise
rather than confrontation, the meeting expressed intentions to
educate women in their rights, arguing that such rights would
'help women to better carry out her duties as mother and as
educator' (Parca, 1976, p.75). In 1909 the Alliance for Suffrage
wrote a protest manifesto to the opening session of parliament in
which the rights and duties of women to deal with public matters
were affirmed. The following year at the Socialist Party Congress,
Anna Kuliscioff presented a motion on the importance of the vote
as a means of defending women's work. Meanwhile the Italian
parliament was busy debating a bill which aimed to extend the
right to vote to the illiterate, but not to women. And when Socialists called for a women's suffrage amendment, Prime Minister
Giolitti refused on the grounds that giving political rights to
women would have been a 'leap in the dark'. The bill awarding
political rights to illiterates but not to women was passed.

Nationwide organisation to agitate for woman's suffrage was
interrupted by the First World War and it was not until four years
later that a bill extending the right to vote to women came before
the Italian parliament. Its passage was prevented when D'Annunzio's
attack on Fiume (1919) precipitated the dissolution of parliament.
Further possibilities for women obtaining the vote were for over

twenty years in the control of the Fascists who came to power
following Mussolini's 1922 March on Rome.

FASCISM AND ITALIAN WOMEN

The achievement of female support was, for Benito Mussolini, one
of the bases of his conquest of power. In a troubled country faced
with economic crisis and recovering from a war which had cost half
a million dead and a similar number of wounded, Mussolini exalted
woman as heroine and transmitter of Italian greatness. Acting in a
role of spokesman for and protector and exalter of thousands of
widows and orphaned girls, Mussolini generated the so-called three
M charisma of Mussolini, Maschio, Marito - Mussolini, Male, Husband
(Maciocchi, 1976, p.58). In his initial programme the 'Duce' pro-
mised woman's suffrage and in 1923 he made a long ambiguous
speech at the IX Congress of the International Alliance for Suffrage
(quoted in Maciocchi, 1976, p.39), saying, amongst other things:
> I think that allowing women to vote, first in administrative
> and then in general election, will not have catastrophic
> consequences . . . but beneficial ones . . ., because in
> the exercise of these new rights the woman will introduce
> her fundamental qualities of moderation, common sense and
> wisdom . . . And now let me direct, on this occasion, my
> thoughts to the millions of mothers and wives who have
> suffered in silence and with dignity the sacrifices and sorrows
> of the Great War and that are not represented here and who
> have co-operated to preserve the rhythm of national life.

In June 1923 a bill was proposed which gave women the vote in
local, but not general elections. All women of the lower classes were
excluded and only seven categories of the remainder could vote:
(1) women holders of military decorations; (2) holders of civil
honours; (3) mothers of war dead; (4) widows of war dead; (5)
women recognised as head of a family; (6) women with primary school
leaving certificates, and (7) women who paid more than 40 lire in
annual taxes. These categories included a total of one million out
of a population of twelve million Italian women. In 1925 this proposal became law, and enabled some women to vote in local elections.
It was a supreme farce, coming from a regime which in 1926 introduced exceptional laws preventing Italians from voting at all. In
the following period, Fascist policy was directed at returning women
to their homes. Women were gradually excluded from paid employment, from the schools, and from the professions and were exhorted
to concentrate on producing babies by slogans such as 'Make babies,
make a lot of babies, large numbers means power!' (Ibid. p.55).

In 1927 women's wages were reduced to half those of men. A law was
introduced prohibiting women from teaching humanities in the high
schools; in 1933 women were excluded from employment in the civil
service except for such feminised grades as secretary, typist or
librarian. Part of Mussolini's war preparation involved the exaltation
of reproduction with slogans such as 'maternity represents for women

what war represents for men' and prizes were awarded to prolific
mothers. During the production of this misogynous propaganda,
Mussolini was supported by the Catholic Church and by the En-
cyclicals of Pius IX who, in exchange for the Lateran Pact Concordat,
hastened to produce the encyclical of 'Casti Connubi' (1930). This
document characterised marriage as the cradle of procreation. In
1931 whilst Fascism was excluding women from public life, Pius IX
produced the 'Quadragesimo Anno' encyclical in which he asserted
(quoted in Maciocchi, 1976, p.49):

    Mothers have to work at home . . ., the fact that they,
    owing to father's low salary, are obliged to work outside
    their home . . . represents an . . . element of disorder,
    which has to be removed by any means.

Between Fascism and Catholicism, Italian women spent many years
confined to the home and subjected to the Duce-husband. Women
had no rights and were oppressed both by the system of Fascism
and by the male head of household. Only after the suffering of the
Second World War and experience in the Resistance movement did
women finally, on 1 February 1945, acquire the right to vote. In
1946, after decades of delay, Italian women were able to exercise
the elementary voting rights which had been denied for nearly a
century. During the general election of 1946, 27 million Italians
voted of whom 52.2 per cent were women. Thus began the history
of formal political participation by Italian women.

THE ITALIAN REPUBLIC: PARTY SYSTEM AND POLITICAL SPECTRUM

The new Italian Republic faced severe socio-economic problems
ranging from economic reconstruction to industrialisation. These
were aggravated by both domestic and international political problems. Geographical location and the events of the world war brought
Italy under the political influence of the USA and its allies, with
immediate repercussions for Italian internal equilibrium. The twenty
years of Fascist rule had destroyed previously existing party structures. Only during the Resistance movement did the three main
tendencies of the Italian political system re-emerge. These Catholic,
Marxist and secular tendencies respectively formed the bases of a
Christian Democratic party, of Socialist and Communist parties, and
of various secular parties. The Christian Democrats (Democrazia
Cristiana, or DCs), previously the Popular Party of Don Sturzo,
were closely linked with the Catholic church and able to use church
organisation to obtain widespread support amongst various social
classes. The Socialists and Communists had had experience of pre-
Fascist organisation as the Italian Socialist Party (Partito Socialista
Italiano or PSI) and the Italian Communist Party (Partito Comunista
Italiano or PCI). Organised in 1921, the PCI was fiercely persecuted
by Mussolini and later played a decisive role in the Italian Resistance,
presenting itself to the Republican electorate as a representative of
the working class. Its influence became particularly strong in the

Northern and Central parts of post-war Italy. Secular tendencies
were represented by two minor parties: the Republican Party
(Partito Republicano Italiano or PRI) which had a long tradition
of opposing the Monarchy and the Liberal Party (Partito Liberale
Italiano or PLI) which was based on support from the northern
industrial middle class. In 1948, dissent within the PSI produced
the moderate socialist Social Democratic party (Partito Socialdemo-
cratico Italiano or PSDI). On the fringes of the political system
were what still remained of the Monarchists (Partito di Unità Mon-
archica or PDIUM) and of the Fascists, now called the Social Movement (Movimento Sociale Italiano or MSI). In addition, a number of
minor parties have come and gone from the extreme left of the
Italian political spectrum over the past thirty years.[1]

At national level Italy has a form of cabinet government led by a
Prime Minister chosen by the majority party or coalition in the
Chamber of Deputies. (There is also an indirectly-elected President
who is titular head of state.) No one party has ever achieved an
absolute majority, hence coalitions have been the rule since 1948.
The largest party, the DC's, have never been out of government, having formed coalitions with the Centre-Right through the
1950s and early 1960s, and the Centre-Left until the mid 1970s.
DC coalition partners have tended to be rewarded for these partner-
ships by steadily decreasing electoral support. This, combined with
gradual decline in DC electoral fortunes and a general increase of
those of the PCI, led in the late 1970s to a series of governments
based upon PCI abstention in the Chamber. This somewhat half-
hearted 'historic compromise' proved unsatisfactory to all involved
and in the spring of 1980 a Centre-Left coalition was formed, possibly also reflecting a strengthening of the PSI. Italian governments are habitually short-lived, with a turnover of more than one
per year between 1948 and 1979. The parliaments, which are
elected for five-year terms, have been rather more stable although
early elections were held in 1972, 1976 and again in 1979. The
apparent instability of the system is to some extent counterbalanced
by a highly centralized, if often inefficient and out-dated, system
of public administration. An intermediate level of regional governments provided for in the 1946 constitution came into operation
during the 1970s and this provides the PCI with the opportunity
to dispose of significant political power, particularly in the industrialised regions.

The system of elections is based on a highly complex law which
enables the rather large array of parties to achieve parliamentary
representation. The electoral mechanism for the Chamber of Deputies
or lower house, involves a list system of proportional representation
based on large constituencies. A modified form of proportional
representation is used for the less important Senate or upper house.
When choosing deputies the voter expresses both a party preference and within the party list, a candidate preference. The vote
for the party list takes precedence and must not be endangered
by intra-list battles for the highest number of preference votes.
Only about 30 per cent of the voters actually use the preference

vote (D'Amato, 1974, p.90). Very strong party loyalty and consistently high voter turnout helps maintain the fragmented character of the Italian party system. Thus, between 1948 and 1979 Italy
has had, on average, seven parties represented in parliament.
Italian multipartism is of a highly polarised type, perhaps best
described by Sartori as being a sort of 'polarised pluralism' (Sartori,
1976, pp.131-45). According to Sartori's typology the salient
characteristics of the Italian party system are a high level of
fragmentation and an ideological distance between the parties.
Other characteristic features are the presence of important anti-
system parties (the PCI and MSI), the existence of bilateral opposition, the centre placement of one party (the DCs), centrifugal
drive, some ideological (i.e. not pragmatic) patterning of politics,
and the presence of an irresponsible opposition (the PCI until
1975-6).
   In 1948 the DCs came very close to obtaining 50 per cent of the
vote but since then it has averaged less than 40 per cent, although
it has never been out of power. By contrast the PCI achieved
between 19 and 35 per cent of the vote over the same period(Table
9.1).
   Centrifugal trends in the post-war period are evident in the
electoral performance of the Italian parties. In 1948 the centre
coalition parties (DCs, Social Democrats, Republicans and Liberals)
obtained a total of 62 per cent of the vote; by 1953 their share
had dropped below the 50 per cent mark. The main beneficiaries
of these centrifugal forces, have been the more extreme parties,
Between 1946 and 1972 the PCI's share of the vote rose steadily
from 19 to 27 per cent of the total. In 1971 the neo-Fascist MSI
nearly doubled its previous share of the vote, from 5 per cent to
almost 9 per cent. The 1976 elections apparently confirmed the
predictive power of the centrifugalism hypothesis. The PCI gained
six percentage points, leaping to an unprecedented peak of 34.4
per cent; the DCs dropped to 38.7 per cent and whilst the Liberals
almost disappeared (1.3 per cent), the neo-Fascist right retained
a respectable 6 per cent of the total vote. The logic of centrifugalism seemed irrefutable. But in the 1979 elections, the PCI dropped
back to 30 per cent, the DCs maintained their 38 per cent, the
MSI slipped to its 1960s share of 5 per cent whilst the Liberals
and Social Democrats both gained a little, thus reversing previous
trends of steadily losing votes to the larger parties. Fragmentation
of the Italian party spectrum has apparently taken place such that
in 1979 there were centripetal rather than centrifugal electoral
changes (Martinelli and Pasquino, 1978, passim). Furthermore the
irresponsible opposition itemised by Sartori as characteristic of
the PCI and the far Right has evaporated in the face of recent
PCI electoral policy changes. The only distinctive features of
'polarised pluralism' evident at the time of writing are the central
place of the DCs, some ideological patterning of politics, and the
presence of irresponsible opposition - but now with the PCI's former place usurped by small extreme Left organisations (the Radicals of Pannella) and the extreme Right (the MSI of Almirante).

The ideological distance between the parties is still apparent, but has been substantially reduced. [2]

Table 9.1   Electoral results 1946-79 in the lower chamber in percentages

Parties	1946	1948	1953	1958	1963	1968	1972	1976	1979
Communist (PCI)	18.9	} 31.0	22.6	22.7	25.3	26.9	27.2	34.4	30.4
Socialist (PSI)	20.7		12.7	14.2	13.8		9.6	9.6	9.8
Social Democrat						14.5			
(PSDI)	–	7.1	4.5	4.5	6.1		5.1	3.4	3.8
Republican (PRI)	4.4	2.5	1.6	1.4	1.4	2.0	2.9	3.1	3.0
Christian									
Democrat (DC)	35.2	48.5	40.1	42.4	38.3	39.1	38.8	38.7	38.3
Liberal(PLI)	6.8	3.8	3.0	3.5	7.0	5.8	3.9	1.3	1.9
Monarchist									
(PDIUM)	2.8	2.8	6.9	4.8	1.8	1.3	–	–	0.6*
Neo-Fascist (MSI)	–	2.0	5.8	4.8	5.1	4.5	8.7	6.1	5.3
Others	11.2	2.3	2.8	1.7	1.2	5.9	3.8	3.4	6.9

*   New party called National Democracy (DN)
Source: Official Election Results (Ministero degli Interni)

Table 9.2   Distribution of votes for DC+PCI, the mass parties and the small parties in the lower chamber

Election	DC+PCI	Mass parties (DC+PCI+PSI)	Small parties
1948	79.5	79.5	20.5
1953	62.7	75.4	24.6
1958	65.1	79.3	20.7
1963	63.6	77.4	22.6
1968	66.0	80.5*	19.5
1972	66.0	75.6	24.4
1976	73.1	82.9	17.1
1979	68.7	78.5	21.5

*   Includes the PSDI which formed a common slate with the PSI known as PSU.
Source: Calculated from Official Election Results (Ministero degli Interni)

Within this spectrum one of the most telling influences on the form and content of women's political participation has, of course, been the role of the Catholic church. So central is organised Catholicism to the Italian political life that it requires examination in its own right.

THE CATHOLIC CHURCH AND THE DCs

In a country recently emerged from war and Fascist rule only one
organisation had an advantaged position in the socialisation of
the female electorate and its mobilisation in support of a particular
party. The organisation was the Catholic church, and the party
was the Christian Democrats. In countries with a strong and continuous Catholic tradion, the religious motivation of women voters
has often been decisive for the electoral victory of Catholic inspired
parties. In addition, post-war Italian political life was marked by
bitter struggle between Catholicism and Marxism, and the Catholic
hierarchy regularly intervened against the Communist Party, and
in support of the DCs during electoral campaigns (Dogan, 1955,
1968, 1969, 1971, passim). Church influence was obviously directed
at both sexes, but affected women's behaviour more as a result of
a complex series of historically and socially decisive motivations
(Magli, 1964, passim). The result was to incline women toward
opting out of politics, a consequence of which was that their
electoral decisions were easily influenced. Whilst full analysis of
the feminine condition in industrial and post-industrial society is
beyond the scope of this text (see Barbero Beerwald, 1976) there
are certain characteristics of that condition which are instructive
here. These include a history of domestic seclusion and ignorance
due to low or non-existent levels of education and exclusion from
the labour market. Such factors have not only led women to opt
out of politics but also have made them prey to closed belief systems
(Giannini Bellotti, 1973, passim). Thus it is hardly surprising that
Italian women in the 1950s and the 1960s were readily influenced
by a church which provided a strong ideological structure and was
often the only extra-familial point of reference (Dogan, 1971, passim).
    Both parish organisations and Catholic Action (Azione Cattolica
or AC) mobilised women's votes for the DCs (Manoukian, 1968
p.361). AC's role was decisive for DC electoral success. In 1946
AC had an enrollment of 151,000 men and 370,000 women (Table
9.3), and 90 per cent of the women members of the DCs were also
members of Catholic Action. DC origins were common amongst the
women who directed the Feminine Democratic Movement after the
Second World War. They were closely bound by the Church and
followed Pius XII's calls for women to enter the political sphere as
though it were a field of the 'apostolate' and 'Christian testimony'
(Menapace, 1974, p.54). The electoral success of the DCs in the
1958 general elections doubled the number of women members and
strengthened the mobilising capacity of Catholic Action. These
were the years of the Catholic's anti-Community crusades, years
of bishops' warnings, and of the excommunication of the Communist-
supporting Catholics. Women were the symbols of the war against
the Muscovite Bear, the bulwark of the defence of family and
religion. In the 1950s female attendance at religious services was
very high, with 80 per cent of women attending Mass 'often' as
opposed to 57 per cent of men. The influence of the clergy on
women's electoral behaviour was strengthened by devotion to the

church, and the connection between religious attendance and DC voting became a fact of Italian voting behaviour. Women's disproportionate (relative to men's) involvement in religious attendance remains true in the current period of declining Church attendance, although the fall-off in their participation has been rather more dramatic than that for men (Table 9.4). Women's regular attendance at Mass dropped from 80 per cent in 1956 to 37 per cent in 1973.

Table 9.3   Male and female membership of Catholic Action

Periods	Men	Women
1946	151,000	370,000
1953	272,000	570,000
1963	320,000	651,000
1969	183,000	459,000
1973	395,000*	

* In the 1970s AC and official data do not give the distinction between sexes;
Source: Weber (1977), p. 65

Table 9.4   Male and female participation in the Catholic church (in percentages)

Periods	Men		Women	
	every week	never	every week	never
1956	57	43	80	20
1961	45	55	51	49
1973	29	71	37	63
1975	25	75	35	65

Source: DOXA, 1961; 1973; 1976

By contrast, the other large party, the PCI, had no such far-reaching social base amongst women. The trade unions, which were the basis of Communist organisational efforts, were monopolised by men. In Italy more than in other countries, women were kept out of the productive process and their presence in the occupational world is still very patchy. The occupational segregation of women in Italy is of sufficient importance to merit examination before proceeding to an analysis of the connection between the female electorate and the Italian parties.

OCCUPATIONAL SEGREGATION AND GENDER

Official statistics on Italian women's employment indicate a fall in the proportion of employed women from 26 per cent of the total female population in 1936 to 20 per cent in 1951 to 18 per cent in 1971, followed by a slight increase, to 21 per cent in 1978. Official statistics therefore suggest that women's employment in Italy has not followed the same trend as that which is evident in other industrial societies (in which steady increases have led to a stable 30 per cent plus of women in paid employment outside the home). Between the 1950s and the 1970s the number of Italian women in the employed labour force declined by more than one million. This decline was due to the progressive exclusion of women from the industrial sector without an equivalent accompanying take-up by the service sector. The official statistical position is not a complete one, however. It is widely believed that the number of Italian women in paid employment has steadily increased and that this increase has taken place within the illicit, sweated, uninsured labour market which involves piece-work or day work carried out in the home. Some estimates put the numbers of women so-employed at more than four million (Weber, 1979, p.24). Women also comprise more than 80 per cent of other categories of home workers (Cutrufelli, 1977, p.76).

Occupational segregation on the basis of sex is also indicated by the concentration of women in less qualified jobs and in their departure from the official labour market after the birth of the first child. Women's exit from officially recorded paid employment during their first pregnancy is often a definitive one and is the basis of the 'dromedary curve' of female occupation (Padoa Schioppa, 1977, p.41; Zincone, 1978, p.73).

Thus women who have been expelled from the official labour market return to the unofficial one and represent 70 per cent of this second market, which involves an estimated total of more than 6 million Italians (Frei, 1975, passim). If we consider this 'underground' labour supply, then women's employment is about 30 per cent of the total and thus at much the same level as in other industrialised societies.

Similarly to other countries, the services sector has been the preferred place of female employment during the 1970s. Women have increased their presence there from 31 per cent to 35 per cent in 1975. In agriculture, women comprise 32 per cent of those economically active, but are confined to the tasks requiring low qualifications. In industry women comprise up to 22 per cent of the work force but are particularly concentrated in clerical and typist categories of employment. Only 5 per cent of women with degree level qualifications have a chance of employment at managerial level. Chance is the operative word here. The reality is that women are two out of every one thousand managers. Geographically 23 per cent of the female working class is concentrated in the rich, industrial north, 19 per cent in the centre and only 14 per cent in the poor agricultural south of Italy (Weber, 1978b, passim).

A widespread lack of professional qualifications and low levels of
education are direct causes of female concentration in the less well-
paid occupational grades. Of those women employed in industry, 60
per cent have a primary school diploma and only 6 per cent a high
school one (Zincone, 1978, p.68). In agriculture, 42 per cent of
women are illiterate and 58 per cent have only a primary school
diploma. Women's university matriculation has, however, shown
a great increase over the last thirty years. There were 38,208
women registered in 1951 (26 per cent of the total), 210,833 in 1971
(37 per cent of the total), and this rose to 40 per cent in 1978
(Weber, 1978b, p.75). Increased educational opportunity has yet
to lead to a high presence of women in the professions, however.
Only 9 per cent of doctors, 6 per cent of notaries, 10 per cent of
lawyers and 5 per cent of architects are women (Parca, 1976,
p.151). Inspection of the lower levels of every category of employment reveals a concentration of women in the non-specialised grades.
The segregation and under-qualification of women is exacerbated
by the domestic burden and the lack of mitigating social services.
Italian workers' absenteeism is, as a result, disproportionately
female. The non-justified absence level in industry was 13 per cent
overall, whilst the rate for women was 19 per cent (Weber, 1979,
p.25). It is apparently the obligations of domestic labour which
are responsible for women's absence from work for periods of
between an hour and a whole day. Children's illnesses and housework obligations are the most common justifications given. Household
responsibilities also account for women's non-availability for over-
time and for their lack of timetable mobility (Zincone, 1978, p.69).

Ironically, protective legislation has exacerbated the weak
position of Italian women and only since 1977 has there been equal
pay legislation. The equal pay law (Legge de Parita, 9 December
1977) repealed statutes banning women's participation in night
work and in heavy jobs and prohibits sex-discrimination in the
labour market. Its passage has been too recent for its benefits to
be assessed, and it will, in any case, not contribute to the
solution of the serious problem of women's exploitation in the
sweated, uninsured 'black economy'. 1974 statistical evidence
suggests that almost 10 per cent of those women officially recorded
as full-time housewives were in reality employed in this market
(ISTAT, 1975, passim). Frei puts the percentage as high as 15
(Frei, 1978, p.87). Whatever the exact figure, it is a fact that
the textile and shoe industries are major employers of women home
workers. These are often women who have been dismissed and
then re-engaged at half their former wages to perform their duties
at home. The Italian 'black economy' is a highly profitable growth
area in which wages are consistently inferior to published contract-
ual ones. It is women who monopolise this work (CENSIS, 1978).
A 1973 law (Legge sul Lavoro a Domicilio, 18 December 1973)
designed to control and protect home work has not been applied,
largely because of the complicity of those women who prefer an
underpaid job at home to a properly paid one in a factory.

The weak position of Italian women workers is underlined by the fact that Italy has the second highest level of female unemployment in Europe (12.6 per cent) (CEE, 1979): 47 per cent of those regist- ered on special first employment youth lists at employment agencies are women, and women were 56 per cent of the two million unem- ployed in 1978 (Weber, 1979, p.25).

A bill addressing this problem and guaranteeing part-time employ- ment for women and youth was proposed in 1980. Several related bills are before the Italian parliament at the time of writing and agreements between government and the trade unions suggest the possibility of the protection and regulation of previously unregulated part-time work. Despite the fact that there are only temporary advantages in part-time work, and that women's acceptance of it confirms their dual function and institutionalises attendant weak- nesses, part-time work is not without short-term advantages for women. Large numbers of housewives who express willingness to work outside their homes for up to half a day could be recruited into the workforce via part-time jobs. European occupational trends point to the increasing feminisation of part-time employment, and it is only in the long run that its disadvantages in terms of occupa- tional segregation and the inhibition of career advancement become evident (Weber, 1979, p.24). In Italy the sexist attitudes of employers and work colleagues combined with the weight of the cultural traditions of Italian Catholicism produce a sexually oppres- sive reality which is very difficult to combat by legal means. Female occupational segregation and its accompanying disadvantage depends to a large extent on this sexism and a substantial cultural change is necessary before any attempts at modification will be successful.

ITALIAN PARTIES AND THE FEMALE ELECTORATE

Having established the close relationship between the DCs, Catholic Action and the Roman Catholic church in Italy, we may now turn to the interaction between the masses of Italian women and the party structure. Discussion of women's membership is necessarily confined to the PCI and the DCs because the other parties provide only limited and partial membership information.

Table 9.5   Female membership of Communist Party (PCI) and Christian Democrats (DC) as a percentage of total membership in selected years

	PCI	DC
1959	25.9	34.5
1963	25.2	35.4
1967	23.9	35.9
1971	23.5	37.3
1975	23.5	37.5
1978	24.6	37.6

Source: Radi (1975), p. 26

Table 9.5 shows the higher proportionate membership in the DCs compared to the PCI. DC women constituted an average of 36 per cent of the membership between 1959 and 1978. This proportion increased from 35 per cent in 1959 to 38 per cent in 1978. In the PCI, on the other hand, women comprised an average of 24 per cent of the membership over the same period. This proportion declined steadily between 1959 and 1975, rising slightly only in 1978. Data on the occupational status composition of the DCs indicate a fall in working-class membership and amongst those employed in agriculture (Table 9.6). The data also show an increase in the proportions of clerical and service workers and a large presence of housewives, although this declined steadily between 1962 and 1975 (Poggi, 1968, p.422; Parisi, 1979, p.31).

Table 9.6   Membership of DC, by occupational status (percentage of total)

	1962	1968	1975
Farmers	12.0	11.1	9.0
Working class	17.0	15.0	13.0
Middle-class	11.7	12.0	13.3
Upper-class	3.0	4.1	5.8
Housewives	25.8	25.4	22.8
Others	30.5	32.4	36.1
Total	100.0	100.0	100.0

Source: Radi (1975), p. 26

Despite its avowed working-class constituency, the PCI has only a low membership of working women. Housewives comprise 50 per cent of women members of the PCI and 13 per cent of its total membership (Table 9.7). By comparison with the DCs who use Catholic women as a recruitment source, the PCI have been tardy in tackling the question of women's participation. Communist women, organised in separated cells, have been ignored since 1962 by a party apparently too busy dealing with political and trade union problems. A supporting organisation and source of PCI recruitment has been provided by the Union of Italian Women (UDI) which had about 400,000 members in the 1950s and, on average, 200,000 in the following decades. But the UDI plays only a subordinate role in PCI strategy and has only limited mobilisation capacity. The UDI has been a source of female leadership recruitment for the PCI, however. Amongst the Communist women deputies in 1976, only one had not been a member of the UDI (Weber, 1977, p.23).

Neither of the two main parties are remarkable for the presence of women in leading party roles, although the record of the PCI is rather better than that of the DCs.

Table 9.7 Membership of PCI by occupational status (percentage of total)

	1956	1963	1974
Farmers	35.0	26.0	21.0
Working-class	40.0	40.0	40.0
Middle-class	2.0	2.0	5.0
Housewives	4.0	13.0	12.0
Others	9.0	19.0	23.0
Total	100.0	100.0	100.0

Source: Ufficio Elettorale PCI (1975)

Women have comprised between 5 and 6 per cent of the members of the Central Committee and 'Direzione' of the PCI since 1946, but no women were members of these bodies between 1956 and 1962 (Guadagnini, 1980, p. 20). The proportions of women members of the provincial federal committees of the PCI have ranged between 10 and 13 per cent in the post-war period.

Whilst at least some relationship between the proportion of women members and leaders is discernible in the PCI, no such positive correlation is visible in the DCs. Despite comprising an average of 34 per cent of the membership, women were only 2 per cent of the DC leadership in 1976, and this represented a decline from 3.4 per cent in the 1946–63 period (Weber, 1977, pp. 26–7). Women have always been absent from the DCs' National Council of Direction. When leadership is defined as the total of a party's successful women candidates plus those women occupying party posts at the decision-making level, PCI but not DC women leaders appear to be on the increase (Table 9.8).

Table 9.8 Women in the leadership of the PCI and the DCs as a percentage of the total leadership

	PCI	DCs
1946-63 (average)	8.9	3.4
1972	7.7	2.3
1976	13.1	2.0

Source: Weber (1977), pp. 26-7

WOMEN IN ELECTED OFFICE

Trends of women's representation in the Chamber of Deputies show
a fairly steady decline between the 1948 and 1968 parliaments with
an upturn in 1972, a large increase in 1976 and a slight decline in
1979. Women formed 7.8 per cent of the deputies elected in 1948,
5.7 per cent in 1953, 4.1 per cent in 1958, 4.6 per cent in 1963,
2.8 per cent in 1968, 4.1 per cent in 1972, 8.5 per cent in 1976
and 8.2 per cent in 1979 (Guadagnini, 1980, p.21).

In the 1979 Chamber, women comprised 17.6 per cent of the PCI
deputies, 3.4 per cent of the DC deputies, 1.7 per cent of PSI
deputies; and 7.1 per cent, 3 per cent, 50 per cent (of 2) and
16.6 per cent respectively of PRI, MSI-DN, PR and DP deputies
(ibid.). A paucity of data prevents examination of the characteristics of women deputies from the Socialist and minor parties, but
examination of those from the PCI and DC parliamentary groups
reveals certain similarities. Guadagnini (ibid., pp.4-5), found
that over half of the women Communist deputies in 1979 came from
posts in the UDI and are either holding or have held posts in local
administration or at the lower levels of the party. Christian Democrat women deputies have backgrounds of holding office in the
Catholic associations or in the DC women's movement.

Through the 1950s and 1960s there was little alteration in the
structure or characteristics of women deputies as a whole (apart
from their declining numbers) and turnover amongst women was
lower than in the chamber as a whole. During the 1970s an influx
of women deputies was combined with an increased rate of turnover
(ibid.). For Guadagnini the most outstanding characteristic of the
new women deputies is the high proportion of professional politicians to be found amongst them, a feature more pronounced in the
PCI than in the DC; 52.7 per cent of the PCI and 44 per cent of
DC women deputies had held offices in local government at some
time before achieving national electoral success in 1979. In addition
66.6 per cent of the PCI women and 22.2 per cent of the DC women
had previously held or still hold office in their parties (ibid.,
p.24).

Women have held responsible positions within the parliament.
Nilde Jotte (PCI) was elected president of the Chamber of Deputies
in 1979 and Maria Martini (DC) was vice-president ('Women of
Europe', 1979, no. 10, p.19). However, the government which
took office in the spring of 1980 contained no women ministers and
only two of fifty-six under-secretaries of state were women ('Women
of Europe', 1980, no.14, p.19). An under-secretariat for women's
status established by Andreotti in 1978 to look into problems of
women's status was disbanded by Cossiga in 1979 and its duties
were assigned to newly created ad hoc committees in the Health,
Employment, Justice and Education Ministries ('Women of Europe',
1979, n.11, p.7).

Such data as are available on the proportions of women in local
government office suggest that local politics provide Italian women
with few more opportunities for exercising political leadership than

do national politics. Guadagnini (1980, p. 26) found that in 1977 women comprised 3. 8 per cent of Communali administratori, 3. 3 per cent of Assessori and 1. 5 per cent of mayors. There are about 695,000 women in the civil service (approximately one-third of the total) with the lowest proportion of women to be found in the legal administration. 236 of 6425 judges and 14 of 1,130 magistrates are women ('Women of Europe', 1978, n. 4, p. 8).

Italian government, in common with government everywhere, has always been in the hands of men and there is evidence to suggest that this corresponds to the wishes of Italian women. The available data indicate that up to 30 per cent of Italian women believe that 'Politics is a man's affair' and as many as 51 per cent are unwilling to take steps to modify the masculine domination of political life (PRAGMA, 1976). However, recent events have tended toward breaking down the traditional isolation of Italian women from the political arena. Although their long-term effect on political participation is difficult to assess, both the 1974 divorce referendum and the 1978 legislation on abortion apparently brought large numbers of Italian women into political activity.

DIVORCE, ABORTION AND FAMILY LAW

The 1929 Lateran Pact Concordat, which outlines the basis of Italian church-state relations remains in force in contemporary Italy. The Concordat delegated to the church the power to dissolve marriages through the institution of the annulment of the 'holy tie' under certain very restricted conditions. Since 1946 the DCs have been firm opponents of any proposal which would have led to state regulation of the dissolution of marriage, a position taken in order to avoid irritating the ecclesiastical hierarchy. Only in 1970 did parliament approve the divorce law (Legge sul Divorzio, 18 December 1973) which instituted civil divorce after a five-year separation. The reaction of the clergy was immediate: groups of Catholics, guided by their bishops and priests and supported by a large part of the DCs began campaigning for the abrogation of the new law via a referendum. Gabrio Lombardi chaired the mobilising committee which declared itself to be in battle against the break-up of the family. Another well-known leader (Fanfani) appealed for a 'union against divorce which could prevent the escape of Italian women from their homes' (Weber, 1977, p. 34). A period of activism lasted from early 1971 to 12 May 1974 – the date of the referendum. The most conservative Catholic forces led the campaign and attempted to inform the population about divorce. Survey evidence for the period indicates that before the antidivorce campaign only 12 per cent of Italians knew of the law's existence and understood its contents (Marradi, 1974, p. 592).

12 May 1974 is often taken as the starting date of a new era in Italian political culture. In the event, 59. 3 per cent of the voters declared against the abrogation of the divorce law. It was not repealed despite widespread church, DC, Monarchist and neo-

Fascist Right campaigning. For the first time large numbers of women electors were unwilling to obey blindly the exhortations of the clergy.

12 per cent of men and 13 per cent of women abstained from voting on the divorce referendum. 44 per cent of the women interviewed by DOXA (ibid., p.623) declared themselves to be in favour of the law. Research undertaken by the author on the results at polling stations situated in the maternity hospitals of several large urban areas (thus comprising an electorate of about 98 per cent women) gave very interesting results, if somewhat limited in their statistical usefulness (see below pp. 203-4). Between 70 and 80 per cent of this maternity hospital electorate were against abrogation (Table 9.9). Another surprising result was observed at a polling station in Ivrea at which a whole convent of nuns had voted. This station declared 54 per cent against the abrogation of the law, indicating that at least some of the nuns were demonstrating rather remarkable independence of mind (Weber, 1977, p.39). On the occasion of the divorce referendum Italian women often not prepared to follow their church and possibly indicated a new receptiveness to secular and rational influences.

Table 9.9   Referendum on divorce (1974): national results and female results, in maternity hospitals, as a percentage of the total electorate

	Percent for the abrogation of the law	Percent against the abrogation of the law
Italy (national results)	40.7	59.3
Maternity hospitals:		
in Bologna	19.3	80.7
in Florence	28.8	71.2
in Turin	15.8	84.2

Source: Weber (1977), p. 71

Equality of rights and duties for women in the family were recognised by the legislature on 23 April 1975 when the new family law (Legge sul Dirrito di Famiglia, 23 May 1975) was approved. This law, passed after a thirty-year delay, asserts the equality of spouses in marriage and in their responsibilities regarding their children's education. The woman's right to maintain her name and to add it to that of the husband is recognised (art. 143) although children of both sexes still take their father's name (Remiddi, 1976, p. 39). Women may now, for reasons of work, reside in a different locality to their husbands, and spouses share responsibility for decisions about their children except 'in cases of serious danger for the child, when the father can take urgent

steps that cannot be deferred' (arts. 135 and 136). Thus paternal
authority has been abolished for everyday problems but retained
in the case of extraordinary circumstances. 'Community of Property'
has been recognised, with goods owned jointly regardless of who
has been responsible for purchase. This is a double-edged weapon
as although it protects housewives from possible abuses of husband-
ly power and from desertion, it ties them to a family conceived of
as a place of production of goods and services (Zincone, 1978,
p.67). All in all the new family law is to the advantage of Italian
women though it clearly reflects the ambivalence of a legislature
still mainly comprised of men. The new family law and the law on
equal pay mentioned above provide a legal basis for an equality
between the sexes which has yet to come.

Also of prime importance to Italian women was the abortion law
(Legge sul Interruzione Volontaria della Gravidanza, 22 May 1978)
finally passed on 22 May 1978. This law aims to regulate what should
be an important personal choice made in complete liberty and which
is in fact prey to bureaucratic procedures and to social pressures
of all kinds. A clause allowing medical and health staff to opt out
on grounds of conscience means that the law has been widely
inapplicable in the public hospitals, and illegal abortions continue
to be carried out in Italy. The majority of doctors take advantage
of the conscience clause, thus the few hospitals performing abortions are overcrowded and have extensive waiting lists. A year
after the law was passed only a few thousand abortions had been
performed in public hospitals compared to an estimated three
million illegal abortions in 1970 (Foletti and Boesi, 1972, p.19).
The Italian law does not solve the problem of illegal terminations
of pregnancy although, ironically, it may have been in advance of
women's demands. DOXA found that 90 per cent of the women
surveyed in 1973 were against abortion on demand. The proportion
fell to 76 per cent in 1975 and to 23 per cent in 1978 (DOXA, 1978).
This dramatic shift in public attitudes bears witness to the effect
of widespread public discussion of a problem which had previously
been closely tied to the fear and therefore the silence of millions
of women.

It is lack of information and fear which remain the salient features
of the political attitudes of Italian women. Makno found that only
11 per cent of women said that they often read newspapers, 23
per cent read them occasionally (one a week), and 66 per cent
never read them (Makno, 1977). Apparently the main sources of
information for most Italian women are 'chats in the family and with
neighbours' and the television; 30 per cent of housewives do not
read the newspapers 'because there is the television', despite
evidence that only 18 per cent of housewife-viewers are able to
have a full understanding of the language used in television broad-
casts (ibid., 1977). This widespread lack of information must be
set against the paucity of women in active political and social
participation. Only 6 per cent of Italian women have ever taken
part in any form of political organisation; 24 per cent would like
to participate, but do not know what in particular to do; and more

than half believe that they would not like to be politically active.
The feminist movement which started more than ten years ago has
had little success in mobilising the mass of Italian women. It
numbers only a few thousand middle- and upper-middle-class
women, and is judged negatively by 70 per cent of Italian women
(Weber, 1977, pp.45-7).

THE ITALIAN WOMEN'S LIBERATION MOVEMENT

The first Italian feminist groups were formed following events
within the student movement in 1968. Since its birth Italian feminism
has reflected Liberal/Marxist divisions in the political culture. To
these have been added the radical inspiration of the United States
feminists. As early as 1966 the DEMAU (Demystification of Author-
itarianism) group carried out the first analysis of women's exclusion
from society (Spagnoletti, 1971, passim). But it was only between
1968 and 1970 that several women split from the student movement
and formed separate groups. In 1971 at Trento women formed the
first 'self-governing' separatist group. At the end of 1970 the
Rebellion (Rivolta) group, was formed. Rivolta rejected all ideological links as reflection of sexual hierarchy and it met in small
groups which discussed members' common experiences of oppression (Lonzi, 1970, 1971, passim). Following Rivolta's example, a
number of women's self-knowledge (auto-consciousness) groups
were created which all elaborated more or less sophisticated, Marxist
derived analyses of the condition of woman. Other groups produced
different theories which followed radical and liberal ideas. In 1970
the WLD (Woman's Liberation Movement) was founded in Rome.
Linked to the Radical Party the WLD had an American inspiration
and was characterised by its interest in the abortion question. It
collected signatures and applied political pressure for a liberalisation of abortion legislation. In fact, it was from the organisation
of clinics for illegal abortion with good standards of care and low
prices, followed by the arrest of WLD and Radical leaders that the
campaign for abortion rights began. This campaign eventually led
to the 1978 law. In Padua during the same period the Feminine
Struggle Movement (Lotta Femminile) later Feminist Struggle (Lotta
Femminista) was organised. Its members held that conventional
work must be eschewed as it was 'by participating in the revolutionary fight and not in capitalist production that women will conquer
the right to be human beings' (Frabotta, 1973, p.177). They also
opposed demands for wages for housework (Dalla Costa, 1975, 1977,
passim). That debate caused disputes inside the women's movement
which led to the first clear splits. Until 1973, apart from some
minor ideological disagreements, Italian feminists were able to present
a united front. That unity broke down when the revolutionary
proposals of Lotta Femminista were presented. Many groups declared
that they were opposed to these goals and produced alternative
proposals. The WLD, for example, demanded the introduction of 50
per cent women's quotas for available jobs (Zincone, 1978, pp.77-87).

Work, seen as either a means of oppression or of emancipation was
the central dividing issue of the feminist debate.
   Even the abortion issue could not generate complete unity. The
feminist group of Cherubini Street in Milan declared opposition to
the abortion campaign on the grounds that it did not tackle the
question of a different sexuality, and served only to institutional-
ise the traditional masculine one ('Sottosopra', 1975). Thus self-
help, followed by self-knowledge, followed by self-analysis,
switched the attention of the women's movement from the external
sphere to the internal one of small groups. Paradoxically it was the
women's movement itself which urged women to refuse to participate in politics, contending that the 'personal' was a sufficiently
political sphere and accepting implicitly that politics was a matter
for men. Although radical and other politically active women,
particularly those on the left of the political spectrum were trying
to intervene via bills, petitions etc., the rest of the movement
dropped out of the political arena.
   Rape is another issue which has generated activism amongst
Italian feminists. Here again, unity has been elusive and groups
are divided over support for a UDI proposed bill designed to
increase the success of rape prosecutions and which would allow
the victim to remain anonymous. Disagreement is over whether
legislative solution is possible or whether feminists should eschew
involvement in a system in which sexual violence is only one of
many violent threats to women.
   The contemporary Italian women's movement demonstrates strengths
and weaknesses in political terms. Its strength is apparent in the
success of the divorce and abortion campaigns whilst its weakness
is clear in its inability to recruit amongst the mass of Italian women.
As the movement has grown it has become self-divided and its most
successful expression has been at the cultural level. The amorphous-
ness and inward-looking mature of the movement leave it ill-
equipped to move into the formal political arena, and internal
pressures to keep clear of organised politics are strong (Zincone,
1978, p.87). Nevertheless women's movement members have entered
the trade unions and the political parties and have obliged them to
deal with traditionally feminine matters. The debate over part-time
work is a case in point here.

THE VOTING BEHAVIOUR OF ITALIAN WOMEN

The latest census indicated that there are 29,933,960 Italian women
(ISTAT, 1979) and that women comprise 51 per cent of the population. Apart from the few thousand women active in the women's
movement, and the estimated two million or so who are members of
parties and trade unions, there are some 26 million Italian women
who are excluded from political life. More than twelve million of
these are housewives, that is, in the situation of home reclusion
described by feminist writers (Balbo, 1976, passim). This home
reclusion unites millions of housewives in their lack of information,

in their alienation from the outside world and in their political inactivity, irrespective of geographical and class differences. Research undertaken by the author on housewives has shown that their socio-economic characteristics have very little bearing on their political attitudes (Weber, 1978b, p.56). Despite residence in different parts of Italy, in towns or villages, in flats of different status and despite membership of different social classes, the housewives covered in the large national survey used had similar political attitudes: 72 per cent had never been interested in political matters, 62 per cent had never read the newspapers, 90 per cent had never engaged in any political activity, even attending election meetings. The only source of information was the television watched by 60 per cent of women. The other activity which united Italian housewives is attendance at church services: 93 per cent declared they were of the Catholic faith, 30 per cent attended church services once or twice a week (Weber, 1977, pp. 14–17).

A culture which differentiates between feminine and masculine roles and encourages feminine indifference to politics is common to all western countries. In Italy this has a special salience due to the determinant influence of the Roman Catholic church (Dogan, 1969, 1968, passim). To the extent that religious influences bear upon women's voting behaviour, they bear more heavily upon housewives who are often the least well-informed and educated of Italian women. The observed relationship between religiosity and DC preference is a strong one with 70 per cent of religious housewives favouring the DCs. Actual voting choices are more difficult to estimate, however, as more than half of the women interviewed refused to reveal their voting choice in the most recent elections. Of the remainder, 23 per cent voted for the DCs, 14 per cent for the PCI and 6 per cent for the PSI, with only a total of 3 per cent choosing the other parties (Weber, 1980).

Table 9.10   Female tendency to concentrate votes on the two major parties, DC and PCI, in Italy and in maternity hospitals

	DC+PCI (1968)	DC+PCI (1972)	DC+PCI (1976)	DC+PCI (1979)*
Italy (national average, men and women)	66.0	65.8	73.1	68.7
Maternity hospitals (average)	71.3	71.3	74.3	69.3

* new data, unpublished
Source: Weber (1977)

Two constant features of post-war Italian electoral behaviour research are women's tendency to concentrate their votes on the two biggest parties and the saliency of religiosity for the DC vote. Table 9.10 indicates that while the tendency for the electorate as a whole to concentrate their votes began only in 1976, it had been present amongst women voters at least ten years before that. This concentration was also reflected in the electoral returns of the special polling stations placed in the maternity hospitals of some of the major Italian cities. The statistical significance of these results is limited by a number of factors (see below) but they are helpful in the interpretation of the women's vote.

Table 9.11   Result of political elections in maternity hospitals: in Turin, in Florence, in Bologna (1968-76)

	PCI	DC	PSI	Others	Total	Number of voters
1968						
Turin	24.5	39.7	14.5	21.3	100	320 women, 4 men
Florence	38.0	38.1	9.3	14.6	100	266 women, 6 men
Bologna	47.1	23.6	6.6	22.7	100	191 women, 8 men
1972						
Turin	39.6	26.2	11.5	22.7	100	121 women, 2 men
Florence	45.9	32.8	7.0	14.3	100	296 women, 5 men
Bologna	49.7	23.4	5.0	21.9	100	157 women, 7 men
1976						
Turin	56.1	18.7	8.1	17.1	100	131 women, 9 men
Florence	50.7	27.3	7.7	14.3	100	254 women, 7 men
Bologna	51.3	19.6	15.6	15.5	100	186 women, 8 men

Source: Weber (1977), pp. 74-90

Dogan's research indicated that more than half of the female electorate expressed a preference for the DCs, and this was confirmed by later surveys (Dogan, 1969, p.365). The process of concentration of the women's vote began in 1968 with a gradual transfer of votes from the DCs to the PCI which culminated in the years between 1975-6. The maternity poll data show a sharper trend than the national one (Table 9.11). The maternity poll data are very limited. They were obtained from four polling stations in the maternity hospitals of three cities in the 1968-76 period. Pre-1968 data was unobtainable due to lack of access to municipal archives. In addition many towns did not have separate maternity hospitals prior to 1968. Thus analysis derived from the maternity poll data is restricted in its time and area. The areas considered are interesting in that one (Bologna) had been a long-term PCI power base and two (Florence and Turin) saw PCI victories in 1975-6. In Turin there were two maternity hospitals, one situated in a poor area which contained many immigrants and one used mainly by middle-class women. Florence and Bologna had just one maternity hospital each, thus servicing women of all social classes except the upper-class members who prefer private clinics. Thus the sample is limited in time, in extent, and in the social position and of course the age of its subjects. The results, however, are not without interest. In all three centres the PCI obtained a gradual increase in its share of the vote and one which was higher than that achieved nationally (Table 9.1 and 9.11). The DC vote declined in all three centres by a greater amount than in its national performance. The PSI, on the other hand followed the national trend. All other parties received too few votes to be analysed, underlining the low women's support for the minor parties.

Women's support for the two major parties and their dislike of the smaller ones is easily attributable to their low levels of political knowledge which prevents them from knowing and assessing the platforms of the less familiar and less well-publicised parties. It is possible that preference for the major parties with their clear ideological stands and their monolithic structures gives women the feeling of being protected. In the case of the DCs and the PCI we must add that both are catch-all parties capable of adapting their platforms to current issues (Sartori, 1976, p.138). In this view women's turn from the DCs to the PCI during the 1970s may have been the result of a pragmatic search for solutions to problems of inflation and criminality which apparently loomed large in the minds of Italy's women voters (Weber, 1977, passim).

Women's declining support for the DCs may be due either to declining Catholic influence or to the transformation of the DCs from a religious to a more evidently conservative force. It is also possible that Italian women, like many Italian men, have been disappointed by the performance of DC government over the last decade. It is, after all, women who first feel the effects of rising prices and growing unemployment.

The transfer of women's votes from the DCs to the PCI is not necessarily an indicator of a secularisation process amongst Italian women. It could easily indicate a lack of information, emotional electoral behaviour and a preference for reassuring ideologies rather than cultural pragmatism. The economic crisis and the decline in religiosity have undoubtedly been determinant contributors to women's disaffection from the DCs and their increasing preference for the PCI. Smaller parties were penalised by this and the increased concentration on the two major parties was a constant feature up until and including the 1976 General Election. In 1979, however, the PCI suffered slight losses, the DCs slighter gains, and allegiance appeared to shift to the smaller parties. However the trend to cultural secularisation and ideological dissipation which became apparent in the divorce referendum will almost certainly continue. The Direction of such a trend is toward the decreasing importance of the sex variable in political behaviour. The sex variable, although still strong in Italy, is gradually giving way to such determinants as class and occupational status. For years the DC vote depended upon women's cultural subordination. Now it is coming increasingly to rely on non-religious factors (for both men and women). This should not be taken to mean that Italian women are losing their preference for totalistic belief systems, however; support for the PCI suggests a strong residual attraction to an encompassing ideology.

Rapid evolution in Italian society enables us to foresee changes, particularly amongst younger voters who have been more subject to mass media influences and less to religious ones. Younger voters who have experienced some sex-equality of educational provision show similar voting patterns for both sexes. The saliency of the sex variable in the prediction of political behaviour is undoubtedly due to differentiated political socialisation. As more women have access to education more will go out to work and isolation in the home will come to a gradual end. This should provide a basis on which participation differences between the sexes grow smaller and lead eventually to Italian men and women making party choices on an increasingly similar basis.

NOTES

1 Two additional parties were present in 1946 which were to disappear in the following period: The Action Party (Partito di Aziona or PdA), a lay party which had played a role in the Resistance movement; and the Common Man Party (Partiti dell'Uomo Qualunque or UQ), a Centre-Right organisation representing the claims of the 'generally dissatisfied'.
2 An example of reduction in ideological distance may be found in the PCI at the time of the 1976 elections, and also in later PCI support (via abstention in parliament) for the DC government.

BIBLIOGRAPHY

Balbo, L. (1976), 'Stato de famiglia', Etas, Milan.
Barbero Beerwald, I. (1976), 'Donna e società industriale' (bibliografia ragionata), Valentino, Turin.
CEE (1979), 'Bollettino', Brussels.
CENSIS (1978), 'Rapporto sull'economia sommerse', Rome.
Cutrufelli, M.R. (1977), 'Operaie senza fabrica', Riuniti, Rome.
Dalla Costa, M. (1975), 'Le operaie della casa', Marsilio, Padua.
Dalla Costa, M. (1977), 'Potere femminile e souversione sociale', Marsilio, Padua.
D'Amato, L. (1974), 'Il voto di preferenza degli italiani', Griuffre, Milan.
Dogan, M. (1955), 'Le donne italiane tra cattolicesimo e marxismo', in A. Spreafico, and J. La Polombara (eds), 'Elezioni e comportmento politico in Italia', Communità, Milan.
Dogan, M. (1968), 'Un fenomeno di atassia politics', in M. Dogan, and O. Petracca (eds), 'Partiti politici e strutture sociali in Italia', Communita, Milan.

Dogan, M. (1969), 'Gli atteggiamenti politica delle donne in Europa e negli Stati Uniti', in R. Boudon, and P.F. Lazarsfeld (eds), 'L'analisi empirica nelle scienze sociale', vol. I, Il Mulino, Bologna.

Dogan, M. (1971), 'Charisma and breakdown of traditional alignments in M. Dogan and R. Rose, (eds), 'European Politics', Little, Brown Boston.

DOXA (1961), (1973), (1976), (1978), Bolletini, Milan.

Foletti, L. and Boesi, C. (1972), 'Per il diritto di aborto', Savelli, Rome.

Frabotta, B. (1973), 'Feminismo e lotta di classe', Savelli, Rome.

Frei, L. (1975), 'Il potenziale de lavoro in Italia', ISVET, Rome.

Frei, L. (1978), 'Nuovi sviluppi delle ricerche sul lavoro femminile', Angeli, Milan.

Giannini Bellotti, E. (1973), 'Dalla parte delle bambine', Feltrinelli, Milan.

Guadagnini, M. (1980), 'Politics without women: the Italian case'. Paper presented to the joint workshops of the European Consortium for Political Research, Florence.

ISTAT (1971), 'Censimento generale della popalzione', Rome.

ISTAT (1975), 'Annuario statistico italiano', Rome.

ISTAT (1979), 'Annuario statistico italiano', Rome.

Lonzi, C. (1970, 'Sputiamo su Hegal', Rivolta, Milan.

Lonzi, C. (1971), 'La donna clitoridea e la donna vaginale', Rivolta, Milan.

Maciocchi, M.A. (1976), 'La donna nera', Feltrinelli, Milan.

Magli, I. (1964), 'La donna un problema aperto', Vallecchi, Florence

Manoukian, A. (ed.) (1968), 'La prezenza sociale della DC e del PCI', Il Mulino, Bologna.

Makno (1977), Bolletini, Milan.

Marradi, A. (1974), 'Analisi del referendum sul divorzio', in 'Rivista Italiana di Scienza Politica', 3.

Martinelli, A. and Pasquino, G. (eds) (1978), 'La politica nell'Italia che cambia', Feltrinelli, Milan.

Menapace, L. (1974), 'La Democrazia Cristiana', Mozzotta, Milan.

Mozzoni, A.M. (1892), 'I socialisti e l'emancipazione della donna', Panizza, Alessandria.

Padoa Schioppa, F. (1977), 'La forza lavoro femminile', Il Mulino, Bologna.

Parca, G. (1976), 'L'avventurosa storia del femminismo', Mondadori, Milan; 'Plusvalore femminile', Mondadori, Milan.

Parisi, A. (ed.) (1979), 'I Democristiani', Il Mulino, Bologna.

Poggi, G. (ed.) (1968), 'L'organizzazione partitica del PCI e della DC', Il Mulina, Bologna.

PRAGMA (1976), Rome.

Radi, L. (1975), 'Partiti e classi sociali in Italia', SEI, Turin.

Remiddi, L. (1976), 'I nostri diritti', Feltrinelli, Milan.

Sartori, G. (1976), 'Parties and Party Systems', Cambridge University Press, New York.

'Sottossopra' (1975), Milan.

Spagnoletti, R. (1971), 'I movimenti femministi in Italia', Savelli, Rome.

Ufficion Elettorale della DC, Rome.

Ufficio Elettorale del PCI, Rome.

Weber, M. (1977), 'Il voto delle donne', Biblioteca della Libertà, Turin.

Weber, M. (1978a), Le casalingne e la politica, 'Argomenti Radicali', 5.

Weber, M. (1978b), Precaria, Sottoocupata, sottopagata, 'Mondo Economico', 25.

Weber, M. (1979), Part-time: una soluzione de parte?, 'Mondo Economico', 14.

Weber, M. (1980), Il comportamento politico delle donne in Italia, in A. Marradi (ed.), Il Mulino, Bologna, in press.

'Women of Europe' (1978), no. 4 Commission of the European
                                 Communities, Brussels.

———   (1978), no. 9

———   (1979), no. 10

———   (1979), no. 11

———   (1980), no. 14

Zincone, G. (1978), Costruzione e costrizione della donna in Italia, in G. Zincone (ed.), 'Un mondo di donne', Biblioteca della Libertà, Turin.

10 SWEDEN
Maud Eduards

HISTORICAL BACKGROUND: The Right to Vote

Historically, Swedish women's wish for equality with men has been
expressed in several ways including demands for the suffrage.
Women were granted the right to vote in local government elections
in 1862, but only a small number were so enfranchised. Only unmarried women, over 25 years old could meet the qualifying conditions, which specified the level of payment of tax. It was more
than ten years later that married women acquired the same rights.
The first bill to give women both an equal franchise with men and
the right to stand for electoral office was presented by a Liberal
member to the Swedish parliament in 1884. The Constitutional
Committee, then considering the question of women's suffrage,
rejected the bill. In their words, as reported by Wahlström (1933,
pp. 58-9): 'women in our country had not yet expressed any opinions on this matter'. The resolution was defeated in the Lower
House by a vote of fifty-three to forty-four, and by a voice vote
in the Upper House.
  The most influential women's rights organisation, the Fredrika-
Bremer Association, was founded in 1884, but, in general, women
did not become interested in the suffrage issue until quite a few
years later. Then, in the first initiative taken specifically by
women in 1889, the Association sent a letter to the government demanding that women be given the vote for members of the Lower
House. During this early period women's suffrage was not strictly
a party question. However, by the early 1900s both the Liberal
and the Social Democratic parties had included it in their party
programmes. But the Social Democratic Party, from which most
support might have been expected, concentrated its energies
mainly upon the expansion of the male suffrage. Although it was
still mainly middle-class liberal women who campaigned most
actively for the issue, by the early years of the twentieth century
interest in the question had extended to women of all political
persuasions.
  In 1903 the National Association for Women's Suffrage (LKPR),
an umbrella organisation for a number of local suffrage organisations, was established. LKPR aimed to bring together women of
different political opinions, but, despite the fact that some of its
members were Social Democratic women, it retained its middle-class
flavour. The tactics used by Swedish women to fight for suffrage
were basically peaceful, although at times they lobbied intensively.
Using such devices as resolutions to parliament, pressure applied

through the parties, delegations, meetings, mass rallies, petitions
and, in 1905, a letter to the king, they kept women's suffrage
on the political agenda.

A first result of these early activities was the suffrage reform
of 1907-9. That reform gave almost all men the right to vote in
elections for the Lower House. Those who continued to be dis-
qualified were those in receipt of welfare payments. From 1907,
the Liberal and Social Democratic Parties repeatedly united in
parliament in pressing for both women's suffrage and the right
for women to stand for electoral office (Kvinnors röst och rätt,
1969, p. 11). In 1908, in the last election held under the old suffrage rules, these two parties substantially increased their representation in the Lower House. One year later, the Lower House
adopted a motion on women's suffrage, and in the same year,
qualified women electors were given the right to stand for electoral
office at local level. However, the Upper House continued to
block the extension of the suffrage to women in general. The
Liberal government of Karl Staaf presented the first government
bill on women's suffrage in 1912. Once more it was defeated in the
Upper House. During the First World War, the issue lay dormant.
Then, in 1917, Liberals and Social Democrats authored a resolution demanding votes for women. Although there was still strong
opposition in parliament from the Right, eventually, in 1919, a
government bill, presented by the coalition of Liberals and Social
Democrats was passed in both Houses. In effect this bill was the
first phase in progress toward a change in the constitution.
Following the elections of 1921, the suffrage proposal was brought
before parliament for final consideration. Although some members
still remained unconvinced, a change in the Constitution was
strongly supported in both Houses.

SOCIO-ECONOMIC BACKGROUND

Swedish women fought for the right to education at the same time
as they fought for their political rights. Primary school education
was compulsory for both sexes as early as 1842, but the right to
higher education was still blocked for many years after that date.
It took almost 100 years before the principle of equal access for
boys and girls to all kinds of education was obtained. At the time
of writing, there is no formal discrimination against women. All
education is legally available, without restriction, for both sexes.

Starting at the age of seven, all children go through a nine-
year basic compulsory education. The upper secondary school,
with about twenty different forms of specialisation, entails two,
three or four years of study. Almost as many girls as boys continue into secondary education, but girls tend to choose shorter
courses than boys. Moreover, when it comes to choice of study
areas, boys prefer technology, construction, forestry, etc. while
girls choose nursing, pre-school teaching, textiles and services.

Differences between men and women are also obvious in higher education. From 1976 to 1978 48 per cent of the entrants to universities were women. But in 1976 only 40 per cent of the graduates were women. After graduation, women tend to obtain lower paid jobs than men with equivalent training (SOU, 1979, pp. 22, 24). The same pattern is evident in the labour market in general. Women are heavily concentrated in those occupations traditionally regarded as 'women's work', such as nursing, teaching and social welfare. In 1974, 81 per cent of all female labour was employed in eleven occupations of this kind. The same professions employed only 20 per cent of the male work force (Sandberg, 1975, p. 19).

The Swedish labour market has been subject to an equal pay for equal work law since 1960. In spite of this, in 1977 the average yearly income for men was nearly twice that of women (Statistisk Årsbok, 1979, p. 346). The discrepancy is partly accounted for by the fact that women tend to work on both a part-time basis and in low-paid sectors. But industries also differ in their practices. In the mining, quarrying and manufacturing industries, in 1977, women took home an hourly wage which was 10 per cent lower than the men's. Greater differences may be found in the graphic industry, for instance, in which, in 1977, the wage difference between men and women was 20 per cent (Statistisk Årsbok, 1979, pp. 257-9).

Whereas, twenty years earlier barely 40 per cent of women worked outside the home, by 1978, 71 per cent of women between 16 and 64 years old were in paid employment. In comparison 88 per cent of men in the same age group were employed. The newcomers to the labour force have been mostly married women. By 1980 two-thirds of all married women were employed. But, because many of these women are employed on a part-time basis, in effect, two labour markets exist - one for full-time men and one for women working part-time while taking responsibility for home and family. The increase in women's paid employment over the last ten years has taken place mainly in the public sector. Yet women working for the national government still have subordinate positions. They are promoted less often than men and account for only 4 per cent of the higher positions in the civil service (SOU, 1979, 43, p. 76). In force from July 1980, a new act (Equality between Men and Women in the Labour Market) attempts to remedy some of the more obvious injustices. The law prohibits sex discrimination in employment, and exhorts employers to take active measures to promote equality. It has also established a new institution, the ombudsman for equality, whose job it is to see that employers conform to the law.

Family structure in Sweden has moved away from the traditional nuclear form. Thirty-three per cent of all households in 1975 were single person households. Thirty-three per cent had two members, whilst only 3 per cent had five or more members. Large families are rare. In 1975 half of all Swedish families included only one child. Single parents with children are a common family pattern. These single parents are almost all women, and in 1975 they comprised 12 per cent of all households. It is also common for men

and women to live together without being married. Sweden's rate
of non-married cohabitees is the highest in the world, closely
followed by Denmark. As a result, the proportion of children born
out of wedlock increased during the 1970s from 18 to 35 per cent
of all births (SOU, 1979, p. 62). Although the number of day
nurseries and day care centres increased in the 1970s, in 1977
public nursery facilities were only available for one-third of the
pre-school children of parents in paid employment (ibid p.65).

VOLUNTARY ASSOCIATIONS AND TRADE UNIONS

Sweden is a group-oriented society. Only 21 per cent of the
population do not belong to some kind of organisation. There is,
however, a difference between men and women in their membership of organisations. Women participate in almost all organisations
less than do men, the exception being in those organisations which
are religion- or temperance-based (Table 10.1).

*Table 10.1   Percentage of the Swedish population belonging to organisations by type of
organisation and gender*

Type of organisation	Sex	
	Male %	*Female* %
NONE	13	29
ONE or MORE	87	71
Job-related organisations	68	33
Religious and temperance	8	9
Other voluntary organisations	61	52
Political party	9	8

Source: Pestoff (1977), p. 173

Over the last ten years women have increasingly joined trade
unions. By 1980 40 per cent of all union members were women.
Yet, despite their increasing membership, women do not have a
proportional share of offices in the higher levels of the union
hierarchies. For instance, the Central Organisation of Salaried
Employees (TCO) has 57 per cent of women members, but in 1979,
had only 29 per cent of women in its congressional delegation and
14 per cent on its managing board. A slightly better situation
pertains in the Confederation of Professional Associations (SACO)/
National Federation of Government Officers (SR). That union, with
a female membership of 33 per cent, had 24 per cent of women
amongst its congressional delegates. and 3 per cent on its managing board. The position was worse in the Confederation of Trade
Unions (LO) itself, where there were no women on the managing
board (Statistisk Årsbok, 1979; TCO, SACO, SR, internal data).

In general women have tended to take a less active role in the trade unions than have men. In 1970, the proportion of men who had held some kind of trade union office was five times higher at 16 per cent than that of women. Women's lack of activity in trade unions is probably, however, overrepresented in this figure. Women in older age groups have seldom worked in paid employment. In the political parties, although fewer of both sexes were involved, the proportion of men who had held some kind of party office (at 5 per cent) was less than twice that of women (Johannson, 1971, p. 64). Differences in the activity rates of women members of trade unions and women members of political parties may be partially explained by the numbers of women who work part-time. For them economic activity is not a central part of their lives. Concomitantly, the concern of the parties for such matters as day care centres and welfare services, may attract women into activity.

THE SWEDISH POLITICAL SYSTEM

Elections to the parliament (Riksdag) and to the local county and municipal councils are held every third year, using a form of proportional representation introduced in 1909. The system allows parties to present lists of candidates. Although voters retain the formal right to delete or add names to the lists, they may not vote for or against individual candidates. It is, however, possible for factions within the parties to register their displeasure with official party lists by presenting alternative lists.

The party spectrum in parliament has been constant for decades, with five parties – the Conservative Party, the Centre Party, the Liberal Party, the Social Democratic Party and the Left Party Communists represented. State financial support for the parties and the necessity to gain 4 per cent of the total vote before they may take a seat, makes it difficult for new parties to gain representation.

In recent years, the party spectrum has narrowed to two major blocks. On the one hand the middle-class block consists of the Conservative, Centre and Liberal parties. On the other, the socialist bloc comprises the Social Democratic Party and the Left Party Communists. Until 1976 the Social Democratic Party and the Communists held the majority of seats, but from the early 1970s the Centre-Right parties steadily increased their representation. Following the 1976 election the three middle-class parties formed the government. However, in the 1979–82 parliament, the Social Democrats gained the largest proportion of votes – 43.2 per cent. The Conservatives followed with 20.3 per cent, the Centre Party with 18.1 per cent and the Liberals with 10.6 per cent of the votes. With only 5.6 per cent of votes the Left Party Communists had the smallest representation.

The Left-Right dimension in Swedish party politics was dominant until the beginning of the 1970s. Then the nuclear energy issue provided a further ideological dimension to party competition. That dimension is concerned with the future shape of Swedish society, whether it should be highly industrialised, nuclear energy-based and technologically advanced, or whether it should be a self-supporting society with small-scale production and no nuclear power. In March 1980, the issue of nuclear power was submitted to a referendum. This was only the fourth time in Swedish history that a referendum had been held. The pro-nuclear parties included the Social Democrats, the Liberals and the Conservatives, while the Centre and Communist parties opposed it. The referendum showed a majority of the population to be in favour of nuclear power ('Dagens Nyheter', 1980).

WOMEN IN THE PARTIES

The status of women has become an issue of considerable importance to the political parties. With the exception of the Conservatives, who emphasise the importance of the family, all the parties claim to support reforms favourable to women. However, they maintain different concepts of the strategy necessary for women to gain equality. Whereas the Centre Party focusses on the reform of family life, the Liberals emphasise equal opportunity, the Social Democrats want equality of men and women within equality of the classes, and the Communists regard the liberation of women as both an integrated part of the class struggle and an ideological struggle in its own right.

The Conservatives do not mention women as a separate subject in their programme, but the Liberals and Communists have been vociferous on the subject. Among other things, the Liberal Party promoted a general law against sex discrimination and legislation on equal pay. Both the Liberals and Social Democrats have translated their concern into action with the party structures. In 1972 the Liberals decided in principle that there should be a minimum of 40 per cent of women on district boards. The Social Democrats, also decided, in 1972, that women's representation within the party should increase at all levels. In the same year the Communist Party Congress recommended that women should be elected, both inside and outside the party, in proportion to their party membership.

It is not easy to calculate the exact number of women members of the political parties. Estimated figures for 1979, including women and youth leagues (Table 10.2) indicate that the proportion of women members ranges from 50 per cent of the Conservative Party to 34 per cent of the Left Party Communists. The Communists are the only party not to have a women's league. Women's membership in the Centre Party is predominantly in the women's league, with only 10 per cent (approximately 14,000) of women being members of the party rather than the league.

The extent to which the women's leagues have influenced the political parties is difficult to judge. During the first decades of

Table 10.2   Women party members (including women's leagues and youth league members)
and women on the boards of the five largest parties

Party	Women's league members* 1977	Women party members 1979 %	Women board members 1979 %
Conservative	63,000**	50	37
Centre	74,000	43	24
Liberal	(29,000)***	45	45
Social Democrat	47,000	40	31
Left Party Communists	—	34	26

*Women's leagues were founded on the following dates: Conservative, 1920; Centre, 1933;
Liberal, 1935; Social Democrats, 1920.
**Women party members are registered as members of the women's league.
***No registration of members.
Source: 'Siffror om män och kvinnor' ('Men and Women — key figures'), 1979, p. 281

their existence they were forced to assume a subordinate position
within the parties. But, more recently, it seems that the Social
Democratic women's league, with its programme for a socialist
family policy and its call for more women to join the ranks of the
party, has forced the Social Democrats to take a stand on the
issue of equality. Even the Conservative Party has received demands from its women's league to formulate an action programme
for attaining equality between men and women. On the whole, the
Swedish women's party organisations tend to be more militant
about the position of women in society than their respective parties, and therefore help to generate internal debate.

The Liberal and Centre Parties allow their women's leagues one
representative on the national party executive board, the Conservative Party includes three such representatives, the present
and two vice-presidents of the women's league. Only the president
of the Social Democratic women's league is not an ex officio member of the party board. She has the right to be present and to
participate in meetings but not the right to vote.

Although many attempts have been made to unite women active
in party politics into one group, these have been unsuccessful.
Hardly any co-operation takes place between women across parties.
However in 1979, for the first time, women in the five established
parties joined together to demand increased representation for
women in politics. Other attempts at co-operation have followed.

WOMEN AS CANDIDATES

In terms of party lists women have a smaller percentage of the
positions which are most likely to be elected than they have of
the positions less likely to be elected. For instance, in 1952 there
were between 15 and 18 per cent of women on the party lists, but

only 12 per cent were elected (SOU, 1958: 6, pp. 326-7). In 1966 the number of women found in list positions least likely to be elected was twice as large as the number of women in positions most likely to be elected (Barkfeldt, 1971, p. 167). Because women are placed in the marginal positions, parties which win are likely to have an unexpectedly high number of women in the legislative bodies. Those parties which lose are likely to have few women representatives.

Attempts to include more women in parliament, through the use of alternative women's lists, indicates a reaction, regardless of party adherence, to the fact that most politicians are men. As early as 1927 a women's list was presented in the Stockholm Community Council election. Women's lists were also presented in the parliamentary elections of 1936, 1938 and in several of the following elections. In one district in both the 1973 and 1976 elections, a woman's list was presented as an alternative to that of the Conservative Party.

WOMEN IN ELECTORAL OFFICE

Women's representation on elected bodies is well documented and the data is easily accessible. Following the 1976 elections one in four of the members of national, regional and local elected bodies were women. Women have gradually increased their representation in parliament from a few per cent in the first election in 1922 to over 28 per cent in that of 1979 (Table 10.3). Between 1970 and 1973 there was a sharp increase of 50 per cent in women's representation. This increase may have been partly due to the emergence of feminism at that time, but can also be ascribed to the sudden electoral success of the Centre Party. Those candidates for that party who were in the most marginal positions on the lists were elected. They were often women.

The parties have not been equally active in attempting to elect more women to Parliament. The Farmers' Union (the present Centre Party) and the Communists (Left Party Communists) had exclusively male members of parliament up until the 1960s. In the 1970 election the Centre Party elected nine women members (12.7 per cent of their seats in parliament). In 1973 they elected twice as many (Table 10.4). Since 1973 the Centre Party has had the highest proportion of women in parliament. The relationship noted in other countries, such as France and England, where right-wing parties are found to exclude women from candidacy, does not therefore seem to hold true for Sweden (Eduards, 1977, p. 44).

If the ratio of women in parliament to party membership is taken, then the Left Party Communists have the best record. With 34 per cent of women members its representation has been 25 per cent women. On the other hand, the Conservatives with 50 per cent women members, return only 22 per cent women MPs.

Table 10.3   Parliamentary composition by sex: 1922-80*

Year	Upper House**		Lower House		Parliament as a whole		
	Total number	Women	Total number	Women	Total number		%
1922	150	1	230	4	380	5	1.3
1925	150	1	230	5	380	6	1.6
1929	150	1	230	3	380	4	1.1
1933	150	1	230	5	380	6	1.6
1937	150	—	230	10	380	10	2.6
1941	150	—	230	18	380	18	4.7
1945	150	2	230	18	380	20	5.3
1949	150	6	230	22	380	28	7.4
1953	150	6	230	28	380	34	8.9
1957	150	10	231	29	381	39	10.2
1959	151	11	231	31	382	42	11.0
1961	151	11	232	32	383	43	11.2
1965	151	13	233	31	384	44	11.5
1969	151	17	233	36	384	53	13.8
1971					350	49	14.0
1974					350	74	21.1
1977					349	80***	22.9
1980					349	97***	27.8

* The table shows the composition of parliament at the beginning of the spring sessions following the elections to the Lower House. The two-chamber parliament was abolished when Sweden became unicameral in 1970.

** The election procedure for the Upper House involved one quarter of the house being indirectly elected every second year.

*** Including 'stand-ins' for members of government.

Source: 'Riksdagsmannavalen', Swedish Official Statistics and 'Allmänna Valen', Swedish Official Statistics.

Table 10.4   Women members of parliament. Percentage of total seats by party in selected years

Party	1948 %	1964 %	1976 %	1979 %
Conservative Party	8.7	9.1	16.4	21.9
Farmers' Union/Centre Party	0	0	27.4	31.3
Liberal Party	12.3	7.0	23.1	23.7
Social Democratic Party	11.6	21.2	22.4	27.3
Communist Party/Left Party Communist	0	12.5	23.5	25.0

At county council level the proportion of women members has gradually increased. Beginning with six women elected to these councils in 1919, by 1979 31 per cent of their membership were women (Table 10.5). In particular, between 1976 and 1979, women's representation increased by more than 25 per cent. The rate of change varies considerably between counties. In 1979, in five counties out of the twenty-three, women were just over 35 per cent of members. The lowest proportion was 21 per cent.

Table 10.5   Percentage of women on county councils by party

Party	1970 %	1973 %	1976 %	1979 %
Conservative Party	12.3	13.5	15.9	27.0
Centre Party	17.2	23.2	28.9	34.9
Liberal Party	15.5	14.9	22.9	28.8
Social Democratic Party	15.4	18.8	24.9	31.5
Left Party Communists	6.1	19.0	28.1	34.3
All parties	15.3	19.0	24.4	31.1

Source: Landstingsfakta 1976:2.

The pattern of women's representation on county councils is similar to that at national level. Since 1970 the Centre Party has had the largest number of women representatives, followed by the Left Party Communists. The sudden jump in the numbers of women representatives between 1976 and 1979 was due to the Conservative Party almost doubling the number of its women representatives.

At municipal level, in the early 1970s nine out of the 464 municipalities had no women members. By 1979 all municipal councils had female representatives. However, there was still a large variation between municipalities. Those with the highest proportion of women members (in the county of Stockholm) had up to 50 per cent of women members. The lowest proportions were between 14 and 15 per cent. Traditionally, variations could be correlated with urban and rural communities. During the 1920s and 1930s, in the cities, women's representation on the municipal councils was three or four times as large as in the rural communities. By 1966 the differences had become much smaller. Fourteen per cent of members of city councils were women compared to 12 per cent on municipal councils.

Those municipalities which elect the largest proportion of women have some common characteristics. They have a large service sector, which suggests they have a large percentage of women in the work force. They tend also to have a high per capita income, a young population and a metropolitan location. There is a positive but not strong correlation between a socialist bloc majority

(Social Democratic and Left Party Communist) and the proportion of women on municipal councils. Conversely, there is a strong negative correlation between the dominance of the Centre Party and the Christian Democratic Party and the proportion of women members of municipal councils. This correlation exists despite the fact, as shown in Table 10.6, that the Centre Party has as high a proportion of women representatives as the other parties. The explanation may be that where the Centre Party is dominant, in rural communities, it has few women representatives, but in the urban areas, where it does not form the majority on the municipal councils, it has a proportionately larger number of women as representatives. Overall the pattern of women's representation at municipal level is similar to that at national level, with the largest proportion of women members coming from the Centre Party, and the lowest number stemming from the Communists. It is noticeable that both the Social Democrats' and the Conservative Party's proportion of women representatives increased between 1974 and 1977 (Table 10.6).

Table 10.6   Female municipal council members by party, 1971, 1974, 1977, 1980 (total only) in percentages

Party	1971	1974	1977	1980*
Conservative Party	12.3	17.5	23.0	
Centre Party	15.6	18.3	23.2	
Liberal Party	13.8	15.7	22.6	
Social Democratic Party	14.4	17.3	23.6	
Left Party Communists	9.3	14.2	21.9	
Christian Democrats	8.7	7.2	9.3	
Others	7.0	14.0	17.8	
Total	14.0	17.1	22.9	29.8

* Official statistics for 1980 not available.
Source: 'Kommunala förtroendemän' (1971), 'Kommunalt förtroendevalda' (1974 and 1977)

WOMEN IN GOVERNMENT

Sweden is no exception to the general rule that few women are allowed to serve in government. The first woman entered government in 1947 and since that time only twenty-four women have been cabinet members. The Social Democratic government, from 1973 to 1976, consisted of three women and sixteen men. In the non-socialist, three-party government, following the 1976 election, there were five women and fifteen men. The non-socialist coalition, following the 1979 election, had 21 members, five of which were women.

The term 'politics' has often been interpreted to include only
electoral bodies and political parties. However, in the case of
Sweden, it is important to also include other powerful organisations
within the term, and to consider both electoral and organisational
'channels' in politics. As Holter (1971, p. 7) has pointed out:

In Scandinavian political discussions, it has been recurrently
asserted that parliament as an institution is becoming less powerful, that important decisions to an increasing degree are taken
outside this body, and that the parliament is losing influence
vis-à-vis a strong governmental apparatus, as well as powerful
economic forces.

Interest groups have formalised their relationship to the Swedish
state apparatus through regular nominations to committees, through
representation on boards, and through consultative procedures.

The way in which the representation and influence of women in
politics has been affected by these corporatist tendencies in
society is a problem which has been the subject of attention in all
the Scandinavian countries (Hernes and Voje, 1977; Sinkkonen,
1977). In the case of Sweden, Holter suggested in 1971, that
whilst the proportion of women representatives in the electoral
bodies was increasing, albeit slowly, in all Scandinavian countries,
the number of women on the boards of banks, insurance companies and in industry was nil (Holter, 1971, p. 7). It should also
be noted that women's share of important offices is decreasing in
some organisational areas. For instance, between 1958 and 1972,
the number of women members of the Confederation of Trade
Unions increased by about 200,000, but women's share of the important offices in the Confederation actually decreased (Qvist,
1974, p. 83).

In a society with corporatist tendencies, organisations may be
integrated in the political decision-making process in a number of
ways, and at national regional or local level. Olof Ruin has pointed
out that organisations may be empowered to make decisions themselves, on behalf of a government, or they may be represented
on different governmental bodies (Ruin, 1974, p. 172). Two examples of organisational influence, those of public commissions and
lay boards, will suffice to illustrate how integration via representation may occur at national level.

The public commissions play an important role in Swedish politics. Political decisions are prepared in the commissions before
they are presented to parliament. Compromise between the parties and organisations on the solution of problems also occur in
these commissions. Their proposals are then further debated
through consultative procedures with government agencies, institutions, organisations and other concerned parties.

The initiative to create a commission usually comes from the
government, although proposals to establish commissions may
come through parliament. The directive establishing a new commission is drawn up by the ministry concerned and it also selects
the commission staff. Commissions may comprise purely civil ser-
vant membership or have a mixed membership drawn from mini-

stries, parliamentary parties and interest groups.

The proportion of women members of the commissions is very low (Table 10.7). In the ten years from 1965 to 1975 the proportion of women members rose from 6 per cent to 11 per cent. A detailed study of women on department-initiated commissions reveals a traditional pattern of representation. Of the four women on the commissions in 1925, two were from the Department of Welfare and two came from the Department of Education. These departments still have the highest number of women on their commissions. Until the 1960s women were only occasionally members of those commissions initiated by Departments of Defence and Communications and the Foreign Office. Where do the women nominated onto the commissions come from? In 1974 an unpublished study by the Committee on Equality between Men and Women came to the conclusion that 14 per cent of the women members were nominated by labour organisations, 6.4 per cent came from ministries and governmental agencies, and 27 per cent were nominated through the political parties, and voluntary organisations. Hence it is through the political parties and voluntary organisations that the highest percentage of women reach the commissions.

Table 10.7　Members of public commissions

Year	Total number of members	Women	% total
1925	488	4	0.8
1935	896	29	3.2
1945	2,188	69	3.2
1965	4,035	239	5.9
1975/6	5,465	602	11.0

Source: Eduards (1980), p. 23

Most state administrative agencies in Sweden have a lay board of directors. Thus the highest decision-making level of the agency is comprised of members who are not directly employed by the agency. The lay boards first became prominent in conjunction with the crisis administration of the Second World War. A second upswing in their numbers occurred during the 1960s. To simplify matters, one may say that the boards fulfil two functions, one representative and one administrative. On the one hand representatives from different groups in society (political parties, organisations etc.) are allowed to influence the activity of agencies. On the other, the agency is able to receive the benefit of outside expertise.

Women have been consistently under-represented on lay boards (Table 10.8). Of those women members of the boards the majority are politicians. In 1975, of the twenty-eight female 'laymen' fourteen were members of parliament, and in 1976, whereas 71 per

cent of the women on the boards were politicians only 19 per cent
came from other organisations and 10 per cent from the civil
service. In all, in that year, of the total 6.4 per cent of women
on lay boards, 4.5 per cent came through the electoral channel
and 1.2 per cent through the organisational channel. It may be
that democratic procedures favour female political participation
and hence more women come through the electoral channel, or the
explanation for the differences between the electoral and organisational channel may rest in the area of relative power. It may be
that the 'more power, the fewer women' and the organisational
channel has more power than the electoral channel. Further analysis is necessary before deciding on the explanation.

Table 10.8   Board members in central state agencies

Year	Total number of members	Women	%
1950	120	7	5.8
1965	281	7	2.5
1975	436	28	6.4

Source: Eduards (1980), p. 28

VOTING BEHAVIOUR

Following the granting of female suffrage, for a long period women
exercised their right to vote less than did men. In the first election in 1921, there was an almost 15 per cent difference between
men and women's voting rate. The difference has successively
decreased since that election, and in 1976 women in fact voted at
a slightly higher rate than men (Table 10.9). Although the difference is only a couple of percentage points, young women have
a higher voting turnout than young men. Both married men and
married women vote more often than single men or women. For
instance, in 1964, 91 per cent of married men, 90 per cent of
married women, 76 per cent of single men and 74 per cent of single
women voted. By 1976 the proportions of voting among all four
groups had risen, so that 97 per cent of both married men and
women, 89 per cent of single men and 90 per cent of single women
voted. Women in the higher socio-economic groups also participate
more often than women in the middle economic groups and women
workers. But, because voter turnout in Sweden is so high, the
difference in voting turnout between men and women is only
marginal.

Table 10.9   *Voting turnout in parliamentary elections. Percentage of eligible voters, by sex*

Year	Men	Women	Difference M-W
1921	62.0	47.2	14.8
1924	60.0	46.7	13.3
1928	72.6	62.7	9.9
1932	73.1	62.5	10.6
1936	78.6	70.7	7.9
1940	72.6	68.1	4.5
1944	74.8	69.2	5.6
1948	84.9	80.7	4.2
1952	80.8	77.5	3.3
1956	81.5	78.2	3.3
1958	79.3	75.6	3.7
1960	87.1	84.8	2.3
1964	86.9	84.8	2.1
1968	91.6	90.7	0.9
1970	90.4	89.0	1.4
1973	92.0	91.9	0.1
1976	93.9	94.3	(−) 0.4

Source: 'Riksdagsmannavalen', Swedish Official Statistics, and 'Allmänna Valen', Swedish Official Statistics.

ISSUE ORIENTATION

Swedish men and women have differed over the years in their orientation to specific issues. For example, in the 1922 referendum on prohibition, 59.1 per cent of men but 41.5 per cent of women voted against prohibition of alcohol. On that occasion many women's organisations protested that the votes of men and women were counted separately. Women feared that if they did not vote against prohibition as men wished, their own votes would be given half the weight of men's. This was the last time that ballot papers differentiated by gender were used in a referendum.

In the late 1970s the nuclear power issue illustrated the continuing differences in the orientation of the two sexes. 46 per cent of women but only 31 per cent of men voted against nuclear energy in the referendum in March 1980 ('Dagens Nyheter', 1980). In May 1979 51 per cent of the women compared to 41 per cent of men considered employment to be one of the most important election issues. Women also gave medical care and the environment higher priority than did men. It is not surprising that more women than men thought that the question of sex equality was one of the three most interesting questions in the then forthcoming election, but the proportion of both (5.5 per cent of women and 2.7 per cent of men) was very small. On the other hand men were more interested in fiscal policy than were women.

These differing issue orientations are not, however, reflected in voting behaviour in elections. Historically it may have been true that Swedish women tended to prefer right-wing parties. In 1946 and 1948, public opinion polls showed that women tended to prefer the Conservative Party. The same polls also showed that the non-socialist parties had a larger proportion of female supporters than did the socialist parties (Ingulfson and Hagman, 1950, pp. 146-7).

But surveys conducted during the 1970s found no discernible difference between men and women's voting behaviour. Although the surveys showed that the Communist Party, in 1973, received 3 per cent of women's votes compared to 5 per cent of men's, generally speaking men and women tended to have the same attitudes to the parties (Petersson and Särlvik, 1975, p. 79).

CONCLUSION

The political role of the Swedish woman is in many ways similar to the role of her sisters in other industrialised countries. There are, however, some differences. In the first place, the parties are relatively sensitive to the women's issue. On average, 30 per cent of the membership of the country's elected assemblies are women. Furthermore, the electoral success of women of the Centre Party seems to contradict the proposition that socialist parties nominate more women to candidacies than do right-wing parties. The Centre Party's record in 1979 seems to contradict the proposition that parties which win elections are more likely to increase their proportion of women representatives than are parties which lose. That party increased its proportion of women representatives both in 1973 when it won seats and in 1979 when it lost seats. This suggests that procedures which normally work against the selection of women cease to function once the proportion of women reaches a certain level.

Once in parliament the strong party loyalty which is characteristic of Swedish party politics has meant that collaboration between women across party lines has been the exception. In the past women MPs have not voted against their parties on women's issues. But there is hope for the future. Since March 1980 women from the five parties in parliament have held discussions on how to unite across party lines on issues concerning women. Things may therefore be changing. In the second place Sweden has a weak women's movement. In addition to the older established women's organisations of the Fredrika-Bremer Association, and the Swedish Women's Left Federation (founded in 1914 to promote the issues of peace and women's role) the first modern women's organisation, Group B, came into being in 1968. The Group describes itself as an independent, socialist women's organisation, but, on the whole, feminist ideas were not widespread in the first half of the 1970s.

Women who were active in the 'new' Swedish women's movement of that time, were anxious to display their loyalty to various left-

wing groups. Faced with the choice between class struggle and
the women's struggle, in solidarity with their male colleagues,
women gave the class struggle higher priority. Party loyalty was
also evident here.

During the late 1970s feminism claimed more public attention.
Women's culture festivals, women's camps, women's houses in
several towns, 'women's struggle for peace' and women's courses
at universities were expressions of these new ideas. But the work
was still performed in small and dispersed groups and the activity
was more often directed inwards towards the groups' members
than outwards towards changing the surrounding society. At the
time of writing, there is no strong, coherent feminist movement
in Sweden.

However, the nuclear power issue has, possibly for the first
time ever, created an atmosphere congenial to an active and comprehensive co-operation between women. The issue has shown
that the traditional Left-Right continuum of politics does not always prevail in Sweden. It has demonstrated that issues exist
which cross party lines, and in which men's and women's opinions
are noticeably different. Aware of these differences, the parties
supporting nuclear power attempted to defuse them by appointing
women to prominent positions on their referendum campaign
committees.

Thirdly, the political role of women in Sweden must be seen in
relation to the recent idea that militant feminism has no place in
Swedish political life. The general consensus is that women's
liberation has already been taken care of by society. The struggle
for women's liberation has been co-opted by the parties and political institutions. Hence, it is labelled as 'work' towards increased
equality between men and women, and must occur in an orderly
way. Women's demands are to be met with the help of reformist
laws on sexual equality, by government contributions to companies employing the under-represented sex, and through institutions such as the Committee on Equality between Men and Women.
This institution is composed of representatives from the five
political parties in parliament and is therefore an institution of
compromise. There seems to be a tacit agreement between politicians that the demands of women must not be met in a manner
which is to the detriment of men. One sex must not 'win' at the
expense of the other. The official view is that both men and women
should be able to work together to improve the situation of both
sexes, that sex roles are an encumbrance and sexual discrimination must be eradicated.

The consequence for women of this Swedish consensus are both
positive and negative. The declarations by the governmental
authorities that they wish to see equality between the sexes is,
without doubt, a good way to influence public opinion. There is
however, much more said than done, and the public commitment
helps to pacify the women's movement. The former chairperson
of the Committee on Equality between Men and Women, Karin
Anderson pointed out the problem ('Svenska Dagbladet', 1979,

11 April): 'it is difficult to fight for something about which there is formal unity. All parties are for equality between the sexes'. Nor is it always clear that the parties intend action to be effective. As Cheri Register (1977, p. 113) has said, in comparing the Swedish to the American women's movement:

The fact that the government has introduced particular reforms to the benefit of women does not necessarily mean that they fully accept it as a just cause. It can also be interpreted as a preventive measure necessary to divert more radical claims and conflicts which could lead to still larger divisions.

It is likely to be difficult in the future to interrupt a chain of behaviour characterised on the one hand by governmental authorities who are, at least in terms of attitudes, positively disposed to equality between the sexes, and on the other by a women's movement which is not strong enough to influence women active in the political parties to go against party solidarity. The demands of women are, therefore, likely to be channelled via the parties, take a more sexually neutral form, and be presented as the national viewpoint. Some women will be satisfied but the future may not be better for the majority of women.

Two trends already seem discernible leading to two components of a future scenario. In the first, an increasing incorporation of organisations into the political power apparatus signifies an increase in the number of civil servants and experts and thus increased access to channels of influence for the male-dominated sphere of the establishment. In the future political parties will have less and less control over the economy, and will devote their time to issues dealing with ethics and the division of power in society - issues such as equality between men and women. Women will be allowed into the popularly elected channel of influence but will not be given any real influential power over the future course which society will take. That chain of behaviour will hence be left intact.

The second trend and component entails a deviation from this traditional pattern of behaviour. Women and the women's movement, activated by the nuclear power issue, together with the growth of other extra-parliamentary groups, may create increased demands on the political parties and the labour unions. Women will change by going out into the public sphere. Men will also have to change by assuming some of the responsibility for the private sphere - the children and home. The parenthood insurance scheme, introduced in 1974, can be seen as a first step in this direction. On the birth of a child the parents have the right to divide seven months of paid parenthood leave of absence from work between themselves. Ten per cent of fathers have taken advantage of this right. This leave of absence can be seen as an attempt to change the attitudes of fathers with regard to child-rearing responsibilities, and, thereby, an attempt to change the division of labour in the private sphere (Sandberg, 1975, p. 71).

For women, the future may bring an increased equality in the political parties and elected bodies and/or increased equality within the family. But, as the locus of power shifts within Swedish society it may be that women will continue to be denied access to the genuinely powerful agencies of decision making.

BIBLIOGRAPHY

'Allmänna Valen' (1970-76), SOS, Statistiska Centralbyran, Stockholm.
Barkfeldt, Bengt, et. al. (1971), 'Partierna nominerar, Den Kommunala självstyrelsen' 3, Almqvist & Wiksell, Uppsala.
Dagens Nyheter (1980), 3 July.
Eduards, Maud (1977), 'Kvinnor och politik, Fakta och förklaringar', Liber Förlag, Stockholm.
Eduards, Maud (1980), 'Kvinnorepresentation och kvinnomakt, Forskningsrapport 1980:2', Statsvetenskapliga institutionen, Stockholms universitet.
Hadenius, Axel (1978), Ämbetsverkens styrelser, 'Statsvetenskaplig tidskrift', no. 1, pp. 19-32.
Herman, Sondra R. (1976), Sweden: A Feminist Model?, in Lynne B. Iglitzin and Ruth Ross, (eds), 'Women in the World, A Comparative Study', Clio Books, Oxford.
Hernes, Helga and Voje, Kirsten (1977), The representation of women in public policy-making: the Norwegian case. Paper prepared for the ECPR workshop on Women in Politics, West Berlin.
Holter, Harriet (1971), Sex roles and social change, 'Acta Sociologica', 1-2, pp. 2-12.
Ingulfson, Hans and Hagman, Rolf (1950), De svenska partiernas sociala och andra grundvalar in Elis Haståd, (ed.),'Gallup och den svenska valjarkaren - nagra studier om opinionsmatningar', Uppsala.
Johannson, Sten (1971), 'Politiska resurser', Allmänna Förlaget, Stockholm 1972.
'Kommunala förtroendemän 1971', Parti-kön-alder, Kommunforbundet, Stockholm 1972.
'Kommunala Valen' (1919-1966), SOS, Allmänna val, Statistiks Centralbyrån, Stockholm.
'Kommunalt förtroendevalda 1974', Parti-kön, Kormunförbundet, Stockholm 1975.
'Kommunalt förtroendevalda 1977', Parti-kön, Kommunförbundet, Stockholm 1978.
'Kvinnors röst och rätt' (1969), Allmänna Förlaget, Stockholm.
'Landstingsfakta 1976:2', Landstingsförbundet, Stockholm 1976.
'Levnadsförhållanden, Årsbok 1975', Utveckling och nuläge, SOS, Stockholm 1975.
Pestoff, Victor (1977), Voluntary associations and Nordic party systems, 'Stockholm Studies in Politics' no. 10, Statsvetenskapliga institutionen, Stockholms universitet.
Petersson, Olof and Särlvik, Bo (1975), Valet 1973, Allmänna Valen 1973. Del 3 (SOS), Statistiska centralbyrån, Stockholm.
Qvist, Gunnar (1974), 'Statistik och politik', Landsorganisationen

och kvinnorna på arbetsmarknaden, Prisma, Stockholm.
Register, Cheri (1977),'Kvinnokamp och litteratur i USA och
Sverige', Raben & Sjörgren, Stockholm.
Riksdagsmannavalen (1921-1968), SOS, Allmanna val Statistiska
Centralbyrån, Stockholm.
Ruin, Olof (1974), Participatory democracy and corporativism:
the case of Sweden, 'Scandinavian Political Studies' no. 9.
Sandberg, Elisabet (1975), 'Equality is the Goal, A Swedish Re-
port', Advisory Council to the Prime Minister on Equality be-
tween Men and Women, The Swedish Institute, Stockholm.
'Sex Roles in Transition', A Report on a pilot programme in
Sweden by Rita Liljestrom et al., International Women's Year
1975. Advisory Council to the Prime Minister on Equality between Men and Women.
'Siffror om män och kvinnor' ('Men and Women - Key Figures')
(1979), Nämnden för jämställdhet i arbetslivet, Stockholm.
Sinkkonen, Sirkka (1977), Women's increased political participa-
tion in Finland: Real influence or pseudo-democracy? Paper
prepared for the ECPR workshop on Women in Politics, West
Berlin.
SOU 1958:6, Författningsutredningen: I, Kandidatnominering vid
andra kammarval, Lars Sköld.
SOU 1979:56, Steg på väg . . Nationell handlingsplan för jäm-
ställdhet utarbetad av Jämställdhetskommittén.
'Statistisk Årsbok 1979 ('Statistical Abstract of Sweden 1979'),
National Central Bureau of Statistics.
Svenska Dagbladet (1979) 11 April, Ami Lönnroth intervjuar
Karin Andersson.
Tingsten, Herbert (1973), Political behaviour: studies in election
statistics, 'Stockholm Economic Studies', no. 7, Norstedts,
Stockholm.
Wahlström, Lydia (1933), 'Den svenska kvinnorörelsen', Norstedts,
Stockholm.

11 FINLAND

Elina Haavio-Mannila

SOCIO-ECONOMIC ENVIRONMENT

Finland is a small Nordic country with only 4.8 million inhabitants. Only recently industrialised, it ranks twenty-first in the World Bank list of gross national product statistics. Urbanisation was most rapid in the 1960s when the agricultural population declined from 32 to 18 per cent of the total. By 1978 60 per cent of the population were living in urban municipalities (Alestalo, 1980, p. 105). Finland is homogenous in both its religion and its language: 91 per cent of its people belong to the dominant Lutheran Church and 93 per cent speak Finnish as their first language. The Swedish minority was 6 per cent of the population in 1975.

In 1978 57 per cent of women and 70 per cent of men in the 15 to 74 age cohort were in paid employment ('Position of Women', 1980, Table 19). Amongst married women in the 15 to 64 age cohort, 62 per cent were economically active in 1975. The figure for mothers with children under the age of seven was 61 per cent (Jallinoja, 1980, p. 235). Hence neither marriage nor motherhood exclude women from the economic sector. The difference between the sexes in labour force participation rates is small and the fact that most Finnish women work full-time is a measure of their significance to the national economy.

Although Finland has had an equal pay policy since 1962 (via ratification of the International Labour Conference Equal Pay Agreement) the average incomes of women were only 61 per cent of those of men in 1977 (OSF: 43, 1977, Table 12). Much, but not all of the difference is due to occupational segregation and differential educational qualifications (Jallinoja, 1980, pp. 245-6; 'Position of Women', 1980, Tables 48-57).

Officially excluded from the universities until 1901, women have comprised about 50 per cent of students entering universities and higher professional schools since 1960, and by 1977 were 52 per cent of university graduates. The traditional concentration of women in the arts and humanities is present here although women do comprise some 29 per cent of engineering and science students. Women are more likely to have obtained secondary school qualifications than men and since 1976 have been 60 per cent of those passing the matriculation examination. Similarly, by 1978 33 per cent of Finnish women aged 15 and over, but only 29 per cent of men, had received second-stage vocational education. At that time 3.7 per cent of women and 4.3 per cent of men held university degrees.

The proportion of women members of trade unions has grown steadily since the turn of the century and in 1979 women comprised 42 per cent of the members of the Central Organisation of Trade Unions (SAK). The two periods of greatest increase in the proportions of women members were after Finland's Civil War in 1917 and in the early 1970s (Alakapee and Valkonen, 1979, p. 37). This pattern of growth has meant that women join unions at similar rates to men: in 1978 84 per cent of female and 86 per cent of male wage earners belonged to a union (Saarinen, 1979, p. 3). However the decision-making posts in union hierarchies continue to be male-dominated although there is evidence that women are now gaining a foothold, particularly in the smaller unions (see Haavio-Mannila and Kirkkonan, 1980).

Marriage rates are high with almost 90 per cent of Finnish men and women married by the ages of 35 to 39. The most common family type is the nuclear one of parents plus children, and extended family households are rare. In recent years, however, the proportion of nuclear family households has declined whilst the proportion of childless couples and single-person households is on the increase (Haavio-Mannila and Jallinoja, 1980, p. 102). Societal and familial development in Finland since the Second World War can be summarised in the following way: in the latter part of the 1940s there was a short period characterised by the instability of the family, its most visible symptom being a high divorce rate. From the 1950s through the first half of the 1960s there was a stable phase in family life patterns. This was followed by a period of very rapid change which continued into the 1970s and was most acute between 1968 and 1972, which most affected young people born in rural areas during the post-war baby boom of the late 1940s. Large-scale migration from rural to urban municipalities and to Sweden between 1965 and 1975 mainly involved the young who had to begin family life in new circumstances. The alteration of traditional patterns of family life could be seen in declining fertility and marriage rates, increasing employment of married women, cohabiting, children born outside marriage and divorce. During that period children's day care centres, municipal home helpers, the food production industry, school and workplace canteens and social assistance partly took over some of the traditional caring functions of the family (ibid., pp. 91-4).

Recent Finnish social and economic development has been characterised by rapid change and this has included substantial alterations in the position of women. Lively public discussion on sex roles has accompanied the growing economic independence and ideological liberation of women and combined with the feminist movement has produced accompanying change in the formal political arena.

THE PARTY AND ELECTORAL SYSTEMS

Finland has five main political parties: Conservative, Liberal, Agrarian (Centre), Social Democratic and Communist, reflecting the Socialist/non-Socialist cleavage which exists throughout Scandinavia (Berglund and Lindström, 1978, p. 16), where class is the single most important determinant of voting behaviour. Students of Scandinavian politics see the emergence of the five-party system as a function of the early adoption of proportional representation and the concurrent extension of the franchise (ibid).

In the following analysis Finnish parties are mainly treated in four major groups: (1) Socialist, i.e. the Social Democratic Party and the Democratic League of the People of Finland (Communists); (2) Urban Centre, i.e. the Liberal Party, the Swedish People's Party and the Christian League; (3) Rural Centre, i.e. the Agrarian/Centre Party and the Finnish Rural Party; and (4) Conservatives, i.e. the National Coalition Party and the Constitutional People's Party. Historical trends and the limited support of many of the smaller parties[1] are such that clustering the parties into four main groups considerably eases analysis. Naturally such clustering conceals important differences, most notably those between Finnish and Swedish speakers and Communists and other socialists. Where these differences are relevant to women's political participation, the parties will be analysed separately.

The Finnish electoral mechanism enables voters to cast ballots for individual candidates thus determining their positions on party lists. This would appear to be advantageous to the success of women candidates as voters may by-pass the party bureaucracy and directly influence the sex distribution of parliament. The country is divided into fifteen electoral districts each of which chooses between eight and twenty-five members of the 200 member legislative assembly (the Eduskunta or parliament).

Members of parliament (MPs) get a salary for their work which is comparable to that of higher civil servants. Electoral campaigns are partly financed by money the parties receive from the state. Campaigns are closely fought and highly visible and about 15 per cent of the candidates are elected. The more than 10,000 municipal councillors are elected in the same way as MPs. Finnish representative assemblies have lately declined in importance vis-à-vis other decision making bodies. Important decisions are made in the incomes policy negotiations between trade unions, employers' organisations and representatives of the state. Participants in these meetings are not elected and those involved are seldom women. A similar absence of women from important committees of state should also be noted.

WOMEN AS PARTY PARTICIPANTS

Survey evidence suggests that Finnish women feel more solidarity with or loyalty toward family, nation, ethnic groups, friends, local community, region or province, and church or religious organisations than do Finnish men. Sex differences are minimal in work place solidarity and men are more likely than women to express solidarity with a political party. Some 30 per cent of women and 33 per cent of men claim to be loyal to a political party whilst 31 per cent of women and 27 per cent of men have no such loyalties (see Haranne and Allardt, 1974). Contrary to common stereotypes about the lack of interest in politics amongst women, Finnish women express party choices more often than men (Table 11.1). The percentage of women among people not indicating support for any party is lower than for the sample as a whole.

Table 11.1   The proportion of women among supporters of different parties in Finland in 1966 and 1974 in percentages (N)

Party	1966	1975
Socialists		
Democratic League of the People of Finland	51(203)	43(133)
Social Democratic Union of Workers and Small Farmers	54(37)	56(18)
Social Democratic Party in Finland	50(477)	46(366)
Urban Centre		
Liberal Party	59(91)	61(46)
Swedish People's Party in Finland	43(73)	59(27)
Rural Centre		
Centre Party	49(290)	54(201)
Finnish Rural Party	–	42(31)
Conservatives		
National Coalition Party	57(209)	54(138)
Other Parties	65(20)	61(38)
No party support	49(150)	49(226)
Total	51(1550)	50(1224)

Sources: Pesonen (1972), p. 354, and Pesonen and Sänkiaho (1979), p. 118

Table 11.1 also shows which parties include the most women amongst their supporters. In 1966 the highest proportion of women was amongst supporters of the Conservatives (57 per cent) and the lowest amongst supporters of the Swedish People's Party (43 per cent). In 1975 the highest figures were for the Liberal and Swedish People's parties and the lowest for Rural and Communist parties. When the parties are combined into the four major groups mentioned above, the percentages of women are as follows:

	1966	1975
Socialists	50	46
Non-Socialists, total	52	54
of which Urban Centre	52	60
Rural Centre	49	52
Conservatives	57	54

The non-Socialist parties appear to attract more women than the Socialist parties and differences between these two party blocs increased between 1966 and 1975. Cleavages between Swedish and Finnish speakers, the urban and rural population, Communist and non-Communist Socialists are also reflected in the sex division of party support.

Data collected on the voting behaviour of men and women suggests that there are no sex differences in leftist voting behaviour amongst Finnish manual workers. Table 11.2 indicates that support for leftist parties is as common amongst women as men when

Table 11.2   Voting for leftist parties by occupation and sex in Finland in 1972 in percentages (N)

	Farmers	Manual Workers	White Collar Employees	House-wives	Stud-ents	Pen-sioners	T
Men	6(67)	77(125)	29(76)	(−)	66(9)	64(25)	48(302)
Women	13(71)	77(62)	30(106)	36(55)	11(9)	52(23)	37(326)

Source: Scandinavian Welfare Survey, Erik Allardt (1976), Helsinki University

controlled for socio-economic group. Overall differences in men's and women's votes for the Socialist parties may be accounted for by the uneven distribution of men and women between white and blue collar occupations, the effect of the housewives vote and the students' and pensioners' votes.

Using material collected in 1975, Matheson found the employed women exhibit similar proportions of preferences for Socialist parties to men and held that this was due to the precarious position of women in the underpaid routine grades of white collar employment (Matheson, 1979, pp. 68-9). The working-class women respondents to Matheson's survey were not only generally (ibid., pp. 69-71):

more prone to indicate party preference . . . but for all respondents who were economically active, women had lower 'no preference' rates than men. Among all social classes and class (categories) women showed a greater tendency to abstain than did men. More significantly . . . there was no appreciable difference in overall socialist party preference between men and women. In fact, in all three (categories) there is a slight tendency for the percentage to be greater for women than for men.

The most notable differences have to do with support within the left. Men have a greater tendency to support the SKDL (Democratic League of the People) than do the women in all groups, with the greatest measure of support coming from the men in the unskilled worker category.

Matheson concludes his observations by remarking (ibid., p. 71):

Thus the strong relationship between sex and the opportunity structure tends to find white collar men in this sample less disposed to favour the socialist parties and more disposed to identify with the National Coalition Party. Perhaps the study has detected a slight 'proletarianisation' effect on women workers engaged in routine non-manual tasks. If this finding hold up under further scrutiny, hunches about the embourgeoisement of the white collar workers may have to be revised as long as the dimension of sexist bias is overlaid on the dimension of workplace alienation. Paradoxically as long as the marketplace is inundated by underpaid, underchallenged females, the probability may remain that support for the socialist parties will be high.

The higher participation of women in the membership and decision-making bodies of the non-Socialist parties is evident in the data presented in Table 11.3. The proportion of women members is highest in the Christian League and in the National Coalition Party (Conservative), somewhat lower in the Centre and Liberal Parties and clearly lowest in the three leftist parties and the Swedish People's Party. Women are underrepresented amongst those officially attending the conferences of all parties and the discrepancy increases at the level of party council and again at the level of party government. The Socialist parties on the whole have fewer women in leadership positions than do the non-Socialist parties, but this must be seen in the light of their proportions of female membership.

Women's sections in the Finnish political parties first appeared at the beginning of the twentieth century, first in the Social Democratic Party and then in the Swedish People's Party. The present women's leagues of the Conservative and Liberal Parties have later establishment dates but their predecessors, the Finnish Party and the Young Finnish Party had women's organisations before 1917. The purpose of women's sections has been to recruit women into political activity, to give women the opportunity to become acquainted with the rules of the political game and to function as a pressure group on women's issues within the party (Means, 1973, p. 95; Ruusala, 1967, passim). They also back women candidates and a number of Finnish women politicians owe their careers to support from the women's sections.

The sex-role policies of Finnish parties have not been subjected to scholarly analysis since the late 1960s, when Terrtu Nupponen analysed party programmes for their sex-role components. Nupponen divided party programmes into three groups according to a classification devised by Edmund Dahlström (1962): those representing conservative, moderate and radical sex-role ideologies.

Table 11.3   The proportion of women members, party conference representatives, party council members and members of party government in the main political parties in Finland in 1979

Party	Members	Total female members %	Representatives in party conference	Percentage of women among Members of party council	Members of party government
Socialists					
Communist Party of Finland	48,642	29	16	–	4
Democratic League of the People of Finland	55,223	32	24	16	16
Social Democratic Party in Finland	99,659	35	19	14	8
Urban Centre					
Liberal Party	20,000	42	29	32	19
Swedish People's Party in Finland	48,454	33	18	28	21
Christian League in Finland	20,150	60	29	20	22
Centre Party	304,325	46	23	25	10
Conservatives					
National Coalition Party	80,938	50	32	16	12

Source: 'Position of Women', (1980), Table 99

She also classified the programmes into those which were family centred, which dealt with problems from feminine perspectives, and which saw women as individuals, and those which sought to eliminate sex-roles. According to conservative ideology a woman's place is in the home, taking care of children. Neither career nor public duties are appropriate and male protection is essential. By this definition, no Finnish party was truly sex-role conservative in 1967. Most parties could be classified in the moderate category, which involved including the following elements in their platforms: (1) vocational training which will protect women in the event of spinsterhood or widowhood; (2) the notion that society has a duty to help women carry out the two female roles of motherhood and paid worker in a manner which leaves the family intact. The bourgeois parties, from the National Coalition Party to the Rural Party were moderate and at the same time family centred (in that they emphasise its significance). Most of the leftist parties were moderate but advocated individual women's rights. The Social Democratic Party, Social Democratic League of Workers and Small Farmers, and Communist Party all fit into this category. Only the Democratic League of the People of Finland exhibited the charac- teristics of Dahlström's radical ideology. Its programmes included giving either men or women the choice between staying at home or being employed. Proposals for social policy reforms were com- mon to all parties, irrespective of their general ideology. The ideology of a particular party did, however determine the context in which the position of women or the equality of the sexes was discussed. Even though all parties advocated improvements in the position of women, not all espoused the principle of equality be- tween the sexes (Nupponen, 1968, pp. 45-6).

Radical elements were found in the programmes of both bourgeois and Socialist parties, Nupponen remarks. The radical programme of the Youth Organisation of the Swedish People's Party, of the Democratic League of the People of Finland and of the Women's Democratic League suggest that it is possible in principle to com- bine radical sex-role ideology with any kind of political ideology (ibid., p. 53).

Recent party policy on women's rights has focused on issues such as abortion and child care provision. In 1980 the Centre Party succeeded in passing legislation which provides a small state-paid salary for a parent (or other relative or 'employee') who stays at home to care for children under two-and-a-half years old, provided there are three children under seven years old in the family. The relative scarcity of such families means that the cost of this legislation is low. In 1970 abortion for social reasons was legalised and in 1972 the Council for Equality was established at the Prime Minister's office. A 1973 law on day care obliged municipalities to investigate the need for and to provide and main- tain subsidised family day care. Financial assistance from the state was supplied to the municipalities for this. In 1975 the last vestiges of gender qualification for state office were abolished. Most of these reforms were initiated and supported by MPs from the socialist parties, but few met with any real opposition. Only in the case of the abortion legislation has there been party opposition - from the Christian League which is campaigning for repeal of the 1970 act. Thus trends in the 1970s suggest that Nupponen's argument that radical sex-role ideologies are compatible with the majority of the Finnish party ideologies continues to find support.

WOMEN IN ELECTORAL OFFICE

Data on Finnish women voters, candidates and office-holders are extensive and these activities may therefore be described in some detail. Available statistics on the proportion of women parliamentary candidates indicate that the proportion rose from 7 to 8 per cent between 1922 and 1936, to 12 per cent after the Second World War, levelling out at between 15 and 17 per cent in the 1950s and 1960s after which it rose to exceed 20 per cent in 1972 (Figure 11.1).

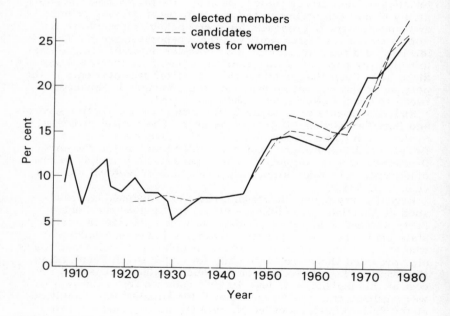

Figure 11.1:
The proportion of women among the candidates and elected members of parliament and of votes cast for women candidates as a proportion of all votes cast in parliamentary elections in Finland.

Table 11.4 *The proportion of votes cast for female candidates as a percentage of all votes cast in parliamentary elections in Finland, by party, and the proportion of women among candidates and elected MPs between 1954 and 1979 in percentages*

Party	1954	1958	1962	1966	1970	1972	1975	1979
Socialists								
Democratic League of the People	23	23	22	18	23	24	28	29
Social Democratic Union of Workers and Small Farmers	–	50	27	37	41	20	–	–
Social Democratic Party	19	18	17	15	23	24	26	33
Urban Centre								
Liberal Party	21	21	18	19	28	36	48	50
Swedish People's Party	10	5	4	8	11	8	16	16
Christian League	–	–	–	–	3	12	22	23
Rural Centre								
Agrarian/Centre Party	8	9	9	11	15	17	21	22
Small Holders' Party, Finnish Rural Party	–	–	5	6	8	12	13	12
Conservatives								
National Coalition Party	20	18	16	17	22	24	27	29
Other parties	16	4	5	1	20	–	14	17
All parties	17.1	16.7	15.5	15.3	19.3	20.9	24.9	27.0
Percentage of women among candidates	15.7	15.1	14.5	16.0	17.3	21.1	24.2	26
Percentage of women elected	15.0	14.0	13.5	16.5	21.5	21.5	23.0	26

Source: Official Statistics of Finland XXIX A

Votes cast for female candidates as a proportion of all votes can be studied for elections since 1954 when voting for individuals became the rule. Until then votes were cast for lists which might include both male and female candidates. In the elections of 1954, 1958, 1962, and 1979 women candidates obtained a disproportionately high share of the vote (Table 11.4), but were less likely to be elected than were male candidates. In the elections of 1966 and 1970 on the other hand, more women were elected than their share of the votes would lead one to expect. In the 1972 and 1975 elections there was almost no difference in the proportions of women amongst candidates, vote receivers and elected members of parliament.

In general, differences in the success rates of men and women candidates in parliamentary elections are minimal. Parties appear fairly skillful at nominating women as candidates in the same proportions as there is support for them in the electorate. Since Finnish women first obtained the vote in 1906 they have been better represented in the parliament than has been the case in any other liberal democracy (Skard, 1980, p. 30; Haavio-Mannila, 1978, p. 352). Only in 1979 did the proportion of women in the Swedish parliament exceed that in the Finnish.

The proportion of women MPs remained fairly stable at its 1907 level of 9.5 per cent (Figure 11.1), during the first half of the century. In 1948 it rose to 12 per cent. The proportion stabilised in the 1950s and 1960s at between 15 and 17 per cent, a similar trend to that of women's share of the candidacies. A sharp increase occurred in 1970 when the percentage of elected women rose to 21.5 even though women were only 17 per cent of the candidates. Growth continued throughout the 1970s and in 1979 fifty-two women (26 per cent) were elected to the parliament.

Patterns of nomination, attracting votes and electoral success for women candidates can be examined by electoral area and party. I have earlier shown (Haavio-Mannila, 1970 and 1978) how support for women in politics has traditionally been stronger in Eastern than in Western Finland, particularly in the non-Socialist parties. This old division seems to be losing importance. Differences between rural and urban areas, and between developed and less developed regions have become more significant: women are nominated, voted for and elected more often in the urban industrialised areas. Support for women as political actors is increasingly positively correlated with the general modernisation of a region.

Table 11.5 indicates that in 1962 women were most likely to be nominated by the National Coalition Party and the Democratic League of the People of Finland, that is by the extreme right- and left-wing parties. The Liberal Party also put forward a fair number of women candidates, whilst the Swedish speakers and Agrarians put forward the fewest women candidates. By 1972 differences between parties in nominating women had diminished. The lowest percentages were in the two agrarian parties and the new Christian League. In 1979 the Liberals, the Social Democrats and the National Coalition Party had the highest numbers of women amongst

Table 11.5 The proportion of women among candidates and elected members and of votes cast for women in parliamentary elections in 1962, 1972 and 1979 by party in percentages

Party	1962			1972			1979		
	Candidates	Votes	MPs	Candidates	Votes	MPs	Candidates	Votes	MPs
Socialists									
Democratic League of the People	19	22	19	21	24	24	26	29	31
Social Democratic League	14	27	100	22	20	–	–	–	–
Social Democratic Party	11	17	16	19	24	27	31	33	31
Urban Centre									
Liberal Party	17	18	15	29	36	57	40	50	75
Swedish People's Party	4	4	–	22	8	10	21	16	22
Christian League	–	–	–	19	12	–	23	23	22
Rural Centre									
Centre Party	12	9	8	19	17	17	23	22	14
Finnish Rural Party	–	5	–	15	12	6	17	12	–
Conservatives									
National Coalition Party	21	16	13	25	24	21	28	29	28
Other Parties	12	5	–	–	–	–	23	17	–
Average	15	15	14	21	21	22	26	28	26

their candidates, and the Finnish Rural Party had the lowest. Comparison of the proportion of women among candidates and those elected by party reveals certain changes in pattern. In the elections of 1962 and 1972 women candidates were more successful in the Socialist parties (except the Liberal Party). By 1979 these differences between Left and Right had diminished. Only in the rural centre were women candidates elected in lower proportions than their candidacies. Centre Party women candidates were not elected to the same extent as their share of the votes would suggest.

Examination of the proportion of votes cast for women candidates by party between 1954 and 1979 indicates a constant increase in the support of women in all parties (Table 11.4). A decline in the proportion of votes for women in the Socialist parties and among the Conservatives in the 1962 and 1966 elections may reflect the impact of the 'Feminine Mystique' period described by Friedan (1963). In the Swedish People's Party the decline was earlier, first becoming noticeable in the elections of 1958 and 1962. The trend 'bottomed' before 1966, possibly because Scandinavian sex-role discussions reached Swedish speakers earlier than it did the rest of Finland. This may also explain the earlier rise in the votes for Swedish People's Party women.

The proportion of women among elected members of parliament by party group between 1907 and 1979 is presented in Figure 11.2. Because of the small number of women elected in each party, the four group party classification scheme outlined above is used here. Until quite recently there have been more women amongst the Socialist MPs, a proportion which was particularly high in the 1920s and the 1950s, compared with that in other parties. These breaks in pattern may well have to do with the differential impact of the two world wars on working-class men and women. The proportion of women amongst Conservative MPs has closely followed the national average. Only in the 1910s was there a sharp unexplained decline. In the 1920s, 1950s and early 1960s the proportion of women among MPs representing the urban centre was low. From 1970 onwards it increased rapidly, mainly due to increases in the number of women Liberal Party MPs. The number of Urban Centre women MPs remains very small, however, and fluctuation there has little effect on the total number of women in parliament. The Rural Centre has returned fewer women MPs throughout this century than have the other party groups, although the proportion has steadily increased.

In summary, once nominated by the parties, Finnish women have been approximately as successful as men in becoming elected to the national legislative body. The proportions of women amongst those nominated, voted for and elected was higher in the Socialist than the non-Socialist parties between 1907 and 1972. Women were, and still are, the least likely to be nominated, voted for and elected in parties of the Rural Centre. And although the impact of the Right/Left cleavage has lost importance, the rural/urban cleavage continues to be an important variable in women's achievement of the electoral office.

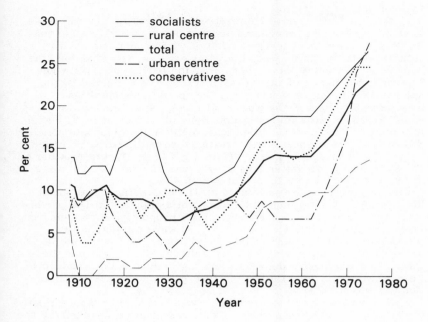

Figure 11.2:
Percentage of women among members of parliament in different party groups in Finland from 1907 to 1979 (three years' gliding averages).

WOMEN IN PARLIAMENT: SOCIAL BACKGROUND AND ACTIVITY

Between 1907 and 1917 women MPs were re-elected more often than men. In the eight elections under consideration women were elected an average of 3.1 times each and men 2.7 times. The average number of diets attended by women was 4.7 and men, 4.3. (Noponen, 1963, p. 82). The first women MPs gained considerable experience in the field of legislation. Even though the representation of women was modest, many were able to influence the legislative work of the diets (ibid.). Women champions of the feminist and labour movement as well as advocates of public education and temperance were elected to the first parliament. About one-third of the first women MPs were housewives or farmers' wives or daughters, that is, without an independent occupation, when first elected. The women MPs from the old bourgeois parties were often teachers, many were also editors and authors. They had, with only one exception, at least junior high school or college education. The average age (37) of women representatives was much lower than that of men (42) (ibid., pp. 82-3).

In the inter-war period the proportion of women MPs employed in public office or professional occupations was higher than that for MPs as a whole. The proportion of women MPs employed in commerce and industry was about the same as, and that for agriculture and forestry lower than, that for parliament as a whole. The male dominance of the Agrarian Party was reflected in the low representation of women from the farming communities. Approximately half of the women MPs originated from the working class, reflecting the higher proportions of women amongst Socialist deputies. National Coalition women MPs were disproportionately drawn from the highest social strata as were the three returned by the Swedish People's Party (ibid., p. 184). During this period the average age of women MPs at the time of first election was, at 38, two years lower than that for all MPs.

Unfortunately, systematic data on the occupations and social backgrounds of later women MPs are not available. In the parliament elected in 1979, there were a high proportion of women from health-related occupations. Six of the 52 were nurses, 4 were physicians, and 1 a pharmacist. In addition 7 had academic degrees in jurisprudence and 8 were editors. More than half the women had university degrees. The high educational standard of Finnish women in general is therefore reflected in the qualifications of women MPs.

Women representatives have been most active over issues related to social and educational policy. Joint research undertaken by the author and Sirkka Sinkkonen during 1979 found support for the hypothesis that women parliamentarians in Finland propose policies which benefit women and other underprivileged groups more frequently than their male colleagues. Issues raised solely by women or initiated by women and brought to the public agenda differed from those raised or initiated by men. Women concentrated to a much greater extent on matters of social legislation while men's policy proposals were focused on developing technological services, transportation, public utilities and economic development.

Women MPs have been most active at three points in time: in the beginning of the twentieth century during the first wave of the women's movement, immediately after the Second World War, and in the 1960s and 1970s during the 'second wave' of the women's movement. The post-war phases of activity were probably related to the general rises in women's activity during wartime.

Our knowledge of women's role in the Finnish parliament is far from complete. In early 1980 there were several women chairpersons or members of important parliamentary committees. Between 1975 and 1979, one of the two vice-chairpersons of parliament was a woman representing the National Coalition Party. When she retired from parliamentary work the position was filled by a man. Vice-presidential status is apparently considered to be appropriate for women and most of the Finnish political parties have women vice-presidents. Finnish governments normally contain two or three women who tend to be Ministers of Health and Social Affairs or

Education, although one of the women ministers in 1980, a Social Democrat, was second Minister of Finance.

WOMEN IN MUNICIPAL COUNCILS

Finnish women fare less well in municipal than general elections. But parties nominate more women and voters support female candidates more frequently than the proportion of elected women suggests. This may be partly explained by the dispersal of votes between relatively unknown local candidates. Men are traditionally more visible than women at local level, and in municipal elections parties are less interested in campaigning for women 'stars' selected to gather votes from the feminine electorate. At the local level the personal characteristics and contacts of the candidate are important and men may have an advantage in this respect. Whilst this pattern holds in the smaller municipalities, it is less apparent in the larger ones. In the largest municipality, Helsinki, women candidates obtained 36 per cent of the votes cast and 35 per cent of the women candidates were elected in 1976.

Table 11.6   The proportion of women members of municipal councils by party in Finland in 1968, 1972 and 1976 in percentages

Party	Year of election		
	1968	*1972*	*1976*
Socialists			
Democratic League of the People	9.3	12.5	16.3
Social Democratic Union of Workers and Small Farmers	15.0	15.6	50.0
Social Democratic Party	12.2	17.8	21.3
Urban Centre			
Liberal Party	23.2	28.6	30.1
Swedish People's Party	10.3	13.9	15.2
Christian Union	−	20.9	29.7
Rural Centre			
Centre Party	8.0	11.6	14.0
Finnish Rural Party	3.5	5.1	6.1
Conservatives			
National Coalition Party	19.4	21.3	23.0
Constitutional People's Party	−	−	14.3
Other parties	−	−	17.7
Total	10.7	14.9	18.2

Source: Official Statistics of Finland XXIX B

The small number of women in municipal councils in Finland might be due to the higher percentage of municipal councillors representing the Centre Party (39 per cent in the country as a whole) than is the case at parliamentary level (18 per cent). In this party the proportions of women among councillors is lower than in most other parties (Table 11.6). Agrarian dominance in councils is accounted for by the large number of small rural communities with their own municipal councils. Whilst Socialist women candidates obtain a higher proportion of votes cast than non-Socialist women in municipal elections, Table 11.6 indicates that the Liberal Party, Christian League and National Coalition Party return more women councillors than the Socialist, agrarian, and Swedish speaker's parties. The Social Democrats return more women than do the Communists. Finally, there are more women councillors in the urban municipalities than in the rural ones (ibid.).

Sirkka Sinkkonen (1979), has outlined the connection between type of municipality and the proportion of women among councillors elected in 1968 and 1976. She found that the proportion of women was highest in the councils of the economically and culturally most developed municipalities. Part of this correlation was interpreted as a result of variations in educational background rather than as an independent result of the development variable. The proportion of people employed in service industries was strongly correlated with the proportion of women councillors in most of the five groups of municipalities Sinkkonen investigated.

Women are less well represented in municipal governments (8.4 per cent) than in the councils (18.2 per cent), but are 22.3 per cent of municipal trustees including committee members not belonging to the councils ('Position of Women', 1980, Table 94). Chairs of various municipal organs are still mainly a male preserve: women are 0.5 per cent of chairpersons of municipal governments, 1.6 per cent of council chairpersons, and hold 4.3 per cent of committee chairs at this level (ibid., p. 191). There are more women among non-Socialist chairpersons of municipal committees than among the Socialist ones. Sinkkonen explains this by the different levels of competition for these seats by men. There is apparently more demand for men for chairpersonships in the parties on the Left than in those on the Right; possibly because the latter are more involved in leading positions in industry and business (ibid., p. 197). Chairwomen of municipal councils, governments and committees have very high educational qualifications and/or a visibly high position in the municipality. In the National Coalition Party the proportion of women with high educational qualifications and occupational positions is higher than is the case in the other parties. This is particularly the case in small towns and in rural areas. Sinkkonen argues that party ideology is not relevant when choosing women for such important municipal positions, possibly because in filling these 'in house' seats, parties need not appeal to women in the electorate in order to maximise their support.

WOMEN AND VOTING

There have been practically no differences in the turnout of men
and women (Figure 11.3) since the 1960s. At that time, possibly
as a result of the impact of 'second wave' feminism, sex discrep-

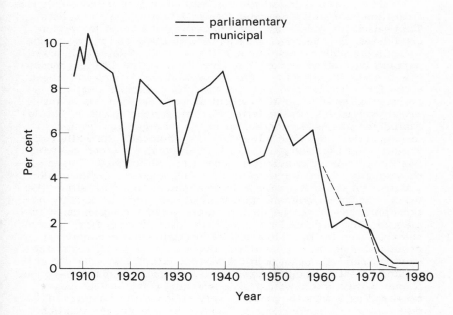

Figure 11. 3:
Difference in the voting activity of men and women in parliamentary elections from 1908 to 1979 and in municipal elections
from 1960 to 1976 in Finland.

ancies in voting turnout disappeared. During the first part of
the twentieth century, however, the political mobilisation of
women was lower than that of men, particularly in the rural municipalities of eastern and northern Finland which are in the least
developed areas of the country. In 1908 the sex differential in
turnout in those communities was 13 per cent while it was 7 per
cent in the urban municipalities and 5 per cent in the rural
municipalities of southern and western Finland (Martikainen, 1978,
p. 25). Thus the political mobilisation of women first took place
in the modernised, developed regions.

By 1951 turnout differences between men and women in Helsinki
could be explained by reference to differences in the age and
marital status of the sexes. According to Erik Allardt (1956, p. 130)

the surplus of women and the high mortality rates of men in Helsinki meant that there were more women in those marital status
and age groups with the lowest turnout rates. When voting rates
were controlled for age and marital status, the sex difference
proved to be very small. The parliamentary elections of 1975 saw
several age cohorts of women utilising their voting right more
frequently than the equivalent male age cohort.

A further interesting element of Finnish voting behaviour arises
from the opportunity for candidate selection within party lists.
This raises the question of who is casting the votes for women
candidates. On the basis of responses to questions in two nation-
wide Gallup polls I have found that women candidates gain more
support from other women than from men. In the 1970 parliamentary election 40 per cent of Finnish women and 7 per cent of men
voted for a female candidate. In the 1976 municipal elections 44
per cent of women and 10 per cent of men cast their votes for
women candidates. In the latter election support given to female
candidates was most pronounced in the younger age groups.
Among women, the most educated, the employed, the white collar
workers and especially those in leading positions voted most frequently for women candidates. More than 50 per cent of each of
these groups voted for women. By a large majority, men in all
groups cast their votes for male candidates. Men with either the
highest or lowest educational qualifications, those in leading positions and those from the working class voted for women most frequently. Women politicians gained the least support from farmers
and from men in the middle-level educational and occupational
groups. Hence there is evidence that men as a group resist the
encroachment of women political participants. This is hardly surprising. Electoral politics are a zero sum game, and for one group
to gain power another must give some up. Once women become
mobilised as voters they may greatly enhance the fortunes of
other women. Clearly those previously in a privileged position
might find this hard to accept and it might be said fairly that
Finnish men have not in general acted as agencies for the elimination of the basis of their special position.

CONCLUSIONS

Finnish women's attainment of basic political rights in 1906 has
been followed by a relatively high proportion of women achieving
electoral office. The comparatively high proportion of women in
the Finnish parliament may well be related to the fact that voting
rights were obtained simultaneously by women and the vast majority of men. Hence the first new male MPs were no better acquainted with political activity than their women colleagues. Women did
not have to compete with an established male political elite on first
entering the legislature.

The importance of the 'second wave' women's movement is evident in the rapid rise in the proportion of women in electoral

office at the beginning of the 1970s. 'Second wave' feminism
emerged in 1965. An 'election victory of women' took place in 1970
when the representation of women in parliament for the first time
exceeded one-fifth of the seats even though only one-sixth of the
candidates were women. The electorate expressed a distinct preference for female candidates. Parties responded to this by mount-
ing more women candidates in subsequent elections, thus producing further growth in the level of women's representation. This
growth in the political visibility of Finnish women coincided with
changes in family life patterns and changes in the position of
women. The activisation of women in politics was thus related to
the relative emancipation and liberation of women in education,
employment and the family.

Early universal suffrage, a relatively lively women's movement,
emancipation in other areas, and both the system of proportional
representation and its candidate preference option have all been
advantageous to the success of women in Finnish politics. Proportional representation often appears to benefit women candidates
(Rule, 1978, p. 10) and when we add to this a predisposition on
the part of half of Finnish women plus one-tenth of Finnish men
to support women candidates we have a powerful explanation for
the relative success of women in Finnish politics.

However, the advantage of Finnish women in politics relative
to women in other countries should not be taken to mean that
political equality there has arrived or is even imminent. At the
highest levels of political office women are conspicuously absent.
The non-directly elected nature of the cabinet, state committees
and sites of corporate power is less favourable to women whose
only route of access to the top elite has been their parliamentary
participation (see Sinkkonen, 1977).

Efforts to increase the proportion of women in the important
decision making bodies within the political system are justified by
two types of arguments: ideological and utilitarian. The ideological
argument is derived from normative theories of democracy which
imply that different groups in society should be represented at
policy-making level in proportion to their numbers. The utilitarian
perspective emphasises the qualitative advantage of recruiting
leaders from the widest possible pool. Women MPs have been more
likely than their male counterparts to pursue policies based on
humanitarian values and which attempt to improve the position of
under-privileged groups. This kind of activity is increasingly
important in the male dominated one-sidedly technological modern
world.

The slightly more conservative political choices of women - defined as observable support for parties of the right - may be
explained by women's position in the occupational system. More
women are white collar employees and full-time housewives than
are men. When statistical controls are applied which take these
factors into account, then women are at least as likely as men to
vote for leftist parties. Amongst housewives, only those married
to white collar workers are more conservative, and they are more

conservative than employed wives of men of this strata.

The main cleavages in support for women in politics used to be those between left and right, Eastern and Western Finland, and Finnish and Swedish speakers. The remaining cleavages are the urban and rural and that between the developed and under-developed regions. Support for women candidates is characteristic of voters in modernised areas, and at the individual level, of women of high social status. Middle-class men are the least likely group to support women politicians.

There are some discrepancies in women's party support and activity. Women vote for, join and are active in the non-Socialist parties more often than in the Socialist ones, but are more likely to hold electoral office as representatives of the Socialist parties. There may well be a larger reserve of qualified women and the competition with men may be milder in the non-Socialist parties. However, traditional Socialist commitment to equality between the sexes is not without importance to the more favourable environment they provide for the representation of women in electoral office. Although the participation of women has increased over time, the increase has been sporadic and there have been phases of stagnation and even retardation. Factors favouring women's participation have included economic growth and modernisation, rapid social and political changes including changes in the general position of women and both the feminist and labour movements. The need for social movements to improve the position of women remains great however, and there is some distance to travel before sex equality is achieved in the political arena.

NOTES

1   In the 1979 parliamentary elections the votes and successful candidates were distributed in the following way between different parties:

Party	Votes per cent	Members elected per cent
Socialists		
Democratic League of the People	17.9	17.5
Social Democratic Party	23.9	26.0
	41.8	43.5
Urban Centre		
Liberal Party	3.7	2.0
Swedish People's Party	4.2	4.5
Christian League	4.8	4.5
	12.7	11.0

Party	Votes per cent	Members elected per cent
Rural Centre		
Centre Party	17.3	18.0
Finnish Rural Party	4.6	3.5
	21.9	21.5
Conservatives		
National Coalition Party	23.8	23.5
Constitutional People's Party	1.2	–
	25.0	23.5
Other Parties	0.8	0.5
	100.2	100.0

BIBLIOGRAPHY

Alakapee, P. and Valkonen, M. (1979), Naiset ammattiyhdistys-
liikkeesṣä, in 'Nainen SAK: laisessa ammattiyhdistysliikkeessä',
Gummerus, Jyvaskylä, pp. 33-204.
Alestalo, M. (1980), Yhteiskuntaluokat ja sosiaaliset kerrostumat
toisen maailmansodan jälkeen, in Tapani Valkonen, et al.,
'Suomalaiset', WSOY, Juva, pp. 102-80.
Allardt, E. (1956), 'Social structur och politisk aktivitet', Söder-
ströms, Borgå.
Allardt, E. (1976), 'Hyvinvoinnin ulottuvuuksia', WSOY, Provoo.
Berglund, S. and Lindström, U. (1978), 'The Scandinavian Party
System(s)', Studentlitteratur, Lund.
Dahlerup, D. (1978), The women's sections within the political
parties in Denmark, Paper presented at ECPR Workshop on
Women as Political Actors, Grenoble, April 6-11.
Dahlström, E. (ed.) (1962), 'Kvinnors liv och arbete', Studieför-
bund Näringsliv och Samhälle, Stockholm.
Eduards, M. (1977), 'Kvinnor och politik', Liber Förlag, Stock-
holm.
Friedan, B. (1963), 'Feminine Mystique', W.W. Norton, New York.
Haavio-Mannila, E. (1970), Sex Roles in Politics, 'Scandinavian
Political Studies', no. 5, pp. 209-39.
Haavio-Mannila, E. (1978), Changes in Sex Roles in Politics as an
Indicator of Structural Change in Society, 'International Journal
of Sociology', VIII, no. 3, pp. 56-85.
Haavio-Mannila, E. and Hallinoja, R. (1980), 'Changes in the Life
Patterns of Families in Finland', Department of Sociology, Uni-
versity of Helsinki, Working Paper 13.

Haavio-Mannila, E. and Kari, K. (1980), Changes in the Life Patterns of Families in the Nordic Countries, 'Yearbook of Population Studies', XVIII, The Population Research Institute, Vammala.

Haavio-Mannila, E. and Kirkkonan, L. (1980), The Role of Trade Unions in Forming Policies Concerning Women. Paper presented at ECPR Workshop on Women and Public Policy, Florence, March 24-29.

Haranne, M. and Allardt, E. (1974), 'Attitudes toward Modernity and Modernization', Research Group for Comparative Sociology, University Helsinki, Research Report 6.

Hjerppe, R. and Schybergson, P. (1977), 'Kvinnorarbete i Finlands industri ca. 1850-1913', Institute of Economic and Social History, University of Helsinki, Communications 5.

Jallinoja, R. (1979), Suomen varhaisen naisasialiikkeen synty, 'Tiede & Edistys', 4, no. 4, pp. 35-41.

Jallinoja, R. (1980), Miehet ja naiset, in Tapani Valkonen, et. al., 'Suomalaiset', WSOY, Juva, pp. 222-50.

Kilpi, S. (1953), 'Suomen työlaisnaisliikkeen historia', Kansankulttuuri, Pori.

Martikainen, T. (1978), 'Ikä ja sioutuminen politiikkaan', Kansalaiskasvatuksen keskuksen julkaisuja 36, Helsinki.

Matheson, D. (1979), 'Ideology, Political Action and the Finnish Working Class', Commentationes Scientiarum Socialium 10, Societas Scientiarum Fennica, Helsinki-Helsingfors.

Means, I. (1973), 'Kvinner i norsk politikk', Cappelens Forlag, Oslo.

Noponen, M. (1963), 'Kansanedustajien sosiaalinen tausta Suomessa', WSOY, Porvoo.

Noponen, M. (1977), 'Politiikka tutkimuksen kohteena', WSOY, Porvoo.

Nupponen, T. (1968), Suomen puolueohjelmat ja sukupuoliroolit, in K. Eskola, (ed.), 'Miesten maailman nurjat lait', Tammi, Helsinki, pp. 45-61.

Official Statistics of Finland XXIX A and B, 'Election Statistics', Central Statistical Office of Finland, Helsinki.

Pesonen, P. (1972), 'Protestivaalit - nuorisovaalit', Ylioppilastuki, Tampere.

Pesonen, P. and Sänkiaho, R. (1979), 'Kansalaiset ja kansanvalta', WSOY, Juva.

'Position of Women' (1980), Central Statistical Office, Statistical Surveys 65, Helsinki.

Rule, W. (1978), 'Socio-Political Environment and the Eligibility and Selection of Women Legislators', Paper presented at Annual Meeting of APSA, New York City.

Ruusala, R. (1967), 'Vasemmiston naisjärjestöjen tavoitteet ja toiminitamenetelmät', University of Tampere, Institute of Political Science, Research Report 4.

Saarinen, J. (1979), Nisten osuus työmarkkinajärjestöjen, puolueiden, maataloustuottajien ja osuustoimintaliikkeiden päättävistä elimistä vuoden 1978 lopussa, Council for Equality, manuscript.

Sinkkonen, S. (1977), Women's Increased Political Participation in Finland. Real influence of pseudodemocracy? Paper presented at ECPR Workshop on Women in Politics, Berlin, March 27-April 2.

Sinkkonen, S. (1979), Modernisaatio, poliittinen ideologia ja naisten edustus kunnallisissa luottamustehtävissä, Kunnallistieteen aikakauskirja, 2, pp. 165-200.

Sinkkonen, S. and Haavio-Mannila, E. (1979), 'Impact of Women MPs and the Women's Movement on Agenda Building', XIth IPSA World Congress, Moscow, August 12-18; also in Finnish in 'Politiikka', 2, 1980.

Skard, T. (1980), 'Utvalgt til Stortinget', Gyldendal Norsk Forlag, Oslo.

12 EASTERN EUROPE

Sharon L. Wolchik

In discussing women's participation in politics in Eastern Europe it is important to keep several factors in mind. The first of these is the diversity in the area. The eight countries in the region (Albania, Bulgaria, Czechoslovakia, East Germany, Hungary, Poland, Romania and Yugoslavia) differ considerably from one another in terms of level of economic development, religious and cultural traditions, and previous social and political history. These differences were particularly marked in the pre-Communist period, when certain countries, such as Albania, Bulgaria, Romania and parts of Yugoslavia, were overwhelmingly peasant societies with very low levels of urbanisation and economic development while others, including Czechoslovakia and Hungary, had levels of economic development and living standards which approximated those found in Western Europe. Although less sharp, many of these differences persist to the present time. In addition, there are still substantial differences between urban and rural areas in many of these countries.

Traditions with respect to women also varied greatly prior to the establishment of Communist systems. Most of the constitutions enacted to govern the new states created after the end of the First World War contained provisions granting women suffrage, but women's actual opportunities to take part in public life depended heavily on social and cultural norms. Women in Czechoslovakia and Germany, for example, had access to education and employment and took an active role in the cultural and political life of their countries, although seldom as elected officials. The situation of women in the Balkans and in rural areas in all countries was far less favourable. Women's activities were particularly restricted in areas where religious customs, such as those of Islam, prescribed a markedly subordinate role for women.

Women's opportunities for political action also varied according to the political climate or type of political regime during this period. In many of these countries, women had organised to promote women's rights prior to the First World War. They also took part in various national and political movements. As the inter-war period progressed, all of these states except Czechoslovakia became increasingly authoritarian, and the activities of women's groups, as well as other voluntary and political organisations, were curtailed.[1]

Given this diversity, one might expect that the way in which women currently participate in politics would vary a good deal from one country to another. In fact, however, although the differences noted above continue to influence many areas of life, their impact on women's political roles has been overshadowed by a feature which is common to all of these states, that is, by the fact that they are all Communist political systems. As such, they share certain political structures and values which are distinct from those found in democratic and other types of political systems. One of the most important is the fact that they are single-party systems in which the Communist party is the leading political force and in which organised opposition is not permitted. They are also systems which have an official ideology, Marxism-Leninism. Together, these characteristics condition the opportunities which women and other citizens have to take part in politics. They also have had an impact on elite policy toward women and led to a common pattern in the way in which women take part in politics.

To what extent do these characteristics of the current political systems encourage women to take part in politics in Eastern Europe? In accordance with Marxism-Leninism, political elites in Eastern Europe have explicitly affirmed their commitment to women's equality in all areas of life, including politics. They have attempted to ensure women's allegiance to the political system and urged women to be more active politically. Because Communist elites, through their ability to use social and economic incentives and manipulate the educational system and mass media, have more tools than leaders in other political systems to use in promoting desired goals, one might expect East European elites to be better able as well as more committed to promote higher levels of activism among women. In particular, the party-based recruitment system means that communist leaders should be able to manipulate the process for selecting candidates for both government and party posts so as to include more women if they so desire.

At the same time, the institution of Communist systems in Eastern Europe has been accompanied by changes in women's lives which may have increased the supply of women available for political activities. As illustrated in greater detail elsewhere (see Heitlinger, 1979; Jancar, 1978; Scott, 1974; Wolchik, 1978a), women's status has changed greatly in these societies, particularly in terms of two factors known to influence levels of political activism: educational access and employment. Communist leaders gave a good deal of attention in the early post-second World War years to eliminating illiteracy, which was particularly great among women, and they have succeeded in reducing the number of illiterates of both sexes substantially.[2] Women's access to secondary and higher education increased dramatically in most countries during the early years of Communist rule and has continued to increase since that time. By 1975 women accounted for approximately one-half of secondary students in all East European countries and from 40 to 60 per cent of all students in higher education (Wolchik, 1978a).

A similar pattern exists in the area of work. Women's employment outside the home increased very rapidly once Communist states were established, primarily due to the need to use all available labour resources to rebuild after the war and meet ambitious economic development plans. The increase in women's entry into the labour force occurred much earlier in the East European states and the Soviet Union than in Western Europe, and women's participation in paid employment in these countries still exceeds levels reached in the West. By the mid-1970's, women comprised over a third of the labour force in all East European countries and close to half of the total labour force in Czechoslovakia and East Germany. The proportion of women in the work-capable ages (generally defined as 15 to 54) who work is also substantially higher in these countries than in Western Europe and the United States, and ranged from a low of 47 per cent in Yugoslavia to approximately 75 per cent in Czechoslovakia and East Germany and nearly 80 per cent in Poland by 1970 (Wolchik, 1978a, p. 65).

Differences between the sexes have not been eliminated completely in either access to education or the labour force. Far more girls in all countries, for example, continue to follow general education programmes at the secondary level than vocational or apprentice training. In higher education, despite the expansion of the number of women students, most women still tend to specialise in those areas, such as education and the humanities, traditionally held to be appropriate for women, as well as in certain disciplines, such as medicine, which have become heavily 'feminised' since the establishment of communist systems. Women are far less frequently found in technical fields.

The effects of continued differences in educational specialisations are evident in the area of work, for there is still considerable sex segregation in the labour force in all East European countries. Women have moved into a somewhat wider range of occupations than in the pre-Communist period, but most women continue to work in highly feminised branches of the economy, such as education and culture, trade and public catering, health, and administrative services. This tendency is also true of women with specialised educations and professional women. In part because the branches of the economy in which women are concentrated have lower than average wage scales, women earn on the average approximately two-thirds the wages that men do. This difference in income, which is also a reflection of the fact that women tend to be assigned to and accept job classifications lower than those for which they are qualified, outright discrimination and the paucity of women who are trained as skilled or highly skilled manual workers, does not vary greatly from one country to another; neither, for those countries for which longitudinal data are available, has it changed significantly over time. The continued inequality of women in the labour force is also reflected in the fact that women are far less likely than men to hold leading economic positions. More women hold such positions in heavily feminised occupations such as teaching and medicine, but even in these cases, men have a much higher likelihood of advancing to leadership positions, despite the fact that they comprise relatively small proportions of the labour forces in these fields. However, the remaining inequalities in these areas do not negate the fact that women's educational levels and rates of economic activity outside the home have increased in all of the countries in the region. I expected that these changes would have a spillover effect into the political sphere, for presumably they provide East European women with greater interest, motivation, and skills to participate in politics than they possessed in earlier periods.

This expectation was only partially fulfilled. While women are somewhat more active politically now than in the pre-Communist period in most of these countries, substantial differences persist in the extent of political activism of men and women, particularly at the elite level. Despite the changes noted above and despite the important differences in the organisation and nature of political life in Communist states, women's political behaviour in Eastern Europe and the Soviet Union displays many of the same patterns evident in women's participation in politics in western democratic countries.

WOMEN'S INVOLVEMENT IN POLITICS AT THE MASS LEVEL

Due to the restrictions on empirical social science research in communist countries, it is difficult to judge the extent of sex-related differences in low-level political activities. This problem is especially severe in assessing attitudes, motivations, and other subjective dimensions of participation, because social scientists seldom conduct research on such topics in these countries, and those surveys which are conducted are not often made public. It is similarly difficult to evaluate possible differences in the political orientations of men and women, for with the exception of Yugoslavia, the political elites in Eastern Europe do not admit that political attitudes, loyalties, or policy preferences should vary by social group. The extensive public opinion polls conducted in Czechoslovakia during the reform period in the late 1960s reveal few systematic differences in men's and women's attitudes on a wide variety of political and social questions (see Piekalkiewicz, 1972, for a summary of these studies), but it is difficult to generalise from these findings because they were obtained in highly unusual political times.

Given the generally higher degree of politicisation and elite efforts to mobilise the population to participate in activities which reaffirm support for the regime, such as voting and attending pre-election meetings, it is not surprising that there is little difference in the extent to which men and women participate in such activities. Information concerning elections in Yugoslavia and the Soviet Union, for example, indicates that sex-related differences in turnout in these countries are indeed minimal (Duverger, 1955, pp. 15-16; Lapidus, 1975, p. 97). The uniformly high levels of voter turnout in these and other Communist countries (virtually all adults of voting age vote) indicate that men and women are

equally mobilised in this respect. However, the generally symbolic nature of elections in these countries and the obligatory
character of the act of voting mean that they are not really a good
indication of participation.

If we turn to such aspects of political involvement as information about and interest in politics, sense of political efficacy, and
participation in less obligatory political acts, the data we have
indicate that sex-related differences have not been eradicated.
Information concerning these aspects of political involvement is
most plentiful in the Yugoslav case. An investigation of the determinants of political participation conducted in that country in the
late 1960s as part of a seven-nation study found that women had
uniformly lower levels of information about politics than men had
and a lower sense of political efficacy. They were also less involved in political activity at all levels (Barbic; Verba, Nie and
Kim, 1978). Although women were less involved than men in all
republics, differences between the sexes were lower in the more
developed republics of Slovenia and Croatia.

Women also spend less time than men on political activities in
the Soviet Union and Czechoslovakia and, in the latter country,
are less interested in political issues (Gordon and Klopov, 1972,
p. 136; Magdolen, 1973, Tables 3 and 4). Czech and Yugoslav
sources indicate that women are also less involved in political
activities in the workplace. In Czechoslovakia, a study of political activism in the workplace conducted in the 1960s found that
women took less interest in methods of improving production, were
less active in factory-level Communist party organisations, and
less frequent participants in factory meetings (Slejska, 1965).
Similar trends are evident in Yugoslavia, where women play a
relatively small role in workers' self-management, particularly in
the executive committees of workers' councils (Pilic, 1969, p. 59).
Statements by party officials which note the low level of women's
activity and emphasise the need for continued educational work
among women are further indications that women's political involvement, beyond ritualised participation as voters, is still perceived
as unsatisfactory in the other countries of the region as well.

Given the importance of the Communist party in East European
societies, one of the most important forms of political participation
is party membership. In the period prior to coming to power and
in the immediate post-Second World War period, most of the Communist parties had separate sections for women. These sections,
which were responsible for mobilising and educating women party
members, were disbanded in the early 1950s along with the broader
mass women's organisations on the grounds that they had fulfilled
their functions and, due to the political maturity of women, were
no longer necessary (see Wolchik, 1978a, Ch.6 for a discussion of
this period in the Czechoslovak case). This action, which reflects
the ambivalence which Marxist leaders have traditionally displayed
concerning separate organisations for any segment of the prole-
tariat, paralleled the dissolution of the women's sections of the
Soviet party which occurred in the 1930s.

As Table 12.1 illustrates, women's proportion of Communist
Party members ranged from approximately 20 per cent in Yugoslavia to approximately 30 per cent in East Germany in the early
to mid-1970s. Seldom have women accounted for more than a third
of all party members. There has been no clear-cut increase in the
proportion of women party members common to all countries, although the degree of variation in this proportion has narrowed
considerably in recent years. Women's lower levels of party
membership hinders their advancement to political offices in all of
these countries: it also impairs women's professional progress, because candidates for most important positions must be party
members.

Table 12.1   Women as a percentage of total members of Communist Parties in the Soviet Union and Eastern Europe

	USSR	Albania	Bulgaria	CSSR	GDR	Hungary	Poland	Romania	Yugoslavia
1950	20.7		13.8	33.0[b]	14.0[a]	28.9	18.0[c]		18.0
1966	20.2[d]	12.5	22.4	27.4	26.5	22.9	19.1	22.4	17.8
1971	22.2	22.0	25.2		29.4[e]	24.0[d]	22.8	23.0	19.5[e]
1975	23.8	24.0[f]	27.6[g]			26.5	23.6		

(a) 1948; (b) 1949; (c) 1951; (d) 1965; (e) 1972; (f) 1974; (g) 1976.
Sources: Burks, 1961, p. 68; Childs, 1969, p. 225; Duverger, 1955, p. 106; Glowny urad
statystyczny, 1973, p. 59, p. 106; 1974, p. 5, p. 25; 1975, p. 5, p. 21; 1976, p. 24; Hoover,
1966, p. 70; 1973, p. 106; 1974, pp. 3-25; 1975, p. 5; Jancar, 1971, p. 36; Keefe, et al.,
1971, p. 115; 1972a, p. 73; Lane, 1971, p. 140; Lapidus, 1975, p. 102; Magyar Szocialista
Munkaspart, 1975, p. 4, p. 20; Nenoff, 1951, p. 28; Radio Free Europe Research, 1970a,
p. 6; 1971a, p. 4; 1976b, p. 3; Rigby, 1968, pp. 360-1; Saveza Komunista Jugoslavije,
1965, p. 65; US Department of State, 1968, p. 57; 1972, p. 30, p. 40; Wrochno, 1971,
p. 98.

As in Western countries, women in Eastern Europe are more
active in non-partisan groups such as school boards, friendship
societies, labour unions, and youth organisations, than they
are in political parties (Duverger, 1955; Jancar, 1978; Wolchik,
1978a). They are also somewhat more active in the minor political
parties which still exist in several of these countries. Women
comprised 40 per cent of the members of the Czechoslovak Peoples'
Party in 1971, for example, a proportion approximately twelve
percentage points greater than their proportion of Community-
party members ('Náse politika', 12 May 1971, p. 5). They are
also more likely to be members of the Peasant party in Poland and
the Christian Democratic party in East Germany than of the Communist parties in those countries (Childs, 1969, p. 113). These
trends may indicate that women in Eastern Europe are more conservative politically. Alternatively, the higher proportion of
women in the minor parties may reflect the fact that these parties
have less prestige and influence than the Communist parties.

WOMEN IN POLITICAL ELITES

As in the West and in the Soviet Union, women in Eastern Europe play a very small role in the exercise of political power. Further women's representation in political elites conforms to the 'law of increasing disproportion' (Putnam, 1976, p. 33), which character-ises the political representation of minorities and women in other societies, i.e., as the importance of the office increases, the number of women declines. Thus women (1) are better represen-ted in the symbolic, or governmental, elites than in the effective, or Communist party, elites at all levels; (2) are more frequently found in the deliberate rather than executive bodies in both types of elites; and (3) play a greater role in leadership at the local than at the national level.

Women have been somewhat better represented in the national governmental elites in Eastern Europe and the Soviet Union than they have in most Western countries, particularly in legislative bodies. There have been no women heads of state in Eastern Europe and few women who have served as ministers. However, one of the deputy heads of the legislatures is frequently a woman, and women have comprised substantially higher proportions of members of the national legislatures in these countries than in most Western states. As Table 12.2 illustrates, women's repre-sentation at this level currently ranges from 14 to 34 per cent.

Table 12.2   Women as a percentage of deputies in national legislatures, Eastern Europe and the USSR

	USSR	Albania	Bulgaria	CSSR	GDR	Hungary	Poland	Romania	Yugoslavia
1948:	24.2^a	7.3		7.1		17.4^b	17.4^c		
1958	27.0	9.0		19.4^d	24.5		4.1^e		6.5
1962	27.0	11.7^f	20.0	20.0^g	27.4^h		13.0^f		19.6^h
1966	28.0	16.7^i	15.2		33.0^i	20.0^i	12.4^j	14.2	17.3^j
1970	30.5		18.4^k	25.7	31.8^k	23.9^k	13.5l	14.0^l	8.3l
1973	31.3^m	34.0^m	19.5	28.6	20.6	28.6^n	20.6		13.6^m

(a) 1946; (b) 1947; (c) 1952; (d) 1960; (e) 1957; (f) 1961; (g) 1964; (h) 1963; (i) 1967; (j) 1965; (k) 1971; (l) 1969; (m) 1974; (n) 1975.

Sources: Institut mezhinarodnigo rabochego dvizheniia., 1972, p. 61; Pierre, 1960, p. 135; Lapidus, 1975, p. 98; Ludz, 1972, p. 200; Childs, 1969, p. 218; Blondel, 1973, p. 160; Matic, 1968, p. 182; 1970, p. 152; 'Encyklopedie modernī ženy', 1966, p. 567; Drejtonia e Statistikes, 1961, p. 49; Staatliche Zentralverwaltung, 1956, p. 137; 1973, p. 513; Glowny urad statystyczny, 1973, p. 56; 1976, p. 21; Savezni zavod za statistiku, 1964, p. 11; 1971, p. 137; 1977, p. 99; Hoover Institution, 1975, p. 5; Keefe et. al., 1971, p. 115; 1972a, p. 32; Radio Free Europe Research, 1971b, p. 22; 1975b, p. 14; 1976a, pp. 1-6; 1976b, p. 3; 'Rude pravo', December 1, 1971, p. 3; November 9, 1976, p. 4; US Department of State, 1965; 1969; 1971.

Given the limited role which the national legislatures play in the formation of policy in most of these countries, women's representation in these largely symbolic bodies is not a true measure of their actual influence at the national level. If we look at women's representation among the effective, or Communist party elites, a very different picture emerges. While women are well represented in the governmental or symbolic elites, they are seldom members of the more important Communist party elites and have been virtually absent from top party positions. A small number of women, such as Alexandra Kollontai and Krupskaya in the USSR, Ana Pauker in Romania, and Marie Švermová in Czechoslovakia, were active in establishing Communist states in their countries and played an important role in political life. However, very few women have served as members of the Politburo, or comparable supreme decision-making bodies of the Communist parties. In 1972, for example, the Politburos of the Albanian, Bulgarian Slovak, East German, and Bulgarian parties each had one woman member. Women were unrepresented in these bodies in Poland, Romania, the Soviet Union, and Yugoslavia in that year (Jancar, 1974a, p. 232). By 1978 two women had been selected for the Politburo in Romania; women thus accounted for eight of the 199 full or candidate members of Politburos in all of Eastern Europe in that year.

The women who have achieved these positions have differed markedly from their male counterparts in terms of previous political experience and social background characteristics. With the exception of women active in the early Communist era, women on these bodies have generally been reputed to have had little influence. Possible recent exceptions to this pattern are Tsola Dragoicheva in Bulgaria and Elena Ceausescu in Romania. A former partisan and member of the central committee of the Bulgarian Communist party since 1937, Dragoicheva has held a number of important party and government posts and has served on the Politburo from 1940 to 1948 and from 1966 to present. Elena Ceausescu, wife of Romanian party leader Nicolae Ceausescu, is held by most analysts to have obtained her high party post by virtue of her relationship to her husband; however, she held a number of important government and party positions prior to her election and is reputed to wield considerable influence in Romania.

Women are somewhat better represented on the central committees of the Communist parties than in the top party bodies. However, as Table 12.3 illustrates, women's proportion of central committee members is far smaller than their number of national legislators and has been below 20 per cent in all countries for which information is available for the post-Second World War period. Given the generally low level of women's representation, there has been some variation within the region. The most striking aspect of this variation is the fact that women are uniformly better represented on the central committees in Eastern Europe than in the Soviet Union. Women have been best represented among central committee members in the GDR and Czechoslovakia throughout this period, and from the mid-1960s to the present, in Bulgaria. Although the proportion of women central committee members in these three

Table 12.3   Women's representation among members of central committees of the Communist parties

	USSR	Albania	Bulgaria	Czechoslovakia	E. Germany	Hungary	Poland	Romania	Yugoslavia
1948	2.5[a]		8.0	13.9[b]	12.3[c]				5.7
1962	3.0[d]		8.6	10.0	11.0[e]	6.7	3.1[f]	5.5[g]	8.4[f]
1971	3.0	15.4	10.5	8.7	12.1	8.6[h]	9.1	6.3[i]	
1976	3.3		10.2	15.0		12.0	8.0[j]	9.1[k]	

(a) 1952; (b) 1949; (c) 1950; (d) 1961; (e) 1963; (f) 1964; (g) 1965; (h) 1970; (i) 1972; (j) 1975; (k) 1974

Sources: Bulgarskata Komunisticheska Partiia, 1948; 1966; 'Current Digest of the Soviet Press', 1976; Duverger, 1955, p. 108; Gesamtdeutsches Institut, 1971, pp. 7-11; Gruliow, 1962, pp. 229-35; Jancar, 1974, p. 159; Komunistická strana Československa, 1949; 1962; 1971; 1976; Ludz, 1972, p. 196, pp. 443-4; Magyar Dolgozok Partja, 1948; Magyar Szocialista Munkaspart, 1962; 1975; Partidul Comunist Roman, 1975; Partidul Munitoresc Romin, 1955; 1965; Pierre, 1960, pp. 129-30; Polska Zjednoczona Partia Robotnicza, 1969; Radio Free Europe Research, 1966; 1970c; 1972a; 1972b; 1976b; Saveza Komunista Jugoslavije, 1965; US Department of State, 1964; 1966.

countries is still far from equal to their proportion of party members of the adult population, women's representation at this level of the effective elite has been considerably higher than that of women in legislatures in the United States and most Western European countries, with the exception of the Scandinavian countries. Women's representation on the central committee has also increased recently in Romania, Poland, Albania, and Hungary, largely as the result of elite efforts to increase women's roles in political life.

As in Western countries and the Soviet Union, women's roles in political leadership in Eastern Europe are greatest at the lower levels, where both the rewards of office-holding and competition for office are lower. Women comprise substantially larger proportions of government leaders at the local level than at the national level in most countries, although women's representation does not vary strictly by level. Women in Poland, for example, comprised from 18 to 25 per cent of deputies at the local level in 1971, compared to 15.9 per cent at the national level (Glowny urad, 1973, pp. 56-60). Women's share of local office holders rose from approximately 27 per cent to 37 per cent in Bulgaria from 1971 to 1974 and reached 40 per cent in Albania in the latter year (Hoover, 1975; see Jancar, 1978, p. 95 for additional information). Women also tend to hold higher proportions of top leadership positions at the lower levels (Wolchik, 1978a; Wronchno, 1969).

In contrast to the Soviet case, where there is currently little variation in women's representation in urban and rural soviets (Lapidus, 1975, p. 99), women in Eastern Europe generally comprise a higher proportion of members of local councils in cities than they do in rural areas (Wrochno, 1969, p. 99; Chovanec, 1974, pp. 130-1). In Yugoslavia, women's representation in both republic and local assemblies has been greatest in the more developed republics of Slovenia and Croatia throughout the post-Second World War era (Savezni zavod, 1958, p. 38; 1964, p. 61, p. 64; 1969, p. 65; 1971, p. 64).

Women also play a larger role in lower level elites in Communist parties. Thus, women in Czechoslovakia generally have been better represented among members of the regional Slovak Communist party's central committee. Their representation among members of regional and district executive party committees consistently has been higher than their representation in higher bodies (Wolchik, 1980). The situation is similar in other East European countries. In Poland, for example, women comprised 10 per cent of all full-time party officials at the county, town, city, and district levels in 1965, compared to approximately 3 per cent of members of the central committee.

However, even at this level, women have seldom served as top leaders; they also appear to be excluded from those positions of regional party leadership, such as district first secretary, which serve as recruiting channels into the central party elite. In the Soviet Union, for example, women accounted for approximately 3

per cent of all obkom, or district, party bureau members in the
25 districts of the RSFSR and Ukranian SSR from 1955 to 1973
(Moses, 1976, p. 530). They have been similarly rare in these
positions in Eastern Europe. Women held none of the leading positions of regional party executive committees in Czechoslovakia in
1962, 1967, and 1971; they were similarly unrepresented in such
positions in Poland in 1967 and 1971. Their representation on
these bodies has been only slightly greater in Bulgaria, where
there was one woman secretary in each of four district party committees in 1965 and one district first secretary in 1971. Women
have occasionally played important roles in republic and district
party bodies in Yugoslavia and Albania, but such women have
been few in number.

Women play the greatest role in party leadership at the level of
local and primary party organisations. However, even at this
level the proportion of women among party officials does not equal
their proportion of party members. In Hungary, for example,
women accounted for approximately 15 per cent of members of
party committees and 8.8 per cent of members of the executive
committees at the local level, and 12 per cent of secretaries of
primary organisations in 1971 (Radio Free Europe Research, 1971b,
p. 14); approximately a quarter of all party members were women
in that year. As in the national elites, women's representation in
party bodies is lower than in governmental elites at these levels.

THE BEHAVIOUR AND BACKGROUNDS OF WOMEN LEADERS

In addition to constituting a smaller group than men, women
leaders behave differently once they become members of the political elite. As in Western countries, women leaders in Eastern
Europe and the Soviet Union tend to be responsible for matters
traditionally viewed as women's concerns and seldom rise to positions of leadership. They also differ from men in terms of their
routes into the elite and the skills they bring with them.

The tendency for East European women to choose or be channelled into certain types of activity once they are in the elite is
evident in the fact, mentioned earlier, that women ministers are
most often responsible for areas such as culture, health, education, and social welfare. It is also evident in the activities of
women legislators. In the Soviet case, women deputies have been
shown to take a more active role in discussions of health, social
welfare, and labour legislation than they do in debates concerning
planning, the budget, or foreign affairs (Lapidus, 1975, pp. 101-
1). Women deputies in Czechoslovakia and Bulgaria appear to
focus on similar issues, for they are overrepresented in relation
to their proportion of total deputies on those committees which
deal with health, welfare, culture, and youth; they are also over-
represented on committees which deal with sectors of the economy
in which women predominate in the labour force, but play very
little role on those committees which deal with overall foreign

and economic policy (Wolchik, 1978a).

The concentration of women deputies in the various chambers of the Yugoslav National Assembly prior to its reorganisation in 1974 further illustrates sex-related differences in political specialisations. Prior to that year, the Yugoslav Federal Assembly consisted of four functional chambers and one general chamber. As Table 12.4 illustrates, women deputies have been consistently concentrated in the largest proportion of deputies in the educational/cultural and social welfare/health chambers; far smaller proportions of women have served in the chambers responsible for economic and organisational/political issues.

Table 12.4   Concentration of women deputies to the national legislature by chamber, Yugoslavia

	1963	1967	1969
Federal	25.2	15.5	36.7[a]
Economic	9.2	2.3	4.1
Educational/Cultural	26.0 ⎤	30.9 ⎤	28.6 ⎤
		53.4		66.6		46.9
Social Welfare/Health	27.5 ⎦	35.7 ⎦	18.4 ⎦
Organisational/Political	12.2	15.5	12.2

(a) Chamber of Nationalities
Sources: From information in Matic (1968); Savezni zavod (1964; 1971)

The extent of sex-related differences in responsibilities among members of the party elites in Eastern Europe is not clear. Moses (1976) and Lapidus (1975) have documented such differences in regional party bodies in the Soviet Union, but comparable data for Eastern Europe have not been gathered. The recent practice of electing the head of the women's organisation to the top party executive organ in several of these countries suggests that there is a sex-related division of labour in top party elites as well, although one cannot really know without information concerning the responsibilities and activities of these bodies.

To a certain extent, the different responsibilities of men and women leaders may reflect the differing skills and experiences men and women bring with them when they enter the elite. As in Western countries and the Soviet Union, women members of the political elites in Eastern Europe differ from their male counterparts in terms of social background characteristics, previous political experiences, and routes into the elite. In both the governmental and party elites, women tend to be drawn from lower status occupations and to have held lower party positions than males.

Male deputies are far more frequently full-time party or governmental officials at the time of their election to the national legislatures in these countries than women. Women deputies, on the other hand, account for a disproportionately large share of those persons of lower socio-economic status chosen for honorific, or symbolic, reasons. The Czechoslovak case is illustrative. Party and governmental officials were the largest single category of male deputies elected to the National Assembly in Czechoslovakia in 1971 (32.9 per cent), but only two of the 90 women deputies had such occupations. Over a half of all women legislators, compared to approximately 20 per cent of all males, were workers. Nearly three-quarters of all women deputies, but slightly less than a third of all men, were either workers or collective farmers ('Rude pravo', December 1, 1971, p. 3).

The social backgrounds of men and women in the party elites also differs. As might be expected, women in the party elites have served more frequently as party officials prior to their selection than have women in the governmental elites. While party activism is an important recruitment channel for women as well as for men, women central committee members who have been political activists tend to have held lower governmental and party posts prior to their selection than their male counterparts. As in the governmental elites, women account for a disproportionately large share of members, including peasants and workers, who are chosen for symbolic reasons. In contrast to men, women who are drawn into central party bodies from other areas of life do not appear to be chosen because they possess valued skills which are needed in the political elite; rather, they are co-opted because they represent certain social categories which must be included in the elite bodies for ideological reasons. While these trends are evident in all of the elites studied, the extent of sex-related differences in occupations and the importance of a career in the party apparatus as a channel into the elite for women differ to some extent from one country to another.[3]

A record of party activism seems to be of most importance for women who aspire to elite positions in Bulgaria and Hungary, and sex-related differences in the occupations of central committee members are lower in these countries than in others. In 1971, for example, one-third of the women members of the Bulgarian Central Committee were party officials; five of the remaining women members held central government posts. The situation was similar in Hungary in 1970, where slightly over half of the women members of the central committee elected in that year (five out of nine) were party officials. However, even in these parties, women tend to hold party posts which are less important than those held by men. One of the five women party officials on the Hungarian Central Committee elected in 1970, for example, compared to over half of the men who worked in the party apparatus, was a central party official. The main exception to this pattern appears in the Bulgarian case, where six of the nine women who were party officials worked in central or district organisations.

Differences in the occupations and degree of party experience of men and women are greater in the Soviet, Polish and Czechoslovak cases. In marked contrast to the situation in Bulgaria and Hungary, women in these countries have not achieved their central committee positions by virtue of long party work. Not one of the seven women full members of the central committee in Poland in 1971, for example, had a career centred in the Communist party apparatus. One-third of the women candidate members had some recorded party experience, but in party organisations at the city or factory level. The situation is similar in Czechoslovakia. Although five of the eight women full members of the 1971 central committee had some party experience, only one of these was a career political activist.

To a larger extent than in Bulgaria or Hungary, women in these countries appear to be chosen for symbolic reasons. Five of the fifteen women members of the Soviet central committee elected in 1971, for example, were workers or collective farmers (Lapidus, 1975, p. 109). Seven of the nineteen women members of the 1971 Polish central committee were drawn from these occupations, while women comprised three of the five workers among the 93 members of the 1971 central committee in Czechoslovakia for whom social background information is available.

The occupations of other women members of the party elites reflect the sex-related differences in educational specialisations and occupations which prevail in these societies. Thus, women who are not party activists or worker-peasant representatives tend to be drawn from those professions in which women predominate in the labour force. The Polish central committee elected in 1968 illustrates this tendency quite clearly. In that year, the three women full members included a lecturer at a medical faculty, a Lodz textile worker, and a central trade union official. In 1971, the seven women full members included, in addition to a central trade union official, two educators and a nurse.

Women members of the party elites also appear to be disproportionately drawn from persons who have had careers in the mass organisations and agitational-propaganda work. Thus, seven of the 27 women members of the Bulgarian 1971 central committee were officials of mass organisations at the time of their selection for the central committee; several of the other women had careers which included lengthy work in such organisations. A similar tendency is evident in Hungary, where two of the five women members (compared to five of the 96 men) of the 1970 central committee were officials of mass organisations at the time of their selection for the central committee and several others had worked in these areas in the past. The tendency to draw women with these specialities into the party elite is also evident in Poland and Czechoslovakia, although to a lesser extent, given the greater proportion of women workers and peasants in the party elites.

Age differences between men and women leaders appear to be lower in Eastern Europe than they are in many western countries. While most women are beyond the prime childbearing ages when they enter the elite, they are not significantly older than their male counterparts. Women in the Hungarian, Czechoslovak, and

Polish central committees discussed above, for example, were slightly younger on the average than male members. Women central committee members in Bulgaria were slightly older on the average than men, but the differences were slight. This pattern may reflect the largely symbolic role most women play in these elites, for most women are not required to serve long apprenticeships as party activists or prove their competence by lengthy work in their professions prior to being selected for political office.

These differences in social background characteristics and previous political experiences which suggest that recruitment criteria are less stringent for women members of the elite, have a negative impact on the success and influence of women once they reach the elite. Given their lower socio-economic status, differing occupations, and less extensive party experience, women lack the skills and resources of their male colleagues and thus do not have the same degree of influence or potential for advancement. The effects of these differences are evident in the shorter tenure and lower re-election rates of women and in their failure to advance to top leadership positions once they are in the elite.

While women members of the party elites have, on the average, higher turnover rates and shorter tenure than men in all of these countries, the extent of sex-related differences in these areas varies considerably. Differences in the tenure and turnover rates of men and women members of the central committee are greatest in Poland and Czechoslovakia, where the occupations of men and women in the party elite diverge most markedly. There is far less difference in the tenure and turnover rates of men and women leaders in Bulgaria and Hungary, where the career patterns and recruitment channels of women more closely resemble those of men (Wolchik, 1978a).

The previous careers and types of political experience of most women members of East European elites appear to put them at a disadvantage in relation to their male counterparts once they are in the elite. Clearly, most women who are workers and peasants will not have the same tools for influencing public policy debates or wielding power as their male colleagues, many of whom are full-time bureaucrats or white collar workers. Nor do women members of the elite have the sophisticated technical or managerial skills which are becoming increasingly important as these countries modernise. Women's concentration in the mass organisations is also a handicap. While work in this area is an important route onto the central committee for women in Eastern Europe, experience in this area is evidently not highly valued in aspirants to the highest decision-making bodies of the party. As Moses (1976) has demonstrated in the Soviet case, careers in these areas seldom lead to positions on the Politburo or other top party bodies in Eastern Europe. The recent practice of electing the head of the women's organisation to the top party decision-making body may indicate a change in this pattern, at least as far as work in the women's organisation is concerned, however, for most of the few

East European women currently in the top party elites achieved their positions by this route.[4]

ISSUE ORIENTATION AND POLICY IMPACT OF WOMEN LEADERS

As we have seen, men and women bring widely different skills and experiences with them when they enter the elites in Eastern Europe. To what extent are these differences reflected in different political attitudes or policy preferences? Do women leaders in these countries have an explicitly feminist orientation to political issues? If so, do differing levels of women's representation in elite bodies lead to observable differences in policy outcomes or the status of women?

Unfortunately, information concerning the political orientations or policy preferences of men and women in East European elites is extremely limited. As in the case of leadership styles and relations within the elite, we simply do not have access to information concerning these aspects of elite behaviour. The concentration of women leaders in certain areas of activity may be indicative of sex-related differences of opinion concerning which issues are important or preferred solutions of particular problems. However, without information on the factors which led to this concentration, it is difficult to judge its meaning, for women may well be channelled into these areas with little real choice.

Given what we know about the determinants of policy preferences and the influence of recruitment channels on the behaviour of political leaders in other contexts, one would not expect great differences in the policy preferences of men and women leaders in these countries. The effects of elite socialisation and role constraints which appear to inhibit the expression of sex-related differences in policy preferences by elites in other countries, might be expected to be particularly great in Eastern Europe, given the predominance of the party as a recruitment channel. The expression of sex-related differences may be further inhibited by the fact that those women recruited from other areas of life do not appear to have the skills or experiences which would have given them an independent power base and by the small absolute numbers of women in any given elite group.

Perhaps the most important impediment to the development or expression of a feminist orientation on the part of women leaders in these countries is the fact that Communist elites do not generally admit that the interests of different social groups may differ or conflict under socialism. Marxist leaders traditionally have been extremely suspicious of the development of particularistic orientations by any segment of the party. During the early Communist period, many of the more powerful women activists in Eastern Europe clearly defined themselves in terms of party-wide tasks rather than as women's advocates. When activists assigned to work with women appeared to be developing too independent an orientation, the women's sections of the party were abolished (see

Meyer, 1974 for a discussion of this orientation; see Stites, 1977; Lapidus, 1978; and Wolchik, 1978a for analyses of the women's sections of the Soviet and Czechoslovak parties). Current Communist leaders often note that women's interests can only be served in the context of society-wide interests. In this context, it is not legitimate to express a clearly feminist orientation to policy-making.[5]

Similar factors inhibit the development of feminist movements in these countries. There is ample evidence that women are dissatisfied with certain aspects of their status but in normal political times they have few channels to articulate their interests or bring them to the attention of the political elites. The official women's organisations do at times appear to serve as advocates of women's interests, but their chief function is to mobilise women to fulfil elite objectives. In the more open political climate in Czechoslovakia in the late 1960s, the women's organisation acted as an interest group. Arguing that women shared certain characteristics which made them a distinct social group, leaders of the organisation articulated and defended women's intersts vis-à-vis the party and government (see Scott, 1974; Wolchik, 1978a). Activities of this type are unusual, however, and generally one cannot view the women's organisations as guardians of women's interests. Nor are women able to organise or form autonomous women's groups independent of the established groups.

There are also more subjective constraints on the development of feminism. The changes in women's lives in these societies were to some extent imposed rather than chosen, and for approximately fifteen years, the very real conflicts arising from the uneven pattern of these changes were not discussed publicly. Since the mid-1960s, it has once again become permissible to discuss difficulties in women's situation. Judging from the types of complaints women raise with leaders of the women's organisations and in letters to the editors of newspapers and magazines, women in these countries are most concerned with problems related to work, child care, and services (Jancar, 1978; Wolchik, 1978a). The activities of the women's organisations in Czechoslovakia in the late 1960s illustrate that women can be mobilised around these issues, but in normal political times, most women do not appear to see these problems as political issues.

Despite, or perhaps because of, the state's formal support for female equality, many women appear to have little interest in the kinds of issues which occupy the attention of western feminists. This lack of interest seems, from unsystematic observation, to be particularly great in the case of younger women (see Jancar, 1978, Ch. 8 for confirming evidence). Thus, while opinion surveys show that women in a number of these countries support and desire greater equality (Bártová, 1972), large groups of women appear to be more concerned with resolving the immediate problems associated with their dual roles at work and in the family than with more abstract issues of equality. This tendency has been reinforced by the current re-emphasis of women's maternal roles which has accompanied the pro-natalist measures enacted in many of these countries. In this situation, the development of explicitly feminist movements in Eastern Europe seems unlikely.

Given the small numbers, differing skills and backgrounds and lower tenure of women members of the elite, as well as the factors which inhibit the development of feminist orientations, it is perhaps not surprising that there are very few observable differences in policy outcomes in elite bodies with varying proportions of women. Differing levels of women's participation in local soviet debates in the USSR appear to lead to variation in the provision of child care facilities (Hough, 1977), but at the national level there is little relationship between the extent of women's representation in party or governmental elites and the extent of child care or other services. There is similarly little relationship between the level of women's representation in the effective elites and women's status in other areas of life. This lack of impact may indicate that other factors, such as demographic and manpower considerations, are of primary importance in determining policy in these areas. However, it may also reflect the fact that, while there is some variation in the extent to which women are represented in the effective elites within the region, women comprise a small number of leaders in all of these countries. In other words, there may simply be too few women in positions of power in any of these countries to have a noticeable impact on policy.

CONCLUSION: EXPLANATIONS AND OUTLOOK FOR THE FUTURE

Despite the important changes in women's status in Eastern Europe and formal elite commitment to women's equality, considerable differences still persist in the rates and kinds of political activity of men and women. Increased educational levels and employment outside the home do have an impact on the rate at which women, as well as men, participate in politics in these countries. Thus, working women with higher education in Yugoslavia have more interest in politics and a somewhat higher level of involvement in politics than women with less education who remain at home (Verba, Nie, and Kim, 1978, pp. 263-4). More highly educated women in the Soviet Union are also more likely than those with less education to be party members (Hough, 1977, p. 130). Sex differences persist at all educational levels, however, and increased education does not lead to as large an increase in political activism for women as it does for men. In the Soviet case, for example, Hough (1977, pp. 131-2) estimates that from 50 to 54 per cent of all men over 30 years of age with higher education were members of the Communist Party in 1970; by contrast, from 14 to 18 per cent of all women over 30 with similar levels of education were party members. Verba, Nie and Kim (1978, pp. 254-65) note that increased education has a greater impact on women's interest in politics than on their actual involvement.

Why have changes in women's status in other areas of life not been translated into the political arena? What leads women in Eastern Europe to perceive themselves and continue to be perceived by others, as unlikely candidates for political office? In looking for explanations for women's lower levels of political activism and representation among political elites, it is more difficult to account for variation within the region than it is to identify common factors which lead to the generally lower levels of activism in all East European countries. Thus, as is not surprising, given the small absolute numbers of women in the elites, there is little relationship between the educational and employment levels of women in particular countries and their representation in either government or party elites. Nor, particularly in recent years, does the extent of women's representation in political elites depend on the country's level of development or previous traditions in regard to women. Although women have been better represented on central committees in Czechoslovakia and East Germany in the post-war period than in most other countries of the region, their representation has been approximately the same in Bulgaria. Most recently, women have been best represented in the party elite in Albania, the least developed and most patriarchal country in the region. As the Albanian case illustrates, the best explanation for variation in the number of women in East European elites is elite-determined demand, as expressed in recruitment policies. Sex appears to be one of the centrally determined norms which govern the selection of candidates for government and party offices in these countries. The recent increase in women's representation among top party as well as government elites in several of these countries coincides with explicit efforts by top party leaders to increase the visibility of women in public life and illustrates the ability of Communist leaders to influence the extent of women's representation.

Given the small numbers of women who are active in politics in all of these countries, particularly at the elite level, the more interesting question is not how to explain the variation in their levels of representation from one country to another but rather why they are generally so little involved in politics in all countries. Analysts have identified a number of possible barriers to women's activism in these societies. Of these, two appear to be most important. First, certain analysts have argued that the particular characteristics of Communist political systems and the nature of political activity in these systems militate against greater involvement of women (see, for example, Jancar, 1978). Thus, the argument is made that the great amount of time required to be a party activist, the mobility needed to develop the broad expertise and experience in diverse geographic regions required of top leaders, and the personal characteristics necessary to climb to the top in communist politics all work against women's advancement to leadership positions. All of these factors undoubtedly inhibit women from taking a more active role in politics in these countries. But, as comparison of women's levels of representation in other countries indicates, women's role in political leadership is not systematically lower in Communist states than in other types of political systems (Wolchik, 1978b). Thus, while the party-based recruitment system in Eastern Europe has not been particularly favourable to women, it is no more of a barrier to women's participation in political leadership than are other political arrangements.[6]

More important in explaining the limited role which women play in leadership in all of these countries are popular attitudes and the legacy of traditional cultures which view different spheres of activity as appropriate for men and women. The influence of these views is evident in many areas of life and limits both the supply of and demand for women activists. Many men and women in Eastern Europe continue to see politics as a man's sphere. Given the different types of educations men and women receive and the occupations women enter, they do not develop the specialities which would be useful politically. Nor, in most cases, are women employed, in jobs which require high levels of political activism.

The impact of traditional sex-role conceptions is particularly evident in roles within the home, for women in Eastern Europe continue to be responsible for child care and housework, despite their employment outside the home and increased educational levels. The persistence of this traditional division of labour within the home poses both objective and subjective barriers to women's political activism in these societies. Given women's 'dual roles' at work and at home, many women simply do not have the free time to engage in politics. Women in Czechoslovakia, for example, are less active politically after marriage and the birth of children (Slejska, 1965); they also identify domestic responsibilities as the main reason for their refusal to accept public functions (Hora, 1972).

While there is little direct evidence, lack of free time and domestic responsibilities appear to be the chief factor responsible for the fact noted above, that increased education and employment outside the home increase women's interest in politics more than their actual levels of involvement. These factors appear to have a particularly negative effect on the political activism of more highly educated women, for there appears to be a trade-off between the demands of a woman's profession and her level of public activism, given the constant demands of home and family. Women in demanding occupations in Czechoslovakia, for example, prefer to use their limited free time to improve their professional qualifications rather than engaging in public activities (Jančovičová, 1974).

Traditional conceptions of women's roles also pose more subjective barriers to women's participation in political leadership, for women are less likely than men to see themselves or be seen by others as appropriate candidates for political offices. Because women are defined primarily in terms of their domestic roles, political leaders in these countries are reluctant to nominate women to responsible leadership posts. In a recent Czechoslovak study, women as well as factory directors identified women's domestic responsibilities as the main impediment to increasing women's share in leadership positions (Hora, 1972). The persistence of these attitudes, and the failure of Communist elites to challenge them in any concerted way, suggest that women's role in the exercise of power in these countries is not likely to increase greatly in the near future. The desire to increase women's visibility in public life, evident in many of these countries in the late 1970s, may lead to increased numbers of women in elite bodies. It is unlikely, however, to result in the selection of women with skills and independent power bases equivalent to those of their male colleagues. Any increase in such women, women who could exercise real power in the effective political elites, may well have to await a more fundamental change in sex-role conceptions which, by eliminating the traditional division of labour within the home, would create a pool of women with the skills, motivations, and experiences necessary for effective leadership. Without such a change, sex will continue to be an important factor determining levels of political activity in these societies.

NOTES

1   The activities of these groups are currently being examined by a number of scholars. See Bruce Garver (1977) for a discussion of the Czech case.

2   The difficulty of this task varied considerably within the region. Both men and women in Czechoslovakia and Hungary had high literacy rates by the 1930s. In Albania, by contrast, over two-thirds of all women over the age of nine were illiterate in 1950; illiteracy was also high among Yugoslav, Bulgarian, and Romanian women. Progress in this area is evident in the fact that female illiteracy declined to 37 per cent in Albania by 1955, to 25 per cent in Bulgaria by 1965 and 15 per cent in Yugoslavia by 1971 (from information in United Nations, 1960, pp. 447-9; 1973, p. 493; UNESCO, 1950).

3   Data concerning the social backgrounds and tenure of members of central committees, unless otherwise noted, are taken from Radio Free Europe Research Reports. See Jancar (1978) and Wolchik (1978a) for more detailed analyses.

4   Women's failure to advance to higher positions also may reflect lower political ambitions. Unsystematic discussions with women leaders in a number of these countries indicate that many women did not actively seek their positions but rather were asked by party leaders to serve (Jancar, 1978; Wolchik, 1978a).

5   Of course, women's leaders may at times further women's interests while couching their suggestions in terms of society-wide interests.

6   The organisational principles of Communist societies do mean that women in these states have fewer opportunities to organise independently than women in democratic political systems.

BIBLIOGRAPHY

Barbic, Ana, The Political Roles of Women in Yugoslav Society, (Mimeographed).

Bártová, Eva (1972), Postoje k problému ženy a rodiny, 'Sociologicky časopis', 8: 44-61.

Blondel, Jean (1973), 'Comparative Legislatures', Prentice Hall, Englewood Cliffs, NJ.

Bulgarskata Komunisticheska Partiia (1948), 'Rezoliutsii na V kongres na BKP', Isdatel'stvo na Bulgarskata Komunisticheska Partiia, Sofia.

Bulgarskata Komunisticheska Partiia (1966), 'For Unity and Cohesion. Materials of the 9th Congress of the Bulgarian Communist Party', Foreign Languages Publishing House, Sofia.

Burks, Richard V. (1961), 'The Dynamics of Communism in Eastern Europe', Princeton, University Press, Princeton, NJ.

Childs, David (1969), 'East Germany', Praeger, New York.

Chovanec, Jaroslav (1974), 'Zastupitelská soustava Československé socialistické republiky', Mladá fronta, Prague.

Drejtonia e Statistikes (1961), (1971/2), 'Anuari Statistikor R. P. SH.', Drejtonia e Statistikes, Tirana.

Duverger, Maurice, (1955), 'The Political Roles of Women', UNESCO, Paris.

'Encyklopedie moderní ženy', (1966), Nakladatelství Svoboda, Prague.

Filipi, Slavko (1967), Membership of the League of Communists of Yugoslavia, 'Yugoslav Survey', 8, pp. 38-48.

Garver, Bruce (1977), Women in Czech Society, 1848-1914. Paper presented at the 1977 annual meeting of the Midwest Slavic Conference, Ann Arbor, Michigan.

Gesamtdeutsches Institut (1971), 'Die Parteiapparat der Deutschen Demokratischen Republik', Gesamtdeutsches Institut, Bundestalt fur gesamtdeutschen Aufgaben, Bonn.

Glowny urad statystyczny (1973), (1974), (1975), (1976), 'Rocznik statystyczny', Glowny urad statystyczny, Warsaw.

Gordon, Leonid Abramovich and Klopov, Eduard Viktorovich (1972), 'Chelovek posle raboty', Nauka, Moscow.

Gruliow, Leo (ed.) (1962), 'Current Soviet Policies', Praeger, New York.

Heitlinger, Alena (1979), 'Women and State Socialism. Sex Inequality in the Soviet Union and Czechoslovakia', McGill-Queens University Press, Montreal.

Hoover Institution on War, Revolution and Peace (1966), (1972), (1973), (1974), (1975), 'Yearbook on International Communist Affairs', Hoover Institution Press, Stanford, California.

Hora, Štefan (1972), 'Za vyššiu účast zamestnaných žien v

riadiacej cinnosti', UV SSZ-Zivena, Bratislava.
Hough, Jerry (1977), 'The Soviet Union and Social Science Theory', Princeton University Press, Princeton, NJ.
Institut mezhinarodnigo rabochego dvizheniia, AN SSSR and Komitet Sovetskikh zhenshchin (1972), 'Zhenshichiny mira v borb'e za stosialnyi progress', Gosudarstvennoe izadatel'stvo politicheskoi literatury, Moscow.
Jancar, Barbara Wolfe (1971), 'Czechoslovakia and the Absolute Monopoly of Power: A Study of Political power in a Communist System', Praeger, New York.
Jancar, Barbara Wolfe (1974), Women and Soviet Politics, in Henry, W. Morton and Rudolf L. Tokes (eds), 'Soviet Politics and Society in the 1970s', Free Press, New York.
Jancar, Barbara, Wolfe (1974a), Women under Communism, in Jane S., Jaquette, (ed.), 'Women in Politics', Wiley, New York.
Jancar, Barbara Wolfe (1978), 'Women Under Communism', Johns Hopkins Press, Baltimore, Maryland.
Jančovičová, Jolana (1974), Problematika ženy v lekarském povolani na Slovensku, 'Sociólogia', 6, pp. 451-9.
Keefe, Eugene, K. et al. (1971), 'Area Handbook for Albania, 1971', US Government Printing Office, Washington, DC.
Keefe, Eugene K. et al. (1972a), 'Area Handbook for East Germany, 1972', US Government Printing Office, Washington, DC.
Keefe, Eugene K. et al. (1972b), 'Area Handbook for Rumania, 1972', US Government Printing Office, Washington DC.
Komunistická strana Československa (1949), 'Protokol IX, sjezdu KSČ.', Svoboda, Prague.
Komunistická strana Československa (1962), 'XXII, sjezd KSC', UV KSČ, Prague.
Komunistická strana Československa (1971), 'XIV, sjezd Komunistické strany Československa', Svoboda, Prague.
Komunistická strana Československa (1976), 'XV. zjazd KSČ. Dokumenty a materialy', Nakladatelstvo Pravda, Bratislava.
Lane, David (1971), 'Politics and Society in the USSR', Random House New York.
Lapidus, Gail Warshofsky (1975), Political Mobilisation, Participation, and Leadership: Women in Soviet Politics, 'Comparative Politics', 8, pp. 90-118.
Lapidus, Gail Worshofsky (1978), 'Women in Soviet Society', University of California Press, Berkeley, Calif.
Ludz, Peter C. (1972), 'The Changing Party Elite in East Germany', MIT Press, Cambridge, Mass.
Magdolen, Ernest (1973), 'Spôsob života zamestnaných žien v mimopracovnom čase', Vyskumný ústav životnej úrovne, Bratislava.
Magyar Dolgozok Partja, (1948), 'I. Kongresszus', Budapest.
Magyar Szocialista Munkaspart (1962), 'A Magyar szocialista munkaspart hara rozatar es dokumentumar, 1956-1962', Kossuth Konyvikiado, Budapest.
Magyar Szocialista Munkaspart (1975), 'XI s'jezd vengerskoi sotsialisticheskoi rabochei partii', Izdatel'stvo politicheskoi

literatury, Moscow.
Matic, Milan (1968), 'Skupstinski izbori, 1967', Centar za strazivanje javnog mnenja, Belgrade.
Matic, Milan (1970), 'Skupstinski izbori, 1969', Centrar za strazivanje javnog mnenja, Belgrade.
Meyer, Alfred, G. (1974), Marxism and the Women's Movement, in Dorothy Atkinson, Alexander Dallin and Gail Warshofsky Lapidus (ed), 'Women in Russia', Stanford University Press, Stanford, California.
Moses, Joel (1976), Indoctrination as a female political role in the Soviet Union, 'Comparative Politics', 8, pp. 525-48.
Nenoff, Dragomir (1951), 'The Bulgarian Communist Party', National Committee for a Free Europe, Research and Information Center, New York.
Partidul Comunist Roman (1975), 'Congresul a XI-lea al Partidului Comunist Roman', Editura politica, Bucharest.
Partidul Munitoresc Romin (1955), 'Congresul a II-lea al Partidului Romin, 23-28 Decembrie, 1955', Editura de stat pentru literatura politica, Bucharest.
Partidul Monitoresc Romin (1965), 'Congresul a III-lea al Partidului Munctitoresc Romin', Editura de stat pentru literatura politica, Bucharest.
Piekalkiewicz, Jaroslaw A. (1972), 'Public Opinion Polling in Czechoslovakia, 1968-69: Results and Analysis of Surveys Conducted During the Dubcek Era', Praeger, New York.
Pierre, Andre (1960), 'Les Femmes en Union Sovietique', Spis, Paris.
Pilic, Andre (1969) 'Karakteristika i problemi ženske radne snage u Jugoslaviji', Institut za Ekonomiska istrazivanje, Belgrade.
Polska Zjednoczona Partia Robotnicza (1969), 'V Sjazd Polskej zjednoczonej Partii robtoniczej', Ksiazka i wiedza, Warsaw.
Putnam, Robert, D. (1976), 'The Comparative Study of Political Elites', Prentice Hall, Englewood Cliffs, NJ.
Radio Free Europe Research (1966), Hungarian Press Summary, no. 281 (8 December).
Radio Free Europe Research (1967), Hungarian Situation Report, 'The New Central Committee of the Hungarian Communist Party' (6 February).
Radio Free Europe Research (1968), Polish Situation Report/35, The New Central Committee of the PUWP (16 December).
Radio Free Europe Research (1970a), Hungarian Background Report/29, 'The HSWP: a Statistical Profile' (20 November).
Radio Free Europe Research (1970b), Hungarian Press Summary 276, (30 November).
Radio Free Europe Research (1970c), Hungarian Situation Report/ 30, 'The New Hungarian Party Central Committee' (9 December).
Radio Free Europe Research (1971a), Rumanian Situation Report/ 7, 'Party Strength and Structure' (22 February).
Radio Free Europe Research (1971b), Hungarian Background Report/112, 'The Hungarian Elections and the New National Assembly' (20 May).

Radio Free Europe Research (1971c), Bulgarian Situation Report/
21, 'The Central Committee Elected at the 10th Party Congress'
(28 June).

Radio Free Europe Research (1971d), Czechoslovak Situation
Report/24, 'The New CPCS Central Committee' (25 June).

Radio Free Europe Research, (1972a), Polish Situation Report/23,
'The new CC of the PUWP' (1 August).

Radio Free Europe Research (1972b), Rumanian Situation Report/
14, 'The National Party Congress' (31 July).

Radio Free Europe Research (1975a), Polish Situation Report/44,
'The National Party Congress' (16 June).

Radio Free Europe Research (1975b), RAD Background Report
(Hungary), 'The New Hungarian National Assembly' (25 July).

Radio Free Europe Research (1976a), Bulgarian Situation Report/
17, 'Election Results and the Pre-election Campaign', (4 June).

Radio Free Europe Research (1976b), RAD Background Report/
140 (Bulgaria), 'The Central Committee after the 11th Party
Congress' (16 June).

Radio Free Europe Research (1976c), RAD Background Report/151
(Bulgaria), 'The BCP Theses on the Party and Mass Organisations' (23 February).

Rigby, T.H. (1968), 'Communist Party Membership in the USSR,
1917-1967', Princeton University Press, Princeton, NJ.

Saveza Komunista Jugoslavije (1965), 'Osmi Mongress SKJ,
Stenografske beliske', Kultura, Belgrade.

Saveza Komunista Jugoslavije (1971), 'Deseti kongres Zveze
Komunistov Jugoslavijii', CZP Komunist, Libliana.

Savezni zavod za Statistiku (1958, 1964, 1969, 1971, 1973, 1977),
'Statisticki godisnjak Jugoslavije', Savezni zavod za statistiku,
Belgrade.

Scott, Hilda (1974), 'Does Socialism Liberate Women?', Beacon
Press, Boston.

Slejska, Dragoslav (1965), Problémy activity žen při účasti na
řizeni v průmyslovém závodu, 'Sociologický časopis', 1, pp.
509-23.

Staatliche Zentralverwaltung fur Statistik, (1956, 1973),
'Statisches Jahrbuch der Deutschen Demokratischen Republik',
Staatverlag der DDR, Berlin.

Stites, Richard (1977), 'The Women's Liberation Movement in
Russia: Feminism, Nihilism, and Bolshevism, 1860-1930', Princeton University Press, Princeton, NJ.

United Nations, (1960, 1973), 'Demographic Yearbook'.

UNESCO (1950), 'Literary Statistics from Available Census
Figures', Education Clearing House, Paris.

US Department of State (1968, 1972), 'World Strength of the
Communist Party-Organisations', US Government Printing
Office, Washington DC.

US Department of State (1964), 'Directory of Hungarian Officials',
US Government Printing Office, Washington, DC.

US Department of State (1965), 'Directory of Czechoslovak Officials', US Government Printing Office, Washington DC.

US Department of State (1966), 'Directory of Polish Officials',
    US Government Printing Office, Washington DC.
US Department of State (1969), 'Directory of Polish Officials',
    US Government Printing Office, Washington DC.
US Department of State (1971), 'Directory of Bulgarian Officials',
    US Government Printing Office, Washington DC.
Verba, Sidney, Nie, Norman H. and Kim, Jae-on (1978), 'Parti-
    cipation and Political Equality: A Seven-Nation Comparison',
    Cambridge University Press, London.
Wolchik, Sharon, L. (1978a), Politics, Ideology and Equality:
    The Status of Women in Eastern Europe, Ph.D. dissertation,
    The University of Michigan.
Wolchik, Sharon L. (1978b), Ideology and Equality: The Status
    of Women in Eastern and Western Europe. Paper presented at
    the annual meeting of the American Political Science Associa-
    tion, New York.
Wolchik, Sharon, L. (1980), The Status of Women in a Socialist
    Order: The Case of Czechoslovakia, 1948-1978, 'Slavic Review',
    38(4), pp. 583-602.
Wrochno, Krystyna (1969), 'Kobiety w Polsce', Wydawnictwo
    Interpress, Warsaw.
Wrochno, Krystyna (1971), 'Problemy prace kobiet', Wydawnictwo
    Zwiazkowe CRZZ, Warsaw.

13 USSR

Joni Lovenduski

HISTORICAL BACKGROUND

In keeping with the Soviet interpretation of the writings of Marx,
Engels and Lenin on the 'women question', a cursory inspection
of the published statistics on women in the USSR suggests that
Soviet women are in a relatively favourable position, by comparison with Western women, in terms of both economic advancement
and access to political office. However, closer scrutiny reveals
broad patterns of disadvantage which are more or less similar to
those found in the West. The evident high visibility of women
becomes less meaningful when placed in the context of the rather
narrow range of representative politics in the Soviet Union. That
context involves a candidate selection system designed in such a
way as to all but specialise in tokenism and it conceals a low level
of female access to policy-making positions in the state and in the
party. Indeed, so startling is women's under-representation at
policy-making levels that a student of Soviet politics could safely
use the absence of women in a high party or state organisation as
an indicator of that organisation's importance. That this is the
case is one of the ironies of development since the installation of
the first government to have produced a policy directed at
women's emancipation.

The USSR has featured an ideological commitment to sex equality since the Bolsheviks came to power in 1917. And the 'woman
question' had exercised at least some members of the Russian
elite since the middle of the nineteenth century. By the 1880s
Russian women were playing a prominent part in the political
parties which were beginning to proliferate. Under the conditions
of Tsarist autocracy the political game was a dangerous one,
characterised by high risks and minimal rewards. Frustrated by
the absence of legitimate channels for political action those desir-
ing change were forced into clandestine revolutionary activity.
The early Populists (People's Will) concentrated on assassination
as their main political weapon and women, possibly because of
their tactical advantage, played a prominent part in terrorist
activities. Sofia L'vovna Perovskaia led the successful plot to
assassinate Alexander II on 1 March 1881, thus carrying off the
dubious distinction of becoming the first Russian woman to receive
capital punishment for a political crime. Women comprised 15 per
cent of the 2564 arrested for political crimes between 1873 and
1879 and were about 30 per cent of the People's Will in the 1870s
(Engel, 1977, p. 348).

The political environment in nineteenth century Russia was
such that any movement for political and legal rights was revolutionary and although an early western-style feminist movement
did appear in the mid-nineteenth century, it remained centred
around the needs of a small educated elite. Women pursing effective political action were rapidly absorbed into nineteenth-century
Russian radical and revolutionary politics, a propensity which
persisted until male suffrage was introduced after the 1905 revolution.

Surprisingly, by the eve of the 1905 revolution, Russian women
were well ahead of their West European counterparts in terms of
their access to university education and about on a par with the
USA in their penetration of, for example, the medical profession.
These educated women developed a feminist movement strongly
influenced by the English suffragettes of the same period. Led by
Anna Milukova, Moscow professional women founded the Union
for Woman's Equality (which later became the All-Russian League
for Women's Equality) in 1905. A separate political party (the
Woman's Progressive Party) appeared at the same time. By 1907
the League had some 80 branches (Rosenthal, 1977, p. 374).
Demands centred around questions of legal equality including suffrage, access to education and employment, divorce reform, and
the availability of birth control. The League's main focus was on
the vote, however, and by 1912 it had succeeded via its alliance
with the Constitutional Democrats (Cadets) in getting the Parliament (Duma) to pass a bill enfranchising women. That bill was
prevented from reaching the statute books by cabinet veto, and
women were only enfranchised with the full-scale revolution of
1917.

With few exceptions, the liberal feminists did not concern themselves with the growing population of Russian factory women who,
by 1885, comprised 22.1 per cent of the industrial workforce in
European Rusia (Glickman, 1978, p. 68). By contrast, pre-1917
Marxist woman leaders were fiercely dedicated to the emancipation
of women workers but had to contend with the fact that women
were low on the priority lists of the predominantly male leadership
(ibid., p. 80) despite the considerable activity of women workers
in the various strike movements of the time.

Women were noticeably less prominent amongst the Marxist
revolutionaries than they had been in the populist movement. Although Vera Zasulich had helped to found the Social Democratic
Workers Party which later split into the Bolsheviks and the Menscheviks, she was something of an exception. Women terrorists
eschewed the Marxist parties and tended to gravitate to the neo-
populist Social Revolutionary Party. Within Social Democracy, the
Bolsheviks tended to lag behind the Menscheviks in the organisation of women, a tendency accentuated by the proletarianisation
of the Bolshevik Party during the post-1905 strike waves
(Rosenthal, 1977, p. 375). Strike literature of the period shows
workers called to action envisaged as male - despite the fact that
demands for paid maternity leave were normally included, and des-

pite considerable participation by women in every type of strike
(Glickman, 1978, pp. 80-2). Slowly the attitudes of at least the
party leaders began to change, however, and Rosenthal (1977,
p. 375) reckons that the first International Woman's Day in 1913
provided a catalyst for Bolshevik feminism. After that date Lenin,
Krupskaia and Inessa Armand founded a women's newspaper,
'Rabotnitsa', under party auspices and the Bolsheviks adopted
a woman's programme.

By the eve of the First World War all the major parties were
committed to sex equality policies of some form or other. In Russia
as in every other country involved, the First World War forced
large numbers of women into the factories. The difference there
was that the largely peasant society contained few prejudices
against women performing heavy labour. By 1917 women comprised
43 per cent of the industrial work force. The high male casualty
rates (approximately half of the 7,500,000 mobilised were reported
dead, missing or wounded) created large numbers of women heads
of household coping on low pay or pensions rendered nearly worth-
less by high inflation rates (ibid., p. 377). Women's sacrifices
during this time brought a Tsarist promise of the franchise which,
had things worked out differently, would have been the crowning
achievement of the liberal feminists, all of whom felt that 'the
vote would be the ultimate panacea for the oppression of women'
(Glickman, 1978, p. 78).

In the event, the revolution came before this conviction could
be put to the test. Tsarist collapse actually began with a demonstration by Petrograd women for peace and bread on International
Woman's Day, 8 March 1917 (23 February, Old calendar). That
demonstration expanded into a general strike which brought down
the old regime and established the ill-fated Provisional Government.
The Provisional Government became the first major power to grant
women's vote. Women continued to organise around women's issues
throughout 1917 and their support was courted by all of the major
parties including the Bolsheviks who took power fairly peacefully
on 7 November 1917 (October 25, old calendar). In December 1917
Lenin's government repealed all Tsarist marriage and divorce laws,
mandated equal pay for equal work, deprived the clergy of their
power to perform marriages, introduced paid maternity leave and
nursing breaks, forbade the sacking of pregnant women and introduced elaborate protective legislation laws. The Bolshevik's
October 1918 Family Code abolished legitimacy distinctions for
children, provided for a wife's control over her own earnings,
abolished unequal paternal authority, liberalised divorce and
explicitly stated that women were expected to engage in paid employment outside the home (Rosenthal, 1977, p. 378). To facilitate the implementation of this legislation Alexandra Kollantai
was appointed First Commissar of Social Welfare. Kollantai immediately set about establishing communal facilities to supply the
domestic labour from which women were to be emancipated. But
the civil war (1918-21) thwarted progress on all fronts. Such communal facilities as were established were ad hoc crisis measures

which no one used unless they had to. The Civil War cost
13,000,000 casualties in a total population of 136,000,000 and
created 7 million homeless children. It also devastated the economy
and left behind a population drastically short of its skilled and
educated members.

The Communist party-led state which emerged attempted to
restore the damage by the introduction of Lenin's New Economic
Policy (NEP) which lasted until 1928. NEP introduced limited private trade in order to provide incentives to work and to production. The over-riding priority was rebuilding the country's
economic base. In a nation isolated from the rest of the world the
social funding needed for women to progress was simply not
available. The makeshift communal facilities of the civil war were
dismantled and the women who worked did so out of necessity.
They were illiterate, unskilled and forced to work mainly at menial
jobs. Protective legislation caused cost-conscious management to
avoid women workers and throughout NEP women were the last to
be hired and the first to be fired (Rosenthal, 1977, p. 380).

Lapidus (1978, p. 138) has found that women did benefit to
some extent in this period from the reallocation of educational resources and from the activity of the Communist Party Women's
Department (Zhenotdel, see below p. 289). Nevertheless, women
in the NEP era experienced little in the way of concrete economic
advancement. By 1928 women comprised only 24 per cent of the
labour force, little more than in 1885. Although illiteracy did fall
during NEP - to 70 per cent from a 1919 high of 90-95 per cent -
substantial improvement in employment rates did not occur until
the ascendancy of Stalin and the abandonment of NEP for the
command economy, five-year plans and forced industrialisation
and collectivisation. The 1929-34 plan called for industrialisation
and collectivisation at the expense of even rudimentary consumer
production, a policy which was continued in subsequent Stalinist
plans, and had only been slightly modified by his death in 1953.
The high demand for labour involved a heavy recruitment of
women who comprised 82 per cent of those entering the work force
between 1932 and 1937 (Sacks, 1978, p. 194). Women as a percentage of the total work force rose from 24 per cent in 1928 to
27.4 per cent in 1932 to 34.7 per cent in 1937 to 39 per cent in
1940 (Lapidus, 1975a, p. 181). Attempts to meet problems arising
from the lack of a skilled labour force included a 1931 effort to
upgrade skills generally, improvements in the education system,
and the introduction of wage differentials to provide incentives.
Factory training schools established female quotas, and women
comprised 50 per cent of their students by 1934 (Rosenthal, 1977,
p. 385). 1934 also saw a new drive to eradicate illiteracy which
increased opportunities for both sexes and included 'affirmative
action' components in the establishment of minimum 'quotas' for
women in universities.

The Second World War years mobilised women both in the industrial work force, where by 1945 they comprised 56 per cent
of the total, and to some extent in the military (Lapidus, 1975a,

p. 181). Soviet Second World War losses totalled some 20 million dead and involved the destruction of most of its industrial heart-land. A population imbalance, already evident after the First World War, was greatly exacerbated and continues to the present day. This shortage of men has kept demand for women's labour high. Reconstruction needs once again pre-empted resources for child-care centres, public dining facilities, modern housing, dom-estic appliances etc. (Sacks, 1978, p. 194) at a time when popula-tion replenishment was a pressing national priority.

Since 1926 there has been a visible deficit of males in the USSR which was intensified by forcible collectivisation and the purges of the 1930s and Second World War losses. In 1946 there were 59 men for every 100 women in the 35-59 age cohort and in 1959 30 per cent of all Soviet 'heads of household' were women (Lapidus, 1976, pp. 304-6). In the post-Stalin era, labour shortages and the declining manpower reserves available from rural migration have brought 18 million more women into paid employment, and since 1970 women have comprised 51 per cent of the work force. Declining birth rates have also been a feature of the Soviet period and were at least partly responsible for the sexual counter-revolu-tion witnessed in the mid-1930s which involved a recidivistic emphasis on the family and the role of woman as mother. A return to traditional views of the family was characteristic of Stalinism and the anticipated post-war population crisis caused a 1944 Family Code revision which made divorce difficult and encouraged the production of 'illegitimate' children.

Thus post-revolutionary Soviet women have been treated by policies which have derived largely from economic, military and demographic events. Policy on women and their changing status appears to have been as much a result of the logic of those events as it has to any Marxist-Leninist commitment to feminine emancipation, sex equality or equal opportunity. This is not to say that the position of women in the USSR has not improved under Soviet rule . . . it patently has improved. The point is, however, that that improvement has always been a by-product of policy designed for some other, 'higher' purpose. In addition as the following sections show, Soviet women, whether as women or otherwise, have had little say in the determination of those 'higher' purposes.

THE CONTEMPORARY SOCIO-ECONOMIC ENVIRONMENT

The advanced nature of the industrial economy of the USSR today was only achieved by dint of considerable human sacrifice. Many of the industrial accomplishments of the 1930s had to be repeated after the devastation of the Second World War. Regime goals were such that industrialism and economic growth became key compon-ents of the official ideology and priority was given to heavy indus-try and the defence sector at the expense of consumer goods and services. There has been a fairly consistent policy of full employ-

ment of women and the need for a skilled labour force has led to
a considerable expansion of educational opportunities for both
sexes. Despite this, most scholars, including Soviet ones, agree
that the available data indicate that women have been consistently
disadvantaged vis-à-vis men in socio-economic terms. This has
been partly attributed to the continuation of the female domestic
burden and partly to what is widely held to be a particularly
pernicious Slavic form of male chauvinism.

David Lane (1978, pp. 273-4) has characterised the contemporary
Soviet system as State Socialist. In such a system ministries and
local authorities own and manage the means of production whilst
central and regional boards determine the prices and output of
individual firms. Industries operate like ministries in the West
with profits and losses accruing to the state. According to Lane
(1978, pp. 273-4) the USSR is 'an administered or command
economy in which the influence of individual consumers and pro-
ducers is replaced by administrative bodies which make decisions
for the whole economy.' Thus:

> industrial enterprises and 'state' farms are organised by the
> government which decides what shall be produced; what pro-
> portion of output is devoted to consumption and investment; it
> is responsible for fixing the price of inputs; raw materials and
> basic wage rates, and outputs; the prices of finished and semi-
> finished products.

Even more than is the case in other systems, the successful
management of the economy is the crucial task of a state socialist
government. Much of the Soviet management policy is political
policy in the sense that it is made by decision makers chosen for
their political acceptability and adherence to party priorities. The
relationship between economic status and political status in the
USSR ought, on this basis, to be a fairly strong one and in the
case of women this supposition is borne out. Women tend to have
low status both in the economic and the political spheres.

The Soviet economy features almost full employment of women
with a participation rate for the 20-55 age cohort which has stabilised at around 85 per cent (Lapidus, 1975a, p. 182). Women's
employment patterns are in some respects similar to those to be
found in the West with women over-represented in the service
sector, amongst lower white collar occupations and in the sub-
professions. The most remarkable differences are a fairly high
proportion (16+ per cent) employed in agriculture, a symptom of
residual backwardness in the Soviet economy, and a high proportion employed in engineering. Women comprise 44 per cent of all
engineers in the USSR, a symptom of the regime's bias toward
heavy engineering and the consequent applied science bias of the
education system (Lapidus, 1976, p. 307). Women were 52 per
cent of those in professional jobs and 63 per cent of those in semi-
professional jobs in 1968 (Dodge, 1978, p. 207) but tend to be
concentrated in certain professions. Dodge (ibid., pp. 208-9)
found that in 1970, a number of professional or semi-professional
occupations were dominated by, i.e. contained between 70 per

cent and 90 per cent, women. These included primary and secondary schoolteaching, heads of primary schools, teachers in industrial education, bookkeepers, technical laboratory workers, econ-
omists and planners, communications workers, physicians, mid-
wives and dentists. Similarly in the non-professional work force
Sacks (1978, p. 202) found that in 1970 working women were concentrated in employment as public dining workers (12.09 per cent
of all working-class women), machine construction and metal workers (10.27 per cent) and communal household and service workers
(16.23 per cent). Women predominated amongst textile workers
(84.8 per cent), garment workers (94.6 per cent), public dining
workers (94.6 per cent), postal workers (89.9 per cent), order-
lies, nurses etc. (98.1 per cent), lab. assistants (90.7 per cent)
and comprised more than 60 per cent of all workers in chemicals,
paper and cardboard, printing, the shoe industry, and of inspec-
tors, sorters and warehouse receivers (ibid., p. 202). Lapidus
(1975a, p. 184) finds a high degree of continuity in this sectoralisation, with changes in the proportion of women in the various
economic sectors between 1940 and 1972 largely corresponding
with changes in women's overall ratio in the work force.

Within the categories of work which have been 'feminised',
women are considerably less likely than men to be in the more
senior, better paid grades. The pattern of vertical occupational
stratification is fairly consistent across the occupational structure
with women being more likely to be found performing the more
menial and poorly paid jobs. Lapidus (1975a, pp. 186-91) has
examined the position of women in agriculture, industrial engineering, medicine and education and scientific work. She found
that in each case the percentage of women becomes progressively
lower as each higher level of the system is reached. In industrial
engineering, despite increasing entry by women and a rise of
women in the higher managerial fields from 13 per cent in 1959 to
16 per cent in 1970, USSR women have still not moved into responsible positions in the numbers one would expect on the basis
of their training and work, and remain largely concentrated in
the technical and clerical categories of occupation.

Although data are somewhat sparse and separate statistics of
men's and women's pay are not published. Soviet social scientists
generally agree that women's earnings are appreciably lower than
those of men. Family budget studies indicate that as a rule the
'second earner', usually the wife, gets about two-thirds of the
income of the 'first earner' (Chapman, 1978, p. 225). Lapidus
(1975a, p. 191) reckons that on the most generous possible cal-
culation, women's earnings are a maximum of 87 per cent of those
of men. Chapman's investigation of equal pay in the USSR found
no evidence of sex-differentiated pay rates for the same jobs.
Rather women's disadvantage came partly from their concentration
in the lower paid occupations and partly from restrictions on a
woman's freedom to take the kind of work she prefers and for
which she is trained. Such restrictions also prevent women from
advancing as fast as men do.

Yet considerable efforts have been made to improve the standard of women's qualifications in the USSR. Education is the main
avenue of upward mobility there and women's access and achievement has consistently improved. Although women's educational
attainment at secondary levels has lagged behind men's, an increasing proportion of women have obtained at least incomplete
secondary education in the Soviet system. The percentage of
those over 10 years old with at least incomplete secondary education rose from 11.4 per cent men and 8.8 per cent women in 1939
to 35.5 per cent men and 32.3 per cent women in 1959 to 47.2 per
cent men and 42.4 per cent women in 1970 (Dobson, 1978, p. 270).
The available data do indicate considerable proportionate fall-off
at the highest levels of educational attainment (see Dodge, 1978,
pp. 212-3) and a relationship between the sectorialisation in the
economy and sex-differentiated subject preferences in the education system (see Dobson, 1978) but the weight of these two factors is insufficient to explain the overall discrepancy in employment.

Restrictions in women's achievement appear mainly to stem from
the nature of the nuclear family and the as yet unameliorated role
of woman as childbearer, child raiser, housewife and worker.
Some evidence also exists of overcrowding in the primarily female
employment sectors which may depress wages (Chapman, 1978,
p. 226). The lack of women in management positions precludes income from big bonus payments and downward pressures on pay
comes from lack of women at the top of each skill pyramid. The
'preferred' economic sectors are those in which women are under-
represented and on top of all this, married women's mobility is
restricted by the locations of their husband's jobs (Lapidus,
1975a, p. 191).

Some 80 per cent of USSR women in the 25-39 age cohort are
married (Lapidus, 1978, p. 252) and facilities to relieve the burden of domestic labour have not appeared in sufficient quantity
and the sexual division of labour in the home continues to persist.
Women in the USSR are still the main servicing agencies of the
nuclear family, spending more time on housework and child care
than their husbands and less on professional activities, self-
improvement, and leisure and even getting one hour per day less
sleep (Lapidus, 1976, p. 308). Solutions to this imbalance appear
to be mainly 'individualistic' and may be found in a rising divorce
rate, late age of marriage and restriction of family size to one or
occasionally two, children. Regime responses are aimed at raising
the fertility rate, lowering the marriage age and introducing
counselling services to increase marital stability (Lapidus, 1978,
p. 303). In short policy initiatives are directed at symptoms of
women's dissatisfaction rather than causes.

Despite what at one time appeared to be a breakdown of barriers
to women's employment in a large number of sectors during the
most acute period of demographic imbalance, there is evidence that
the gradual reassertion of demographic normality has led to the
return of cultural biases toward women's work (Sacks, 1978, pp.
203-4). Rising rates of female labour force participation in the

non-agricultural sector and increased educational attainment by women have not led to the elimination of differences between men and women in the labour force.

This set of differences is reflected in women's participation in the main employment organisations, the USSR trade unions. Women comprise 50 per cent of trade union members, 60.5 per cent of the members of factory and local committees and their auditing commissions, 50.8 per cent of the chairpersons of primary trade union organisations, 55.2 per cent of district and town trade union committees and their auditing commissions. But after this the fall-off begins. Women comprise 46.1 per cent of the republican, territorial and regional trade union councils and their auditing commissions and only 34.5 per cent of the All-Union Central Council of Trade Unions, the VTsSPS (Yemelyanova, 1975, p. 65). The Praesidium of the VTsSPS has a commission for work among women with counterparts in enterprises and on state farms, but the role of Soviet Trade Unions is such that they are unlikely to have much impact on the overall position of women in the economy. The twenty-five Soviet trade unions are partly advisory bodies and partly government agencies (Lane, 1978, pp. 304-5). They are not interest groups in the sense that Western trade unions are, and they are very much in tune with the same state priorities which have led to the disadvantages suffered by employed women. These priorities have to do with the nature of the industrialisation goals, the primacy of which has led to insufficient funding for the sorts of services which are necessary if women are to participate in the economy at the level of their qualifications and abilities. Wages, conditions, industrial growth, etc. are all determined by the Soviet planning mechanism, which, whilst far from perfect, is unlikely to have produced the current relative employment status of the sexes by accident or oversight. As such the economically disadvantaged position of Soviet women must be seen as a direct, if occasionally embarrassing, result of centrally determined policy priorities.

THE PARTY AND ELECTORAL SYSTEMS

The USSR is a one-party state in which electoral competition does not feature. The Communist Party of the Soviet Union (CPSU) leads and directs the state which is federal in structure. The USSR is divided into fifteen Union Republics, some of which contain the twenty Autonomous Republics, eight Autonomous Regions and ten National Areas. Each of these federal units is based on the existence of a 'homogenous national group', having its own written language' (Lane, 1978, p. 143). Of these the Central Asian Republics have presented particular problems of development and assimilation for the regime. Each of the Union Republics (except the Russian Republic - RSFSR) has its own party and central committee, which is formally subject to the Congress of the CPSU and actually subject to the CPSU politbureau. The

RSFSR is directly integrated into the CPSU which is organised on the basis of democratic centralism. In its current form, democratic centralism means that all leading party bodies are elected and must make periodic reports to both electing and higher bodies; that there is strict party discipline with subordination of the minority to the majority will; and that the decisions of higher bodies bind lower ones. Primary party organisations (PPOs) are mainly found at places of work and exist wherever three or more communists are located. PPOs of less than fifteen members elect a secretary and deputy secretary whilst those of fifteen or more elect a bureau or executive. Where membership exceeds one hundred and fifty, the branch qualifies for a full-time salaried official. The PPOs elect delegates to area, district or town conferences which in turn elect delegates to regional conferences. These choose delegates to Republican conferences (except in the RSFSR) which, along with the RSFSR Republican Conference elects delegates to the Congress of the CPSU (ibid. p. 129). These bodies all have secretariats which are regularly in touch with the top party apparat. The Congress elects the Central Committee which in turn elects the politbureau. The internal party elections are formalities with decisions on who the sole candidate should be taken at central level, largely within the highly powerful secretariat. The top level party elite is drawn mainly from the ranks of party and state officials. This 2.1 per cent of the party membership in 1966 made up 40 per cent of the Congress delegates and 81.1 per cent of the full members of the central committee (ibid., p. 142). A successful political career in the USSR is impossible outside the party and depends to a large extent on the holding of certain types of party or state posts.

Elected state offices in the USSR are organised along federal lines taking the form of a hierarchy of councils (soviets). These soviets follow the hierarchy of administrative units, starting with town or rural soviets, then district (raion) soviets, then autonomous region and national area (okrug) soviets, then Autonomous republican, territorial (kray), regional (oblast) and certain major city soviets, then Union Republican soviets. The Supreme soviet of the USSR is the highest legislative body. All soviets are unicameral except the Supreme Soviet which is bicameral. Elections to the soviets are direct and the Supreme elects the Praesidium, the Council of Ministers, the Supreme Court and the Procurator-General. Similar executives, committees and agencies are elected by the Union Republican soviets (ibid., pp. 48-54).

In 1980 there were some 2,210,000 deputies to local soviets, about 3,000 deputies to Union Republican soviets and 1500 deputies to the Supreme Soviet. All are chosen by direct election in single member constituencies. There is only ever one candidate in each constituency and candidate selection is carefully monitored by the party. To be elected, a candidate must receive the approval of 50+ per cent of those registered to vote (as opposed to those voting) which may normally, but not always be assumed.

Elections are frequent with some kind being held in three of
every four years. Polling arrangements are highly convenient
and 99 per cent of those eligible to vote and who have not applied
for an absentee certificate regularly turn out. Elections are
supervised by electoral commissions and involve a considerable
publicity feast for the CPSU. Elected delegates must report back
to their constituents and there is a recall procedure as soviet
delegates are considered to be mandated. Soviet deputies are
occasionally recalled via this procedure. Election campaigns are
state-funded and mainly used to underline the achievements of
the party and the state although there is evidence that some
bargaining with constituents is also involved (see Zaslavsky and
Brym, 1978). Elected deputies do have a role to play and the
overall composition of the Supreme Soviet appears to be determined with some attention to representativeness. The USSR electoral process is not, as some would have it, a meaningless publicity exercise, although it certainly has less to do with determining policy priorities than Western elections do. In the contemporary
USSR, as David Lane (1978, p. 142) writes,

> The Communist Party is an authoritative source of values . . .
> (whilst) . . . the state, or government, has the legal power
> of enforcement. The party mobilises the population towards
> the achievement of particular goals, whereas the state formally
> arranges the administration and enforcement of policy.

Effective political participation normally involves success in both
structures with party membership itself being a prime requisite
not only for high state office, but also for advancement in the
state-run economy. It is rare for Soviet women to achieve high
positions in either structure although significant numbers of
women do appear to rise to about the middle levels of state office.
Within the party, however, even this modest achievement has
eluded women as the following sections of this discussion indicate.

WOMEN IN THE CPSU

There are no data available on women's membership of the pre-
revolutionary Bolshevik party as the first comprehensive census
of party membership was not taken until 1922 when women constituted just under 8 per cent of the membership of the Communist
Party. The composition of delegates to the 6th Party Congress of
the Bolsheviks (August 1917) included ten women amongst 171
delegates, approximately 6 per cent of the total (Lapidus, 1978,
p. 39). A biographical directory of Bolshevik leaders includes a
total of eight women in the pre-revolutionary leadership. Elena
Stasova succeeded Nadezhda Krupskaia (Lenin's wife) as party
secretary in 1917 and was the only woman on the Bolshevik Central Committee until Alexandra Kollantai and Zoia Iankova became
members for a brief period in August 1917. The other three leading women Bolsheviks listed were E.F. Rozmirovich, secretary of
the Duma faction, K.N. Samoilova, the 1911 'Pravda' secretary,

E.B. Bosh and Inessa Armand (ibid., p. 40).

The low proportions of women in the party did concern at least some members of the party leadership and in 1918, at the instigation of the All-Russian Conference of Proletarian and Peasant Women, the party set up a woman's department (Zhenotdel) led by Inessa Armand (Rosenthal, 1977, p. 381). The Zhenotdel's tasks were the education of women and children (largely via the early literacy drives) and the recruitment of women to Communism. During the Civil War Zhenotdel delegates worked in factories as women's stop stewards, taking the side of women workers against male management, setting up factory arbitration committees and combating tendencies to fire women first (ibid., p. 381). On the political front it sponsored women as deputies to local soviets and pressed motions on women's rights at party conferences. Zhenotdel activists were encouraged to organise and construct communal institutions for eating and child care, thus liberating women from household chores.

The Zhenotdel's relationship with the party was never an easy one, however, and it was frequently rebuked for overzealousness. Male communists objected to the attachment of departments usually staffed by Zhenotdel dealing with women's affairs to party committees at all levels. Frequent changes in Zhenotdel leadership diminished its clout in party circles and its effectiveness was considerably limited by the fact that it had no powers of enforcement and had to rely upon the mobilisation of public opinion to get its policies implemented (ibid., p. 382).

The Zhenotdel's tasks became more complex with the assimilation of the Moslem societies of Central Asia. According to Lapidus (1975b, p. 95) the failure of the regime to

destroy or permeate traditional associational networks by a
direct assault on local elites led to a new strategy in which . . .
sex replaced social class as the decisive lever for effecting
social change. The task of the Zhenotdel was . . . to launch
. . . (a revolution) . . . by bringing to Moslem women a vision
of the new possibilities open to them by the establishment of
Soviet power.

Early work amongst Moslem women involved the creation of women's clubs as a focus for illiteracy elimination campaigns and the introduction of basic political education. Later the Zhenotdel moved to a broad attack on the structure of Moslem society encouraging women to make use of the new divorce laws, to join in mass public unveilings and to enter male roles in competition with men. The response to this ranged from selective accommodation to violent hostility - Uzbekistan recorded 203 cases of anti-feminist murder in 1928 (Lapidus, 1975b, p. 95).

Hostility was not confined to Central Asia. During the 1920s there was increasing conflict between Zhenotdel and party and trade union leaders with party leaders regularly expressing worries about 'feminist deviations'. In 1930 the Zhenotdel was abolished by Stalin and its duties assigned to Commissions for the Improvement of the Working and Living Conditions of Women which were attached to local, regional and republican party executive committees (ibid., p. 97).

The impact of the Zhenotdel is difficult to assess in qualitative terms, but certainly its period of existence coincided with a dramatic increase in women's political activity. Between January 1922 and the end of 1930 the proportion of women in the party had nearly doubled, rising from 7.4 per cent to 13.1 per cent (Rigby, 1968, p. 361). The proportions of women deputies to rural soviets increased from 1 per cent in 1922 (White, 1979, p. 88) to 27 per cent in 1934 (Lapidus, 1975b, p. 98). In the urban soviets the similar increase was from 5.7 per cent in 1920 to 32 per cent in 1934. Gail Lapidus (ibid., p. 97) believes that its impact was also evident in more self-assertion by women and points out that within the party its influence was both noticeable and measurable: some 103 resolutions and decrees on women were promulgated by the party during the Zhenotdel's existence as compared to only three since. Certainly there has been no equivalent rise in the proportion of women party members since the abolition of the Zhenotdel.

In 1976 24.3 per cent of all CPSU members were women, involving 5 per cent of all Soviet women in the 30 to 60 age cohort. This compares with 20 per cent of all men in the same age range (Hough and Fainsod, 1979, p. 313). Since 1950 growth in the proportion of women in the party has been more or less steady, if slow. But data produced by Lapidus (1975b, p. 102) shows women suffering disproportionately during the purge years, as well as slight losses in 1952 and 1961. In 1932 women comprised 15.9 per cent of party members, the proportion for 1934 was 16.5 per cent; for 1939, 14.5 per cent; for 1941 14.5 per cent; for 1945, 17 per cent; for 1947, 18.7 per cent; for 1950, 20.7 per cent; for 1952, 19 per cent; for 1956, 19.7 per cent, for 1961, 19.5 per cent. Post-Khruschev a steady pattern of growth has appeared with women comprising 20.6 per cent of the membership in 1966, 20.7 in 1967, 22.2 per cent in 1971 and 23 per cent in 1973.

Even in the Central Asian republics, where intensive efforts to recruit women have been made, the proportions of women's party membership remains low. Statistics on Turkmenistan and Tadzhikistan put the percentage of women party members in the Turkmen party at 18.2 per cent in 1967 and the Tadzhik at 19 per cent in the same year (ibid., p. 105). The underrepresentation of women in the party becomes more striking when demographic factors are taken into account: the chances of being a party member are about one in eight for a man and one in forty for a woman. The overall underrepresentation of women in the party becomes more perplexing when one considers the fact that Komsomol (party youth) membership does not reflect a similar discrepancy. In 1975 women comprised more than 50 per cent of all Komsomol members (Yemelyanova, 1975, p. 66) and Hough (1978, p. 362) found that in schools women comprised 52.4 per cent of members and 57.1 per cent of secretaries of primary Komsomol organisations.

Although possibly less so in recent years, election to party

membership represents a reward for achievement and it is also a
condition for advancement. The very fact that party membership
is necessary for a high managerial position in the state economy
or a similarly prestigious and well remunerated post must make
membership an attractive proposition for both sexes. The low
presence of women in the party is a sensitive indicator of their
prospects elsewhere in the society and indicates a fairly consistent pattern of disadvantage.

Moreover, the picture deteriorates considerably as one ascends
the party hierarchy. Lapidus (1975b, p. 106) found that women
party functionaries were most frequently to be found as secretaries of PPOs. Data on local level functionaries cited by Hough
(1978, pp. 356-7) indicate that in 1976 women comprised 28.8 per
cent of gorkom and raikom level party committees and in 1973 they
were 22.9 per cent of obkom and republican party central committee members. At these levels women appear to be represented
approximately in proportion to their membership. However, as the
levels of party decision making are reached the proportions of
women fall off sharply. In 1972 women comprised 2.2 per cent of
the membership of republican party bureaus and in 1973 they
were 3 per cent of the members of regional bureaus. At the All-
Union level there has only ever been one woman member of the
Politbureau (Ekaterina Furtseva) and there have never been more
than 4.2 per cent of women on the All-Union Central Committee
(ibid., p. 356). Hough's investigations indicate that there has
been no woman head of a central committee department since the
Second World War and only two of 200 deputy department heads
and heads of section have been women (Hough, 1978, p. 357).
Lapidus (1975b, p. 110) found no correlation between women's
central committee and party memberships. A peak of 9.7 per cent
was reached in July 1917 and there were no women on the 40-
member 1921 Central Committee. Rakowska-Harmstone (1970, p.
103) provides evidence that within the Central Asian republics
the promotion of native women has led to a slightly different
pattern with women comprising between 10 per cent and 14 per
cent of the Tadzhik Central Committee Auditing Commission. However, her study indicates that native women feature most in symbolic positions and in areas requiring the local language.

There is also evidence that women's membership in the All-
Union Party Central Committee is largely symbolic. Lapidus (1975b,
p. 108) points out that the Central Committee of the CPSU that
was elected at the 24th Party Congress in April 1971 was (as
usual) dominated by male members of the state and party bureau-
cracies. Only nine of the fifteen women members and candidate
members came from such backgrounds. The other six included
one astronaut, two factory workers, one milkmaid, one brigade
leader from the pig livestock section of a state farm and one loom
operator. The symbolic nature of their presence was confirmed by
the fact that none were identifiable in any directories of prominent
Soviet leaders.

The pattern in the Komsomol hierarchy is similar. Whilst women

comprise approximately half of the heads of primary Komsomol
organisations, they hold only one-third of the key district and
town committee secretaryships and about 30 per cent of the places
on regional, territorial and Union republican central committees
(Yemelyanova, 1975, p. 66). Mickiewicz (1971, p. 61) found that
at the end of the 1960s there were no women first secretaries in
any republic-level Komsomol organisation, no women first or second secretaries of Komsomol organisations in the Estonian or
Latvian Republic or in the Tomsk, Kurst, Pskov or Orlov regional
organisations. A study of Ivanov Oblast, a textile centre, indicated that whilst women comprised 65 per cent of the Komsomol
membership they held only seven of the twenty-four district
secretaryships.
    Possible causes of the underrepresentation of women in the
CPSU are numerous. The commitment involved in being a party
member is high and Hough and Fainsod (1979, p. 313) cite
evidence that women's political activity drops sharply with marriage
and more with the birth of each child. This would explain the discrepancy between women's membership in the Komsomol and the
party, but it sheds little light on the absence of women in leadership roles in either organisation. Similarly White (1979, p. 155)
refers to studies which suggest that Soviet women are slightly
less likely to be interested in politics than Soviet men, but this
only serves to explain part of the lower membership levels. Moreover, it does not explain why, once a commitment is made, membership and presence in the party committees at the lower levels
does not lead to the occupancy of leading positions for women in
the same manner that it does for men.
    The type of data necessary for a full explanation of the dispro-
portions is not available, but there is evidence to support the
hypothesis that early socialisation and the position of women in
the Soviet family is at the root of it. In a study of party careers
in the Russian and Ukranian Republics between 1955 and 1973
Moses (1976) found that typical successful male careers involved
both geographic mobility and administrative flexibility. Typical
male members of Obkom party bureaus were recruited from outside the region and, once assigned, were frequently rotated to
a number of positions of responsibility inside the bureau. By contrast the women members were locals, recruited from lower positions within the bureau and tended to hold only one bureau position during their tenure (usually in indoctrination). Hence, to the
extent that the preferred leader is a 'mobile generalist, tested in
a number of locales', (Moses, 1976, p. 530) the more parochial
women are at a disadvantage. The indoctrination specialism of
women was found to be a fairly typical one, a factor which Moses
attributed to the tendency for women to have had their training
in education or the humanities. Indoctrination officials tended to
be of lower status than those concerned with economics or production engineering. In regions where indoctrination was important
for some special reason, the position was held by a man. The
weight of these two factors appears to be considerable. In the

nineteen years covered by Moses's study only one woman was
elected to the All-Union level from the twenty-five bureaus investigated. Of the twenty-one professional women elected to the All-
Union Central Committee and Central Auditing Commission of the
CPSU between the 20th and 24th Party Congresses, fifteen had
career backgrounds covering industrial, agricultural and political
administration and all had avoided training and careers associated
with indoctrination (Moses, 1976, p. 537). Hough's data on the
RSFSR supports Moses's suggestion that women preponderate
in indoctrination careers. Between 1966 and 1975 women comprised
11.3 per cent of the ideological secretaries of RSFSR regional
party committees, 35 per cent of the heads of science education
departments, and 42 per cent of the fifty-two ideological secretaries of city party committees (Hough, 1978, pp. 359-60).
    Women's lower geographic mobility is likely to be a function of
spouse's career whilst differences in specialisation are traceable
to differences in educational background. There is considerable
evidence of sex-linked differentiation in the occupational preferences of boys and girls, indicating boy's preference for technical occupations and showing girls as giving high valuations to the
'caring' and cultural occupations. These preferences are clearly
reflected in patterns of educational enrolment (see Dobson, 1978).
But, as Lapidus (1975b, p. 107) points out 'it is precisely those
industrial, technical and agricultural specialisations which men
have tended to enter in larger proportions that have the greatest
. . . "professional convergence" . . . with the skills demanded
of political leaders in the Soviet system.'

WOMEN IN ELECTED OFFICE

There has been no sex-differentiated voting behaviour since the
1930s when women's turnout reached the same levels as men's.
In 1975 women comprised 48.1 per cent of deputies to local soviets,
46 per cent of Oblast soviet deputies, 39 per cent of the deputies
to the supreme Soviets of the autonomous republics, 35 per cent
of the deputies to the supreme soviets of the union republics and
31 per cent of the deputies to the Supreme Soviet of the USSR
(Hough, 1978, p. 356). They also comprised 32.2 per cent of the
elected people's judges, 14 of the 45 people's assessors of the
USSR Supreme Court, and 27 women were members of the Supreme
Court (Yemelyanova, 1975, p. 64). The expected pattern of proportionate fall-off is evident throughout the hierarchy of soviets.
Assessing the meaning of these data is problematic. Lapidus warns
that although a clear pattern emerges, the composition of a single
electoral slate and therefore of the soviets themselves is the outcome of political decisions made at higher levels and in which
'neither aspirations of potential candidates nor the preferences of
the electorate is decisive' (Lapidus, 1975b, p. 98). Soviet delegate
composition is intended to provide representation across a wide
range of occupational and social groups, i.e. to be a microcosmic

cross-section of the population. The consistent proportions of women delegates across the various component republics of the USSR suggests that delegate selection is guided by norms for sex composition. For example, the 1975 local election returns showed the proportion of women deputies varying within a very narrow range - from a low of 44.8 per cent in Turkmenistan to a high of 49.4 per cent in the RSFSR (ibid., p. 99). This, plus the relatively high order of women's participation, suggests some degree of regime consciousness of a political need for the visible inclusion of women. What it does not suggest is that women are disposing of significant quantities of political power. Whilst soviets at all levels have, since Stalin's demise, come to play an increasing role in the necessary bargaining processes of the industrial society, they are not now and have never been the site of effective decision-making in the system. The role of women elected to them must therefore be considered within a very narrow political range.

Within that range women's most extensive contribution is at the local level. Local soviets supervise activities concerned with housing, education, culture, health, local industry, trade and social services. The soviets have some amount of scope in police implementation in their localities and they can and probably do exert a certain amount of bargaining power. There is at present no reliable way of estimating the importance of that power, but it is likely to be a factor in many of the areas which most affect people's everyday lives. This is in the nature of local government and it is reasonable to suppose that the USSR is no exception in this regard.

So, the high visibility of women in Soviet local government is not without some political meaning. However closer scrutiny of the data reveals that although the proportion of women deputies to local soviets has steadily increased since their first convocation in 1939 - from 31.1 per cent in 1939 (Yemelyanova, 1975, p. 6) to 49 per cent in 1977 (White, 1979, p. 88) - the role of women in the executive levels of local government has not kept pace. Lapidus (1975b, p. 100) cites work which shows that between 1948 and 1965, twenty-six of a total of 340 members of the city executive and department heads in Leningrad were women. Of these, eight were members 'without portfolio' who served only one term. Six served as one of the four to seven vice-chairpersons of the committee, and one as committee secretary. Seven women headed departments which did not carry executive committee positions. Examination of the executive committee of a Leningrad District Soviet between 1962 and 1966 (three elections) indicated that women were 100 per cent of the clerical staff, from 82 per cent to 92 per cent of the specialists, between 40 and 60 per cent of the directors and deputy directors of divisions and sectors, but only 24 per cent of the top executive personnel (Mickiewicz, 1971, p. 61).

The pattern described above persists throughout the system. Hough's data indicates that in 1973 women comprised only 11 per cent of the RSFSR Oblast soviets executive committees' members and held only 5.5 per cent of the committees' chairs and deputy chairs (Hough, 1978, p. 357). Lennon's data on women in the councils of ministers of the union republics indicates that in the late 1960s women occupied 7.8 per cent of the chairs and deputy chairs of committees and 3.9 per cent of the council memberships (Lennon, 1971, p. 50).

At the All-Union level, only two women have been members of the Council of Ministers since the Second World War, and only seven of between 550 and 560 deputy ministers and deputy chairs of ministries and state commissions of the USSR have been women (Hough, 1978, p. 356).

Moreover Hill's (1972) study of the Supreme Soviet elections of 1966 and 1970 suggests that such clout as could be acquired within the Supreme Soviet was likely to be unavailable to the women deputies. Women deputies experienced higher turnover rates when compared to men and were less likely to be party members.

Hill argues that the main operative variable in selecting deputies for re-election is occupation. Use of this variable favours party officials, state officials, officers in the armed forces and management generally. These 'responsible office holders' are generally male and the bias in their favour translates into a bias against women as holders of particular occupations. This pattern, Hill points out, has implications for the effectiveness of women deputies. In practice those who have gained experience as deputies are likely to form a stable group, and become proficient at dealing with constituents, officials etc. Although no data are available it is likely that this sort of experience may be necessary for promotion to ministerial status, service on Supreme Soviet commissions etc. To the extent that there are indicators of the lower effectiveness of women deputies they tend to confirm these speculations. Hough (1978, p. 356) found that women comprised only 10.5 per cent of all speakers in Supreme Soviet debates between 1966 and 1975, and found no growth in the proportion of women speakers over the period.

The educational and cultural factors which lead to women's preference for lower priority policy areas such as health, education, culture and consumer affairs are evident in the various soviet debates. Women contribute to debates in those areas in proportion to their membership, but play a negligible role in the discussion of the planning and budgetary matters and foreign affairs which have been the priority policy areas of the regime for the past sixty-odd years.

Thus a clear long-term growth of women's involvement in public affairs has not led to their participation in the leading organs of the party or the state. There is little evidence of a positive correlation between participation rates of women and their entry into the Soviet political elite, however defined. As Gail Lapidus (1975b, pp. 108-9) has noted

The role of women in the Soviet Political elite is perhaps best summarised in a biographical directory of Soviet party and government officials, which lists the members of all central government bodies from 1917 and of major party organs from the founding of the Social Democratic party in 1898. Of the approximately 2,100 names included in the directory, 77 or 3.4 per cent were women.

CONCLUSION

Clearly in a one-party state the decisive feminine political participation will be that which takes place within the party. Positions of responsibility and effectiveness in the state bureaucracy, the planned economy and the elective assemblies are all closely controlled by the party. That party has been unable, despite considerable efforts, to recruit women to its membership in any proportion to their presence in the society; and it has been apparently unwilling to promote those recruited into positions in its leadership.

On the face of it women's absence from the USSR political elite may be due to preferences expressed by Soviet women. White (1979, p. 155) refers to evidence that women are less interested in politics than men and that measured differences in political interest decrease but do not disappear when they are controlled for age, education and occupation. However, it must be remembered that these preferences are expressed in a society which despite considerable strides toward sex-equality remains patriarchal in its structure. The available data indicate that women's evaluations of politics as a useful activity are as favourable as those of men and Komsomol participation suggests that there is little difference in the propensity for boys and girls to participate. Additionally, Hough's examination of the day care facilities issue in the RSFSR indicates that where there was both a relevant grievance and a possibility of change women's participation rates rose noticeably (Hough, 1978, pp. 369–70). Hough found that party meetings, trade union meetings and meetings of other Soviet groups featured women speakers in proportion to their presence when the issue was one which could be regarded as of social interest to women. The fact that such meetings are attended by party leaders or their representatives, is to Hough, at least some insurance that the views of women are heard by decision-makers.

Indirect access to elites is, however, a far cry from full women's participation in politics, and it is a disheartening fact that Soviet women's political roles have not even kept pace with their economic ones. The time is long since past when historical explanations are valid. The nuclear family is the norm in the USSR, and the site of the discrepancy is without doubt the female domestic role. Although regime social services have alleviated some of the worst effects of women's role in the family, such services have rarely received high priority. Repeated party decisions to concentrate resources on heavy industry and defence have been implemented at the cost of the emancipation of Soviet women and there is increasing evidence that this will eventually cost the regime dearly.

The low birth-rates of the 1960s means that by the 1980s there
will be critical labour shortage in the European Republics of the
Soviet Union (see Feshback and Rapawy, 1976), one which cannot
be made good by the mobilisation of more women into the economy,
simply because there are so few women not already so mobilised.
There is little doubt that the current leadership is aware of this,
but it is facing a problem for which there is no ideologically acceptable short-term solution, and in which circumstances in which the
dominant industrial priorities of the last half century are unlikely
to be reconsidered. There are no women making the feminist case
in the contemporary Soviet elite[1] and the radicalism of Bolshevik
feminism died with socialist democracy in hte USSR. It is therefore unlikely that the kind of thinking necessary to produce a sustained attack on sex-differentiated domestic roles, not to mention
the concept of domestic roles itself, will emerge. That this
is the case is largely a result of party policy. Sustained efforts
and an active policy of female leadership recruitment could
improve the political visibility of women within a very short period
of time, and the CPSU has the propaganda wherewithal to transmit
successfully a non-sexist ideological message. Budgetary changes
could be made which provide the services for families which were
part of the platform on which the Bolsheviks came to power. That
this would be a costly exercise is not in doubt, but it is less
costly than the under-utilisation of over half the population in a
country plagued by labour shortages.

Such a major alteration in a society in which the rate of change
might best be described as 'glacial' is unlikely however, and the
absence of a woman's movement in the USSR does not augur well
for the improvement of the status and position of Soviet women.
Initiatives which might generate change have not been forthcoming, even if women in the USSR were to begin making radical
feminist demands on the system, their current political position
leaves them ill-placed to press them.

NOTES

1   However press reports in the summer of 1980 indicate that
     feminist ideas have begun to appear in samizdat literature,
     ('Guardian', 31 July 1980).

BIBLIOGRAPHY

Chapman, J.G. (1978), Equal Pay for Equal Work, in Atkinson,
    Dallin and Lapidus (eds), 'Women in Russia', Harvester Press,
    Hassocks, England.
Dobson, R.B. (1978), Educational Policies and Attainment, in
    Atkinson, et al. (eds), op.cit.
Dodge, N.T. (1978), 'Women in the Professions', et al. (eds),
    op.cit.

Engel, B. (1977), Women as Revolutionaries: the Case of the Russian Populists, in Bridenthal and Koonz (eds), 'Becoming Visible: Women in European History', Houghton Mifflin, Boston.

Feltham, A. (1978), Politics and Russian Women: The Dysjunction between Theory and Practice, Paper presented to the European Consortium for Political Research Workshop on 'Women as Political Actors', Grenoble.

Feshback, M. and Rapawy, S. (1976), 'Soviet Population and Manpower Trends and Policy', US Congress Joint Economic Committee Report.

Glickman, R.L. (1978), The Russian Factory Woman, in Atkinson et al. (eds), op.cit.

Hill, R.J. (1972), Continuity and Change in USSR Supreme Soviet Elections, 'British Journal of Political Science', no. 2, pp. 44-67.

Hough, J.F. (1978), Women and Women's Issues in Soviet Policy Debates, in Atkinson et.al., (eds), op.cit.

Hough, J.F. and Fainsod, M. (1979), 'How the Soviet Union is Governed', Harvard University Press, Cambridge, Mass.

Lane, D. (1978), 'Politics and Society in the USSR', Martin Robertson, London.

Lapidus, G.W. (1975a), USSR Women at Work: Changing Patterns, 'Industrial Relations', vol. 14, no. 2, pp. 178-95.

Lapidus, G.W. (1975b), Political Mobilization, Participation and Leadership: Women in Soviet Politics, 'Comparative Politics', vol. 8, pp. 90-118.

Lapidus, G.W. (1976), Changing Women's Roles in the USSR, in L. Iglitzin and R. Ross (eds), 'Women in the World', Clio Books, Oxford

Lapidus, G.W. (1978), 'Women in Soviet Society', University of California Press, London.

Lennon, L. (1971), Women in the USSR, 'Problems of Communism', July-August, pp. 47-58.

Mickiewicz, E. (1971), The Status of Soviet Women, 'Problems of Communism', Sept.-Oct. pp. 59-62.

Moses, J.C. (1976), Indoctrination as a Female Political Role in the Soviet Union, 'Comparative Politics', vol. 8, pp. 525-47.

Rakowska-Harmstone, T. (1970), 'Russia and Nationalism in Central Asia; The Case of Tadzhikistan', Johns Hopkins Press, Baltimore.

Rigby, T.H. (1968), 'Communist Party Membership in the USSR, 1919-1967', Princeton Univeristy Press, Princeton, NJ.

Rosenthal, B.G. (1977), Love on the Tractor: Women in the Russian Revolution and After, in Bridenthal and Koonz (eds), 'Becoming Visible: Women in European History', Houghton Mifflin, Boston.

Sacks, M.P. (1978), Women in the Industrial Labour Force, in Atkinson et al. (eds), op.cit.

White, S. (1979), 'Political Culture and Soviet Politics', Macmillan, London.

Yemelyanova, Y.D. (1975), The Social and Political Activity of Soviet Women, in 'Soviet Women', Progress Publishers, Moscow.

Zaslavsky, V. and Brym, R.J. (1978), The Functions of Elections in the USSR, 'Soviet Studies', vol. XXX, pp. 362-71.

14 JAPAN

Eileen Hargadine

BACKGROUND

In the late 1800s, Japan's self-imposed isolation from the rest of the world ended with the United States' demand for trade access to the island nation. The liberal democratic philosophy that accompanied it was new to the people of this hierarchically structured country. With the introduction of liberalism, the first seeds of the women's movement were sown. As early as 1870, Hideko Fukuda was speaking out for women's equality and independence as part of the Democratic Rights Movement. Apprehensive that the trend toward liberalism would undermine the government's legitimacy, based on the theory of absolute imperial rule, the administration moved to contain it and the embryonic women's movement. The Peace Preservation Law of 1887 was instituted to prohibit secret meetings and associations, publications, and acts disturbing to the public peace. Article 5 specifically forbade women's participation in political activities and associations. Representative political institutions were introduced to the Japanese imperial system with the Meiji Constitution of 1889, and limited popular participation was allowed. Male suffrage was slowly extended, but women remained unable to participate in the growing democracy.

In 1920, Fusae Ichikawa, Raicho Hiratsuka and Mumeo Oku formed the New Women's Organisation (Shin Fujin Kuōkai) to improve women's social and economic conditions. Their first goal was rescission of Article 5 which severely limited women's organised activities. Through petitions and letters, these feminists lobbied for reform, and in spite of police harassment, public hostility and exclusion from political meetings, they won rescission in 1922 (Vavich, 1967, p.412). Soon afterward, factionalism broke up the New Women's Organisation, but the Japanese women's movement had never been a cohesive, unified association. The developing socialist parties soon had women's auxiliaries. They were prevented from collaborating, however, by their parties' placement of other social reforms ahead of suffrage and women's issues. Party consensus, still a major political force, required adherence to the party line and did not allow for individual positions. In spite of the factionalism and dissension, campaigns were waged to extend the right to vote to women, but they were not successful.

Heightened militarism and nationalism in the 1930s and 1940s brought this first era of feminist activity to a close. To mobilise the country behind the war effort, the government brought down controls in all political and social organisations advocating increased civil rights. Nevertheless, a foundation had been laid for women's postwar suffrage and political participation. Women were ready to take advantage of Article 14 of the New Constitution of 1947:

All people are equal under the law and there shall be no discrimination in political, economic or social relations because of race, creed, sex, social status or family origin.

Full civil rights, for women, was part of the United States Occupation plan for restructuring the Japanese government to ensure a stable democracy. The reintroduction of democracy into Japan, required adaptation of its emphasis on individual rights to the Japanese value system stressing the higher importance of society. Loyalty to one's primary group, and its leader, be it political party or company, had traditionally taken precedence over one's personal preferences and, at times, over even family ties (Hargadine, 1980, p.197). The significance of the group has modified the concept of democracy in Japan. It has come to imply consensus building, in which each individual seriously participates then unites to support the group's decision (Beer, 1976, p.105). The implications for women are two-fold: first, as members of a political organisation, they are constrained by its position; and secondly, the political guarantees of equality are mitigated by social consensus on appropriate activities, political or otherwise. Women's roles as wives and mothers are not always compatible with that of professional politicians. Therefore, women's political participation must be examined in the context of the Japanese culture.

WOMEN'S SOCIO-ECONOMIC POSITION

Japanese society is among the most homogeneous in the world. An insular nation of 115 million people, it had little contact with the rest of the world until the late 1800s. The Japanese strong sense of cultural identity effectively isolated the few ethnic Koreans and Chinese who live there. The contemporary Japanese wants, generally, to preserve Japan's national identity as exemplified in its traditions and customs. This densely populated country is relatively affluent and urban. As of 1974, only 12 per cent of those employed were working in agriculture (United States, 1976, p.209). As measured by consumer goods, the urban Japanese are well off; 77.2 per cent of the households contain a colour television, 97.4 per cent have a washing machine, and 95.2 per cent have a refrigerator (Japan, 1976, p.29). Traditional practices have been modified with the industrialisation that produced these consumer products, but there is still a strong sense of cultural heritage.

In order to broaden her practical ability and education, the model Japanese woman is expected to work after graduation from high school, junior college, or university. However, by age 25, she should find a good man, marry, quit work, and have children. If they are financially able to retire this is the sequence most women follow. Ninety-three per cent of the female population is married by age 35,

and the average at marriage is 24.7. The average for men is
slightly higher at 27.0 (Bando, 1977, p.15). Divorce is available
by mutual consent or through the courts, but it is often financially
disastrous for the wife. She rarely receives alimony, or even an
equal share of the accumulated property. A Labour Ministry
survey of widows and divorcees indicated their household expenses
were limited to 63 per cent of the average Japanese household.
These women earned an average monthly salary of only 89,000 yen
($356 or £148). The average female worker does slightly better
with a salary of 94,000 yen ($376 or £157) ('Mainichi Daily News',
12 December 1977). Divorced women have found discrimination in
employment and there is always pressure on women to retire early.
Socially and financially discouraged, only 1.08 divorcees per
thousand of population were recorded in 1975 (Japan, 1977a, p.28).

Children follow almost immediately after marriage; about 80 per
cent of the yearly births are to women between the ages of 25 and
29. The average number of children born to a married couple is
2.12 as of 1972, with the last child born when the mother is 28
years old. The Japanese woman, with a life expectancy of 75.5
years, has about forty-two years left after her last child enters
school and, probably, fifteen years alone with her husband, after
the last child marries (Bando, 1977, pp.4, 17). The nuclear family
is the standard; most families (46.1 per cent) are composed of a
married couple with children. Only 10.8 per cent of the households
are single persons, and only 11 per cent are married couples without children, including couples who had not yet had children, as
well as those who never will (Japan, 1975, p.40). Small families,
and longer life expectancies, leave Japanese women with much time
on their hands. The desire for a better standard of living brings
women back into the work force when they are free of family
responsibilities.

When they marry, or, at the latest have their first child, many
Japanese women retire or are forced out of the work force. Labour
Ministry surveys indicate that at least 29 per cent of Japanese
enterprises have different retirement ages for men and women
(Hanami, 1969, p.8). In 1965 9.4 per cent of 4,000 establishments
surveyed enforced policies requiring retirement upon marriage.
Although it was not compulsory, another 7.5 per cent 'urged'
retirement. These figures are probably conservative because this
policy is not officially sanctioned by the government and has been
contested successfully in the courts (Hargadine, 1980, pp.147-52).
Social pressure to retire is reflected in a 1975 attitude survey of
the general population (Bando, 1977, p.27). 19.2 per cent of the
respondents considered it a 'matter of course' that women quit
working upon marriage or childbirth. Another 60 per cent considered
it 'inevitable', and only 12.6 per cent considered such retirement
'not right'. The responses are indicative of the general consensus
on early retirement for women. Labour statistics for 1974 (United
States, 1976, p.206), reveal that the number of women working
between the ages of 20 and 24 (marriage age) drops, by only 34
per cent, for women aged 25 to 29. In other words, well over half

of the women who begin work after school do not drop out of the labour force. Of those who drop out willingly, or unwillingly, many return to work as soon as their children enter school or are old enough to be left alone after school. Unfortunately the employment opportunities for women are usually limited to temporary, part-time, poorly paid positions.

Women's employment opportunities are limited in part because of this interrupted working pattern. The Japanese employment system discourages job mobility. Ideally one enters a company upon graduation and remains with that company until retirement. There are few company provisions for maternity leave or other long leaves of absence, although the Labour Standards Law provides for six-week pregnancy and maternity leaves. Allegiance to one's employer is rewarded by making seniority a determinant of wages. Disregarding some of the finer details of the employment system, the average woman's home life is not compatible with a well-paid career, secure employment or professional politics. In 1975 women's cash earnings were only 56 per cent of men's (Japan, 1977a, p.19). These low wages reflect a significant portion of employment costs in Japan. In 1975 female workers represented 38 per cent of the labour force. Forty-seven per cent of the women over fifteen were in employment. In comparison, 82 per cent of men of the same age were in paid employment. But whereas, in 1973, 75 per cent of the men were paid employees and 4 per cent were unpaid family workers, the comparable proportions for women were 59 per cent and 25 per cent. Remaining men and women were self-employed (Japan, 1974a, pp.112-14). Thus, a quarter of employed women work unpaid in family businesses or farms. A breakdown of women's wages, as a proportion of total wages, is not available but, if women employees' wages were equivalent to men's, Japan would have higher wage costs. Women's jobs are frequently considered an expendable frill for a company, because the important positions are filled by men. Department stores, which traditionally hired more women than men, are now 'rationalising' their work force and hiring more men as the young women retire ('Mainichi Daily News', 3 August, 1977).

In spite of the evidence that almost half the female population is in the work force and that even during child-bearing years, 44 per cent of them are working, society and employers perpetuate the myth that women are temporary employees. This stereotype of a temporary, less dedicated worker is difficult to overcome, and leaves women underrepresented in technical and management fields. They comprise only 5.8 per cent of managers and officials and 1.4 per cent of engineers and technicians. Women congregate in the more socially acceptable fields of lower school teaching (56.8 per cent) and nursing (97.6 per cent) (United States, 1976, pp.214-15). Women workers are treated as a special class by employers and by law. The Labour Standards Law reinforces this treatment through protective legislation, which limits women's working hours, and forbids their employment under certain conditions. The equal pay provision of the Labour Standards Law is difficult to enforce, because of the difficulty in determining what is equal work. Twenty-

nine per cent of the women workers do belong to unions, but
because Japan's unions are organised on a company basis rather
than along trade or skill lines comparison with other countries
is difficult. Women represent 28 per cent of union membership,
but few women hold leadership positions. The unions do not
provide much recourse for women, and have entered into labour
agreements to retire women workers early (Hargadine, 1980, pp.
148-9). With little support from the government, unions or employers, women's employment opportunities are very restricted, and
this carries over into politics, where their options are also very
limited.

Education plays an important role in employment and professional
possibilities, and Japanese women's rights are legally protected.
The education system is open equally to both sexes, and education is highly valued. However, while higher education represents
the gateway to a rewarding career for a man, it represents part
of a woman's training to be a good wife and mother. In 1975 34.6
per cent of the female high school graduates went on to higher
education, compared with 33.8 per cent of the male graduates, but
the type of institution varied by sex. The post-high school education system is two-tiered. Academically less rigorous junior colleges
are 86.2 per cent female and provide further education for about
45 per cent of women, but only for 3 per cent of men. There,
women specialise in 'home economics'. Women make up only 21 per
cent of the students in the four-year institutions, which lead to
high-level employment opportunities. Within these institutions,
women are usually found in the literature and education departments, which do not develop very marketable skills (Japan, 1977a,
pp. 7-8). In all, only 34 per cent of women attend four-year institutions, compared to 44 per cent of men ('Mainichi Daily News',
10 January 1978).

Women's employment opportunities outside the home are limited
by this educational background, by occupational segregation and
interrupted work patterns. Because there is little rewarding work
available, these restricted opportunities, in turn, encourage women
to stay at home. If women are confined to home, where men help
for an average of seven minutes per day, they cannot participate
in professional politics (ibid.).

THE POLITICAL SYSTEM

Japan's political system is a parliamentary democracy. Law-making
powers reside in a Diet composed of 511 member House of Representatives and a House of Councillors with 252 senators. The Diet
elects one of its members as Prime Minister, and he appoints a
cabinet, the majority of which must also be Diet members. The
House of Representatives is the constitutionally more significant
House because with a two-thirds majority, it can override inaction
or rejection by the Upper House. The Japanese electoral system
is unique. The members of the House of Representatives are elected

from 130 multi-member districts with three to five representatives, but the voters may cast only one vote apiece. Under these rules, party members in the same constituency must compete with each other. For a party to obtain a majority, multiple slates must be run in each district to win an average of two seats per district. This intraparty competition, as well as Japan's group-oriented social structure, has contributed to factional divisions within the parties. Organised around an individual leader, these factions are strong, well disciplined political units which channel financial contributions and patronage to the faction members. In return, members are loyal to the faction leader and will not dissent from the group consensus. These members deliver a solid block of votes for the leader. Between the follower and the leader exists a permanent, functionally diffuse, relationship, embracing personal as well as political considerations. This factionalism is found in all political parties and has its counterparts in the administration and the business world.

Elections for half the House of Councillors' six-year seats are held every three years. Half of these are elected from districts larger than the Lower House, with one to four seats. The remaining seats are elected in a national constituency. The purpose of the large districts and national constituency seats was to encourage the election of unaffiliated statesmen, with wider political appeal than the Representatives with their smaller, more parochial districts. However, independent politicians are a rarity, and lines are drawn along party membership in both Houses. There have been some unexpected side effects of the national constituency. Most politicians have lacked the widespread public recognition for a national seat, but many entertainers, athletes and other public figures have had the requisite following. Parties have found it expedient to ask some of these nationally known 'non-politicians' to represent them, and several of them have been elected. Among the few women senators have been several such talent candidates.

The Liberal Democratic Party (LDP) has controlled both Houses of the Diet for the past twenty-five years, and the party president has been duly elected Prime Minister. Consequently, intra-LDP politics have been of vital national interest and its factional alliances have determined who would be LDP President and Prime Minister. The Liberal Democratic Party is characterised as conservative. It is supported by corporate interests, has a rural, conservative electoral base, and lacks a strong ideological position. Like all Japanese parties, it is not a mass-based organisation. Membership estimates range from 200,000 to 1,000,000, or less than 1 per cent of the population. The LDP is a parliamentary party controlled by Diet members and composed of their individual support organisations (koenkai). The allegiance of the koenkai is more to the individual representative than to the party, which lends credence to the characterisation of the LDP as an alliance of smaller parties. With allied independents, the LDP in 1979 had a slim majority of 258 seats in the 511-member House of Representatives and 163 in the 252-member Upper House. Its representation had slipped over the previous fifteen years and it had failed to garner 50 per cent of the popular vote in elections during the 1970s. However, in the June 1980 election the LDP won a landslide victory with 284 seats in the Lower House.

Opposing the LDP is a wide range of parties from the conservative New Liberal Club to the Japan Community Party (JCP). The New Liberal Club was formed in 1976 when six LDP members withdrew to form an alternative conservative party. In 1980 it won twelve seats compared to its previous four. Moving from right to left along the political spectrum, the Komei Party, as the political arm of the Sokagakkai sect of Nichiren Buddhism, claims to represent the ordinary citizen and to support cleaning up political corruption. Hence comes its name: Clean Government Party. Although officially separated from Sokagakkai, the Komei Party has the support of its strong, effective organisation which claims access to 6 million households (Stockwin, 1975, pp.155–8). As the second largest opposition party, after the 1980 election holding 6 per cent (thirty-three) of the Lower House seats, the Komei Party demonstrates the strength of conservatism in Japanese politics. However, its representation declined by 5 per cent between 1979 and 1980.

More to the left is the Democratic Socialist Party (DSP), formed in 1960 when dissatisfied Japan Socialist Party members left the primary socialist party for a more moderate position and conciliatory politics. Although the DSP's membership is about the same as the Japan Socialist Party's (JSP), it usually receives less than 10 per cent of the popular vote and Diet seats. In 1980 it won thirty-two seats compared to thirty-five in the 1979 election. The strongest opposition party, the JSP, is no more a party of the masses than the LDP. Its membership is only 40,000 and it relies on the General Council of Trade Unions, Sohyo, for electoral and financial support. Espousing a socialist ideology and representing the industrial workers position, the JSP's percentage of the popular vote had declined over the last ten years, and it seemed unable to exploit popular dissatisfaction with LDP policies. However, in 1980, its representation in the Lower House remained stable at 21 per cent of the 511 seats (107). The last major party is the Japan Communist Party (JCP), which has suffered, in national elections, from its adherence to dogmatic ideologies, and its failure to address salient political issues. While it lacks a support group like the JSP's, or the LDP's corporations, the JCP does have a strong grass roots organisation which financially supports the party by selling the JCP newspaper, 'Akahata'. Hostility from the labour unions and the more conservative opposition parties have isolated the JCP, and it has tried to improve its image by disassociating itself from radicalism and violence. In 1980 it held twenty-nine seats in the Lower House, a decline of ten seats from 1979. Occasional coalitions develop among the opposition parties, but there has never been a real alternative to the LDP. Often votes for the Socialist and Communist parties are interpreted as a vote against the LDP, rather than a vote for these parties' policies.

Public interparty legislative politics generally consist of an appro-

priate degree of anti-LDP posturing on the part of the opposition
parties. Then the majority party, occasionally with some opposition
support, passes its legislation. To avoid serious, and, at times,
violent, confrontation politics, before the legislation is presented
in the Diet, the LDP makes concessions to the opposition parties'
views. This exchange of views usually takes place through neutral
intermediaries and private meetings. The parties' public positions
represent intraparty consensuses, and public debate becomes more
repetition of these policies. Only in rare cases of irreconcilable
differences does the opposition resort to disruption of Diet proceedings)Baerwald, 1974, pp. 103-20). In such cases, speakers
have been prevented from reaching the podium and convening the
Diet has been made impossible. The LDP has responded by locking
out the opposition members on occasion. But these confrontations
are infrequent, and, usually, over major policy decisions, such as
the United States-Japan Security Treaty of 1960. Although the LDP
has a controlling majority, the Japanese concept of democracy
implies that a consensus should be reached among all concerned
parties. A simple majority rule is inappropriate, and, when the
LDP forces a vote, without tacit opposition consent, it is severely
criticised by the public.

WOMEN IN NATIONAL POLITICS

Conservative party dominance, and the need for consensus, form
a formidable barrier to women's participation in politics. There is
no strong social consensus supporting such participation, and it
goes outside the normally accepted role for women. None of the
political parties have taken strong positions supporting women, or
women's issues. There was a short-lived Japan Women's Party (JWP),
but it was never taken very seriously. Founded in 1977, it was
dissolved the same year, after it failed to win any seats in the
House of Councillors election. The JSP was organised by Mrs Misako
Enoki, who had also founded Chupiren, Women's Liberation League
Against the Anti-abortion Law and for the Use of the Pill. This
organisation had provided support for women mistreated by their
husbands, and had received lots of press attention for its harassment (through their employers) of some husbands. After national
recognition for this activity, Mrs Enoki took a very combative,
ideologically pure stand, saying that women were superior to men
and therefore, should not seek equality, but superiority. She
received more media attention, but the women's party was relegated
to the political oddity fringe. After losing badly in the House of
Councillors election, Mrs Enoki retired from activist politics to
return to housewifery, and thus complied with the conditions of a
campaign loan from her husband ('Japan Times', 24 July 1977).
This debacle did nothing to improve the public's image of women
politicians, and served to discredit serious women contenders.
Other women's organisations, like Fusae Ichikawa's Fusen Kaikan
(Women's Suffrage Hall) have sponsored electoral candidates, but

their major emphasis is on lobbying, not electoral politics.

Among the major parties there are no sharp differences in their policies on women's issues, their attitudes towards women, or the degree to which women are represented. Ideologically, the JSP and JCP support child care facilities and protection for women workers. These are considered women's issues. Support derives, however, from socialist ideologies, not from a sensitivity towards women. For example, the JSP and JCP do not come out strongly for equal pay for equal work or for equal treatment in the workplace. Rather than address salient women's issues, these parties place higher priority on changing the political and economic systems. Theoretically, these changes should improve women's status, but the women's role as wife and mother is still seen as the one to be protected. In comments on women's place in politics, the JSP's Tosaki Yokoyama opined that women were neither progressive nor dedicated enough for party politics (Jones, 1976, p.222). On the same subject, Masako Kobayashi of the JCP praised women for their work at the local and prefectural level, but criticised their grasp of national policy. Although rationales may differ, there is nominal support for child care facilities and protective labour legislation from all the major parties. However none of them encompasses a non-traditional role for women.

In 1947, in the first general election in which women could vote, thirty-nine women were elected to the House of Representatives, giving them 8 per cent of the seats. This was an all-time high. As Table 14.1 shows, only fifteen women were elected a year later, in the second general election, when their political representation decreased to 3 per cent. Since then, their numbers in the Lower House have fluctuated between seven and twelve or between 1.3 and 2.5 per cent. In the Upper House, as can be seen from Table 14.2, women have done slightly better. However, the House of Councillors is the less influential of the two houses. Women's membership has included a number of 'non politicians' or talent candidates.

In 1975 there were two women representatives each from the LDP, JSP and JCP in the Lower House, with one independent representative. In the 1974 elections to the Upper House one independent, two LDP 'talents', one JSP, and one JCP woman councillor, were elected in the National Constituency, and two JCP and an LDP woman were elected in the prefectural constituency (Baker, 1976, pp.96-7). Proportionately, in 1975, in the Lower House, women comprised less than 1 per cent of the LDP representatives, 1.7 per cent of the JSP, and 5.7 per cent of the JCP. In the Upper House of Councillors in 1974, the Japan Communist Party led the way with four women comprising 13.0 per cent of its senators, and the JSP had three representatives, 6.0 per cent. The DSP and the Komei party had one each 5.0 and 3.0 per cent respectively (Jones, 1975, p.722).

The JCP has the largest proportion of women representatives. It also finances its candidates from central funds. This type of financing is an exception to the common practice of personal and

Table 14.1   Eligible voters, votes cast and voting rates by sex and the number of successful women candidates (General Elections of House of Representatives)

	Eligible voters (millions)		Votes cast (millions)		Voting rates (%)		Women Elected [1]
	Male	Female	Male	Female	Male	Female	
22nd General Election (10 April, 1946)	16	21	13	14	78.5	67.0	39
23rd General Election (25 April, 1947)	20	21	15	13	74.9	61.6	15
24th General Election (23 January, 1949)	20	22	16	15	80.7	67.9	12
25th General Election (1 October, 1952)	22	24	18	18	80.5	72.8	12
26th General Election (19 April, 1953)	22	25	18	17	78.4	70.4	9
27th General Election (27 February, 1955)	24	26	19	19	78.0	72.1	8
28th General Election (22 May, 1958)	25	27	20	20	79.8	74.4	11
29th General Election (20 November, 1960)	26	28	20	20	76.0	71.2	7
30th General Election (21 November, 1963)	28	30	20	21	72.4	70.0	7
31st General Election (29 November, 1967)	30	33	23	24	74.8	73.3	7
32nd General Election (27 December, 1969)	33	36	23	25	67.9	69.1	8
33rd General Election (10 December, 1972)	36	38	25	23	71.0	72.5	7
34th General Election (5 December, 1976)	38	40	27	30	72.8	74.1	7

Source: Election Bureau, Ministry of Home Affairs
[1] 466 seats in total, up to 26th General Election; 467 in total, up to 30th; 486 in total, 31st; 491 in total, 32nd; 511 in total, 33rd; 511 in total, 34th.

Table 14.2 *Eligible voters, votes cast and voting rates by sex and the number of successful women candidates (General Elections of House of Councillors)*

	Eligible voters (millions)		Votes cast (millions)		Voting rates (%)		Total Women Councillors[1]
	Male	Female	Male	Female	Male	Female	
1st General Election (20 April, 1947)	20	21	13	12	68.4	54.0	11
2nd General Election (4 January, 1950)	21	23	16	12	78.2	66.7	12
3rd General Election (24 April, 1950)	22	25	15	14	67.8	58.9	19
4th General Election (8 July, 1956)	24	26	16	15	66.9	57.7	15
5th General Election (2 January, 1959)	26	28	16	15	62.6	55.2	13
6th General Election (1 July, 1962)	27	29	19	19	70.1	66.5	17
7th General Election (4 June, 1965)	28	31	19	21	68.0	66.1	17
8th General Election (7 July, 1968)	32	34	22	24	68.9	69.0	13
9th General Election (27 June, 1971)	34	37	20	22	59.1	59.3	13
10th General Election (7 July, 1974)	36	40	27	29	72.7	73.6	18
11th General Election (10 July, 1977)	38	40	26	28	67.7	69.3	16

Source: Election Bureau, Ministry of Home Affairs.
[1] 252 seats in total: Elections take place every three years for half the seats.

factional responsibility for fund-raising. There is no state provision for funding candidates, and although the election laws have been revised to limit campaign spending, such restrictions are generally ignored. In spite of the 21 million yen ($84,000) limit to expenditures for a House of Councillors' seat, an estimate 100 million yen ($400,000) was the minimum required for a successful campaign in the 1970s (Hrebenar, 1977, p.993). Candidates usually have personal support organisations, not directly affiliated with the party, which provide campaign organisation and funds. The parties are relatively poor providers of campaign financing, but the party faction leaders, who are successful, nationally-known politicians, have access to large sums of money which they distribute among their followers. Because they do not have the image or reputation as serious politicians, women find it particularly difficult to raise funds. Without funds, their low profile and failures only reinforce the negative image of women in politics.

The undivided loyalty and allegiance that membership in a political organisation requires, presents women aspirants to a political career with a real dilemma. As in most countries, there are conflicts between home and career responsibilities. In Japan women are expected to be good wives and mothers, just as men are expected to support their families through hard work outside the home. However, if a woman's first allegiance is to her home, there is little room for the politics, careers and occupations that men pursue. Undivided loyalty and allegiance to one's calling, inside or outside the home, is socially reinforced, to the extent that participation in groups and organisations with crosscutting memberships is relatively rare (Hargadine, 1980, pp.201-5). Women who go into politics must prove their allegiance to the party or organisation, but they risk reproach for neglecting their family responsibilities. For this reason, at least until they prove their commitment, married women are suspect to a degree in professional political circles. There are many single women in politics who feel that the dual responsibilities are incompatible, and, in a sense they have demonstrated their sincerity by remaining single. In politics, as in most professional occupations, only a few women can make the commitment necessary to go outside the expected role of wife and mother.

Although they are not a large component of either the bureaucracy or the judiciary, women do have access to the political system through the other branches of government. The civil service has had a long history of political policy-making through administrative control. In existence before the Second World War, it was the only institution relatively untouched by the Occupation's reforms. Women were not a part of the pre-war bureaucracy, but the Occupation opened it up as part of its policy of introducing democracy and equality. To deal with women's affairs and promote their status, the Women's and Minors' Bureau (WMB) was established in the new Ministry of Labour. This Bureau has provided much of the political expertise in drafting legislation pertaining to women, and it has administered programmes designed to improve women's social, economic and political status. One of its quasi-official roles is that

of representing women's special interests within the government.
As part of a new ministry, the WMB provided access for women
who wanted to pursue civil service careers. Inroads into the other
more established ministries have been very slow. In the 1970s,
women comprised only 0.9 per cent of those employed at the managerial level, a grand total of 1,100 women. In the diplomatic corps,
there was only one woman career foreign service officer until
October 1977, when two women passed its entrance examination.
Some government examinations had been closed to women until
1978, the momentum of International Women's Year compelled the
government to open to women applicants, previously restricted
portions of the administrative service examination. Generally, the
larger, more prestigious agencies are less amenable to women
career civil servants.

Women are slightly better represented in the judicial branch,
where in the 1970s they comprised 2.4 per cent of the judges,
prosecutors and lawyers. At a lower level, they comprised 7.4
per cent of the other judicial workers, including family court
commissioners. The family courts deal with intra-family matters
such as divorce and juvenile delinquency. Women are often shunted
into these courts because the subject matter is deemed appropriate
and women's contributions are valued in this area. About 3,700
women were family court mediators, and they represented 39 per
cent of all mediators. A career in the family court system may
often be a dead-end for a woman. However, increased representation of women may eventually spill over into the regular court
system. It must be remembered that educational and political
institutions have only been open to women for thirty-five years,
and in seniority-conscious Japan, women have not yet earned the
seniority required for many high positions.

WOMEN AND LOCAL GOVERNMENT

With little national, highly visible, political participation by women,
it is not surprising that they have even less representation in the
local assemblies. Since 1955, women have held an average of 1.3
per cent of the seats in the prefectural assemblies. In the town
and village assemblies they had even less: 0.5 per cent of the
seats. In 1977 there were 233 women and 47,381 men in these local
elected bodies. In municipal assemblies, women's representation
has increased slightly from 0.7 per cent in 1955 to 2.0 per cent in
1977. Of the 19,971 municipal representatives, 414 were women
(Japan, 1977a, p.5). Although women tend to be concerned with
local issues, and active in local elections, this activity is not
reflected in the number of women elected.

In local government, in 1975 the JCP had more women assembly
members than any other organised party; 36.9 per cent of the
women were affiliated to the JCP. This is an impressive mobilisation
of women because the Community Party had less than 10 per cent
of the assembly seats. The other major block of local representatives

were the 38.4 per cent of women who were unaffiliated. The remaining 25 per cent were distributed among the other four parties. Women have certainly improved their position within the JCP, but not all of the party members are amenable to women's increased representation. Three per cent of the JCP Diet representatives felt that the number of women in the Diet should be less (Jones, 1975, p.710).

Table 14.3   Number of assembly members of local public bodies by sex

Years	Prefectural Assemblies		Municipal Assemblies		Town or village Assemblies	
	Male	*Female*	*Male*	*Female*	*Male*	*Female*
1955	2,436	32	21,240	158	114,015	455
1960	3,607	36	17,724	190	63,699	275
1965	2,565	41	17,732	198	56,712	311
1968	2,659	37	17,786	225	52,894	272
1971	2,705	26	20,133	350	49,453	198
1975	2,796	32	19,807	360	48,003	217
1977	2,734	34	19,557	414	47,381	233

Note: For a member of the House of Councillors and a headman of the prefecture the eligible age to be elected is 30 years of age and over.
Source: Election Bureau, Ministry of Home Affairs.

WOMEN AND VOTING

In 1946, in their first exercise of suffrage, 67 per cent of women compared to 78.5 per cent of men, turned out to vote (Table 14.1). Originally, a higher percentage of men voted than women. But, gradually, women voted in increasing numbers. Since the late 1960s more women than men have voted in national elections. For instance, in the 1977 House of Councillors election, 67.7 per cent of men voted, compared to 69.3 per cent of women. The higher turnout of women may be related to the number of women left to manage farms in rural areas. In those areas, candidates are more easily able to mobilise voters through social and personal networks, and rural turnout is greater than that of urban areas.

The primary cleavages in Japanese voting behaviour are not upon straight class or religious lines, but upon a traditional attitude / class /rural /urban split. Voters resident in rural areas, with lower educational attainments, seem to favour the conservative parties. The mobilisation of electors by candidates tends to be based on existing social networks. Because residents in rural areas belong to more organisations than do those of urban areas, and because voting tends to be along instrumental lines, it has been suggested that the failure of the LDP to mobilise support in urban areas is due both to its lack of urban social networks, and to its failure to pay attention to policy areas, such as housing and environment. Those parties establishing urban and social networks of their own, such as the Komei Party and the JCP, or able to utilise networks, as the JSP uses the trade unions, have done better in urban than rural areas (Ike, 1978, pp.110-19).

Within these patterns of voting behaviour, it seems that women have not supported the LDP as much as men. In the 1958 House of Representatives election, 60 per cent of men and 53 per cent of women supported the LDP, whereas 26 per cent of men and 24 per cent of women supported the JSP (Scalapino, 1962, p.177). In 1963 47 per cent of men and 40 per cent of women supported the LDP; 22 per cent of men and 21 per cent of women voted for Socialist parties (Tsuneishi, 1966, p.160).

In similar fashion to men's, women's voting has been related to their occupation. Thus in 1958, 61 per cent of women in agriculture supported the LDP compared to 17 per cent who supported the JSP. In contrast, 44 per cent of those in white collar occupations supported the LDP compared to 37 per cent who supported the JSP. As might be expected, within those employed in manual labour, the proportion supporting the LDP decreased further to 39 per cent, although the JSP did not increase its support (34 per cent) (Scalapino, 1962, p.177). Only in the white collar occupational category were women more conservative than men, for whom the comparative figure of support for the LDP was 36 per cent. It would therefore seem inaccurate to consider women in Japan to be more right-wing than men.

ATTITUDES TO WOMEN IN POLITICS

In a survey of female Tokyo residents, in 1972, only 20 per cent of the women had voted for a woman candidate in the local elections (Jones, 1975, p.712). In 1977, a further survey of Tokyo women residents found that, in general, women regarded women politicians to be basically untrustworthy ('Japanese Women', 1 March 1977). These women's opinions indicate the barriers to women's direct participation in political institutions. Some outstanding women may overcome these cultural barriers. For instance, in the 1974 House of Councillors national constituency election, over 70 per cent of the support for four of the winning women candidates, and, over 50 per cent of the support for the other winning woman candidate, may have come from women (Baker, 1976, p.97).

Nevertheless, although Japanese civic culture is actively democratic and sanctions voter participation, women are not thought politically aware and therefore, suitable in general, for public office. This attitude is found in more than one opinion poll. For instance, a public opinion survey by the Komei Party, found that only 14 per cent of the men would answer yes to the question 'Do you think the political consciousness of women is high?' Conversely, 60 per cent answered yes to the question 'Do you think the political consciousness of women is low?' Similarly, the percentages of women answering in the affirmative were 12 per cent and 55 per cent respectively. These questions, which phrased the same proposition in two ways, are indicative of social attitudes (Okamura, 1973, p.74). Other surveys also indicate similar opinions.

A survey of opinion leaders by the Prime Minister's Office suggested that they are not much more open to women's participation than are the general public (Japan, 1977b). Most importantly, 56 per cent of the professionals, politicians, and businessmen surveyed, agreed that the proper place for women was in the home, attending to family affairs, while the men worked outside. Thirty-eight per cent disagreed with that concept and 6 per cent did not reply. Thus, opinion leaders were slightly more conservative than women in general, of whom 49 per cent agreed women should stay at home, 40 per cent disagreed, and 11 per cent did not reply. Although 29 per cent of the opinion leaders were satisfied with the current level of participation, 57 per cent considered there should be more women in elected office. On average, the supporters of an increase in women's political representation favoured an increase to about 11 per cent (Japan, 1977b, passim). A previous survey, in 1972, showed that those opinion leaders, favouring increased participation, in fact, conceived of an appropriate, but limited, role for women in 'women's affairs' such as education, welfare, and social problems (Jones, 1975, p.713). It is evident that there is little support for more active participation by women in professional politics. Society and its leaders encourage women to participate in electing their representatives, but not to seek direct representation.

WOMEN REPRESENTATIVES

The paucity of women in elected political office makes generalisations about women officials difficult. The early women Diet representatives were dominated by the leaders of the pre-war movements for increased civil rights. As they have retired from politics, housewives, teachers and nurses with solid party experience have replaced them. Women who have served more than one term in the Diet range in age from 54 to 80, consistent with the preponderance of Diet members over 50. The most famous woman in politics, Fusae Ichikawa, led the first women's civil rights movement in the 1920s. As an independent, she was a member of the House of Councillors from 1953 to 1971 and has been very critical of all the party organisations and their corruption. She was not re-elected in 1971 and had retired, but was prevailed upon to run again in 1974. She won this election at the age of 81, with the second largest number of votes in the nation-wide constituency. As a literal living legend, Ichikawa has provided a strong example for women in politics. She lives a simple, single life, and eschews the usual driver and car for the subway. By remaining aloof from party politics, she has been a rallying point for women of all parties and ideologies. Unfortunately, there seem to be no women of adequate strength and following to succeed her.

Another leader from the early feminist and birth control movements, Shzue Kato, lost her Upper House seat in 1974. She and
Ichikawa were competing for the same group of voters in the
national constituency. These two women stand out in Japanese
politics. In itself, their individuality is unusual in a political
culture which values anonymity, and discourages individual recognition. Political careers for women are exceptions. A profile of the
average woman holding an elected office should distinguish between
local and national office holders. The women in the Diet are much
older, more seasoned politicians than those at local level. However,
there are few studies of women politicians at any level. One survey,
including National Diet members and local assembly members,
showed that about half the women were under 50 years old. Thirty-
three per cent were between the ages of 50 and 63, and 15 per
cent were between 64 and 71. Thus approximately half the elected
women came of age before or during the war, and half had experience limited to post-war conditions. Most importantly, over 40 per
cent of these elected women were in their first term of office, and
a quarter were only in their second term of office. Yet, unless
women can maintain their positions over several terms, they cannot
develop the political power that comes with seniority in Japan.

More than half the women surveyed were first elected after the
age of 40. A breakdown by party reveals that the more conservative members entered at a later age than the progressives. Whereas most of the LDP women ran for their first election when they
were in their 40s or 50s, the majority of the socialists were in their
30s or 40s. JCP, with over 50 per cent first standing for election,
in their 30s and over 10 per cent in their 20s. All of the women
who entered electoral politics in their 20s were JCP representatives.
Overall, the JCP tends to field younger people, 80 per cent of the
JCP women were under 50. The LDP runs older, more established
candidates. The LDP and JSP members have usually had a previous
career in business, the bureaucracy or the unions and have entered
professional politics later in life. The JCP is a young party, without the pre-war heritage of the LDP and JSP, and its electoral
success began relatively recently. As a result half the JCP women
representatives were in their first term of office. The JCP has
actively promoted women candidates and between 1971 and 1975
doubled the number of their women representatives.

An examination of the activities of women representatives indicates
that they are primarily concerned with stereotyped women's issues.
They deal with education, day care, welfare for the aged, and
children, environmental and consumer issues. They attribute their
expertise in social issues to their personal and family experiences.
These are the areas in which women face the least opposition and,
in which, an activist woman can more easily slip across the boundary between concerned citizen and professional politician ('Japanese
Women', 12 November, 1976).

From a series of interviews with well established, older women in
politics (Carlberg, 1976, pp.233-55), the following picture emerged.

As children, these women had all been exposed to western culture. Their families had adopted many western customs and ideas, including the equality of men and women. Some of them had lived abroad as children and consequently had a more liberal education than most Japanese women. The other striking factor in their backgrounds was encouragement by their fathers to pursue a career. Several fathers had insisted that their daughters go to university, at a time when few women went on to higher education. These women politicians had sought independence through careers outside the usual female occupations, such as teaching. Although based on a very limited sample, it would seem that liberal, western education distinguishes Japan's first wave of politically active women from their less active sisters. Western ideas and culture are no longer a novelty in Japan nor an important factor, but family support for a non-traditional career is still very important.

The attitudes of successful women politicians contrasted with those of the unsuccessful, such as Mrs. Enoki of the Japan Women's Party. They had little of her bitterness and hostility either towards men or towards the political system. They were very conservative in their estimation of the sex discrimination they had personally experienced, quick to point out the problems faced by all professional women, and quick to acknowledge general discrimination against women. Nevertheless, they played down their own particular problems. This moderate attitude is necessary to be effective in the Japanese political system. Confrontation is only condoned in specific ritualised circumstances, such as Diet debate between political parties.

Although women have not participated much in the male domains of the organised political parties, women have organised consumer and environmental groups to pressure the government about specific problems. In 1975, Governor Minobe of Tokyo withdrew his candidacy when his supporting coalition of progressive parties fell apart (Jones, 1976, pp.229-30). He was prevailed upon by a metropolitan citizen's party to run, and he won. The women leaders of this citizen's party criticised the JCP and JSP divisiveness and went on to be politically effective outside the major parties. Boycotts by women's consumer groups focused public attention on food containing cyclamates and on over-priced colour television sets - issues that the government was lax in attending to. Through citizen's movements, women have attacked pollution problems and have forced the removal of a particularly sexist television commercial. However, they have dealt only with narrow issues and not general policies, and there is little indication that they will broaden their line of attack (Tsurutani, 1977, pp.176-212; Jones, 1975, pp.720-1).

These single-issue, loosely organised political activities are more easily reconcilable with women's role as homemaker than are party politics. Middle-class housewives can more easily balance family responsibilities with civic, or volunteer work, than with professional, full-time career. The total dedication required by a political party or a job is difficult for a married woman, and, even if they have the commitment, they are frequently relegated to auxiliary, helping roles. The Japan Communist Party and the Komei Party, which do organise housewives and emphasise grass roots politics, have more active women members than the more elitist LDP, JSP and DSP.

CONCLUSION

In summary, women's contemporary social roles are not compatible with professional politics, as currently practised. As long as the social and political institutions remain the same, women's political participation in the established parties, and in the bureaucracy, will be slight. However, increasing affluence, and smaller families, will free many women to become more involved with citizen's organisations. These organisations do wield political clout on particular issues. Unfortunately, the implication is a continued lack of formal participation, by women, in broader policy determination.

BIBLIOGRAPHY

Baerwald, Hans, H. (1974), 'Japan's Parliament: An Introduction', Cambridge University Press, London.

Bando, Mariko (1977), 'The Women of Japan: Past and Present', The Foreign Press Centre of Japan, Tokyo.

Beer, Lawrence W. (1976), Freedom of Expression in Japan with Comparative Reference to the United States, in Richard P. Claude (ed.), 'Comparative Human Rights', Johns Hopkins Press, Baltimore, pp.99-126.

Baker, Michael K. (1976), 'Japan at the Polls. The House of Councillors Election of 1974', American Enterprise Institute, Washington, DC.

Carlberg (Hargadine), Eileen (1976), Women in the Political System, in Joyce Lebra et al. (eds), 'Women in Changing Japan', Westview Press, Boulder, Colorado, pp.233-55.

Fukui, Haruhiro (1970), 'Party in Power: The Japanese Liberal Democrats and Policy Making', Australian National University Press, Canberra.

Hanami, Tadashi (1969), Women Workers and Retirement after Marriage, 'Japan Labor Bulletin', 8 (May), 7-9.

Hargadine, Eileen (1980), Revising Japan's Labor Standards Law: The Debate over Protective Legislation, Ph.D dissertation, University of Colorado, Boulder, Colorado.

Havens, Thomas R.H. (1975), Women and War in Japan, 1937-45, 'American Historical Review', 80 (October), 913-34.

Hrebenar, Ronald J. (1977), The Politics of Electoral Reform in Japan, 'Asian Survey', 17 (October), 978-96.

Ike, Nobutake (1978), 'A Theory of Japanese Democracy', Westview Press, Boulder, Colorado.

Japan, Prime Minister's Office, 'Statistical Survey' (1974a).

Japan, Ministry of Labor, Women's and Minors' Bureau (1974b),

'Fujin Rodo no Jitsujo' ('Actual Conditions of Women's Labor'), Tokyo.

Japan, Ministry of Foreign Affairs (1975), 'Status of Women in Modern Japan', Tokyo.

Japan (1976), 'Seminar in Public Administration Officers on Women's Problems, 1976 Fiscal Year', Tokyo.

Japan, Ministry of Labor, Women's and Minors' Bureau (1977a), 'Status of Women in Modern Japan', Tokyo.

Japan, Prime Minister's Office (1977b), 'Report on Survey of Opinion Leaders on Women's Problems in Japan', Tokyo.

'Japanese Women' (1975-8), Women's Suffrage Hall, Tokyo.

'Japan Times' (1977), Tokyo.

Jones, H.J. (1975), Japanese Women in the Seventies: Politics, 'Asian Survey', 15 (August), 708-23.

Jones, H.J. (1976), Japanese Women and Party Politics, 'Pacific Affairs' 49, (Summer), 213-34.

Jones, H.J. (1977), Japanese Women and the Dual-Track Employment System, 'Pacific Affairs' 49 (Winter 1976-7): 589-606.

Kirkpatrick, Maurine A. (1975), Consumerism and Japan's New Citizen Politics, 'Asian Survey', 14 (March), 234-46.

Kusano, Kazuo (1973), Industrialization and the Status of Women in Japan, PhD. dissertation, University of Washington, Seattle.

Lebra, Joyce, et al. (eds) (1976), 'Women in Changing Japan', Westview Press, Boulder, Colorado.

'Mainichi Daily News', Tokyo.

Nakane, Chie (1972), 'Japanese Society', University of California Press, Berkeley.

Okamura, Masu (1973), 'Women's Status', International Society for Education, Tokyo.

Patai, Raphael (1967), 'Women in the Modern World', Free Press, New York.

Patrick, Hugh (ed.) (1976), 'Japanese Industrialization and its Social Consequences', University of California Press, Berkeley.

Pittman, Barrie O. (ed.), (1977), 'Equal Pay for Women: Progress and Problems', Hemisphere Press, Washington, DC.

Scalapino, Robert, A. and Junosoke, Masumi (1962), 'Parties and Politics in Contemporary Japan', University of California Press, Berkeley, Los Angeles, California.

Stockwin, J.A.A. (1975), 'Japan: Divided Politics in A Growth Economy', W.W. Norton, New York.

Totten, George Oakley III (1966), 'The Social Democratic Movement in Prewar Japan', Yale University Press, New Haven.

Tsuneishi, Warren N. (1966), 'Japanese Political Style', Harper & Row, New York and London.

Tsurutani, Taketsugu (1977), 'Political Change in Japan: Response to Post-Industrial Change', David McKay, New York.

United States, Department of Labour, Women's Bureau (1976), 'The Role and Status of Women Workers in the United States and Japan: A Joint U.S.-Japan Study', Washington, DC.

Vavich, Dee Ann (1967), The Japanese Women's Movement: Ichikawa Fusae, A Pioneer in Women's Suffrage, 'Monumenta Nipponica',

22, 401-36.
ɔgel, Suzanne H. (1978), Professional Housewife: The Career of
Urban Middle-Class Japanese Women, 'Japan Interpreter', 12
(Winter), 16-43.
tanuki, Joji (1977), 'Politics in Postwar Japanese Society',
University of Tokyo Press, Tokyo.

15 CONCLUSIONS
Joni Lovenduski and
Jill Hills

It is evident that although women's public participation bears m
similarities to that of men, there remain significant differences,
particularly at the upper levels of the hierarchies of political
organisations. More immediately interesting than this however a
the variations in amounts and types of political activity to be fo
amongst women. Clearly the amount of influence any individual
will have will vary according to the type of participation that
individual chooses to undertake, and according to the type of
policy she wishes to influence. This choice will in turn vary acc
ing to the resources and motivation necessary to political partic
ation at the disposal of the individual. As it happens research o
political participation has shown that relatively few people of eit
sex are willing or able to do more politically than vote, and that
many do not even do that.

Willingness to vote is in fact a useful analytical base line here
as an individual's act of casting a ballot for a candidate is of a
qualitatively different order from that of becoming or attempting
to become a candidate for public office. This is because standin
for public office involves considerably more in the way of commi
ment and resources than does making a choice between candidat
By extension, it is possible to conceive of some forms of direct
political action as falling between candidacy and voting in terms
of the demands made on the individual. The logic of ordering
participatory acts in terms of the costs involved enables us to
conceptualise political participation as a pyramidical hierarchy in
which at each level fewer people are able or willing to make the
required investments. The traditional view of this hierarchy ha
deemed voting as at the lowest level of participation and member
of the political elite as the highest. Milbrath (1968) has termed
these levels of activity as 'spectator' and 'gladiator' respectively
and he also includes a transitional level within which participant
were moving up or down the hierarchy. For Milbrath activity at
each level implied activity at all preceding levels. Milbrath confi
his attention to the formal electoral and political process in the
and once the definition of political participation is expanded to
include more informal types of direct political action a simple, si
hierarchical pyramid is no longer an adequate conceptualisation.
Nor does the concept of a single channel of ascent within that
pyramid remain valid (see Verba and Nie, 1972, passim). Whethe
a single or multi-pyramid concept is used, the absence of women
from the political elites at the apex is a noteworthy feature of al
political systems. However the flexibility provided by the multi-

yramid concept enables us to appreciate the significance of
omen's apparent propensity in recent years to favour forms of
rect political action. We are thereby able to examine women's
olitical activity in terms of more than one dimension.

The variation in the extent to, and manner in which women have
een politically active in different countries is almost as great as
at between men and women within nations. The single reliable
onstant is that men and women have different life patterns in
ich of the twenty countries investigated. This difference in
ivate life styles clearly affects public activity and women's
eater domestic seclusion clearly underpins male/female differ-
ices. But the degree of women's privatisation itself varies across
ational cultures, even amongst those women who are economically
tive. Such variation might be expected to be associated with
riations in political participation.

Another significant variable here is that of family structure.
hilst the presence of helpful relatives may lead to the increased
ossibility of political activity on the part of women, the persist-
ice of traditional attitudes toward women in extended family
stems (e.g., as in Japan) is likely to outweigh the effect of
ich an advantage. In any case the nuclear family is the most
mmon family form in the countries considered here. Its attend-
it high levels of privatisation have not been conducive to women's
itry into the political arena. In countries where there is evid-
ice of shifts away from the nuclear family (Sweden, Finland, USA
id Canada) the changes are likely to be at variance in their
ipact on political activism. On the one hand, falling commitment
husbands' economic status with its inhibitions on women's
ographical mobility (Finland, Sweden) would suggest an increase
the incidence of women making careers in politics. On the other
ind, a rise in the number of single-parent families (USA, Canada,
weden, Finland, and Britain) which are normally mother-led would
ive precisely the opposite effect. Finally an increase in the number
dual-career childless couples (Finland, Sweden, USA and West
ermany) might allow women more time for political activity.
cause such shifts as there have been away from the nuclear
mily have taken place relatively recently, interpretations of their
gnificance to women's political behaviour are bound to be spec-
ative. Each such development in family structure has different
id contradictory implications for both men and women.

Responsibilities within the family have normally meant that
creased proportions of women, particularly married women with
ildren, in economic activity will not directly translate into similar
roportions of women in formal political activity. However, women
ive been more likely to penetrate the political sub-elites in the
untries in which they have been most economically active. The
lationship between women's political and economic activism holds
ue across most of Western Europe including Britain, across East-
n Europe and in most of the Soviet Union. Only those countries
ich as Italy where female employment involves large numbers of
omen in home work (and hence increases rather than decreases

their domestic seclusion) are exceptions. The pattern in the
larger English-speaking democracies is slightly different in tha
the more recent increase in women's economic activity has not s
far been reflected in their entry into the political elites, althou
the evidence suggests that token admissions may be beginning
occur. Japanese women, although highly involved in the econon
sector have had a singular lack of access to the political arena.
This might be explained by the numbers of 'employed' women
working unpaid for family enterprises.

The pink collar ghetto is characteristic of all of the states co
sidered in this volume. Although the precise nature of occupati
sectoralisation by sex varies considerably, there is no country
which women do not predominate in certain types of low status
occupation, notably clerical and low-level service employment.
More substantial variations are to be found in access to the hig
status professions. Women comprise about 80 per cent of the
doctors in the Soviet Union, 20 per cent in West Germany and c
9 per cent in the USA; are 40 per cent of the engineers in the
Soviet Union, but virtually none in Britain and the USA. Women
are everywhere poorly represented at higher managerial level.
Part-time employment and interrupted career patterns go some
way toward explaining women's relatively poor showing in the
professions, but these should be seen in conjunction with the o
portunities for marriage, the provision of social services and at
udes to women's role in the family in each nation.

The level of women's access to education, particularly higher
education, has a strong explanatory power when questions of
occupational sectoralisation and low status employment are cons
ered. In most of the countries under consideration, women first
entered further education and higher education at around the
beginning of the twentieth century. They did not enter on the
same terms as men, however, until the 1930s in the Soviet Unio
the post-Second World War era in most of Europe, and have yet
do so in Spain, Italy and some of the less wealthy East Europea
states. Even where women now comprise at least half of univers
undergraduates they do not proceed to higher training in prop
tion to their numbers. In addition women are less likely than m
in each country to obtain posts in the occupations for which the
have trained. Thus 'equal' access to educational provision on a
informal level conceals the persistence of traditional imbalances
subject specialisation between the sexes. Women are more likely
opt for humanities and arts subjects and vocational training for
the caring sub-professions, whilst men pursue the more potenti
lucrative scientific, engineering and technical skills. Substanti
evidence from a number of countries suggests that such prefere
become fixed very early on in a child's education. Even where
regimes have made efforts to overcome sex-segregated subject
choice, those women entering male-dominated occupations have
done little more than pass the point of entry. Those countries
which have made the most consistent efforts in this direction ha
been those suffering from persistent labour shortages and have

erefore had strong motivation to upgrade the skills of the female
our force. Ironically they are also amongst the poorer nations
der consideration and have been the least able to provide the
le-ranging social services necessary for women to use these
portunities to advantage.

Variations in women's educational and employment opportunities
ve not usually been accompanied by substantial changes in the
ision of labour within the family in systems in which nuclear
ilies prevail. And as Pateman (1979, p.21) has written: 'The
rticipation of men in . . . all levels of hierarchical organisations
dependent upon their non-participation (or minimal participation)
domestic labour.' Domestic labour is, or course, normally per-
med by women. Hence, for women, the translation of public
ivity from the economic to the political sphere is impeded by
nestic responsibilities. The impact of the domestic burden upon
men and the cultural attitudes which support her continuing
sponsibility for servicing the family, although by now a truism,
not be overestimated. Otherwise attractive activities such as
se involved in commitment to political or trade union organisa-
ns are likely to be regarded as luxuries by all but the most
termined of women. Thus it is not surprising that in none of
 countries under consideration does women's active political
rticipation take place in the proportions one would expect if the
nslation from economic to political activities were free from family
straints.

The crucial factor of the division of labour within the family
doubtedly explains the decreasing proportions of women as one
ceeds up each national political hierarchy. Nation by nation,
men's patterns of formal political activity takes the form of the
ected hierarchical pyramid. At the base is voting, rising to
ty membership and activism, to office-holding in parties and
al government, to national candidacy, to presence in national
islatures – or in the case of the state Socialist societies, party
tral committee membership and finally to presence at the execu-
e level.

The only political activity apparently not affected by the domestic
e of women is that of voting. The effect of the 'dual burden'
household and employment responsibilities is only visible at the
els at which significiant time and money costs accompany political
ivity. One would not therefore expect to find signtficant dif-
ences in voter turnout between men and women, and this is in
t the case. In most states women first obtained the vote later
n men and tended to be regarded as surrogate voters or, per-
s more accurately, a second electorate. But such differences
there were between men's and women's turnout have all dimin-
ed over the period since women first cast their ballots, and in
ny countries had disappeared by the late 1970s. Where residual
ferences remain these may often be accounted for by the pres-
e in the electorate of women with pre-suffrage socialisation.
Whilst voting turnout differences may now be seen to be unimport-
, many countries manifest significant differences in men's and

women's rates of support for parties on the left of the ideologic
spectrum. Women are often apparently more conservative than n
although when the relevant data are controlled for occupation a
education, many of these ideological differences 'disappear'. Th
societies in which women's greater conservatism is not 'removed
by the application of such statistical controls are those in which
there is both a strong religious influence (normally Roman Cath
and the opportunity of voting for a 'religious' political party, (
France, Spain, and West Germany). In the countries in which s
ideological differences persist between the sexes there normally
remains a linkage between the conservative party, the majority
religion and the age structure of women in the population (Brita
and Finland). It is likely that as religiosity declines, difference
in the conservatism of men and women will also decline.

National variations in the distribution of women's party membe
ships across the ideological spectrum are also amenable to expla
tions based on the religious variable as are differences in the
distribution of men's and women's party affiliations within natio
But the striking feature here is the low proportions of women p
members by comparison with men. Women's share of party memb
ship varies from as little as 13 per cent in the Bavarian based C
to 50 per cent in the traditional Conservative parties of Britain
Australia and Sweden. Although women are more likely to be fo
as members of the parties of the Right, nowhere does their mem
ship of Socialist or Communist parties fall below 20 per cent.
Ironically women's higher proportionate memberships of right-w
parties are not normally reflected at the level of party office-
holding. For example, 32 per cent of women members of the Ital
Christian Democrats hold only 2 per cent of the leadership posit
and the 41 per cent of women RPR supporters in France have
obtained only 14 per cent of that party's executive posts. Amon
Socialist parties it is the Communist parties which appear to ha
been the most systematic in promoting women. However, the Eas
European and Soviet Communist parties, i.e., those in power in
societies in which electoral competition is negligible, have been
less consistent in the promotion of women than have their West
European counterparts.

A major function of political parties is the recruitment of suit
personnel for public office. Whether or not electoral competition
a feature of the political process, political parties normally have
the major say in who the candidates will be. The data available
candidate selection for local or regional office do not enable us
draw conclusions on the process by which, at this level, women
might be excluded. Only in the Soviet Union and Eastern Europ
where nomination is tantamount to election may we determine wo
share of candidacies at sub-national level. In the Soviet Union
women are nominated for and therefore attain local office in nea
proportion to their presence in the population. Via a similarly
controlled nominating procedure the percentage of women holdin
local office in Eastern Europe is higher than anywhere in the We
except Sweden, but remains below 30 per cent except in Bulgar

d Albania where it approaches 40 per cent. In the western liberal
mocracies, in general women hold less than 20 per cent of elected
:al offices and often less than 10 per cent. Rural/urban differ-
ces within countries are reflected here in that women appear
>re likely to be elected from urban than from rural constituencies
'SSR, France, USA, Britain, Finland, Spain, Sweden). These
fferences may be due to obvious transport and communication
fficulties in rural areas or to variations in the persistence of
aditional attitudes toward women between metropolitan and country
mmunities.

There is no state in which parties select women candidates to
and for election to national legislative office in proportion to
eir membership of the population. Furthermore, only in the state
>cialist societies do parties select women as candidates for state
fice in any proportion to party membership. Indeed the Czech,
ingarian and Soviet parties nominate proportionately more women
an are party members. This must however, be seen in the light
the largely symbolic nature of the national legislatures there.
>re telling are the low proportions of women at the upper levels
Communist party hierarchies in these states. Where data are
ailable for the western liberal democracies, they appear to indi-
te that parties resist nominating women for national office. This
most remarkable in Australia where women comprise only 7 per
nt of national candidates although they may be as many as 50
·r cent of party members. In Britain women are between 35 and
per cent of party members but only about 20 per cent of national
ndidates. In France, women, at 16 per cent of the candidates
d over 30 per cent of the party membership are similarly under-
presented. In these and other systems minor parties with relatively
tle chance of electoral success are more likely to put forward
>men candidates.

The reluctance of parties in competitive electoral systems to
·minate women may be due to their perception that women's candid-
ies are less likely to be successful. Whereas lower proportions
women in Britain and France are elected than are nominated, it
noticeable that in Finland women are elected in a similar proportion
their candidacies. Scrutiny of national electoral systems suggests
at parties in simple plurality systems tend to nominate women for
irginal or unwinnable seats and parties facing systems of propor-
>nal representation often place women at less favourable positions
 party lists. The prediction that women candidates will be un-
iccessful therefore often becomes a self-fulfilling prophecy.

Amongst the liberal democracies women's presence in national
gislatures varies from none in the Australian House of Represent-
ives to 3 per cent in the British House of Commons and the French
ssembly, through 5 per cent in Canada and Spain, 7 per cent in
:st Germany, up to 29 per cent in Sweden. As the rather higher
·oportionate presence of women in the legislatures of the state
>cialist societies should be seen in the same light as their candid-
ies, the effective variation in the range of women's access to
itional legislative office is in the order of 30 per cent.

On the face of it variations in the proportions of women in pa
ments may have some association with the type of electoral syst
But these variations are not just a simple function of electoral
systems. Although the two western systems with the highest pe
centage of women national legislators have proportional represe
tion, there are many such systems in which women's representa
at this level remains low. Nevertheless, women consistently app
to do marginally better in systems of proportional representatio
than in those based on simple plurality.

It is likely that a large part of the immediate explanation for
numbers of women in national office rests rather with the reluc
of political parties to promote women than with the mechanics of
the electoral system. Self-selection may also be important here
might be the conditions of campaign finance. In those countries
such as Japan and the USA, where candidates finance their own
campaigns it is likely that women are especially disadvantaged.
The two Scandinavian countries of Finland and Sweden provide
some evidence that where the will to promote women as political
actors is present, it is possible to increase substantially the nu
of women in electoral office within a very short period of time.
possibilities for translating such determination into reality may
according to internal party decision-taking arrangements, and
many party leaders may have found themselves frustrated by th
memberships when attempting to promote women. Hence interna
party structures may also be a significant variable. Certainly t
centralised structure and financing of Communist parties have
enhanced their ability to promote women when they have chosen
do so. Whatever the obstacles, there is little doubt that under
present conditions, commitment on the part of male elites is vit
to the improvement of women's electoral prospects.

At government decision-taking level the only countries in whi
women comprise more than a token proportion of cabinet membe
or their equivalents are Sweden and the USA. Arguably the
American cabinet is amongst the least important political institu
to be found at the apex of any government. And in Scandinavia
countries such as Sweden and Finland, major policy decisions
appear normally to be taken outside the formal institutions of
government. Nowhere does women's representation at parliamen
level lead to similar representation in the executive policy-maki
organs. The one woman head of state, in Britain, has formed a
cabinet in which women have less representation than at any tin
during the last twenty years. It is therefore by no means neces
sary that where women have themselves obtained promotion the
feel obliged to promote women.

On the whole, apart from the anomaly of Mrs Thatcher, scrut
of the gender composition of the hierarchy of political institutio
suggests that the absence of women might well be taken as an
initial indicator of the power, importance or significance of the
relevant institutions. Obvious time and money costs of political
activity for individuals, party reluctance and domestic burdens
all play a part in the inhibition of women's access to public offi

addition the definition of political issues has been largely male
nstructed and may have reduced the motivation of individual
men to become involved. Where issues have had special relevance
women, such as abortion, rape or divorce, then women have
en more politically active. Their political action has taken the
m of demonstrations, mass campaigns and petitions as well as
t of working through the existing political institutions. Although
ch issues may be leading more women to seek access to the formal
itical arena, the existence of feminine direct action over what
ve previously been regarded as personal and private issues
ses the question of whether the traditional separate definitions
public and private life remain valid. In some countries political
rties have responded to women's issues by including them in
ir party platforms, presumably so as not to risk alienating the
nale electorate. Where parties have not responded adequately,
for example in Japan, Canada, France, Australia and West
rmany, women have attempted to form their own parties in comp-
tion with the established ones. Whilst the success of these parties
s been limited, their existence indicates that politicians ignore
e possible rejection by women of traditional politics at their
ril.
Possibly because of the sectoralisation of women's employment in
st industrial societies women's mobilisation over the issue of
ual pay has been less remarkable than that which has taken place
er the so-called private issues. Male-dominated trade unions
ve done little to change this and may, on occasion, have actively
ited women's political mobilisation as women on economic issues,
ling that such considerations only divide the union movement.
e same sectoralisation and union constraints may have prevented
men from realising their special vulnerability to economic reces-
ns such as that in the late 1970s. In each country where data
e available, women's unemployment rates rose more sharply than
n's at that time. Yet in no country was there evidence that women
re beginning to mobilise over the issue.
Despite increasing penetration of the economic sector, women's
rceptions of themselves continue to be rooted in the family.
titudes arising from the division of labour within the family may
th limit women's expectations in the economic sphere and inhibit
ir willingness to attempt reform of their economic condition.
re specifically, women have less information about their rights
d less knowledge and experience of demanding their rights than
n and have a more limited conception of the possibilities for
litical change. It is therefore not surprising that whatever the
onomic gains made by men via political activity, those made by
men have been minute in comparison. Of course men's expectations
the possibilities of reform through political action have often
en inflated and it may be that women are aware of this. If that
the case then the historical message to women is a contradictory
e. On the one hand it appears that only a little can be gained by
aying the political game. On the other hand, non-players are
rticularly penalised. Playing is necessary, but only in order not

to lose ground.

The task facing women is monumental. In order to change an unfavourable economic, social and domestic condition women mu seek not only to enter the political arena in greater numbers, b must also expand it to include 'private' issues on the public age Women currently in positions of political leadership bear major responsibility for initiating this dual strategy. Unfortunately th is evidence that many women in such positions feel little obligat to their sex. This is hardly surprising when so few of these wo directly owe their positions to other women, and are therefore i required to distinguish the special needs of their women constit ents. This suggests that women have never exercised the powe of the vote to its full extent, have never turned the apparent disadvantage of being a second electorate into a political weapo Women's massive voting strength thoughtfully used, or withhelc could activate even apparently moribund political leaders. And may be fairly stated that only when women begin to vote and mobilise as women over the whole range of political issues will political leaders of whichever sex perceive and act upon obligat to women electors. Then and only then will an effective re-orde of public priorities and a redefinition of the political take place.

BIBLIOGRAPHY

Milbrath, L (1968), 'Political Participation', Rand McNally, Chic
Pateman, C (1979), Hierarchical organizations and democratic
    participation: the problem of sex, 'Resources for Feminist Re
    March, pp.19-22.
Verba, S. and Nie, N.H. (1972), 'Participation in America', Ha
    & Row, New York.

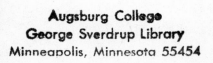